The Controller's Toolkit

Founded in 1807, John Wiley & Sons is the oldest independent publishing company in the United States. With offices in North America, Europe, Asia, and Australia, Wiley is globally committed to developing and marketing print and electronic products and services for our customers' professional and personal knowledge and understanding.

The Wiley Corporate F&A series provides information, tools, and insights to corporate professionals responsible for issues affecting the profitability of their company, from accounting and finance to internal controls and performance management.

The Controller's Toolkit

Christine H. Doxey

WILEY

Library of Congress Cataloging-in-Publication Data:

Names: Doxey, Christine H., 1955- author.
Title: The controller's toolkit / Christine H. Doxey.
Description: Hoboken, New Jersey : Wiley, [2021] | Includes index.
Identifiers: LCCN 2020029244 (print) | LCCN 2020029245 (ebook) | ISBN
  9781119700647 (hardback) | ISBN 9781119700623 (Adobe PDF) | ISBN
  9781119700654 (epub) | ISBN 9781119700586
Subjects: LCSH: Controllership. | Corporate—Finance. | Risk management.
  | Corporate governance.
Classification: LCC HG4026 .D68 2021 (print) | LCC HG4026 (ebook) | DDC
  658.15/1—dc23
LC record available at https://lccn.loc.gov/2020029244
LC ebook record available at https://lccn.loc.gov/2020029245

Cover Design: Wiley
Cover Image: © nasirkhan/Shutterstock

SKY10093817_121324

Contents

Preface

This book provides a comprehensive collection of templates, checklists, roadmaps, review sheets, internal controls, policies, and procedures. These practical and implementable tools will enable aspiring, new, and established controllers to take a significant leap forward as finance and accounting leaders. This book is an excellent reference for all finance and accounting professionals because it provides a wide array of information on technical and "soft" competencies. The contents provide concrete examples and tools on business ethics, corporate governance, regulatory compliance, risk management, security, IT processes, leadership, and financial operations. Anyone wishing to learn more about a specific business process—such as accounts payable, accounts receivable, or payroll—can use this valuable resource to quickly become a subject matter expert.

PART ONE

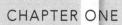

CHAPTER ONE

About This Toolkit

The Controller's Toolkit provides a single source for everything that controllers and finance and accounting professionals need to know to be successful. This toolkit will enable aspiring, new, and current controllers to take a giant leap forward and gain proficiency as corporate leaders.

The comprehensive content provided in this toolkit consists of process flows, checklists, tables of controls, and tables of risks and controls. Each comprehensive table of risks and controls identifies the risks to the business process, recommended policies, controls that will mitigate the risks, and internal control metrics. Besides laying out the accounting and technical requirements of the controllership, this toolkit describes the leadership skills that support the success of a controller's career.

This toolkit is a must-have for accounting and finance professionals wishing to advance their careers and expand their skills and knowledge. This toolkit may also appeal to chief operating officers (CEOs), chief financial officers (CFOs), chief human resources officers, controllers, treasurers, and anyone else who is in the chain of command or who serves as an influencer for corporate finance and accounting processes.

This toolkit is a great reference for many roles within these wide-ranging corporate functions and for companies of many sizes. It can also serve as a training tool, since the content takes a new look at the roles and responsibilities of a controller.

This comprehensive toolkit is organized by specifically defined areas of risk that apply to any company or industry. Each chapter is focused on a business process and includes an overview, a process flow, a table of controls, and a table of risks and controls. The author has included 66 tools, each of which has been designed specifically for controllers to tackle the challenges of a specific business process. Here's how this toolkit is organized.

How This Toolkit Is Organized

Section Number	Area of Risk	Chapter Number	Chapter Title
Introductory Chapters		1	About This Toolkit
		2	Defining the Role of a Controller
1	**Corporate and Reputational Risk**	3	The Controller and Risk Management
		4	The Controller and Ethics
		5	The Controller and Corporate Governance
		6	Entity-Level Controls
2	**Strategic Planning and Mergers and Acquisitions Risk**	7	Strategic Planning and Mergers and Acquisitions
3	**Internal Control Risk**	8	Internal Control Program
4	**Compliance Risk**	9	Regulatory Compliance
5	**Payment Risk**	10	Procure-to-Pay
		11	Hire-to-Retire
		12	Order-to-Cash
6	**Financial Operations Risk**	13	Record-to-Report
		14	Budgets, Forecasts, and Capital Budgeting
		15	Supply Chain Management and Inventory Control
		16	Treasury and Cash Management
		17	Shared Services and Business Process Outsourcing
		18	Dashboards, Data Validation, Analytics, Metrics, and Benchmarking
7	**Information Technology Risk**	19	Information Technology Controls and Cybersecurity
8	**Business Continuity and Physical Security Risk**	20	Business Continuity and Physical Security
9	**Leadership and Change Management Risk**	21	Leadership and Managing Change
		22	Trends, Process Transformation, and Digitization

2

Defining the Role of a Controller

 OVERVIEW

The controllership function is carried out by a controller, which usually is the individual in charge of and with authority over the processes related to finance and accounting. A controller has the main goal of keeping the company's bottom line secure by accurate internal controls and well-defined financial operations. But a good controller needs to be aware of all areas of risk that may impact a company and its ongoing success.

The role of the controller is often defined as being a business partner to other functions and divisions within an organization. In many organizations the role of the finance professional is defined as being a business partner to the organizations supported.

Controllers are faced with much broader challenges and opportunities in today's business world and are being asked to take on additional responsibilities outside of the traditional "chief accounting officer" role. Controllers are connected to most of the key business processes within an organization. Controllers provide the stewardship and accountability systems that ensure that the organization is conducting its business in an appropriate, ethical manner.

Controllers and their staffs should also provide the information, analysis, and advice that will enable the organization's operational management to perform effectively. This means understanding the impacts that the supply chain can have upon the accounting processes for the organization.

Controllers are process driven and are always looking for practical tools to manage their areas of responsibility and to advance their careers. These tools can extend the competencies and efficiencies of corporate and controllership processes, which fall under the umbrella of governance, risk management, and compliance (GRC).

CONTROLLER'S TOOL 1 – SUGGESTED JOB RESPONSIBILITIES FOR A CONTROLLER

Introduction. Monster is a global online employment solution for people seeking jobs and employers. Monster has expanded from its roots as a job board to a global provider of a full array of job-seeking, career-management, recruitment, and talent-management products and services. Monster recommends the following list of job responsibilities for a controller:

Suggested Job Responsibilities for a Controller

- Achieves budget objectives by scheduling expenditures, analyzing variances, and initiating corrective actions.
- Provides status of financial condition by collecting, interpreting, and reporting financial data.
- Prepares special reports by collecting, analyzing, and summarizing information and trends.
- Complies with federal, state, and local legal requirements by studying existing and new legislation, anticipating future legislation, enforcing adherence to requirements, filing financial reports, and advising management on needed actions.
- Ensures operation of equipment by establishing preventive maintenance requirements and service contracts, maintaining equipment inventories, and evaluating new equipment and techniques.
- Completes operational requirements by scheduling and assigning employees and by following up on work results.
- Maintains financial staff by recruiting, selecting, orienting, and training employees.
- Maintains financial staff job results by coaching, counseling, and disciplining employees and by planning, monitoring, and appraising job results.
- Protects operations by keeping financial information and plans confidential.[1]

CONTROLLER'S TOOL 2 – CORE COMPETENCIES OF A CONTROLLER

Introduction. Within their companies, controllers are always looked upon as accounting and financial leaders. Many controllers are thought of as the chief accounting officer. I recently authored a blog entry for Nvoicepay that highlights the 15 leadership skills that a controller should have. Controllers should have a blend of skills from two key areas: (1) accounting and business knowledge, and (2) leadership and influence, as listed below.[2]

---

[1]Monster (n.d.). Controller job description sample. Monster website, Job Description Templates (accessed March 8, 2020). https://hiring.monster.com/employer-resources/job-description-templates/controller-job-description-sample.
[2]Doxey, Chris (2017). 15 leadership skills every controller must have. Nvoicepay website (June 29; accessed March 8, 2020). https://www.nvoicepay.com/resources/blog/15-leadership-skills-controllers-must-have.

Accounting and Business Knowledge

1. Cost Control. As an example, a cost-control process would be implemented for a major project to monitor cost performance, ensure changes are recorded accurately, prohibit unauthorized changes, inform stakeholders of cost changes, maintain expected costs with acceptable limits, and monitor and document reasons for favorable or unfavorable cost variances. As a controller, you're responsible for controlling cost. This involves developing policies and procedures, systems, processes, and metrics to make sure that costs are under control.

2. Internal Controls and Compliance. A controller usually has overall responsibility for the internal controls program and processes for their organization. This means that the design, development, and testing of the operational effectiveness of each control is the responsibility of you and your team. If you work for a publicly traded company, you'll also need to prepare all of the quarterly and annual reporting requirements for Sarbanes–Oxley (SOX).

3. Financial Reporting and Adding Value. Controllers and their staffs typically drive the fiscal closing process and are always looking for ways to streamline the process and provide the results sooner through automation and a quicker closing process.

4. Corporate Transaction Processes. Controllers have ownership of corporate transaction processes, which include accounts payable, accounts receivable, payroll, travel and expense (T&E), general accounting, and others. There are always large opportunities for streamlining these processes, as evidenced by automation and transformation initiatives in the procure-to-pay (P2P) and order-to-cash (O2C) processes.

5. Corporate Knowledge. Controllers should have an excellent knowledge of what their companies do and how they are organized. What is the culture of the company? How is the company organized? How quickly do decisions get made?

6. Efficiency Improvements. Along with having a solid knowledge of the corporate transaction processes that are the backbone of your company, you should always look for ways to improve them through process efficiencies and automation. Are there ways to combine similar processes into a shared services organization? Can you reduce manual invoices through implementing an e-invoicing solution? Can you streamline your payment process by implementing e-payment solutions or even outsourcing your payment process?

7. Analytics. A savvy controller is driven by analytics and metrics. The results of a well-developed metrics program will indicate how well your company's business processes are working and where improvements were successfully implemented. Metrics will also reveal problem areas and should have the analytics to drill down to find the solution.

Leadership and Influence

8. Business Partnerships. Since a controller oversees the accounting processes for a company, maintaining good business partnerships is a key success factor. You should identify your areas of influence and ensure you have a good relationship or partnership with the leadership in other departments. Key departments usually include information technology (IT), legal, human resources (HR), business ethics, supply chain, and procurement.

9. Communication. Communication is a personal process that should be appropriate for both the audience and situation. Choosing the wrong communications channel could send the wrong message. For example, a decision that dramatically impacts a person's career should never be delivered via an impersonal form letter. It's always good to consider how it would feel to be on the receiving end. Think about it: If you were being recognized for outstanding work or many years of service, would a personal thank-you note or an e-mail be more meaningful to you?

10. Active Listening. The concept behind active listening is encouraging the speaker to state what they really mean and stems from the work of counselors and therapists. The goal of active listening is to help associates express themselves, offer suggestions, and get to the root of a matter.

1. Listen for the content of the message and organize it into key components.
2. Listen for feelings about the key points being conveyed.
3. Ensure that you respond to feelings appropriately and with compassion.
4. Be cognizant of any overreaction to the situation.
5. Watch verbal and nonverbal signals and be prepared to reconvene the discussion if necessary.
6. Repeat and paraphrase the key points that were conveyed.
7. Wait until the speaker is finished.
8. Do not plan your response until the speaker is finished.
9. Never interrupt to state you own opinion.
10. Maintain eye contact if you are in a face-to-face meeting.

11. Leadership Style. Based on an analysis of all the leadership styles, it makes sense that a controller should be flexible, understand his or her own core leadership style, value team members, and be cognizant of all factors impacting a situation. Although situational leadership is touted as the best leadership style, the situation should not change one's core values or ethics. Great leaders have an in-depth understanding of which leadership style works best for them.

12. Motivation and Inspiration. Motivation involves using words and examples that give your team the will to accomplish an objective or take action. Motivation occurs when one has confidence, feels a sense of belonging to a solid team, and has good leadership. Motivation is nurtured by constant reinforcement, a level of trust, and loyalty to the organizational leader, the company, or both. True team motivation occurs when team members motivate each other.

13. Managing Change. One of the major challenges of change management is assessing readiness for change. Unfortunately, this assessment does not always take place and the risks associated with the change are not always properly addressed. The goal of assessing change readiness is to identify specific issues and to plan for and address those issues so that risks are minimized. If that assessment does not take place, performance improvement may either be delayed or not achieved, and associated costs can be higher than expected.

14. Emotional Intelligence. Psychologist and author Daniel Goleman is cochair of the Consortium for Research on Emotional Intelligence in Organizations, based at Rutgers University. He first brought the term *emotional intelligence* to a wide audience with his 1995 book of the same name. According to Goleman, the chief components of emotional intelligence are self-awareness, self-regulation, motivation, empathy, and social skills.

15. Building a Strong Team. Choosing the right team members is critical to being a good controller. Unless your staff is competent, cohesive, communicative, and committed, you will not be able to fulfill your controllership responsibilities.

CONTROLLER'S TOOL 3 – THE CONTROLLER'S BUSINESS PARTNERSHIP MATRIX

Introduction. Controllers should consider building business partnerships with the organizations included in the table below. This business partnership matrix was developed to provide a listing of potential business partnership organizations. The matrix also includes the areas of influence that will drive the business partnership. Although the areas of influence will differ in public and private companies, the value of a business partnership can be critical to the success of a controller.

Suggested Business Partnership Organization	Area of Influence
HR and Benefits	■ HR and Payroll Internal Controls ■ Entity-Level Controls ■ HR Policy ■ HR Policies to Support Internal Controls, Such as Policies for Corporate Cardholder Agreements ■ Controller Staff Development and Training Programs ■ Benefit Plan Decision Making ■ Pension Plan Investment Analysis and Decision Making ■ Sarbanes–Oxley 302 and 404
Facilities	■ Physical Security Controls ■ Facility Strategy 　▪ Closing Old Facilities 　▪ Building New Facilities ■ Capital Budgets ■ Depreciation Analysis ■ Risk Management ■ Insurance Plans ■ Asset Impairment ■ Sarbanes–Oxley 302 and 404

Suggested Business Partnership Organization	Area of Influence
Supply Chain	■ Supply Chain Internal Controls ■ Supply Chain Strategy ■ Logistics Outsourcing Strategy ■ Inventory Control ■ Inventory Fraud Detection and Prevention ■ Operational Metrics and Reporting ■ Risk Management ■ Sarbanes–Oxley 302 and 404
Legal and Risk Management	■ Entity-Level Controls ■ Risk Management ■ Insurance ■ Record Management ■ Contract Compliance ■ Regulatory Compliance Issues ■ Fraud Detection and Prevention ■ Sarbanes–Oxley 302 and 404
Compliance	■ Regulatory Compliance Applicable to the Organization ■ Address Compliance Issues and Ensure the Implementation of Corrective Action Plans ■ Sarbanes–Oxley 302 and 404
Internal Audit	■ Control Self-Assessment Programs ■ Address Control Issues and Ensure the Implementation of Corrective Action Plans ■ Recommend Audit Plan and Focus ■ Sarbanes–Oxley 302 and 404
Ethics and Compliance	■ Entity-Level Controls ■ Entity-Level Control Questionnaire ■ Ethics Hotline Issues ■ Whistleblower Protection ■ Fraud Detection and Prevention ■ Tone at the Top ■ Sarbanes–Oxley 302 and 404
Security and Investigations	■ Ethics Hotline Issues ■ Fraud Detection and Prevention ■ Security Controls ■ Physical Security ■ Protection of Company Data

Information Technology	■ Develop IT Strategy
	■ IT Controls
	  ■ System Access Controls
	■ Reporting and Metrics
	■ Selection of ERP Systems
	  ■ Cost Analysis
	  ■ Functionality
	■ Financial Systems
	■ Capital Budget
	■ Asset Impairment
	■ IT Business Continuity Plan
	■ Sarbanes–Oxley 302 and 404

CONTROLLER'S TOOL 4 – THE CONTROLLER'S SPAN OF INFLUENCE

Introduction. The controller position impacts nearly every aspect of the organization. The role of the controller now requires broad interpersonal skills. It is important to build relationships with the management or senior team members of every function within the organization. As an example, if there is a large investment in inventory, the controller should establish a relationship with the inventory controls manager and the materials manager for the organization. The wider range of functions managed by the controller means a broader range of functional knowledge. In general, the controller should be familiar with enterprise resource planning (ERP) systems, internal auditing, and the organization's functional and administrative areas.

The Controller's Span of Influence

- Ensure that regulatory and compliance requirements are followed across all divisions.
- Attend and participate in interdepartmental meetings.
- Support strategic planning and ensure that corporate budgets are linked to the planning process.
- Provide opinions on the effectiveness of other departments.
- Implement and manage the company's internal program and ensure that controls are operating effectively.
- Implement and manage the effectiveness of corporate policies, including:
  - Delegation of authority policy
  - Segregation of duties policy
  - Internal controls policy
- Develop enhanced internal control programs and remediation activities to address control weaknesses.
- Develop and implement organization-wide metrics, scorecards, and analytics.
- Acquire and approve insurance coverage.
- Conduct public offerings.
- Deal with investors and lenders.
- Determine credit limits for strategic customers.
- Invest pension funds.
- Invest surplus funds.
- Administer changes to the pension plan.
- Maintain employee files.

Corporate and Reputational Risk

 SECTION INTRODUCTION

"We are living in a trust paradox," said Richard Edelman, CEO of Edelman, a global communications firm. "Since we began measuring trust 20 years ago, economic growth has fostered rising trust. This continues in Asia and the Middle East but not in developed markets, where national income inequality is now the more important factor. Fears are stifling hope, and long-held assumptions about hard work leading to upward mobility are now invalid."[1]

The trust of employees, shareholders, and customers drives corporate and reputational risk. Reputational risk has traditionally been seen as an outcome of other risks and not necessarily as a stand-alone risk. This view has been gradually changing, because it is increasingly clear that reputation is critical to the viability of a company.

Reputational risk refers to the potential for negative publicity, public perception, or uncontrollable events to have an adverse impact on a company's reputation, thereby affecting its revenue. A controller can mitigate reputational risk through risk management processes, code of conduct, ethics, corporate governance, and the implementation and ongoing validation of entity-level controls. Mitigating reputational and corporate risk is an ongoing process that is critical to the success of a company.

---

[1]Edelman (2020). 2020 Edelman Trust Barometer reveals growing sense of inequality is undermining trust in institutions. January 19, 2020, Edelman website, accessed April 10, 2020, https://www.edelman.com/news-awards/2020-edelman-trust-barometer.

CHAPTER THREE

The Controller and Risk Management

 OVERVIEW

Companies of all sizes are subject to a variety of risks. Among them are legal, regulatory, strategic, operational, financial, and reputational. Each functional organization is subject to one or more of these types of risk, each of which may impact the company's bottom line. Companies use a number of tools, such as insurance, establishment of reserve funds, and investment policies (including options and futures), to address some of their risks.

The controller should ensure that the organization's internal controls properly address risk by conducting a risk assessment and analysis of the relevant risks that may impact the achievement of company objectives. Furthermore, economic, industry, regulatory, operating, and compliance impacts are always changing. A controller should establish the appropriate methodology to assess and react to different kinds of risk.

RISK MANAGEMENT PROCESS FLOW

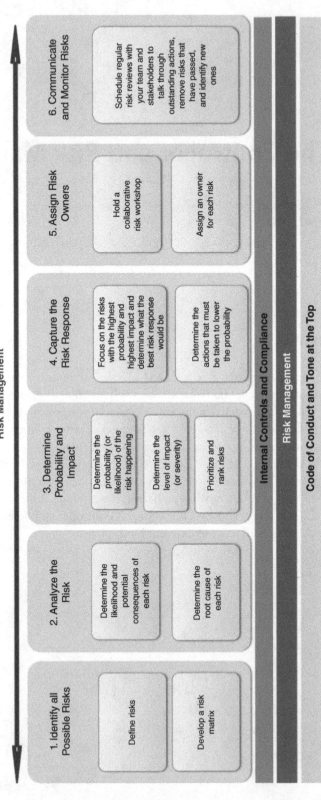

Risk Management

1. Identify all Possible Risks
- Define risks
- Develop a risk matrix

2. Analyze the Risk
- Determine the likelihood and potential consequences of each risk
- Determine the root cause of each risk

3. Determine Probability and Impact
- Determine the probability (or likelihood) of the risk happening
- Determine the level of impact (or severity)
- Prioritize and rank risks

4. Capture the Risk Response
- Focus on the risks with the highest probability and highest impact and determine what the best risk response would be
- Determine the actions that must be taken to lower the probability

5. Assign Risk Owners
- Hold a collaborative risk workshop
- Assign an owner for each risk

6. Communicate and Monitor Risks
- Schedule regular risk reviews with your team and stakeholders to talk through outstanding actions, remove risks that have passed, and identify new ones

Internal Controls and Compliance

Risk Management

Code of Conduct and Tone at the Top

RISK MANAGEMENT DEFINED

Risk management is a process for identifying, assessing, and prioritizing risks of different kinds. Once the risks are identified, the risk manager will create a plan to minimize or eliminate the impact of negative events. Risk management can also be defined as the process of assessing risk and acting in such a manner, or prescribing policies and procedures, so as to avoid or minimize loss associated with such risk. Risk management is not a regulatory requirement but is an important focus of all types of organizations.

The Committee of Sponsoring Organizations of the Treadway Commission (COSO) defines enterprise risk management (ERM) as follows:

> Enterprise risk management is a process, effected by an entity's board of directors, management, and other personnel, applied in strategy setting and across the enterprise, designed to identify potential events that may affect the entity, and manage risk to be within its risk appetite, to provide reasonable assurance regarding the achievement of entity objectives.

The Global Association of Risk Professionals (GARP) defines risk management in this way:

> Risk management is a structured approach to monitoring, measuring, and managing exposures to reduce the potential impact of an uncertain event happening.

When developing a risk management plan, a controller should consider the factors that may create risk. These factors are:

- Inadequate management reporting and monitoring
- Inadequate financial performance metrics
- Operational issues due to poor internal controls
- Legal and regulatory violations
- Incorrect financial reporting due to management overrides or fraudulent activities
- Excessive bad debt and inventory write-offs
- Internal and external fraud
- Breaches of confidentiality
- Lack of quality control
- Lack of a business continuity plan

After considering the risk factors above, a controller should develop a risk policy that outlines the risk management framework of an organization in relation to its objective. Risk policies will vary across industries and companies based on the ability to absorb losses and the rate of return an organization seeks from operations.

CONTROLLER'S TOOL 5 – TYPES OF RISK

Introduction. Besides the types of risk identified in this book, there are other types of risk that controllers should consider when defining a risk management process for their companies. These types of risk are provided below.

Type of Risk
Operational Risk. Operational risk is a potential risk of loss resulting from inadequate or failed internal processes, from people and systems, or from external events. The result of unmanaged operational risk is an operational failure.
Financial Risk. Financial risk is sometimes referred to as treasury risk. Hedging attempts to reduce financial risk by matching a position with an opposite and offsetting position in a financial instrument that tracks or mirrors the value changes in the position.
Fraud Risk. Fraud risk is a potential violation of the organization's ethics and compliance standards, business practice requirements, financial reporting integrity, and other objectives.
Market Risk. Market risk deals with the different types of financial market risks, such as interest rate risk, equity risk, commodity risk, and currency risk.
Credit Risk. Credit risk is the risk of loss due to nonpayment of a loan, bond, or other credit instrument.
Commodity Risk. Commodity risk is a potential loss from an adverse change in commodity prices.
Currency Risk. Currency risk management focuses on the fluctuations in currency values (see Financial Risk).
Project Risk. Project risk is the risk associated with not completing a project within the expected timeline and budget.
Technology and Software Risks. Technology and software risks are associated with implementation of new technology or software and the impact that the implementation may have on the organization.

 ## CONTROLLER'S TOOL 6 – RISK MANAGEMENT FRAMEWORKS

Introduction. There are several risk management frameworks that a controller should consider when developing an internal controls structure to mitigate specific areas of risk across the company. The type of framework selected will depend upon company strategy and customer requirements. As the company works with the risk management team, it should consider the risk events that can be fatal to the company and jeopardize its survival.

Multiple studies have found that people overestimate their ability to influence events that, in fact, are heavily determined by chance. We tend to be overconfident about the accuracy of our forecasts and risk assessments and far too narrow in our assessment of the range of outcomes that may occur.[1]

---

[1]Kaplan, Robert S. and Mikes, Anette (2012). Managing risks: A new framework. *Harvard Business Review* (June; accessed April 28, 2020). https://hbr.org/2012/06/managing-risks-a-new-framework.

Type of Risk Management Framework	Overview
ISO 31000:2018 https://www.iso.org/standard/65694.html	This updated standard now defines risk as the "effect of uncertainty on objectives," with a focus on the effect of incomplete knowledge of events or circumstances on an organization's decision-making. This requires a change in the traditional understanding of risk, forcing organizations to tailor risk management to their needs and objectives – a key benefit of the standard. Jason Brown explains: "ISO 31000 provides a risk management framework that supports all activities, including decision-making across all levels of the organization. "The ISO 31000 framework and its processes should be integrated with management systems to ensure consistency and the effectiveness of management control across all areas of the organization." This would include strategy and planning, organizational resilience, IT, corporate governance, HR, compliance, quality, health and safety, business continuity, crisis management, and security.[2]
COSO Enterprise Risk Management – *Integrating with Strategy and Performance* (2017) https://www.coso.org/Pages/default.aspx	"In keeping with its overall mission, the COSO board commissioned and published in 2004 *Enterprise Risk Management – Integrated Framework*. Over the past decade, that publication has gained broad acceptance by organizations in their efforts to manage risk. "However, also through that period, the complexity of risk has changed, new risks have emerged, and both boards and executives have enhanced their awareness and oversight of enterprise risk management while asking for improved risk reporting. This update to the 2004 publication addresses the evolution of enterprise risk management and the need for organizations to improve their approach to managing risk to meet the demands of an evolving business environment. The updated document, titled *Enterprise Risk Management – Integrating with Strategy and Performance*, highlights the importance of considering risk in both the strategy-setting process and in driving performance.[3]"
National Institute of Standards and Technology (NIST) Risk Management Framework https://www.nist.gov/system/files/documents/2018/03/28/vickie_nist_risk_management_framework_overview-hpc.pdf	The selection and specification of security controls for a system is accomplished as part of an organization-wide information security program that involves the management of organizational risk – that is, the risk to the organization or to individuals associated with the operation of a system. The management of organizational risk is a key element in the organization's information security program and provides an effective framework for selecting the appropriate security controls for a system – the security controls necessary to protect individuals and the operations and assets of the organization.[4]

[2]Tranchard, Sandrine (2018). The new ISO 31000 keeps risk management simple. ISO website, News (February 15; accessed March 24, 2020). https://www.iso.org/news/ref2263.html.

[3]COSO (n.d.). Guidance on enterprise risk management. COSO website (accessed March 24, 2020). https://www.coso.org/Pages/erm.aspx.

[4]NIST (2016). FISMA implementation project, risk management framework (RMF) overview. NIST website, Projects (accessed March 24, 2020). https://csrc.nist.gov/projects/risk-management/risk-management-framework-(RMF)-Overview.

CONTROLLER'S TOOL 7 – CONSIDERATIONS FOR MANAGING RISK WITH AN ENTERPRISE RISK MANAGEMENT MODEL

Introduction. The following tool provides an approach to consider when implementing an ERM model. ERM aims to attain informed business decisions by evaluating total returns relative to total risks, which can be determined by asking these questions:

I. Internal Environment

1. What is the overall risk appetite of the organization?

2. How committed is the board of directors (BoD) to establishing a risk management philosophy?

3. Are there integrity, ethical values, and a commitment to competence in the organization?

4. Is the assignment of authority and responsibility over risks well managed? Who manages this process?

5. What is the organizational structure of the company and departments?

6. What HR standards related to risk management are currently in place?

II. Objective Setting

7. How well are strategic and related objectives defined?

8. How is the achievement of these objectives monitored?

9. What activities are on your risk management goal sheet for this year?

10. What does the company need to do well over the next year in order to succeed and reach its goals? What factors do you consider to be critical to your company's success in the next year?

11. What areas would you like to see moved to the next level of performance?

12. What could prevent you from achieving your goals (e.g. people, processes, funding, etc.)?

III. Event Identification

13. How do internal and external forces impact the risk profile?

14. What other event identification techniques are in place (e.g. self-assessments, SOX, report reviews, trend reporting, fraud hotline, etc.)?

15. How are deficiencies captured and reported?

16. How does the organization distinguish between risks and opportunities?

IV. Risk Assessment

17. What does management perceive to be the largest risks to the company, in terms of significance and likelihood?

18. What do managers perceive to be the biggest risks within their areas of control? Please provide examples.

19. Thinking of other areas within the company, how well does management receive information from shared services groups (e.g. IT, finance, HR)?

20. What additional information would management like to have accessible in order to better perform its responsibilities?

21. In management's opinion, what areas or processes are most susceptible to fraud?

22. Is management aware of any instances of fraud within the company? What/how/who?

V. Risk Response

23. How are risks monitored and reported within the organization?

24. How effectively are identified risks managed?

25. What is management doing specifically to manage identified risks (e.g. financial statement variance reporting, trend reporting, credit reporting, insurance policies, legal, BoD involvement and reporting)?

VI. Control Activity

26. What is management's assessment of the effectiveness of overall controls in preventing risks and carrying out risk activities within your organization?

27. How are the defined control activities tested?

28. What type of review process takes place for policies and procedures?

29. What type of review process takes place for IT application controls and the IT general control environment?

30. What components are included in the company's entity-level controls program?

VII. Information and Communication

31. How does the organization/department capture information and communicate related risk?

32. What communications barriers are present within the organization?

33. What ongoing monitoring activities are in place (e.g. compliance monitoring, Internal Audit (IA), risk management group, BoD monitoring, etc.)?

TABLE OF CONTROLS – RISK MANAGEMENT

Process: Risk Management

1. Governance and ownership of the risk management process are clearly established.

2. Roles and responsibilities for the risk management process are clearly defined.

3. Risk management processes begin and end with clearly defined business objectives.

4. The risk management model to be used is defined and communicated to executive management for approval and implementation.

5. A risk rating system is defined in relation to organization's objectives and considers all types of risks applicable to the company. Risk rating scales are tied to the company's risk management model and establish risk tolerances and are determined based on the calculated or perceived severity of the consequences. Leading indicators are used to provide insight into potential risks using market, industry trends, and weather and world health impacts.

6. A risk portfolio is developed to support decision-making. This portfolio is updated on an annual basis.

7. Action plans and remediation activities are in place to address potential risks.

8. Risk-based internal controls are prioritized based on mitigating risk. All companies, regardless of size, structure, nature, or industry encounter risks at all levels within their organizations. Risks affect each company's ability to survive, successfully compete within its industry, maintain financial strength and a positive public image, and maintain the overall quality of its products, services, and people. Since there is no practical way to reduce risk to zero, management should determine how much risk should be prudently accepted and strive to maintain risk at acceptable levels by considering the implementation of risk-based controls.

9. Risk assessment plans and schedules are communicated to the audit committee, the BoD, and executive management. A schedule is in place to ensure that a risk assessment is conducted in a timely manner.

10. Significant risks are communicated to executive management and the BoD when they are identified.

TABLE OF RISKS AND CONTROLS – RISK MANAGEMENT

Process: Risk Management			
Process Risk	**Recommended Policies**	**Internal Controls**	**KPIs**
1. The value of a risk management process is limited. The owner of a risk assessment must clearly communicate its purpose, process, and expected benefits. The right parties must be engaged to ensure relevant input, informed assessment, and meaningful and actionable results.	■ Risk Strategy ■ Risk Tolerance Statement ■ Risk Management Policy ■ Risk Assessment Policy ■ Internal Controls Policy	1. Governance and Ownership 2. Roles and Responsibilities 3. Risk Management Processes 4. Risk Management Model 5. Risk Rating System 6. Risk Portfolio 7. Action Plans and Remediation Activities 8. Risk-Based Controls 9. Risk Assessment Plans and Schedules 10. Communication of Significant Risks	■ Number of Risks Identified per Period ■ Number of Risks Requiring Remediation ■ Number of Risks That Occurred More than Once ■ Predicted Risk Severity Compared to Actual Severity ■ Number of Risks That Were Not Identified ■ Cost of Risk Management ■ Number of Risks Mitigated
2. Results are difficult to use. Failure to effectively organize and manage the volume and quality of assessment data makes interpreting that data a challenge. Tools, templates, and guidance are necessary to ensure consistency in data capture, assessment, and reporting.	■ Risk Strategy ■ Risk Tolerance Statement ■ Risk Management Policy ■ Risk Assessment Policy ■ Internal Controls Policy	3. Risk Management Processes 4. Risk Management Model 5. Risk Rating System 6. Risk Portfolio 7. Action Plans and Remediation Activities 8. Risk-Based Controls 9. Risk Assessment Plans and Schedules	■ Number of Risks Identified per Period ■ Number of Risks Requiring Remediation ■ Number of Risks That Occurred More than Once ■ Predicted Risk Severity Compared to Actual Severity ■ Number of Risks That Were Not Identified ■ Number of Risks Mitigated
3. Results of the risk assessment are not acted upon. Lack of clarity and accountability around objectives frequently leads to a failure to follow through on assessment findings.	■ Risk Assessment Policy ■ Internal Controls Policy	2. Roles and Responsibilities 3. Risk Management Processes 5. Risk Rating System 6. Risk Portfolio 7. Action Plans and Remediation Activities 8. Risk-Based Controls 9. Risk Assessment Plans and Schedules 10. Communication of Significant Risks	■ Number of Risks Identified per Period ■ Number of Risks Requiring Remediation ■ Number of Risks That Occurred More than Once ■ Predicted Risk Severity Compared to Actual Severity ■ Number of Risks That Were Not Identified ■ Number of Risks Mitigated

Process: Risk Management			
Process Risk	**Recommended Policies**	**Internal Controls**	**KPIs**
4. Risk is overcontrolled, resulting in excessive costs and stifled innovation. Lack of an effective risk assessment process and defined risk tolerance could result in an organization overcontrolling a risk, which could place an excessive cost burden on the organization and/or stifle its ability to seize opportunities.	▪ Risk Strategy ▪ Risk Tolerance Statement ▪ Risk Management Policy ▪ Risk Assessment Policy ▪ Internal Controls Policy	1. Governance and Ownership 2. Roles and Responsibilities 3. Risk Management Processes 4. Risk Management Model 5. Risk Rating System 6. Risk Portfolio 7. Action Plans and Remediation Activities 8. Risk-Based Controls 9. Risk Assessment Plans and Schedules 10. Communication of Significant Risks	▪ Cost of Risk Management
5. Risk assessments become stale, providing the same results every time. Without their data capture, process, and reporting being refreshed from time to time, risk assessments may lose relevance.	▪ Risk Management Policy ▪ Risk Assessment Policy ▪ Internal Controls Policy	7. Action Plans and Remediation Activities 8. Risk-Based Controls 9. Risk Assessment Plans and Schedules 10. Communication of Significant Risks	▪ Number of Risks Identified per Period ▪ Number of Risks Requiring Remediation ▪ Number of Risks That Occurred More than Once ▪ Predicted Risk Severity Compared to Actual Severity ▪ Number of Risks That Were Not Identified ▪ Cost of Risk Management ▪ Number of Risks Mitigated
6. Risk assessment is added onto day-to-day responsibilities without being integrated into business processes. While tools and templates are helpful to ensure consistency in data capture, assessment, and reporting, it is important that the risk assessment process be anchored and integrated into existing business processes.	▪ Risk Management Policy ▪ Risk Assessment Policy ▪ Internal Controls Policy	1. Governance and Ownership 2. Roles and Responsibilities 3. Risk Management Processes 4. Risk Management Model 5. Risk Rating System 6. Risk Portfolio 7. Action Plans and Remediation Activities 8. Risk-Based Controls 9. Risk Assessment Plans and Schedules 10. Communication of Significant Risks	▪ Number of Risks Identified per Period ▪ Number of Risks Requiring Remediation ▪ Number of Risks That Occurred More than Once ▪ Predicted Risk Severity Compared to Actual Severity ▪ Number of Risks That Were Not Identified ▪ Cost of Risk Management ▪ Number of Risks Mitigated

Process: Risk Management			
Process Risk	**Recommended Policies**	**Internal Controls**	**KPIs**
7. Too many different risk assessments are performed across the organization. A shared approach should be defined for performing risk assessments, using common tools or templates, common data sets (e.g. risk categories, libraries of risks and controls, rating scales), and flexible hierarchies to enable streamlined data capture, an integrated assessment process, and flexible reporting.	■ Risk Management Policy ■ Risk Assessment Policy	2. Roles and Responsibilities 3. Risk Management Processes 4. Risk Management Model 5. Risk Rating System 6. Risk Portfolio 7. Action Plans and Remediation Activities 8. Risk-Based Controls 9. Risk Assessment Plans and Schedules 10. Communication of Significant Risks	■ Number of Risks Identified per Period ■ Number of Risks Requiring Remediation ■ Number of Risks That Occurred More than Once ■ Predicted Risk Severity Compared to Actual Severity ■ Number of Risks That Were Not Identified ■ Cost of Risk Management ■ Number of Risks Mitigated
8. Risk assessments are not structured to prevent the next big failure. As risk assessment provides a means for facilitating the discussion around key risks and potential control failures, it helps reduce the risk of breakdowns, unanticipated losses, and other significant failures. Risk assessments need to invoke the right subject-matter experts and consider not only past experience but also forward-looking analysis.	■ Risk Strategy ■ Risk Tolerance Statement ■ Risk Management Policy ■ Risk Assessment Policy ■ Internal Controls Policy	1. Governance and Ownership 2. Roles and Responsibilities 3. Risk Management Processes 4. Risk Management Model 5. Risk Rating System 6. Risk Portfolio 7. Action Plans and Remediation Activities 8. Risk-Based Controls 9. Risk Assessment Plans and Schedules 10. Communication of Significant Risks	■ Number of Risks Identified per Period ■ Number of Risks Requiring Remediation ■ Number of Risks That Occurred More than Once ■ Predicted Risk Severity Compared to Actual Severity ■ Number of Risks That Were Not Identified ■ Cost of Risk Management ■ Number of Risks Mitigated

Process: Risk Management			
Process Risk	**Recommended Policies**	**Internal Controls**	**KPIs**
9. Key principles are not put to work. With organizations facing a fluid and seemingly endless array of risks and obligations, these key principles should be leveraged to provide the consistent platform necessary to effectively manage these risks in a cost-effective and sensible way.	■ Risk Strategy ■ Risk Tolerance ■ Statement ■ Risk Management Policy ■ Risk Assessment Policy ■ Internal Controls Policy	4. Risk Management Model 5. Risk Rating System 6. Risk Portfolio 7. Action Plans and Remediation Activities 8. Risk-Based Controls 9. Risk Assessment Plans and Schedules 10. Communication of Significant Risks	■ Number of Risks Identified per Period ■ Number of Risks Requiring Remediation ■ Number of Risks That Occurred More than Once ■ Predicted Risk Severity Compared to Actual Severity ■ Number of Risks That Were Not Identified ■ Cost of Risk Management ■ Number of Risks Mitigated

CHAPTER FOUR

4

The Controller and Ethics

 OVERVIEW

In this chapter we'll define the requirements for an ethics program that supports the company's tone at the top and ensures corporate compliance. We'll demonstrate how tone at the top can impact the external perception of the company and influence the attitude of employees and dedication to internal controls. A code of conduct is defined as the policies and procedures that support the organization's tone at the top.

The connection between fraud and the tone at the top of an organization has received a great deal of attention over the last few years. Tone at the top refers to the ethical atmosphere that is created in the workplace by the organization's leadership. Whatever tone management sets will have a trickle-down effect on employees of the company. If the tone set by managers upholds ethics and integrity, employees will be more inclined to uphold those same values.

As a best practice, many organizations integrate ethics and compliance requirements into all business processes. Controllers need to ensure that an environment of ethics and compliance is embedded within their areas of responsibility. A controller plays a key role in managing all internal control initiatives in private and public companies. These initiatives usually include the deployment of ethical standards and/or a code of conduct for the organization. The controller may work with the organization's ethics and/or compliance officer to ensure that the tone at the top is embedded in internal controls programs.

ETHICS PROGRAM PROCESS FLOW

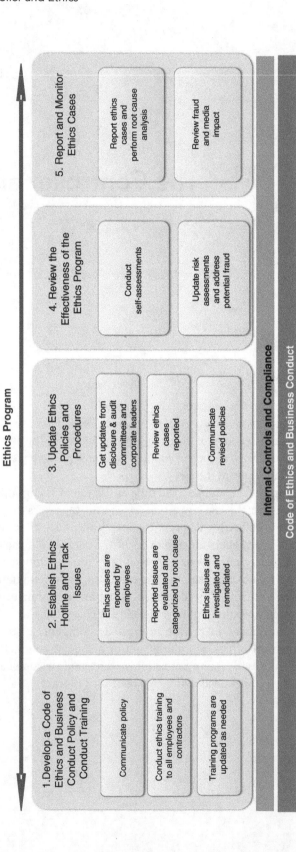

Ethics Program

1. Develop a Code of Ethics and Business Conduct Policy and Conduct Training

- Communicate policy
- Conduct ethics training to all employees and contractors
- Training programs are updated as needed

2. Establish Ethics Hotline and Track Issues

- Ethics cases are reported by employees
- Reported issues are evaluated and categorized by root cause
- Ethics issues are investigated and remediated

3. Update Ethics Policies and Procedures

- Get updates from disclosure & audit committees and corporate leaders
- Review ethics cases reported
- Communicate revised policies

4. Review the Effectiveness of the Ethics Program

- Conduct self-assessments
- Update risk assessments and address potential fraud

5. Report and Monitor Ethics Cases

- Report ethics cases and perform root cause analysis
- Review fraud and media impact

Internal Controls and Compliance

Code of Ethics and Business Conduct

Code of Conduct and Tone at the Top

WHAT IS TONE AT THE TOP?

The tone at the top establishes the integrity of a company and directs how employees, shareholders, and stakeholders of a company will behave. A tone at the top focused on personal salary and greed that supports and overlooks fraudulent activities results in a company that may behave the same way. A tone at the top that is focused on doing the right thing for employees, shareholders, and stakeholders results in a company that has an environment of openness and honesty. As Michael Volkov of the Volkov Law Group states, "Compliance professionals frequently cite "tone-at-top" as an essential component of a compliance program. It sounds good and a few quick sentences on the topic is usually all that is provided when explaining what this means."[1]

Business owners and managers affect an organization's ethical culture by implementing practices, policies, and procedures – and equally importantly, by following them. Properly setting the tone at the top of a business can help to send a clear message, reinforcing the owners' and managers' commitment to integrity and ethical values. Tone at the top must be constantly communicated and enforced so that there is a clear understanding of the company's emphasis on ethical behavior. Employees must understand the consequences if there is a violation of this organization-wide requirement.

 ## EXAMPLE – CODE OF CONDUCT: MCI

Several codes of conduct are provided in the reference section of this chapter. But as a compelling example, we are providing the code of conduct that was used at MCI (formerly WorldCom) below. Much of the content of this code were taken from the code of conduct that Michael Capellas developed when he was CEO of Compaq Computer Corporation (acquired by Hewlett-Packard). When Capellas became CEO of MCI, he knew that one of his most important actions would be to establish a foundation of ethics and integrity at the company.

He hired an ethics officer from Boeing and started a company-wide campaign to communicate the company's tone at the top. Every employee attended web-based quarterly training sessions and was tested at the end of every session. Additionally, employees were often asked to recite all 10 components of the company's code of conduct by Capellas:

1. Do what you say and say what you do.
2. Treat each other with dignity and integrity.
3. Everyone should be comfortable to speak his or her own mind.
4. Management leads by example.
5. Follow company policy and regulatory requirements.
6. Avoid conflicts of interest.
7. Establish metrics and report results accurately.
8. Focus on what is important and not what is convenient.
9. Be loyal to your families, your company, yourselves.
10. Do the right thing because it's the right thing to do.

---

[1]Volkov, Michael (2012). How to define "tone-at-the-top." *Corruption, Crime & Compliance* blog (September 30; accessed March 24, 2020). https://blog.volkovlaw.com/2012/09/how-to-define-tone-at-the-top.

THE REACTION TO UNETHICAL BEHAVIOR

The federal government and the accounting industry have responded to the erosion of public trust in the accuracy of financial reporting results by enacting legislation and standards that specifically address management's responsibilities.

The Sarbanes–Oxley Act of 2002 (SOX) addresses publicly held entities and identifies the CEO and CFO as the primary parties responsible for setting the tone at the top of an organization; moreover, it holds them personally accountable for accurate financial reporting and discovering and disclosing fraudulent behavior. Even though SOX applies to publicly held companies, many privately held companies and organizations have implemented its internal control requirements as best practices. And many private companies strongly embrace its internal control requirements if there are plans to become public.

An overview of Sections 302 and 404 of SOX is provided for your reference in the figure in the next section. The main requirements of Sections 302 and 404 are the annual management assessment process and the quarterly certification process (respectively). An example of a quarterly internal control certification process is included in the figure.

Both processes require the statements that the tone at the top is ethically sound and that no fraudulent activities have occurred during the reporting period.

Establishing (and continually reviewing) a code of conduct, ethics policy, and statement of business principles identifies and documents exactly what behaviors are acceptable within an organization. HR policies that reflect these protocols can ensure that the company is adequately protected from unethical behavior, and implementing such policies related to hiring, training, and promoting staff can keep unethical individuals from joining an organization or obtaining a position of trust.

A COMPARISON OF SARBANES–OXLEY SECTION 302 AND SECTION 404

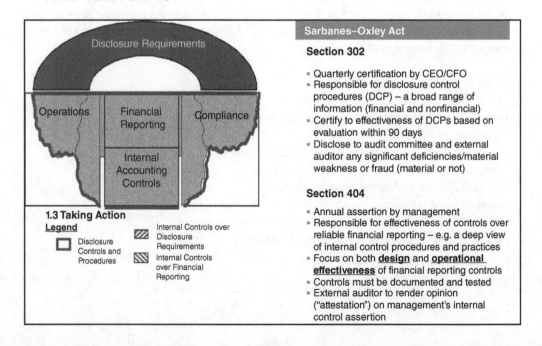

SARBANES–OXLEY AND WHISTLEBLOWER PROTECTION

SOX encourages the disclosure of corporate fraud by protecting employees of publicly traded companies or their subsidiaries who report illegal activities. Section 806 of SOX authorizes the US Department of Labor to protect whistleblowers against employers who retaliate and further authorizes the US Department of Justice to criminally charge those responsible for the retaliation.

Under Section 806 of SOX, an employee engages in protected whistleblower conduct by providing information about matters that he or she reasonably believes are violations of:

- Federal mail, wire, bank, or securities fraud statutes
- Federal law relating to fraud against shareholders
- Any rule or regulation of the Securities and Exchange Commission (SEC)

 ## CONTROLLER'S TOOL 8 – ETHICS TRAINING PROGRAMS

Introduction. An ethics training program is more effective when employees can apply the concepts to their work environments. Examples include the discussion of case studies and role playing exercises. Training is often the responsibility of an ethics or compliance officer and should be provided quarterly and at least annually. An ethics training program should focus on the required behavior within specific situations, such as when and how to report fraud. Some companies focus on their training efforts after a significant event has occurred. These companies refer to the significant event during the training so that employees have a real-life point of reference. The list below provides recommendations to consider when implementing an ethics training program.

1. Ethics programs should target the required behavior.
2. Ethics programs should include a process for asking questions and getting management action to correct possible weaknesses in procedures.
3. Ethics training participants must perform the specified behavior by responding to case studies or role playing.
4. Training programs should include examples where the particular behavior is demonstrated by people who are similar to the participants.
5. Training instructors should review and positively reinforce behaviors learned by participants.
6. Training program participants should experience and learn to cope with the stresses associated with ethical behavior by assessing their own emotional and physical states.
7. The general principles of codes of conduct should be an integral part of the strategic planning process.

CONTROLLER'S TOOL 9 – KEY CONSIDERATIONS AND HOW TO MANAGE AN ETHICS HOTLINE

Introduction. Tips from employees are one of the best ways that unethical behavior and fraud is detected, according to the Association of Certified Fraud Examiners. Under current US Sentencing Guidelines, a corporation convicted of a federal offense may seek leniency if it has maintained an effective program to prevent and detect violations of criminal laws. To take advantage of this provision, the company must prove that it has the following requirements in place and is properly managing its ethics hotline.

1. **Management and Training**. The ethics hotline is managed by a senior staff member and often by the legal department of the ethics office. Ensure that employees with a propensity to commit crimes are not given discretionary authority. Determine whether the hotline should be managed within the company or by a third party. Train the hotline staff with specific scripts to assure employees that there will be no retaliation.

2. **Tone at the Top.** Promote the tone at the top as part of the culture of company. Ethics line procedures and visibility will likely reduce the prospect of criminal activity.

3. **Communication.** Provide effective communications and training for the ethics program. Publicize the hotline using posters, intranet notices, and employee fraud awareness training. Publicizing the hotline is required by US Sentencing Guidelines.

4. **Alleviate Fear of Retribution.** Ensure that the ethics hotline is a system that allows employees to report misconduct without fear of retribution. Employees need to know that all communication will be kept in the utmost confidence and that a proper investigation will take place. Provide other options for employees to use to report an issue, such as e-mail and postal mail.

5. **Response and Reporting.** Provide adequate methods for responding to ethics violations that have been reported. Establish an easily accessible channel with a toll-free number and test the hotline to make sure that it's working. Be sure to validate caller wait times. Identify the types of issues that require immediate visibility. Establish procedures for escalating and reporting issues to executive management, audit committees, and disclosure committees. Ensure there is a reporting process in which issues may be reported by type, such as employee issues, misconduct, violation of accounting policies and practices, supplier contracts, transaction processing issues, and potential evidence of fraud or collusion.

6. **Validate Effectiveness.** The ethics hotline and process should be tested on an annual basis as part of the entity-level controls program.

 ## CONTROLLER'S TOOL 10 – TONE AT THE TOP AND THE TONE IN THE MIDDLE

Introduction. In his article entitled "Ethics and the Middle Manager: Creating 'Tone in the Middle,'" Kirk Hanson listed eight specific actions that top executives should take that will demonstrate the commitment of their company and themselves to ethics and compliance. His recommendations are listed below.

1. Top executives must themselves exhibit all the tone at the top behaviors, including acting ethically, talking frequently about the organization's values and ethics, and supporting the organization's and individual employee's adherence to these values.

2. Top executives must explicitly ask middle managers what dilemmas arise in implementing the ethical commitments of the organization in the work of their groups.

3. Top executives must give general guidance about how values apply to those specific dilemmas.

4. Top executives must explicitly delegate resolution of those dilemmas to the middle managers.

5. Top executives must make it clear to middle managers that their ethical performance is being watched as closely as their financial performance.

6. Top executives must make ethical competence and commitment of middle managers a part of their performance evaluation.

7. The organization must provide opportunities for middle managers to work with peers on resolving hard cases.

8. Top executives must be available to middle managers to discuss the hardest cases, to provide coaching, and to help resolve those cases.

TONE AT THE TOP AND US SENTENCING GUIDELINES

In November of 1991 the US Sentencing Commission adopted new sentencing guidelines (the Guidelines) applicable to all organizational defendants in criminal cases. The Guidelines substantially increase the financial penalties for corporations whose employees engage in unlawful conduct that is ostensibly intended for the corporation's benefit.

The Guidelines are the product of the US Sentencing Commission, which was created by the Sentencing Reform Act of 1984. Following the savings and loan crisis of the 1980s, the US Sentencing Commission responded to the public's frustration with the criminal justice system by releasing the Federal Sentencing Guidelines for organizations, which imposed harsh penalties on organizations whose employees or other agents have committed federal crimes. The Guidelines – comprising seven steps for mitigating the risk of such crimes – include implementing compliance standards and procedures, assigning compliance oversight responsibility to high-level personnel, avoiding delegation to individuals prone to committing crimes, providing information and training on standards, establishing systems for monitoring and reporting criminal conduct without fear of reprisal, enforcing standards and assigning responsibility for detecting offenses, and taking all reasonable steps to guard against offenses in the future.

The US government would also appear to believe that a company's ethics and compliance culture are set by the very top levels of management because the US Sentencing Guidelines states: "High-level personnel and substantial authority personnel of the organization shall be knowledgeable about the content and operation of the compliance and ethics program . . . and shall promote an organizational culture that encourages ethical conduct and a commitment to compliance with the law."

While the Guidelines apply to all corporations, the larger the organization, the more formal the program should be, and the greater the penalty for failure to comply. Formal policies and procedures, and extensive communication programs, are expected of a large, publicly traded corporation. The expectations are not as extensive for a small business.

 TONE AT THE TOP AND THE FOREIGN CORRUPT PRACTICES ACT

If top management is not fully committed to an ethical environment, the lack of tone at the top will be evidenced throughout the company, specifically in middle management. As noted above, the US Sentencing Guidelines mandate that the highest levels of management promote and encourage not only ethical conduct but a commitment to comply with the Foreign Corrupt Practices Act (FCPA) itself.

When passed in 1977, the FCPA was characterized by the American Bar Association as the most extensive application of federal law to the regulation of business since the passage of the 1933 and 1934 securities acts.

Congress acted decisively to restore the reputation of American business and eliminate improper payments to foreign governments, politicians, and political parties. In fact, the FCPA is actually an amendment to the 1934 Securities Exchange Act and is administered by the SEC.

The FCPA contains both provisions against bribery and rules establishing accounting standards. The accounting rules apply only to companies that are required to report financial information under the securities laws. These accounting and record-keeping rules are broad. Your accounting advisor or securities lawyer can advise you if you think that you may be subject to these requirements. Summaries of the fundamental objectives of the FCPA, which are legal requirements, are included below

 ANTI-BRIBERY PROVISIONS OF THE FCPA

The FCPA generally applies to all US corporations, partnerships, and other business organization (generically, a "company"), as well as all persons acting on behalf of those entities. For purposes of this discussion, suffice it to say that the FCPA applies to a US company and its corporate subsidiaries, as well as their officers, directors, agents, and shareholders. The FCPA prohibits any payment or offer of payment to a "foreign official" for the purpose of influencing that official to assist in obtaining or retaining business for a company. The act applies to any act or event that is "in furtherance of" a payment to a foreign official. Further, the payment clause of the FCPA is broadly phrased. It covers not only the actual payment of money, but also the offer, promise, or authorization of the payment of money and the offer, gift, promise, or authorization of the giving of "anything of value." The act also applies to payments to foreign officials, foreign political parties, officials of foreign political parties, and candidates for foreign political office.

RECORD-KEEPING REQUIREMENTS OF THE FCPA

In addition to its anti-bribery provisions, the FCPA also imposes certain accounting requirements on companies. Specifically, the FCPA requires that a company maintain books, records, and accounts that, in reasonable detail, accurately reflect the transactions and dispositions of that company. In order to comply with these requirements, it is imperative that company employees, agents, and others acting on its behalf maintain complete and accurate records with respect to all transactions undertaken on behalf of the company.

 ## GUIDELINES FOR FCPA COMPLIANCE

The consequences of failing to comply with the FCPA are potentially disastrous for a company and its employees. Violation of the FCPA and related laws by a company employee can result in millions of dollars in fines against the company and can subject the employee to prosecution, criminal fines, and imprisonment, as well as disciplinary action by the company, including dismissal. Note that the FCPA states that fines and penalties imposed upon individuals may not be paid directly or indirectly by any corporation for which they may have acted.

 ## THE DODD–FRANK ACT

The Dodd–Frank Act (fully known as the Dodd–Frank Wall Street Reform and Consumer Protection Act) is a US federal law that places regulation of the financial industry in the hands of the government.

The legislation, enacted in July 2010, aims to prevent another significant financial crisis by creating new financial regulatory processes that enforce transparency and accountability while implementing rules for consumer protection.

To both ensure cooperation by financial insiders and fight corruption in the financial industry, the Dodd–Frank Act contains a whistleblowing provision. This means that persons with original information about security violations can report the information to the government for a financial reward.

 ## THE WHISTLEBLOWER PROTECTION ACT OF 1989

The Whistleblower Protection Act of 1989 is a US federal law that protects federal whistleblowers who work for the government and report agency misconduct.

A federal agency violates the Whistleblower Protection Act if agency authorities take (or threaten to take) retaliatory personnel action against any employee or applicant because of disclosure of information by that employee or applicant.

Whistleblowers may file complaints that they believe reasonably evidences a violation of a law, rule, or regulation; gross mismanagement; gross waste of funds; an abuse of authority; or a substantial and specific danger to public health or safety.

THE FALSE CLAIMS ACT

Under the False Claims Act, 31 USC §§ 3729–3733, those who knowingly submit, or cause another person or entity to submit, false claims for payment of government funds are liable for three times the government's damages plus civil penalties of $5,500 to $11,000 per false claim. The False Claims Act explicitly excludes tax fraud.

The False Claims Act contains qui tam, or whistleblower, provisions. Qui tam is a unique mechanism in the law that allows citizens with evidence of fraud against government contracts and programs to sue, on behalf of the government, in order to recover the stolen funds. In compensation for the risk and effort of filing a qui tam case, the citizen whistleblower (or "relator") may be awarded a portion of the funds recovered, typically between 15% and 25%. A qui tam suit initially remains under seal for at least 60 days, during which time the Department of Justice can investigate and decide whether to join the action.

TABLE OF CONTROLS – ETHICS PROGRAM

Process: Ethics Program

---

1. Ethics and Compliance Program. The company has implemented an ethics and compliance program with responsibilities defined for oversight of the programs. The company's code of conduct is widely published to all employees, shareholders, and suppliers.

2. Ethics Hotline Instructions. Instructions to access the company's hotline are widely published to all employees, shareholders, and suppliers.

3. Hotline Inquires. Hotline inquiries are categorized, reported, and acted upon in a timely manner (within 24 hours).

4. Charters and Plans for Ethics and Compliance Functions. The ethics and compliance departments have charters in place. Their charters are approved by the ethics and compliance steering committee.

5. Updates from Disclosure and Audit Committees. The ethics and compliance departments receive updates and minutes resulting from disclosure committee and audit committee meetings.

6. Updated Risk Assessments. Plans are in place in which the ethics department interacts with ethics line management to ensure that compliance issues are included in the applicable risk assessment.

7. Monitored Disputes. The ethics and compliance departments monitor the company's dispute portfolio for developments that suggest systemic issues.

8. Input from Corporate Leaders. The ethics and compliance departments receive systematic input from the company's business leaders, corporate staff, and others on trends and changes in the company's risk profile.

9. Ethics and Compliance Steering Committee. This committee is put in place by the assigned executive to oversee the management and effectiveness of ethics and compliance programs. The ethics and compliance steering committee is responsible for reviewing, revising, and adopting standards for conduct and procedures.

10. Corporate Policy Approval. All compliance policy efforts are coordinated through the assigned executive with formal approval performed by ethics and compliance steering committee. New compliance policy proposals are prepared as needed for the committee. Subject matter experts have been appointed to review the necessity for and content of company policies.

11. Reviews for Effectiveness. Independent examination of the effectiveness of the company's ethics and compliance programs are conducted and the results are provided to the chief ethics officer and the audit committee of the board.

TABLE OF RISKS AND CONTROLS – ETHICS PROGRAM

Process: Ethics Program

Process Risk	Recommended Policies	Internal Controls	KPIs
1. The company is vulnerable to inefficient and fraudulent processes. A poor ethics program is one that ultimately allows fraudulent, inappropriate, and/or inefficient and wasteful activities to exist unchecked or unidentified, causing harm to one or more of the organization's stakeholders.	■ Code of Ethics and Business Conduct ■ Ethics Policy and Procedure ■ Whistleblower Protection Policy ■ Internal Controls Policy	1. Ethics and Compliance Program 2. Ethics Hotline Instructions 3. Hotline Inquires Are Categorized and Addressed 4. Charters and Plans for Ethics and Compliance Functions 5. Updates from Disclosure and Audit Committees 6. Update Risk Assessments 7. Monitor Disputes 8. Input from Corporate Leaders 9. Ethics and Compliance Steering Committee 10. Corporate Policy Approval 11. Reviews for Effectiveness	■ Number of Ethics Issues Reported by Period ■ Number of Ethics Hotline Calls ■ Number of Root Causes of Ethics Issues by Type ■ Number of Fraudulent Activities ■ Value of Fraudulent Activities ■ Number of Ethics Issues Remediated ■ Percentage of Employees Trained ■ Revenue Impact of Ethics Violations ■ Media Impact of Ethics Violations ■ Risk Assessment Results ■ Self-Assessment Results
2. Low employee morale causes negative consequences. Negative consequences can occur, ranging from lowered employee morale to criminal and civil exposure, including possible exclusion from government programs.	■ Code of Ethics and Business Conduct ■ Ethics Policy and Procedure ■ Whistleblower Protection Policy	1. Ethics and Compliance Program 2. Ethics Hotline Instructions 3. Hotline Inquires Are Categorized and Addressed 7. Monitor Disputes 10. Corporate Policy Approval 11. Reviews for Effectiveness	■ Number of Ethics Issues Reported by Period ■ Number of Ethics Hotline Calls ■ Number of Root Causes of Ethics Issues by Type ■ Number of Fraudulent Activities ■ Value of Fraudulent Activities ■ Number of Ethics Issues Remediated ■ Percentage of Employees Trained ■ Revenue Impact of Ethics Violations

Process: Ethics Program

Process Risk	Recommended Policies	Internal Controls	KPIs
3. There is no corrective action or response to offenses. When offenses are discovered, swift and appropriate actions must be taken. An adequate investigation of potential violations must be timely, and when inappropriate actions are discovered the individuals involved must be disciplined in accordance with the compliance and ethics program, and corrective actions must be put into place.	■ Code of Ethics and Business Conduct ■ Ethics Policy and Procedure ■ Whistleblower Protection Policy	1. Ethics and Compliance Program 2. Ethics Hotline Instructions 3. Hotline Inquires Are Categorized and Addressed 7. Monitor Disputes 10. Corporate Policy Approval 11. Reviews for Effectiveness	■ Number of Ethics Issues Reported by Period ■ Number of Ethics Hotline Calls ■ Number of Root Causes of Ethics Issues by Type ■ Number of Fraudulent Activities ■ Value of Fraudulent Activities ■ Number of Ethics Issues Remediated
6. There is no code of conduct. Without standards of conduct and comprehensive, clear, and accurate compliance and ethics policies and procedures, a compliance and ethics program is nonexistent.	■ Code of Ethics and Business Conduct ■ Ethics Policy and Procedure ■ Whistleblower Protection Policy ■ Internal Controls Policy	1. Ethics and Compliance Program 4. Charters and Plans for Ethics and Compliance Functions 5. Updates from Disclosure and Audit Committees 11. Reviews for Effectiveness	■ Number of Ethics Issues Reported by Period ■ Number of Ethics Hotline Calls ■ Number of Root Causes of Ethics Issues by Type ■ Number of Fraudulent Activities ■ Value of Fraudulent Activities ■ Number of Ethics Issues Remediated ■ Percentage of Employees Trained ■ Revenue Impact of Ethics Violations ■ Media Impact of Ethics Violations ■ Risk Assessment Results ■ Self-Assessment Results

Process: Ethics Program

Process Risk	Recommended Policies	Internal Controls	KPIs
4. Ethics training programs are poor or lacking. Programs have poor/incorrect/ inadequate content (in general or for the specific audience). The trainer is unqualified and/or the train-the-trainer content is diluted. There is a lack of variation in education (training sessions, memos, postings, one-on-one instruction, Web-based training, etc.).	▪ Code of Ethics and Business Conduct ▪ Ethics Policy and Procedure ▪ Whistleblower Protection Policy ▪ Internal Controls Policy	1. Ethics and Compliance Program 2. Ethics Hotline Instructions 3. Hotline Inquires Are Categorized and Addressed 4. Charters and Plans for Ethics and Compliance Functions	▪ Percentage of Employees Trained ▪ Revenue Impact of Ethics Violations ▪ Media Impact of Ethics Violations ▪ Risk Assessment Results ▪ Self-Assessment Results
5. There are concerns with confidentiality. Employees are concerned that their names will appear on a report.	▪ Whistleblower Protection Policy	1. Ethics and Compliance Program 2. Ethics Hotline Instructions 3. Hotline Inquires Are Categorized and Addressed	▪ Number of Ethics Issues Reported by Period ▪ Number of Ethics Hotline Calls ▪ Number of Root Causes of Ethics Issues by Type ▪ Number of Ethics Issues Remediated
6. Retaliation can occur. Employees do not often report misconduct since they are concerned about retaliation by their superior and/or coworkers.	▪ Code of Ethics and Business Conduct ▪ Ethics Policy and Procedure ▪ Whistleblower Protection Policy	1. Ethics and Compliance Program 2. Ethics Hotline Instructions 3. Hotline Inquires Are Categorized and Addressed	▪ Number of Ethics Issues Reported by Period ▪ Number of Ethics Hotline Calls ▪ Number of Root Causes of Ethics Issues by Type ▪ Number of Fraudulent Activities ▪ Value of Fraudulent Activities ▪ Number of Ethics Issues Remediated ▪ Percentage of Employees Trained

Process: Ethics Program

Process Risk	Recommended Policies	Internal Controls	KPIs
7. **Proper dissemination of policies and procedures is lacking.** Employees are not aware of the company's ethics program and what to do if there is an issue.	▪ Code of Ethics and Business Conduct ▪ Ethics Policy and Procedure	1. Ethics and Compliance Program 2. Ethics Hotline Instructions 3. Hotline Inquires Are Categorized and Addressed 4. Charters and Plans for Ethics and Compliance Functions 5. Updates from Disclosure and Audit Committees 6. Update Risk Assessments. 7. Monitor Disputes 8. Input from Corporate Leaders 11. Reviews for Effectiveness	▪ Number of Ethics Issues Reported by Period ▪ Number of Ethics Hotline Calls ▪ Number of Root Causes of Ethics Issues by Type ▪ Number of Fraudulent Activities ▪ Value of Fraudulent Activities ▪ Number of Ethics Issues Remediated ▪ Percentage of Employees Trained ▪ Revenue Impact of Ethics Violations ▪ Media Impact of Ethics Violations ▪ Risk Assessment Results ▪ Self-Assessment Results
8. **Policies and procedures are inaccurate, highly theoretical, not tailored, and/or out of date.** Policies become outdated and do not address current ethics concerns.	▪ Code of Ethics and Business Conduct ▪ Ethics Policy and Procedure	1. Ethics and Compliance Program 4. Charters and Plans for Ethics and Compliance Functions 5. Updates from Disclosure and Audit Committees 6. Update Risk Assessments 7. Monitor Disputes 8. Input from Corporate Leaders 9. Ethics and Compliance Steering Committee 11. Reviews for Effectiveness	▪ Number of Ethics Issues Reported by Period ▪ Number of Ethics Hotline Calls ▪ Number of Root Causes of Ethics Issues by Type ▪ Number of Fraudulent Activities ▪ Value of Fraudulent Activities ▪ Number of Ethics Issues Remediated ▪ Percentage of Employees Trained ▪ Revenue Impact of Ethics Violations ▪ Media Impact of Ethics Violations ▪ Risk Assessment Results ▪ Self-Assessment Results

CHAPTER FIVE

The Controller and Corporate Governance

 OVERVIEW

Corporate governance refers to the body of guidelines, systems, policies, procedures, and practices by which private and public organizations are structured. Corporate governance is also the system by which organizations are controlled and managed. A structure of corporate governance builds in accountability for a company's employees, management team, board of directors, governing boards, and shareholders.

Applied Corporate Governance, the digital publisher and training company, describes corporate governance as follows:

"In essence we believe that good corporate governance consists of a system of structuring, operating, and controlling a company such as to achieve the following:

- A culture based on a foundation of sound business ethics
- Fulfilling the long-term strategic goal of the owners while taking into account the expectations of all the key stakeholders, and in particular:

  - Consider and care for the interests of employees, past, present, and future
  - Work to maintain excellent relations with both customers and suppliers
  - Take account of the needs of the environment and the local community
  - Maintain proper compliance with all the applicable legal and regulatory requirements under which the company is carrying out its activities."

CORPORATE GOVERNANCE PROCESS FLOW

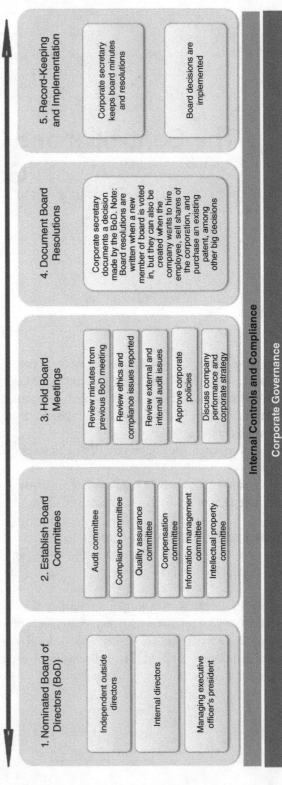

Corporate Governance

1. Nominated Board of Directors (BoD)

- Independent outside directors
- Internal directors
- Managing executive officer's president

2. Establish Board Committees

- Audit committee
- Compliance committee
- Quality assurance committee
- Compensation committee
- Information management committee
- Intellectual property committee

3. Hold Board Meetings

- Review minutes from previous BoD meeting
- Review ethics and compliance issues reported
- Review external and internal audit issues
- Approve corporate policies
- Discuss company performance and corporate strategy

4. Document Board Resolutions

- Corporate secretary documents a decision made by the BoD. Note: Board resolutions are written when a new member of board is voted in, but they can also be created when the company wants to hire employee, sell shares of the corporation, and purchase an existing patent, among other big decisions

5. Record-Keeping and Implementation

- Corporate secretary keeps board minutes and resolutions
- Board decisions are implemented

Internal Controls and Compliance

Corporate Governance

Code of Conduct and Tone at the Top

THE 1992 CADBURY COMMITTEE

The definition of corporate governance most widely used is "the system by which companies are directed and controlled," coined by the Cadbury Committee in 1992. The committee was set up in May 1991 by the Financial Reporting Council, the London Stock Exchange, and the accountancy profession to address the financial aspects of corporate governance. The committee's objective was to raise the standards of corporate governance and the level of confidence in financial reporting and the audit process. Some highlights of their report follow.

"Corporate governance is the system by which companies are directed and controlled. Boards of directors are responsible for the governance of their companies. The shareholders' role in governance is to appoint the directors and the auditors and to satisfy themselves that an appropriate governance structure is in place. The responsibilities of the board include setting the company's strategic aims, providing the leadership to put them into effect, supervising the management of the business, and reporting to shareholders on their stewardship. The board's actions are subject to laws, regulations, and the shareholders in general meeting.

"Within that overall framework, the specifically financial aspects of corporate governance (the committee's remit) are the way in which boards set financial policy and oversee its implementation, including the use of financial controls, and the process whereby they report on the activities and progress of the company to the shareholders.

"The role of the auditors is to provide the shareholders with an external and objective check on the directors' financial statements which form the basis of that reporting system.

"Although the reports of the directors are addressed to the shareholders, they are important to a wider audience, not least to employees whose interests boards have a statutory duty to take into account."[1]

In December 1992, the Cadbury Committee published its Code of Best Practice. The recommendations, which largely reflected perceived best practice at the time, included separating the roles of CEO and chairman, having a minimum of three nonexecutive directors on the board, and the formulation of audit committees.

THE INTERNATIONAL FINANCE CORPORATION AND THE GLOBAL CORPORATE GOVERNANCE FORUM

The Global Corporate Governance Forum is the leading knowledge and capacity-building platform dedicated to corporate governance reform in emerging markets and developing countries. The forum offers a unique collection of expertise in, experiences in, and solutions to key corporate governance issues from developed and developing countries.

The forum's mandate is to promote the private sector as an engine of growth, reduce the vulnerability of developing and emerging markets to financial crisis, and provide incentives for corporations to invest and perform efficiently in a transparent, sustainable, and socially responsible manner. In doing so, the forum partners with international, regional, and local institutions, and draws upon on its network of global private-sector leaders.

---

[1]The Cadbury Report. The University of Cambridge – Judge Business School (accessed July 30, 2020). http://cadbury
.cjbs.archios.info/report.

THE ORGANIZATION FOR ECONOMIC COOPERATION AND DEVELOPMENT AND CORPORATE GOVERNANCE

According to the Organisation for Economic Co-operation and Development, "Corporate governance involves a set of relationships between a company's management, its board, its shareholders, and other stakeholders. Corporate governance also provides the structure through which the objectives of the company are set." The means of attaining these objectives and the process for monitoring the performance are also defined within a corporate governance structure.

While the conventional definition of corporate governance acknowledges the existence and importance of other stakeholders, there is still focus on the traditional debate on the relationship between disconnected owners (shareholders) and often self-serving managers. Indeed it has been said, rather ponderously, that corporate governance consists of two elements:

1. The long-term relationship, which has to deal with checks and balances, incentives for managers, and communications between management and investors
2. The transactional relationship, which involves dealing with disclosure and authority

CORPORATE GOVERNANCE IN PRACTICE

Publicly traded companies have placed their corporate governance structures on their corporate websites. We'll explore examples that will look at the public view of corporate governance for some of the largest and well-known companies in the United States.

The Coca-Cola Company states its commitment to a structure of corporate governance as follows:

"The Coca-Cola Company is committed to sound principles of corporate governance. The Board is elected by the shareowners to oversee their interest in the long-term health and the overall success of the business and its financial strength. The Board serves as the ultimate decision-making body of the company, except for those matters reserved to or shared with the shareowners. The Board selects and oversees the members of senior management, who are charged by the Board with conducting the business of the company. The Corporate Governance Guidelines, along with the Charters of the each of the Board Committees and the key practices of the Board provide the framework for corporate governance at The Coca-Cola Company."

The Coca-Cola Company includes the following sections on its Corporate Governance web page:

- Certificate of incorporation
- Bylaws
- Guidelines
- Committee charters
- Code of business conduct
- Reporting of accounting issues

- Public policy engagement
- Contact the Board

IBM defines corporate governance as "the set of processes, customs, policies, laws, and institutions affecting the way a corporation is directed, administered, or controlled. Principal stakeholders are the stockholders, management, and the board of directors. Other stakeholders include employees, suppliers, customers, banks and other lenders, regulators, and the community at large." IBM further states that corporate governance is "the relationship between stockholders, directors, and management as set forth in the corporate charter, bylaws, corporate governance guidelines, and applicable rules and regulations."

Caterpillar's statement on corporate governance is "Caterpillar's corporate governance program ensures we serve the interests of stockholders and other stakeholders with the highest standards of responsibility, integrity, and compliance with all laws. These standards are guided by our board of directors and global management team, who work to oversee the company's actions, performance, and governance policies." Caterpillar also provides the following highlights on its Governance web page:

- Our Code of Worldwide Business Conduct, first published in 1974 and last amended in 2010, sets a high standard for honesty and ethical behavior by every employee.
- In 1999, the Caterpillar board developed and published guidelines on corporate governance, which among other provisions includes the establishment of a fully independent board of directors, with the sole exception of its chairman, and a fully independent compensation committee.
- In advance of the 1999 report of the Blue Ribbon Committee on Audit Committee Effectiveness, Caterpillar had already implemented many of its recommendations, including a fully independent audit committee with a financial expert as chairman.
- In 1993, Caterpillar's Board adopted written charters for each of its committees, which the recently passed Sarbanes–Oxley Act only now makes mandatory.
- In 1992, the Caterpillar Board adopted a confidential voting policy for shareholders.
- While not required by law, Caterpillar established share ownership guidelines in connection with stock option grants for corporate officers and directors over a decade ago. All of Caterpillar's equity-based compensation plans have been approved by shareholders. Furthermore, Caterpillar has never offered golden parachutes to any company officers and has never repriced stock option grants.
- On June 17, 2005, Caterpillar Inc. executed a fourth amended and restated version of its Shareholder Rights Plan with Mellon Investor Services LLC. The modified agreement moved the final termination date of the Shareholder Rights Plan from December 11, 2006, to June 30, 2005, terminating the Shareholder Rights Plan approximately 17 months earlier than the original agreement and subsequent amendments had specified.
- Company policy requires former senior manager level (or higher) employees of our outside auditor to wait three years before being eligible for certain management-level positions at Caterpillar and requires rotation of outside auditor partners in compliance with the requirements of the Sarbanes–Oxley Act of 2002.

WHEN CORPORATE GOVERNANCE IS FLAWED

The March 2004 edition of the *CPA Journal* included Jorge E. Guerra's article "The Sarbanes–Oxley Act and Evolution of Corporate Governance," in which Mr. Guerra cites *Corporate Governance*,[2] whose authors provide a comprehensive list of the most common transgressions to existing corporate governance rules:

- Executive compensation grossly disproportionate to corporate results
- Stock promotion, such as initial public offerings (IPO), that has gone to an extreme in the creation of very questionable or unproven business concepts
- Misuse of corporate funds
- Trading on insider information, particularly by managers exercising stock options that have rewarded short-term thinking
- Misrepresentation of the true earnings and financial condition of too many companies
- Obstruction of justice by concealing activities or destroying evidence

Mr. Guerra notes that these transgressions are mainly due to these factors:

- Passive, nonindependent, and rubber-stamping boards of directors
- Nonaccountable CEOs and senior management involved in serious conflicts of interest
- Transaction-driven investment bankers and market-makers, and biased and nonindependent investment analysts
- Nonindependent public accounting firms
- Regulators paying more attention to the manifestations of the problem than to the systemic conflicts of interest at the core of poor governance practices

Mr. Guerra states that regulators must take the following actions:

- Strictly enforce new rules issued as directed by the Sarbanes–Oxley Act aimed at transparent financial reporting and effective internal controls.
- Monitor and take necessary action to avoid the negative impact of unintended consequences from the application of Sarbanes–Oxley dispositions.
- Actively enforce laws and regulations relating to board of director and auditor independence from management.
- In rule-making activities, prioritize the shareholder's ability to monitor the board of directors' structure, operation, and performance.
- Ensure that the financial markets' self-regulatory organizations (SRO) adopt strict governance listing requirements.
- Effect the necessary changes in the operation of the financial markets to guarantee a market free of the conflicts of interest now widespread.

---

[2]Colley, John L., Doyle, Jacqueline L., Stettinius, Wallace, and Logan, George (2003). *Corporate Governance*. McGraw-Hill Executive MBA Series, p. 229.

He also states that boards of directors must take the following actions:

- Restructure the board of directors and the audit committee to effectively undertake the new responsibilities assigned by the Sarbanes–Oxley Act.
- Review the structure and operation of the nominating and compensation committees to eliminate even the appearance of conflicts of interest.
- Review existing corporate governance policies to ensure the inclusion of corporate governance "best practices".
- Eliminate even the appearance of conflicts of interest when dealing with management performance and compensation.
- Decide how to give shareholders direct input into the governance of the corporation.
- Educate board members in the responsibilities they must fulfill as fiduciaries of the stockholders.

Lastly, Mr. Guerra states that investment banks, market-maker firms, mutual fund managers, and investment analysts must take the following actions:

- Create and strictly enforce firewalls to eliminate conflicts of interest that result when investment bankers pressure investment analysts for directed company evaluations.
- Change the transaction-driven approach to a "put-the-investors-first" approach when effecting market transactions.[3]

CONTROLLER'S TOOL 11 – THE SARBANES–OXLEY ACT OF 2002 AND CORPORATE GOVERNANCE

Introduction. In his book "The Effect of SOX on Internal Control, Risk Management, and Corporate Governance Best Practice," David A. Doney states, for fraudulent "The effect of the Sarbanes–Oxley Act of 2002 (SOX) has been dramatic and global. SOX enhanced the regulatory framework for investor protection and confidence. SOX has required or encouraged a variety of best practices related to management accountability, auditor independence, audit committees, internal control reporting, risk management, and improvement of financial processes."[4]

SOX has required best practices as included below:

- **Disclosure Committees.** A cross-functional group of top-level managers that meets to discuss pending public disclosures, including quarterly and annual financial reporting.
- **Representation Letters.** To support the certification by the CEO and CFO and ensure that material information is made known to them, a variety of senior finance and operations managers sign representation letters regarding financial reporting matters relevant to their areas of responsibility.

---

[3]Guerra, Jorge E. (2004). The Sarbanes–Oxley Act and the evolution of corporate governance. *CPA Journal* 74, no. 5 (May): 14–15. https://search.proquest.com/openview/65c09128152f297efebcc472b1472530/1?pq-origsite=gscholar&cbl=41798.

[4]Doney, D.A. (2011). The effect of SOX on internal control, risk management, and corporate governance best practice. In: *Best-Practice Approaches to Internal Auditing*, 53–58. Bloomsbury. http://dx.doi.org/10.5040/9781472920409.0013.

■ **Improvement of Finance Organization.** Many companies expanded the number and quality of financial personnel, particularly with respect to US Generally Accepted Accounting Principles and SEC reporting requirements.

SOX has 11 titles that shaped the way corporate America approaches corporate governance and internal controls:

1. **Public Company Accounting Oversight Board**
   ■ Title I consists of nine sections and establishes the PCAOB to provide independent oversight of public accounting firms providing audit services ("auditors"). It also creates a central oversight board tasked with registering auditors, defining the specific processes and procedures for compliance audits, inspecting and policing conduct and quality control, and enforcing compliance with the specific mandates of SOX.

2. **Auditor Independence**
   ■ Title II consists of nine sections and establishes standards for external auditor independence to limit conflicts of interest. It also addresses new auditor approval requirements, audit partner rotation, and auditor reporting requirements. It restricts auditing companies from providing nonaudit services (e.g. consulting) for the same clients.

3. **Corporate Responsibility**
   ■ Title III consists of eight sections and mandates that senior executives take individual responsibility for the accuracy and completeness of corporate financial reports. It defines the interaction of external auditors and corporate audit committees, and specifies the responsibility of corporate officers for the accuracy and validity of corporate financial reports. It enumerates specific limits on the behaviors of corporate officers and describes specific forfeitures of benefits and civil penalties for noncompliance. For example, Section 302 requires that the company's "principal officers" (typically the CEO and CFO) certify and approve the integrity of their company financial reports quarterly.

4. **Enhanced Financial Disclosures**
   ■ Title IV consists of nine sections. It describes enhanced reporting requirements for financial transactions, including off-balance-sheet transactions, pro forma figures, and stock transactions of corporate officers. It requires internal controls for assuring the accuracy of financial reports and disclosures, and mandates both audits and reports on those controls. It also requires timely reporting of material changes in financial condition and specific enhanced reviews by the SEC or its agents of corporate reports.

5. **Analyst Conflicts of Interest**
   ■ Title V consists of only one section, which includes measures designed to help restore investor confidence in the reporting of securities analysts. It defines the codes of conduct for securities analysts and requires disclosure of knowable conflicts of interest.

6. **Commission Resources and Authority**
   ■ Title VI consists of four sections and defines practices to restore investor confidence in securities analysts. It also defines the SEC's authority to censure or bar securities professionals from practice and defines conditions under which a person can be barred from practicing as a broker, advisor, or dealer.

7. **Studies and Reports**
   - Title VII consists of five sections and requires the comptroller general and the SEC to perform various studies and report their findings. Studies and reports include the effects of consolidation of public accounting firms, the role of credit rating agencies in the operation of securities markets, securities violations and enforcement actions, and whether investment banks assisted Enron, Global Crossing, and others to manipulate earnings and obfuscate true financial conditions.

8. **Corporate and Criminal Fraud Accountability**
   - Title VIII consists of seven sections and is also referred to as the Corporate and Criminal Fraud Accountability Act of 2002. It describes specific criminal penalties for manipulation, destruction, or alteration of financial records or other interference with investigations, while providing certain protections for whistleblowers.

9. **White Collar Crime Penalty Enhancement**
   - Title IX consists of six sections. This section is also called the White Collar Crime Penalty Enhancement Act of 2002. This section increases the criminal penalties associated with white-collar crimes and conspiracies. It recommends stronger sentencing guidelines and specifically adds failure to certify corporate financial reports as a criminal offense.

10. **Corporate Tax Returns**
    - Title X consists of one section. Section 1001 states that the CEO should sign the company tax return.

11. **Corporate Fraud Accountability**
    - Title XI consists of seven sections. Section 1101 recommends a name for this title as Corporate Fraud Accountability Act of 2002. It identifies corporate fraud and records tampering as criminal offenses and joins those offenses to specific penalties. It also revises sentencing guidelines and strengthens their penalties. This enables the SEC to resort to temporarily freezing transactions or payments that have been deemed "large" or "unusual."

CONTROLLER'S TOOL 12 – EXAMPLES OF BOARD COMMITTEES

Introduction. This tool provides a series of 10 examples of board committees in place for several well-known companies. I am also providing the board committees for today's Big Four technology companies: Amazon, Apple, Google, and Microsoft.

According to a survey issued by Harvard Law School, "Amid sustained and unprecedented change, board committee structures stayed largely the same over the past six years. Across all industries, boards primarily rely on the three "key" committees generally required by the stock exchanges – audit, compensation, and nominating and governance."[5]

---

[5]Klemash, Steve W., Huennekens, Kellie C., and Smith, Jamie (EY Center for Board Matters; 2018). A fresh look at board committees. Harvard Law Forum on Corporate Governance (July 10; accessed April 28, 2020). https://corpgov.law.harvard.edu/2018/07/10/a-fresh-look-at-board-committees.

1. **Amazon**
   - Audit committee
   - Nominating and corporate governance committee
   - Leadership development and compensation committee
2. **Apple**
   - Audit and finance committee
   - Compensation committee
   - Nominating committee
3. **Caterpillar**
   - Audit committee
   - Compensation and human resources committee
   - Public policy and governance committee
4. **Coca-Cola**
   - Audit committee
   - Executive committee
   - Committee on directors and corporate governance
   - Finance committee
   - Human capital management and compensation committee
   - Management development committee
   - Public issues and diversity review committee
   - Public issues and sustainability committee
5. **Facebook**
   - Audit & risk oversight committee
   - Compensation, nominating, & governance committee
6. **Google**
   - Audit committee
   - Leadership development and compensation committee
   - Nominating and corporate governance committee
   - Executive committee
7. **IBM**
   - Audit
   - Directors and corporate governance
   - Executive compensation and management resources
8. **Microsoft**
   - Audit committee charter and responsibilities calendar
   - Compensation committee charter
   - Governance and nominating committee charter
   - Regulatory and public policy committee charter
9. **Walt Disney Company**
   - Executive committee
   - Audit committee
   - Compensation committee
   - Governance and nominating committee
10. **Zoom Video Communications**
    - Compensation committee charter
    - Audit committee charter
    - Nominating and governance committee charter

TABLE OF CONTROLS – CORPORATE GOVERNANCE

Process: Corporate Governance

1. Create a BoD. Many privately held companies may already have a board, but make sure the board is composed primarily of independent outside directors. These directors should be like a portfolio of investments that are varied and balanced. Directors should be leaders from a variety of industries who provide value, contacts, opportunities, and plenty of objective advice.

2. Develop Policies and Procedures. Policies and procedures establish operational requirements for the organization. The board of directors should approve this document and provide oversight in its application.

3. Develop an Internal Controls Program. Develop an internal controls program to determine if policies and procedures are working. Policies and procedures should be updated if there are ongoing internal controls issues.

4. Implement a Financial Accounting System. The financial accounting system and processes are usually the responsibility of the controller. It is important to establish the proper policies and procedures to ensure that all transactions are reported in the organization's financial statements and the financial overrides cannot be made to falsify financial results.

5. Establish a Culture of Honesty and Accountability. Management needs to establish a culture of doing the right thing through the tone at the top. This culture will become embedded in the organization and positively impact the reputation of the company.

6. Establish a BoD Approval Process.

    a. The board approves the annual budget and five-year strategic plan, along with the annual financial plan objectives. The board constructively reviews management's planned decisions, strategic initiatives, and major transactions, and probes for explanations of past results (e.g. budget variances).

    b. The board approves any financial commitment and/or spending over $50M relating to expenditures, commitments, leases, general purchases, and disposals per the delegation of authority policy.

    c. The board approves any consultant commitment and/or spending over $1M relating to outside consultants and contractor services.

    d. The board approves any financial commitment over $5M for spending overruns and revisions relating to expenditures, commitments, leases, general purchases, disposals, purchase or sale of equity securities or interests, loans, guarantees of indebtedness, and charitable contributions budget in accordance with the delegation of authority policy.

    e. The board approves any financial commitment over $50M relating to acquisitions, mergers, consolidations, divestitures, reorganizations, purchases or sales of business or product line, joint ventures, and any combination of these activities per the delegation of authority policy.

    f. The board must be informed of any financial commitment over $50M for spending relating to legal settlements per the delegation of authority policy.

7. Establish Audit Committee Responsibilities. The audit committee of the board must approve of any financial commitment for spending relating to nonaudit accounting and tax or consulting services offered by the external auditor per the delegation of authority policy.

    a. The audit committee has oversight for all significant related-party transactions. A process exists for informing the board of significant issues on a timely basis.

    b. The audit committee provides oversight to support ethical behavior in the company. The audit committee is sufficiently involved in evaluating the effectiveness of the code of conduct. The audit committee takes steps to ensure an appropriate code of conduct.

8. Establish Risk Committee and Process. The risk committee of the BoD reviews the quarterly risk assessment prepared by management. This committee meets six times a year and reports to the board on any significant issues.

   a. The risk committee of the board, company general counsel, CFO, and independent auditors have a comprehensive risk assessment process and make major business decisions only after analyzing risks and potential benefits. The risk committee and other respective committees review these decisions and issues prior to presentation to the board.

9. Ensure Board Committee Independence.

   a. All committees are composed of independent directors. Composition of the board includes a sufficient number of independent directors to serve on key committees.

   b. Each committee reports to the BoD on a regular basis and more frequently when the topic necessitates it. The committees are sufficient, in subject matter and membership, to deal with important issues adequately. They report results and major issues back to the board as a whole.

10. Provide Board Updates. The board is provided regular updates on progress on achieving the yearly objectives set by management and information on significant transactions anticipated in the next quarter. The board regularly receives key information, such as financial statements, major marketing initiatives, and significant contracts or negotiations. The audit committee receives quarterly and annual financial statements, 10-Ks, and other significant SEC filings. Board members can request more frequent or detailed financial information if needed.

11. Define General Counsel Roles and Responsibilities. General counsel attends the monthly board meetings to discuss significant litigation. There are scheduled board meetings each year.

12. Establish a Code of Conduct. Policies regarding ethics and professional conduct are communicated and accessible from company websites and ongoing publications. The board specifically addresses management's adherence to the code of conduct and is required to approve and disclose any waivers of the code.

13. Define Corporate Secretary Responsibilities. The corporate secretary of the board maintains a listing of open actions requiring management follow-up. Most follow-up items are from committees. The board issues directives to management detailing specific actions to be taken as needed and ensures that appropriate follow-up is taken.

14. Establish Controller and CFO Accountability. The controller and CFO attend monthly company leadership meetings and are viewed with the same regard as division heads within the organization.

   a. The controller and CFO are knowledgeable about complex accounting issues relevant to the organization.

   b. Protocol exists for the selection of accounting principles.

   c. Valuable assets, including intellectual assets and information, are protected from unauthorized access or use.

   d. Financial management reports quarterly on financial results or sign-offs on 10-Qs for public companies.

   e. Reporting responsibilities for the corporate office versus operating units are clearly defined. If the accounting function is decentralized, operating management signs off on reported results. Unit accounting personnel also have responsibility to central financial officers.

   f. For the finance departments (including accounting, treasury, taxes, and financial reporting) there are job descriptions encompassing defined responsibilities and tasks for management positions, including clearly defined supervisory and reporting responsibilities. The knowledge and skills required for the position are clearly defined.

15. Establish Accountability of Key Corporate Officers. Officers meet with key operational personnel in person quarterly. Senior managers frequently visit subsidiary or divisional operations. Group or divisional management meetings are held frequently. There are regularly established staff meetings.

TABLE OF RISKS AND CONTROLS – CORPORATE GOVERNANCE

Process: Corporate Governance

Process Risk	Recommended Policies	Internal Controls	KPIs
1. **Lack of company oversight and accountability.** Responsibilities are unclear and management has no accountability for their actions.	■ Organizational and Salary Structure ■ Job Descriptions ■ Performance Ratings Drive Salary Increases	1. Create a BoD 2. Establish Policies and Procedures 3. Develop an Internal Controls Program 4. Implement a Financial Accounting System 5. Establish a Culture of Honesty and Accountability 6. Establish a BoD Approval Process 7. Establish Audit Committee Responsibilities 8. Establish a Risk Committee and Process 9. Ensure Board Committee Independence 10. Provide Board Updates 11. Define General Counsel Roles and Responsibilities 12. Establish a Code of Conduct 13. Define Corporate Secretary Responsibilities 14. Ensure Controller and CFO Accountability 15. Ensure Accountability of Key Corporate Officers	■ Number of Ethics Issues Reported by Period ■ Number of Ethics Hotline Calls ■ Revenue Impact of Ethics Violations ■ Risk Assessment Results ■ Self-Assessment Results

Process: Corporate Governance

Process Risk	Recommended Policies	Internal Controls	KPIs
2. **Lack of budgets and attention to financial results.** The company is not financially responsible and doesn't focus on spending or financial results. As a result, financial results may be misstated and company funds may be used for personal reasons.	■ Roles and Responsibilities for Budgets ■ Monthly Budget and Forecast Reviews	3. Develop an Internal Controls Program 4. Implement a Financial Accounting System 5. Establish a Culture of Honesty and Accountability 6. Establish a BoD Approval Process 7. Establish Audit Committee Responsibilities 14. Ensure Controller and CFO Accountability 15. Ensure Accountability of Key Corporate Officers	■ Budget Accuracy Percentage ■ Variance Amount per Financial Close ■ Number of Remediation Issues ■ Number of Ethics Issues Reported by Period ■ Number of Ethics Hotline Calls ■ Number of Post-close Adjustments ■ Value of Post-close Adjustments
3. **Executives are overcompensated due to inconsistent job descriptions and pay grades.**	■ HR Policies and Procedures ■ Organizational and Salary Structure ■ Job Descriptions ■ Performance Ratings Drive Salary Increases	3. Develop an Internal Controls Program 4. Implement a Financial Accounting System 5. Establish a Culture of Honesty and Accountability 6. Establish a BoD Approval Process 7. Establish Audit Committee Responsibilities 14. Ensure Controller and CFO Accountability 15. Ensure Accountability of Key Corporate Officers	■ Average Percentage of Salary Increases per Financial Period ■ Number of Promotions per Quarter ■ Number of Instances Where Salaries Are Above Pay Grades
4. **Unfair hiring practices leaves process open to nepotism.**	■ HR Policies and Procedures ■ Hiring Approval Process	3. Develop an Internal Controls Program 4. Implement a Financial Accounting System 5. Establish a Culture of Honesty and Accountability 6. Establish a BoD Approval Process 7. Establish Audit Committee Responsibilities 14. Ensure Controller and CFO Accountability 15. Ensure Accountability of Key Corporate Officers	■ Number of Ethics Issues Reported by Period ■ Number of Ethics Hotline Calls ■ Number of Ethics Issues Remediated ■ Average Percentage of Salary Increases per Financial Period ■ Number of Promotions per Quarter ■ Number of Instances Where Salaries Are Above Pay Grades

Process: Corporate Governance

Process Risk	Recommended Policies	Internal Controls	KPIs
5. **The lack of a strategic plan results in conflicting company priorities.**	■ Roles and Responsibilities for Budgets ■ Monthly Budget and Forecast Reviews	3. Develop an Internal Controls Program 4. Implement a Financial Accounting System 5. Establish a Culture of Honesty and Accountability 6. Establish a BoD Approval Process 7. Establish Audit Committee Responsibilities 14. Ensure Controller and CFO Accountability 15. Ensure Accountability of Key Corporate Officers	■ Budget Accuracy Percentage ■ Variance Amount per Financial Close ■ Number of Remediation Issues ■ Number of Ethics Issues Reported by Period ■ Number of Ethics Hotline Calls ■ Number of Post-close Adjustments ■ Value of Post-close Adjustments
7. **No tone at the top is set.** This results in negative employee behavior and little pride in the company.	■ Code of Ethics and Business Conduct ■ Ethics Policy and Procedure ■ Whistleblower Protection Policy ■ Internal Controls Policy	1. Create a BoD 2. Establish Policies and Procedures 3. Develop an Internal Controls Program 4. Implement a Financial Accounting System 5. Establish a Culture of Honesty and Accountability 6. Establish a BoD Approval Process 7. Establish Audit Committee Responsibilities 8. Establish a Risk Committee and Process 9. Ensure Board Committee Independence 10. Provide Board Updates 11. Define General Counsel Roles and Responsibilities 12. Establish a Code of Conduct 13. Define Corporate Secretary Responsibilities 14. Ensure Controller and CFO Accountability 15. Ensure Accountability of Key Corporate Officers	■ Number of Ethics Issues Reported by Period ■ Number of Ethics Hotline Calls ■ Number of Root Causes of Ethics Issues by Type ■ Number of Ethics Issues Remediated

Process: Corporate Governance

Process Risk	Recommended Policies	Internal Controls	KPIs
8. **The company has a poor reputation and competitive image.** The company loses its competitive edge and revenue growth is diminished.	■ Code of Ethics and Business Conduct ■ Ethics Policy and Procedure	1. Create a BoD 2. Establish Policies and Procedures 3. Develop an Internal Controls Program 4. Implement a Financial Accounting System 5. Establish a Culture of Honesty and Accountability 6. Establish a BoD Approval Process 7. Establish Audit Committee Responsibilities 8. Establish a Risk Committee and Process 9. Ensure Board Committee Independence 10. Provide Board Updates 11. Define General Counsel Roles and Responsibilities 12. Establish a Code of Conduct 13. Define Corporate Secretary Responsibilities 14. Ensure Controller and CFO Accountability 15. Ensure Accountability of Key Corporate Officers	■ Number of Ethics Issues Reported by Period ■ Number of Ethics Hotline Calls ■ Number of Root Causes of Ethics Issues by Type ■ Number of Fraudulent Activities ■ Value of Fraudulent Activities ■ Number of Ethics Issues Remediated

Process: Corporate Governance

Process Risk	Recommended Policies	Internal Controls	KPIs
9. **There are no internal controls or audit processes.** Regulatory and legal risks are high due to potential lawsuits and compliance issues.	■ Code of Ethics and Business Conduct ■ Ethics Policy and Procedure ■ Whistleblower Protection Policy ■ Internal Controls Policy	2. Establish Policies and Procedures 3. Develop an Internal Controls Program 4. Implement a Financial Accounting System 5. Establish a Culture of Honesty and Accountability 6. Establish a BoD Approval Process 7. Establish Audit Committee Responsibilities 8. Establish a Risk Committee and Process 9. Ensure Board Committee Independence 10. Provide Board Updates 11. Define General Counsel Roles and Responsibilities 12. Establish a Code of Conduct 13. Define Corporate Secretary Responsibilities 14. Ensure Controller and CFO Accountability 15. Ensure Accountability of Key Corporate Officers	■ Number of Ethics Issues Reported by Period ■ Number of Ethics Hotline Calls ■ Number of Root Causes of Ethics Issues by Type ■ Number of Fraudulent Activities ■ Value of Fraudulent Activities ■ Number of Ethics Issues Remediated ■ Percentage of Employees Trained ■ Revenue Impact of Ethics Violations ■ Media Impact of Ethics Violations ■ Risk Assessment Results ■ Self-Assessment Results

CHAPTER SIX

Entity-Level Controls

 ## OVERVIEW

Entity-level controls determine how effectively internal controls are working at the organizational level. In contrast, activity-based controls focus on the governance and control environment of the entity. The concept of entity-level controls is somewhat complicated, since these controls focus on the organizational level. They often referred to as "soft" controls.

Entity-level controls have a pervasive influence throughout all organizations. If they are weak, inadequate, or nonexistent, they can impact material weaknesses relating to an audit of internal control. Weak entity-level controls can also lead to material misstatements in the financial statements of the company. The presence of material misstatements could result in receiving an adverse opinion on internal controls and a qualified opinion on financial statements.

ENTITY-LEVEL CONTROLS PROCESS FLOW

Entity-Level Controls

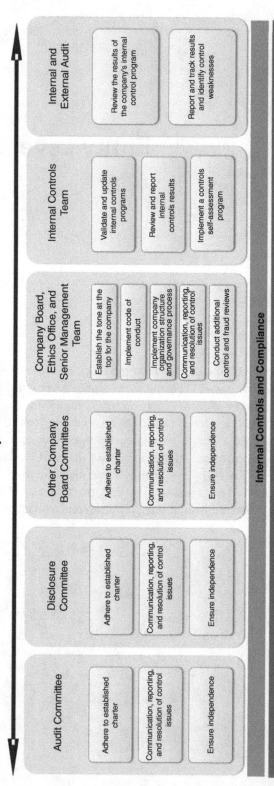

Audit Committee
- Adhere to established charter
- Communication, reporting, and resolution of control issues
- Ensure independence

Disclosure Committee
- Adhere to established charter
- Communication, reporting, and resolution of control issues
- Ensure independence

Other Company Board Committees
- Adhere to established charter
- Communication, reporting, and resolution of control issues
- Ensure independence

Company Board, Ethics Office, and Senior Management Team
- Establish the tone at the top for the company
- Implement code of conduct
- Implement company organization structure and governance process
- Communication, reporting, and resolution of control issues
- Conduct additional control and fraud reviews

Internal Controls Team
- Validate and update internal controls programs
- Review and report internal controls results
- Implement a controls self-assessment program

Internal and External Audit
- Review the results of the company's internal control program
- Report and track results and identify control weaknesses

Internal Controls and Compliance

Corporate Policies – HR, Delegation of Authority (DoA), Segregation of Duties (SoD), and Systems Access

Code of Conduct and Tone at the Top

COSO Framework

BENEFITS OF ENTITY-LEVEL CONTROLS

There are several benefits to implementing an effective entity-level controls program that are applicable to all types of organizations. These benefits include:

- Reduction of the likelihood of a negative risk event by establishing and reinforcing the infrastructure that sets the control consciousness of the organization
- A more effective and efficient evaluation strategy for companies conducting evaluations of internal controls
- Increased effectiveness and efficiency of management's risk assessment and controls evaluation
- Enforcing adherence to an internal controls framework, such as COSO's
- The highlighting of potential problems that require a revision of existing internal controls programs at the activity level that results from an assessment of entity-level controls

Diagram of the Scope of Entity-Level Controls

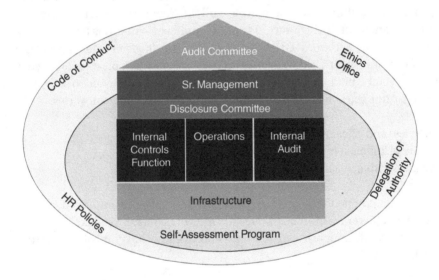

WHY IS THE COMMITTEE OF SPONSORING ORGANIZATIONS OF THE TREADWAY COMMISSION FRAMEWORK IMPORTANT TO ENTITY-LEVEL CONTROLS?

Entity-level controls, along with all other internal controls, should be evaluated by independent auditors according to the Statement on Auditing Standard (SAS) 109 (AU 314) issued by the American Institute of CPAs (AICPA). SAS 109 stipulates that "auditors should obtain an understanding of the five components of internal control sufficient to assess the risk of material misstatement of the financial statements whether due to error or fraud, and to design the nature, timing, and extent of further audit procedures."

This section will focus on the COSO framework, since an evaluation of entity-level controls is essentially determining how effectively the COSO framework is working within an organization.

As defined on COSO.org, COSO was originally formed in 1985 to sponsor the National Commission on Fraudulent Financial Reporting, an independent private sector initiative that studied the causal factors that can lead to fraudulent financial reporting and developed recommendations for public companies and their independent auditors, for the SEC and other regulators, and for educational institutions. The COSO framework helped emphasize the balance sheet review process required by the former Digital Equipment Corporation (DEC). This quarterly process reviewed the status of internal controls across the company.

The National (Treadway) Commission was jointly sponsored by five major professional associations in the United States: the American Accounting Association, the AICPA, Financial Executives International, the Institute of Internal Auditors, and the National Association of Accountants (now the Institute of Management Accountants). The commission was wholly independent of each of the sponsoring organizations and included representatives from industry, public accounting, investment firms, and the New York Stock Exchange.

The COSO framework is the internal controls framework that has been utilized since the implementation of the Sarbanes–Oxley Act of 2002. The diagram below provides a pictorial view of the COSO framework. COSO defines internal controls as a process, affected by an entity's board of directors, management, and other personnel, and designed to provide reasonable assurance regarding the achievement of objectives in the following categories:

- Effectiveness and efficiency of operations
- Reliability of financial reporting
- Compliance with applicable laws and regulations

Although the components apply to all entities, small and mid-sized companies may implement them differently from large ones. Its internal controls may be less formal and less structured, yet a small company can still have effective internal control. A diagram of COSO framework is included.

Control Environment

The control environment sets the tone of an organization, influencing the control consciousness of its people. It is the foundation for all other components of internal control, providing discipline and structure.

Control environment factors include the integrity, ethical values, and competence of the entity's people; management's philosophy and operating style; the way management assigns authority and responsibility, and organizes and develops its people; and the attention and direction provided by the board of directors. Components of a control environment are

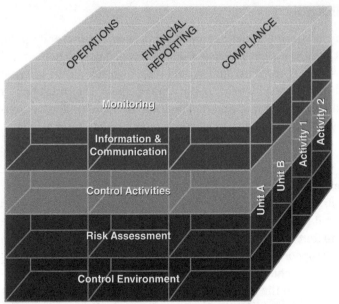

tone at the top, commitment to internal controls, and following a controls self-assessment (CSA) program.

Risk Assessment

Every entity faces a variety of risks from external and internal sources that must be assessed. A precondition to risk assessment is establishment of objectives, linked at different levels and internally consistent.

Risk assessment is the identification and analysis of relevant risks to achievement of the objectives, forming a basis for determining how the risks should be managed. Because economic, industry, regulatory, and operating conditions will continue to change, mechanisms are needed to identify and deal with the special risks associated with change. An internal controls program should be developed to identify and address risk.

Control Activities

Control activities are the policies and procedures that help ensure management directives are carried out. They help ensure that necessary actions are taken to address risks to achievement of the entity's objectives. Control activities occur throughout the organization, at all levels and in all functions. They include a range of activities as diverse as approvals, authorizations, verifications, reconciliations, reviews of operating performance, security of assets, and segregation of duties. A Controls Self-Assessment (CSA) program is an excellent example of a control activity.

Information and Communication

Effective communication also must occur in a broader sense, flowing down, across, and up the organization. All personnel must receive a clear message from top management that control responsibilities must be taken seriously. They must understand their own role in the internal control system, as well as how individual activities relate to the work of others. They must have a means of communicating significant information upstream. There also needs to be effective communication with external parties, such as customers, suppliers, regulators, and shareholders.

Monitoring

There is synergy and linkage among these components, forming an integrated system that reacts dynamically to changing conditions. The internal control system is intertwined with the entity's operating activities and exists for fundamental business reasons. Internal control is most effective when internal controls are built into the entity's infrastructure and are a part of the essence of the enterprise. Built-in internal controls support quality and empowerment initiatives, avoid unnecessary costs, and enable quick response to changing conditions.

There is a direct relationship between the three categories of objectives, which are what an entity strives to achieve, and components, which represent what is needed to achieve the objectives. All components are relevant to each objective's category. When looking at any one category – the effectiveness and efficiency of operations, for instance – all five components must be present and functioning effectively to conclude that internal control over operations is effective. In conclusion, all five components represent the COSO internal control framework.

 CONTROLLER'S TOOL 13 – IMPLEMENTING AN ENTITY-LEVEL CONTROLS FRAMEWORK

Introduction. Since entity-level controls focus on the effectiveness of corporate governance and corporate internal controls requirements, it is important to test the effectiveness of the controls. Many companies deploy a questionnaire and then use the results of the questionnaire to validate the controls. Others rely on the questionnaire alone, which is not a recommended approach. In practice, many organizations follow the COSO model, as described in the last section, when implementing an entity-level controls framework.

I. **Control Environment**
   - Integrity and ethical values
   - Management commitment to competence
   - An effective BoD
   - Management's philosophy and operating style
   - Organizational structure
   - Assignment of authority and responsibility
   - Organization around the HR department.

II. **Risk Assessment**
   - Entity-level objectives
   - Process-level objectives
   - Risk identification and analysis
   - Managing change
III. **Information and Communication**
   - Quality of information
   - Effectiveness of communication
IV. **Control Activities**
   - Process controls
V. **Monitoring**
   - Ongoing monitoring activities
   - Evaluation of internal control system
   - Reporting deficiencies

CONTROLLER'S TOOL 14 – EXAMPLES OF ENTITY-LEVEL CONTROLS

Introduction. Here are some examples of entity-level controls that controllers should consider in the monitoring process. These controls support the requirements of an internal controls framework and indicate how well the concept of tone at the top has been embraced by the company.

Corporate Governance

Please refer to Chapter 5 for a full discussion of corporate governance.

- Which policies does the company have in place?
- Are the policies comprehensive – in other words, do they include a code of ethics and conduct and other relevant policies?
- Are the policies made available on the company website?
- Are employees properly advised of the policies annually, and is there evidence of training and acknowledgement by employees maintained in company files?

Operating Reviews

- Has the company performed a top-down risk assessment of financial statements and identified the significant and material processes and transactions?
- Are there regularly scheduled monthly operating reviews, and are the results documented with operating issues identified and follow-up measures detailed?

- Are there explanations for any significant operating variances?
- Are there minutes and documentation to support the reviews?

Personnel Assessment and Systems Investment

- Does the company require skilled, qualified, and experienced personnel in key positions?
- Are professional accounting designations required for senior finance roles?
- Does the company maintain ongoing training and certifications?
- Are the financial and operating systems adequate to support the transaction volume and complexity of the business operations?

Tone at the Top

Please refer to Chapter 4 for a full discussion of tone at the top. This control would involve a subjective analysis of the emphasis and seriousness that senior management displays towards internal controls and compliance. This can be quite easy to determine based on the results of the tests mentioned above, but can also be supported by reviewing the following:

- Has the company implemented the appropriate internal control framework?
- Does the company have the requisite amount of independence in the audit, finance, and other functional areas as evidenced by the organizational chart?
- Are meeting minutes documented for each BoD meeting?
- Do the CEO and president participate in the follow-through and implementation of internal control reviews, gaps, and remediation? Is this documented?

Additional Entity-Level Controls

Depending upon the complexity of the organization, there are additional considerations to include in the continuous monitoring of entity-level controls as listed below. These controls can be included in the specific internal control programs for the applicable business processes.

- Controls over management override
- Company's risk assessment process
- Centralized processing and controls, including shared service environments
- Controls to monitor results of operations
- Controls to monitor other controls, including activities of the internal audit function, the audit committee, and the self-assessment programs
- Controls over the period-end financial reporting process
- Policies that address significant business control and risk management practices
- Internal audit
- Ethics hotline
- Code of conduct
- IT environment and organizations

- Self-Assessment
- Disclosure committee
- Oversight by the board or senior management
- Policies and procedures manual
- Variance analysis reporting
- Remediation mechanism
- Management triggers embedded within IT systems
- Internal communication and performance reporting
- Tone at the top
- BoD and audit committee reporting
- External communication
- Segregation of duties
- Account reconciliations
- System balancing and exception reporting
- Change management
- Risk assessment methodology
- Corporate governance
- Delegation of authority policies
- Hiring and retention practices
- Fraud prevention/detection controls and analytical procedures

TABLE OF CONTROLS – ENTITY-LEVEL CONTROLS

Process: Entity-Level Controls

1. BoD and Audit Committee Oversight. The BoD and the audit committee have oversight over all significant related party transactions. A process exists for informing the BoD of significant issues on a timely basis. The BoD/audit committee provide oversight to support ethical behavior in the company. The BoD and audit committee are sufficiently involved in evaluating the effectiveness of the code of conduct. The BoD/audit committee take steps to ensure an appropriate code of conduct. The ethics committee chairperson communicates the results of ethics violations noted and investigated during the scheduled monthly committee meetings.

2. Company Policies and Procedures. Company policies and procedures regarding ethics and professional conduct are communicated and are accessible from company websites and ongoing publications. The BoD specifically addresses management's adherence to the code of conduct and is required to approve and disclose any waivers of the code.

3. Corporate Secretary Responsibilities. The corporate secretary of the BoD maintains a listing of open actions requiring management follow-up. Most follow-up items are from committees. The BoD issues directives to management detailing specific actions to be taken as needed and ensures that appropriate follow-up is taken.

4. Risk Committee Responsibilities. The risk committee of the BoD and the general counsel and the CFO for the company, along with its independent auditors, have a comprehensive risk assessment process and make major business decisions only after analyzing risks and potential benefits. The risk committee and other respective committees review these decisions and issues prior to presentation to the BoD.

5. Responsibilities of the CFO and Finance Executives. The vice president of accounting and the controller attend monthly company leadership meetings and are viewed with the same regard as division heads within the organization.

a. The CFO is knowledgeable about complex accounting issues relevant to the organization.

b. Financial management reports quarterly on financial results and signs off on 10-Qs.

c. A protocol exists for the selection of accounting principles.

d. Reporting responsibilities between the corporate office and operating units are clearly defined. If the accounting function is decentralized, operating management signs off on reported results. Unit accounting personnel also have responsibility to central financial officers.

6. Protection of Assets. Valuable assets, including intellectual assets and information, are protected from unauthorized access or use.

7. Corporate Officer and Management Reviews. Key corporate officers meet with key operational personnel in person quarterly. Senior managers frequently visit subsidiary and/or divisional operations. Group and/or divisional management meetings are held frequently. There are regularly established staff meetings. Management meets weekly with the financial reporting group and resolves issues on a timely basis.

Management performs a thorough and timely review of all financial results. Managers do not ignore signs of inappropriate practices. Management has analyzed, on a formal or informal basis, the tasks comprising particular jobs, considering such factors as the extent to which individuals must exercise judgment and the extent of related supervision. For the finance departments, HR has documented evidence in personnel files that the personnel in all supervisory positions have the requisite knowledge and skills as described in the job description.

8. Operating Personnel Business Performance Reports. Operating personnel submit weekly, monthly, and quarterly operating reports, which are discussed with corporate personnel during recurring weekly, monthly, and quarterly business performance reviews.

9. Organizational Structure and Responsibilities. The company maintains organizational charts depicting reporting responsibilities (by department and individual) for the overall organization, each functional area, and each business unit, including finance, tax, treasury, and financial reporting departments. Key areas of senior management responsibility and control are defined and communicated. The organizational structure is appropriately centralized or decentralized, given the nature of the entity's operations. The structure facilitates the flow of information upstream, downstream, and across all business activities.

10. Defined Skills and Job Descriptions. Managers ensure that requisite skills are reflected in job openings when posted. Managers participate in the review and interviewing process to ensure adequately skilled personnel are hired. Evidence exists indicating that employees hired appear to have the requisite knowledge and skills. Job descriptions specify knowledge and skills needed and these descriptions are used in making hiring, training, promotion, and termination decisions.

11. Integrated Internal Controls Program. The organization's managers are responsible for integrating effective internal controls into all company operations. This responsibility includes identifying, assessing, and managing risks related to their business objectives. The resulting internal control activities must be monitored to verify that they are effective and working as intended.

12. Strategic Plans. Strategic plan objectives are assigned to the management team for planning and implementation. These objectives are linked to the budget process and forecasts. Budget results are periodically reviewed to ensure that objectives are met.

TABLE OF RISKS AND CONTROLS – ENTITY-LEVEL CONTROLS

Process: Entity-Level Controls			
Process Risk	Recommended Policies	Internal Controls	KPIs
1. Lack of strategic planning. A strategic plan may not be established for the organization, which could impact the company's structure, priorities, and budget process. The lack of strategic planning could also result in hiring too many employees for a department or project.	▪ Strategic Planning Roles and Responsibilities ▪ Strategic Plan Road Map ▪ Strategic Planning Communication Process	1. BoD and Audit Committee Oversight 2. Company Policies and Procedures 3. Corporate Secretary Responsibilities 4. Risk Committee Responsibilities 5. Responsibilities of the CFO and Finance Executives 6. Protection of Assets 7. Corporate Officer and Management Reviews 8. Operating Personnel Business Performance Reports 9. Operating Structure and Responsibilities 10. Defined Skills and Job Descriptions 11. Integrated Internal Controls Program 12. Strategic Plans Linked to Budgets and Forecasts That Are Periodically Reviewed	▪ Percentage of Strategic Deliverables Achieved ▪ Percentage Budget Accuracy ▪ Percentage Revenue Increase

Process: Entity-Level Controls			
Process Risk	**Recommended Policies**	**Internal Controls**	**KPIs**
2. Lack of accountability. Inadequate entity-level controls can impact the organization's metrics process and create a lack of management accountability.	■ Roles and Responsibilities for Budgets ■ Monthly Budget and Forecast Reviews	5. Responsibilities of the CFO and Finance Executives 6. Protection of Assets 7. Corporate Officer and Management Reviews 8. Operating Personnel Business Performance Reports 9. Operating Structure and Responsibilities 12. Strategic Plans Linked to Budgets and Forecasts That Are Periodically Reviewed	■ Budget Accuracy Percentage ■ Variance Amount per Financial Close ■ Number of Remediation Issues ■ Number of Ethics Issues Reported by Period ■ Number of Ethics Hotline Calls ■ Number of Post-close Adjustments ■ Value of Post-close Adjustments ■ Value of Fraudulent Activities ■ Risk Assessment Results ■ Number of Remediation Activities from the Internal Audit Process
3. Controls do not effectively mitigate risk. Control objectives and activities may be established without considering risk. Without proper controls and risk assessment activities, the company may not meet its objectives, its reputation may be significantly damaged, or there could be regulatory violations resulting in significant fines.	■ Internal Controls Policy ■ Risk Management Policy and Process	1. BoD and Audit Committee Oversight 2. Company Policies and Procedures 4. Risk Committee Responsibilities 5. Responsibilities of the CFO and Finance Executives 6. Protection of Assets 7. Corporate Officer and Management Reviews 8. Operating Personnel Business Performance Reports 9. Operating Structure and Responsibilities 11. Integrated Internal Controls Program	■ Value of Fraudulent Activities ■ Value of Fraudulent Activities ■ Risk Assessment Results ■ Number of Remediation Activities from the Internal Audit Process

Process: Entity-Level Controls			
Process Risk	**Recommended Policies**	**Internal Controls**	**KPIs**
4. The audit committee is not independent and may not be properly focused on the company's control environment. Audit committee members may not be qualified for their positions if there are poor selection processes. The audit committee may not have a documented charter and may be unclear regarding their responsibilities.	■ Audit Committee Charter ■ Internal Audit Planning Process	1. BoD and Audit Committee Oversight 2. Company Policies and Procedures 3. Corporate Secretary Responsibilities 4. Risk Committee Responsibilities 5. Responsibilities of the CFO and Finance Executives 6. Protection of Assets 7. Corporate Officer and Management Reviews 8. Operating Personnel Business Performance Reports 11. Integrated Internal Controls Program	■ Value of Fraudulent Activities ■ Value of Fraudulent Activities ■ Risk Assessment Results ■ Number of Remediation Activities from the Internal Audit Process
5. Ineffective internal audit department. The internal audit function may lack independence and may develop an incomplete audit plan for the organization. The internal audit function may make adjustments to the audit plan due to coercion from management.	■ Audit Committee Charter ■ Internal Audit Planning Process	1. BoD and Audit Committee Oversight 2. Company Policies and Procedures 3. Corporate Secretary Responsibilities 4. Risk Committee Responsibilities 5. Responsibilities of the CFO and Finance Executives 6. Protection of Assets 7. Corporate Officer and Management Reviews 8. Operating Personnel Business Performance Reports 9. Operating Structure and Responsibilities 11. Integrated Internal Controls Program	■ Value of Fraudulent Activities ■ Value of Fraudulent Activities ■ Risk Assessment Results ■ Number of Remediation Activities from the Internal Audit Process

Process: Entity-Level Controls			
Process Risk	**Recommended Policies**	**Internal Controls**	**KPIs**
6. No tone at the top. This results in negative employee behavior and little pride in the company.	▪ Code of Ethics and Business Conduct ▪ Ethics Policy and Procedure ▪ Whistleblower Protection Policy ▪ Internal Controls Policy	1. BoD and Audit Committee Oversight 2. Company Policies and Procedures 5. Responsibilities of the CFO and Finance Executives 6. Protection of Assets 7. Corporate Officer and Management Reviews 8. Operating Personnel Business Performance Reports 9. Operating Structure and Responsibilities 10. Defined Skills and Job Descriptions 11. Integrated Internal Controls Program	▪ Number of Ethics Issues Reported by Period ▪ Number of Ethics Hotline Calls ▪ Number of Root Causes of Ethics Issues by Type ▪ Number of Ethics Issues Remediated
7. No internal controls or audit processes. The lack of these processes will result in regulatory and legal risks that are high due to potential lawsuits and compliance issues.	▪ Internal Controls Policy	1. BoD and Audit Committee Oversight 2. Company Policies and Procedures 4. Risk Committee Responsibilities 5. Responsibilities of the CFO and Finance Executives 6. Protection of Assets 7. Corporate Officer and Management Reviews 8. Operating Personnel Business Performance Reports 9. Operating Structure and Responsibilities 11. Integrated Internal Controls Program	▪ Value of Fraudulent Activities ▪ Number of Fraudulent Activities ▪ Value of Fraudulent Activities ▪ Revenue Impact of Ethics Violations ▪ Media Impact of Ethics Violations ▪ Risk Assessment Results ▪ Number of Remediation Activities from Self-Assessment Results

Strategic Planning and Mergers and Acquisitions Risk

 SECTION INTRODUCTION

The strategy of an organization is formalized by the development of the strategic plan. The purpose of strategic planning is to set the company guidelines and policies that serve as the foundation for all other planning activities within the organization. The strategic plan focuses on the needs, goals, opportunities, and risks facing the company. The strategic plan also identifies the key decisions that are needed to achieve the company's goals.

The strategic plan establishes the strategy for the organization for one to five years and is supported by divisional or budget unit plans that span one to three years. The annual budget process and monthly forecast process should also be linked to the strategic planning process.

The outcome of a strategic plan has four basic outcomes and benefits to the organization:

1. Helps management or an entrepreneur to clarify, focus, and research their business's or project's development and prospects.
2. Provides a considered and logical framework within which a business can develop and pursue business strategies over the next three to five years.
3. Serves as a basis for discussion with third parties such as shareholders, agencies, banks, investors, and the like.
4. Offers a benchmark against which actual performance can be measured and reviewed.

CHAPTER SEVEN

Strategic Planning and Mergers and Acquisitions

 ## OVERVIEW – STRATEGIC PLANNING

Depending on the size of the organization, the controller may be assigned the role of the primary contact that is responsible for assembling and maintaining the plan and developing the financial schedules and statements to support the strategic plan. Here are some additional key tasks:

- Verify the sales and production plans.
- Validate that expense levels are in proportion to other activities.
- Ensure that there is sufficient funding for the projected activity or program.
- Determine if the plan meets the organization's requirement for return on investment (ROI).
- Determine that other financial ratios and metrics are reasonable.
- Ensure that the strategic, development, and operational plans link together.
- Ensure that organizational changes are documented and well communicated.
- Drive the budget process considering the budget process required by the company.

 ## THE STRATEGIC PLANNING PROCESS

According to the Small Business Administration (www.sba.gov), a strategic plan is an essential road map for business success: "This living, breathing document generally projects 3–5 years ahead and outlines the route a company intends to take to reach, maintain, and grow revenues."

This definition can be applied to organizations of all sizes. In their book *Corporate Strategic and Operational Controls*, John Kyriazoglou and Frank Nasuti suggest a strategic planning methodology that includes the following six steps.

1. Prepare for Strategy
2. Articulate the Mission, Vision, and Values
3. Assess the Situation
4. Develop Strategies, Goals, Objectives, and Budget
5. Write the Strategic Plan
6. Evaluate the Effectiveness of the Strategic Plan[1]

[1]Kyriazoglou, John, and Nasuti, Frank. (2012). *Corporate Strategic and Operational Controls*. The Institute for Internal Controls (U.S.A.). http://www.theiic.org/publicationsbookstore/bookstore2.html.

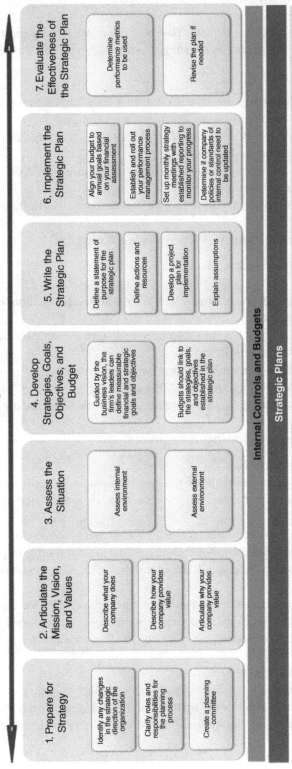

STRATEGIC PLANNING PROCESS FLOW

Strategic Planning

1. Prepare for Strategy
- Identify any changes in the strategic direction of the organization
- Clarify roles and responsibilities for the planning process
- Create a planning committee

2. Articulate the Mission, Vision, and Values
- Describe what your company does
- Describe how your company provides value
- Articulate why your company provides value

3. Assess the Situation
- Assess internal environment
- Assess external environment

4. Develop Strategies, Goals, Objectives, and Budget
- Guided by the business vision, the firm's leaders can define measurable financial and strategic goals and objectives
- Budgets should link to the strategies, goals, and objectives established in the strategic plan

5. Write the Strategic Plan
- Define a statement of purpose for the strategic plan
- Define actions and resources
- Develop a project plan for implementation
- Explain assumptions

6. Implement the Strategic Plan
- Align your budget to annual goals based on your financial assessment
- Establish and roll out your performance management process
- Set up monthly strategy meetings with established reporting to monitor your progress
- Determine if company policies or standards of internal control need to be updated

7. Evaluate the Effectiveness of the Strategic Plan
- Determine performance metrics to be used
- Revise the plan if needed

Internal Controls and Budgets

Strategic Plans

Code of Conduct and Tone at the Top

STEP 1 – PREPARE FOR STRATEGY

The first step in developing a strategic plan is to determine if the organization is ready to initiate the process. Kyriazoglou and Nasuti suggest a seven-step process during the preparation stage, as summarized below:

1. Identify any changes in the strategic direction of the organization.
2. Clarify roles and responsibilities for the planning process.
3. Create a planning committee (see "Sample Strategic Planning Committee Charter," below).
4. Develop a profile for the organization.
5. Identify the information needed to complete the planning process.
6. Deploy a strategic readiness checklist.
7. Deploy a planning tool to ensure that all the components of the plan are identified.

Sample Strategic Planning Committee Charter

The strategic planning committee shall:

- Define the planning process and establish roles and responsibilities for the development and execution of the plan.
- Ensure that all critical business issues are reviewed, documented, and included in the strategic plan for the organization.
- Oversee the strategic planning process for the organization.
- Provide expertise throughout the planning process.
- Ensure that the strategic plan is communicated throughout the organization.

Sample Strategic Planning Readiness

Overall Corporate Strategy
- What is the future direction of the organization in terms of developing new product, entering a new market, increasing current market share, developing corporate competence, and capacity?
- Is everyone in the organization aware of the company's direction?
- What support is needed by the employees of the organization to implement the strategy?
- Do the employees understand the organization's vision, mission, values, and industry direction?
- How much emphasis should be placed on innovation within the organization?
- Has the organization identified potential partners and competitors?
- Has the organization identified a company to acquire or merge with?

Business Unit Strategy
- Is the strategic plan being developed at the headquarters level or at the business-unit level?
- Does the business unit have its own vision, mission, and plan? If so, are the business unit's visions, missions, and plans aligned with the strategic plan developed by headquarters?

- What resources should be invested in innovation?
- What types of innovation should the organization focus on?
- How will this innovation align with the organization's strategy?

Risk Management
- Is risk addressed in the strategic plan?
- Does the strategic plan create any new risks for the organization?
- Are there new compliance issues that need to be considered?

Human Resources Management
- Does the strategic plan require additional resources or new levels of competencies within the organization?
- Does the organization need to hire new talent or should the organization implement a training and development plan?
- Are employees compensated according to professional and industry markets?

Management and Performance
- Does management establish performance requirements for employees?
- Do performance requirements align with the organization's strategic plans?
- Is the management team of the organization held accountable for meeting the goals and objectives defined in the strategic plan?

 ## STEP 2 – ARTICULATE THE MISSION, VISION, AND VALUES

After the organization determines it is ready to initiate the strategic planning process, the planning team develops the mission and vision for the organization.

The Mission Statement

The mission statement focuses on the purpose, business, and values of the organization. A mission statement also defines the organization's purpose and primary objectives. A mission statement is a combination of what the organization does and how and why it does it, expressed in a way that encapsulates the values that are important. Here's how to write a mission statement in three easy steps:

1. Describe **what** your company does.
2. Describe **how** your company provides value.
3. Articulate **why** your company provides value.

The Vision Statement

The vision statement provides a description of success for the organization. Vision statements also define the organization's purpose, but in this case the vision statement describes success in terms of the organization's values rather than bottom-line measures. (Values are guiding beliefs about how things should be done.)

The vision statement communicates both the purpose and values of the organization. For employees, it gives direction about how they are expected to behave and inspires them to give their best. Vision statements are written for customers, employees of corporations, trade partners, the media, and shareholders. Nonprofit organizations write vision statements to clarify and emphasize their future goals and the benefits that would be derived from donations.

The Values Statement

A values statement provides the guiding principles that facilitate the implementation of the mission and vision defined in the strategic plan.

A study by Edwin Giblin and Linda Amuso of California State University published in *Business Forum* concluded that values have to be internalized by employees in organizations to be real, and that rarely happens.

The idea of establishing and communicating corporate values was popularized by management gurus Tom Peters and Bob Waterman, and thousands of management consultants have created a healthy business working with leaders developing corporate values. In fact, corporate values are often used to establish both the tone at the top and the strategic plan.

STEP 3 – ASSESS THE SITUATION

This step of the planning process determines the current state of the organization. Before completing an organizational analysis it is important to consider external and internal environmental factors defined a.

The Internal Environment

The internal environment includes the factors that impact the organization's success. The company's internal strengths and weaknesses can significantly impact the outcome of the plan process.

The planning team should be aware of any cultural issues, internal control issues, or communication weaknesses that may impact the process. The following factors are important indicators of the internal environment and should be considered in a strengths, weaknesses, opportunities, and threats (SWOT) analysis:

- Internal control environment
- Quality controls
- Product issues
- Patent status
- Research and development status
- Supplier issues

- Foreign market status
- Plant capacity
- Management team stability
- Change management and flexibility

The External Environment

The external factors below should be considered when an organization is developing its strategic plan and should be the focus of a **p**olitical, **e**conomic, **s**ocial-cultural, and **t**echnological (PEST) analysis.

- Markets (customers)
- Competition
- Technology
- Supplier markets
- Labor markets
- Economy
- Regulatory environment

STEP 4 – DEVELOP STRATEGIES, GOALS, OBJECTIVES, AND BUDGETS

This step in the planning process focuses on developing the specific strategies, goals, objectives, and budgets for the strategic plan.

Strategies

Strategies are implemented by means of programs, budgets, and procedures. Implementation involves organization of the firm's resources and motivation of the staff to achieve objectives. The way in which the strategy is implemented can have a significant impact on whether it will be successful. In a large company, those who implement the strategy likely will be different people from those who developed it.

For this reason, care must be taken to communicate the strategy and the reasoning behind it. Otherwise, if the strategy is misunderstood or if lower-level managers resist its implementation because they do not understand why a particular strategy was selected, the implementation might not succeed. This is why the strategic plan must be communicated to all levels of the organization. Additionally, the owners of executing the plan must be aware of their deliverables.

Goals and Objectives

Guided by the business vision, the firm's leaders can define measurable financial and strategic goals and objectives. Financial objectives involve measures such as sales targets and earnings growth. Strategic objectives are related to the firm's business position, and may include measures such as market share and reputation.

Budgets

Budgets are an integral part of running any business efficiently and effectively. They serve as a plan of action for managers as well as a point of comparison at the period's end. Budgets should link to the strategies, goals, and objectives established in the strategic plan. In fact, the strategic plan should drive the organization's annual budget.

 ## STEP 5 – WRITE THE STRATEGIC PLAN

The final strategic plan includes several of the following components, depending on the type of organization and the level of complexity:

According to Stephen M. Bragg in his book *The Controller's Function: The Work of the Managerial Accountant* "the strategic plan of an organization must contain six elements", as summarized below:

1. **Statement of Purpose.** The statement of purpose for the strategic plan.
2. **Actions.** Specific actions should be defined in this section of the plan. The actions should be specific enough to be defined in terms of resource availability.
3. **Resources.** This section defines the resources needed to complete the actions defined within the plan.
4. **Goals.** The goals define the level of accomplishment expected from the actions required.
5. **Time Frame.** The time schedules or the project plan that should be followed.
6. **Assumptions.** The assumptions establish the scenario and conditions that the strategic plan is based upon.

The table of contents for a strategic plan expands upon these elements. The table of contents that follows represents a complete strategic plan for an entire organization."[2]

 ## CONTROLLER'S TOOL 15 – SAMPLE STRATEGIC PLAN TABLE OF CONTENTS

Introduction. Here is an example of a table of contents that can serve as a template when developing your own strategic plan. This suggested approach will help you to keep your strategic planning process organized.

---

[2]Bragg, Steven M. (2011). *The Controller's Function: The Work of the Managerial Accountant*, 4th edition. Wiley.

Sample Strategic Plan Table of Contents

1. Executive Summary. This is written to the scope and level of content that would allow an "outsider" to read the summary and grasp the mission of the organization, its overall major issues and goals, and key strategies to reach the goals.

2. Authorization. This section includes all of the necessary signatures from the BoD (if applicable) and other top management designating that they approve the contents and support implementation of the plan. This section may also include the members of the strategic planning committee.

3. Organizational Description. This section describes, for example, the beginnings and history of the organization, its major products and services, highlights and accomplishments during the history of organization, and so on.

4. Mission, Vision, and Values Statements. These statements describe the strategic foundation of the organization. After approval, these statements are typically placed on the company's website.

5. Goals and Strategies. This is a list of all of the major strategic goals and associated strategies identified during the strategic planning process.

6. Assumptions. This is a list of all the assumptions that were made in developing the plan.

7. Risks Analysis. This includes the organizational risks and how they will be addressed.

8. Budget. The annual budget is included in the strategic plan. This section should contain pertinent analysis that compares the current year's budget to the previous year's budget. Significant increases should be explained and tied to goals and strategies. The budget section of the strategic plan may include staffing plans.

9. Major Company Initiatives. This section provides a listing of all major company projects to be implemented during the life of the strategic plan (one to five years). The listing may contain IT projects, outsourcing or offshoring plans, or merger and acquisition activities plans.

10. Supporting Organizational Plans. This section includes the plans for business development and for operations.

11. Supporting Exhibits. This optional section should include the results of a SWOT and/or PERT analysis, project plans for major company initiatives, and communication plans.

STEP 6 – EVALUATE THE EFFECTIVENESS OF THE STRATEGIC PLAN

The effectiveness of the strategic plan must be monitored to determine if revisions must be made. Monitoring the plan includes the following steps:

1. Define parameters to be measured.
2. Define target values for those parameters.
3. Perform measurements.
4. Compare measured results to the predefined standard.
5. Make necessary changes.

When evaluating the effectiveness of the strategic plan, the organization should determine the performance metrics that will validate the effectiveness of the plan. These metrics are usually reported in an organizational scorecard.

Examples of performance metrics are as follows:

- Number of improvements after budget and performance reviews
- Well-defined business objectives for all departments
- Number of hours spent on strategic reviews
- Percentage of investments that have exceeded targets
- Changes in stock price
- Situations where the corporate strategy was not followed
- Cash-flow improvements
- Profit/revenue by function
- Profit by new products and services
- Total profits/revenues/ROI
- Market-share increase
- Changes to customer base
- Customer satisfaction

TABLE OF CONTROLS – STRATEGIC PLANNING

Process: Strategic Planning

1. Communication of Company Mission. The organization's mission is well stated and communicated to all stakeholders.

2. Periodic Review of Company Objectives. There is a periodic review to determine if the objectives of the plan have been achieved. A quarterly review is a recommended best practice.

3. Performance Metrics. Performance metrics are assessed during periodic reviews. Organizational changes are well communicated and anticipated results are measured by performance metrics and methods such as a balanced scorecard.

4. Action Plans. Action plans are developed to ensure that remediation activities are defined and addressed within the defined time frame.

5. Environment Risks. Environmental risks are included and appropriately addressed in the strategic plan or by the development of contingency plans.

6. Identification of Key Programs. The strategic plan has identified key programs that need to be implemented so that the organization can meet its goals.

7. Detailed Project Plans. Detailed project plans are defined for key programs and are reviewed on a quarterly basis. Project plans have project managers and sponsors.

8. Defined Budgets. All applicable budgets are defined and linked to the strategic plan and reviewed through the controller's organization at least monthly

9. Plans Are Revised When Justified. The strategic plan is revised throughout the fiscal year if there are any significant changes within the organization. All revisions to plans are approved by executive management.

TABLE OF RISKS AND CONTROLS – STRATEGIC PLANNING

Process: Strategic Planning

Process Risk	Recommended Policies	Internal Controls	KPIs
1. **Lack of strategic plan.** A strategic plan may not be established for the organization, which could impact the company's structure, priorities, and budget process. The lack of strategic planning could result in hiring too many employees for a department or project.	■ Strategic Planning Roles and Responsibilities ■ Strategic Plan Road Map ■ Strategic Planning Communication Process	1. Communication of Company Mission 2. Periodic Review of Company Objectives 3. Performance Metrics 4. Action Plans 5. Environmental Risks 6. Identification of Key Programs 7. Detailed Project Plans 8. Defined Budgets 9. Plans Are Revised When Justified	■ Percentage of Strategic Deliverables Achieved ■ Percentage Budget Accuracy ■ Percentage Revenue Increase ■ Percentage of Company Goals Achieved
2. **Company goals and objectives are not achieved.**	■ Strategic Planning Roles and Responsibilities ■ Strategic Plan Road Map ■ Strategic Planning Communication Process	1. Communication of Company Mission 2. Periodic Review of Company Objectives 3. Performance Metrics 4. Action Plans 6. Identification of Key Programs 7. Detailed Project Plans	■ Percentage of Strategic Deliverables Achieved ■ Percentage Budget Accuracy ■ Percentage Revenue Increase ■ Percentage of Company Goals Achieved
3. **There are no operational performance metrics.**	■ Monthly Review of Operational Performance Metrics	3. Performance Metrics 4. Action Plans 6. Identification of Key Programs 7. Detailed Project Plans	■ Percentage of Cost Savings ■ Percentage of Cycle Time Improvements ■ Percentage of Company Goals Achieved
4. **Budgets and spending do not link to the strategic plan.** Overspending can be a significant result.	■ Budget and Forecast Review Process ■ Operational Spending Reviews	7. Detailed Project Plans 8. Defined Budgets	■ Percentage of Strategic Deliverables Achieved ■ Percentage Budget Accuracy ■ Percentage Revenue Increase ■ Percentage of Company Goals Achieved

Process: Strategic Planning

Process Risk	Recommended Policies	Internal Controls	KPIs
5. **Critical company programs are not implemented in time or at all.**	■ Strategic Planning Roles and Responsibilities ■ Strategic Plan Road Map ■ Strategic Planning Communication Process	3. Performance Metrics 4. Action Plans 6. Identification of Key Programs 7. Detailed Project Plans 8. Defined Budgets	■ Percentage of Strategic Deliverables Achieved ■ Percentage Budget Accuracy ■ Percentage Revenue Increase ■ Percentage of Company Goals Achieved
6. **Business continuity plans are not developed or implemented.** Environmental risk needs to be considered in the planning process.	■ Business Continuity Planning Policy	5. Environmental Risks	■ Percentage of Critical Operations with Contingency Plans ■ Percentage of Contingency Plans Test

 ## OVERVIEW – MERGERS AND ACQUISITIONS

The strategic planning initiative may result in the organization's pursuit of an M&A (mergers and acquisitions) activity. This effort may be led by the controller from start to finish. M&A refers to the management, financing, and strategy involved with buying, selling, and combining companies. M&A strategy refers to the driving idea behind a deal. Strategic buyers are more likely to be other companies, and these deals are called strategic M&A. Financial buyers are interested in performing M&A transactions for the purpose of financial return, such as increasing operating cash flow.

Merger: A merger is the combination of two or more entities into a single entity, with the resources of the original entities being pooled into the new entity. The intent of a merger is that the parties enter into the transaction on approximately equal terms.

Acquisition: When a buyer decides to engage in an acquisition, it should be done in a methodical manner and not in reaction to a sudden opportunity. This requires a long-term commitment to reviewing the range of possible acquisition opportunities, based on what is needed in an acquisition target.

The M&A process from the seller's and the buyer's perspective are depicted in the following figures.

MERGERS AND ACQUISITIONS PROCESS FLOW – SELLER

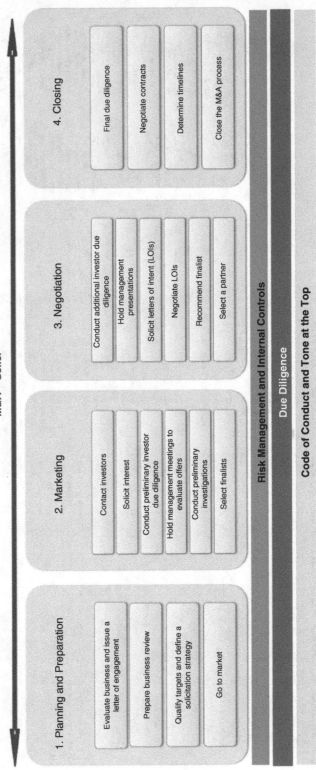

M&A – Seller

1. Planning and Preparation
- Evaluate business and issue a letter of engagement
- Prepare business review
- Qualify targets and define a solicitation strategy
- Go to market

2. Marketing
- Contact investors
- Solicit interest
- Conduct preliminary investor due diligence
- Hold management meetings to evaluate offers
- Conduct preliminary investigations
- Select finalists

3. Negotiation
- Conduct additional investor due diligence
- Hold management presentations
- Solicit letters of intent (LOIs)
- Negotiate LOIs
- Recommend finalist
- Select a partner

4. Closing
- Final due diligence
- Negotiate contracts
- Determine timelines
- Close the M&A process

Risk Management and Internal Controls

Due Diligence

Code of Conduct and Tone at the Top

MERGERS AND ACQUISITIONS PROCESS FLOW – BUYER

M&A – Buyer

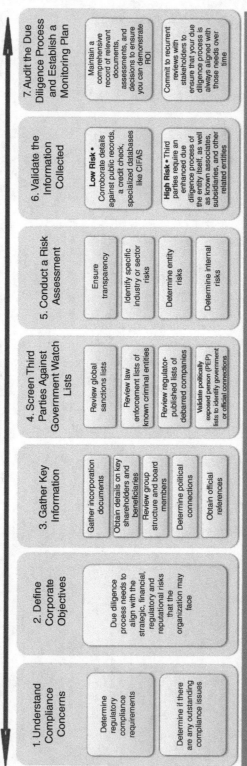

1. Understand Compliance Concerns

- Determine regulatory compliance requirements
- Determine if there are any outstanding compliance issues

2. Define Corporate Objectives

- Due diligence process needs to align with the strategic, financial, regulatory and reputational risks that the organization may face

3. Gather Key Information

- Gather incorporation documents
- Obtain details on key shareholders and beneficiaries
- Review group structure and board members
- Determine political connections
- Obtain official references

4. Screen Third Parties Against Government Watch Lists

- Review global sanctions lists
- Review law enforcement lists of known criminal entities
- Review regulator-published lists of debarred companies
- Validate politically exposed person (PEP) lists to identify government or official connections

5. Conduct a Risk Assessment

- Ensure transparency
- Identify specific industry or sector risks
- Determine entity risks
- Determine internal risks

6. Validate the Information Collected

- **Low Risk** ● Corroborate details against public records, a credit check, specialized databases like CIFAS
- **High Risk** ● Third parties require an enhanced due diligence process of the entity itself, as well as known associates, subsidiaries, and other related entities

7. Audit the Due Diligence Process and Establish a Monitoring Plan

- Maintain a comprehensive record of relevant documents, assessments, and decisions to ensure you can demonstrate ROI
- Commit to recurrent reviews with stakeholders to ensure that your due diligence process is always aligned with those needs over time

Risk Management and Internal Controls

Due Diligence

Code of Conduct and Tone at the Top

CONTROLLER'S TOOL 16 – MERGERS AND ACQUISITIONS DUE DILIGENCE CHECKLIST

Introduction. The following due diligence checklist should be used as a master list of possible due diligence items that should be investigated when initiating an M&A activity. It is rarely necessary to use the entire list. Instead, select only those items that appear to be most relevant to the current acquisition target.

Synergies

- Itemize the synergies that will be created by the acquisition. Split the synergies list into those based on identifiable cost reductions and those based on possible revenue increases.
- How well do the products, personnel, and geographic coverage of the acquirer and acquiree fit together?

Market Overview

- What is the size of the market?
- How is the market segmented?
- What is the market's projected growth and profitability?
- What are the factors affecting growth and profitability?
- What are the trends in the number of competitors and their size, product innovation, distribution, finances, regulation, and product liability?

Corporate Overview

- What are the company's core competencies?
- Does the company maintain any strategic alliances?
- When and where was the company founded, and by whom?
- What is its history of product development?
- What is the history of its management team?
- Has the corporate location changed?
- Have there been ownership changes?
- Have there been acquisitions or divestitures?
- What is its financial history?

Culture

- What type of command structure is used? Does it vary by department?
- Is there a set of standard policies and procedures that govern most processes? How closely do employees adhere to it?
- What practices does the company use to retain employees?
- What types of social functions do employees engage in as a group?
- Does the company generally promote from within or from the outside?
- What types of training does the company require of its employees?
- What types of indoctrination programs are used for new employees?

- What types of awards and ceremonies are used to recognize employee achievements?
- What level of customer service is the company accustomed to provide? Does it support "above and beyond" levels of support and publicize these efforts?
- What dress code does it allow? Does this vary by location?
- What type of feedback mechanisms are used to discuss issues about employee performance?
- How does the company disseminate information to its employees? Is it a more formal method, such as a monthly newsletter, or more informal employee meetings?
- What is the physical environment? Does the company emphasize low costs with cheap furnishings or more expensive surroundings?
- Is there a sense of urgency in completing tasks, or is the environment more relaxed?

Personnel

- Obtain a list of all employees, their current compensation and compensation for the prior year, dates of hire, dates of birth, race, sex, and job titles.
- Obtain a list of all inactive employees that states the reason for their inactive status and the prognosis for their return.
- Obtain copies of the I-9 forms for all active employees.
- Obtain copies of any employment agreements.
- Obtain copies of performance evaluation criteria and bonus plans.
- Obtain copies of any noncompete, intellectual property, and/or confidentiality agreements. Also obtain copies of noncompete agreements that currently apply to terminated employees.
- Obtain copies of any salesperson compensation agreements.
- Obtain copies of any director compensation agreements.
- Summarize any loan amounts and terms to officers, directors, and employees.
- Obtain any union labor agreements.
- Determine the number of states to which payroll taxes must be paid.
- Obtain a copy of the employee manual.
- Conduct background investigations on principal employees.
- Summarize the names, ages, titles, education, experience, and professional biographies of the senior management team.
- Obtain copies of employee resumes.
- Determine the employee turnover rate for the past two years.
- Obtain a list of all involuntary terminations within the past year, stating the reason for termination and the age, sex, race, and disability status of each person terminated.
- Obtain a copy of the organizational chart.

Benefits

- Review accrued 401(k) benefits. What is the company contribution percentage? What is the level of employee participation?
- Obtain copies of all pension plan documents, amendments, and letters of determination.
- Obtain copies of the pension assets, liabilities, expenses, and audits for the past three years.
- Determine the funding status of the company pension plan and the 10-year projected cash expense associated with it.

- Itemize all fringe benefits, along with current and projected employee eligibility for and participation in each one.
- Obtain a list of all former employees using COBRA coverage and the dates on which their access to COBRA coverage expires.
- Itemize all executive perquisites above the standard benefits package and the extent of these expenses for the past two years.

Intellectual Property

- Review all current patent, trademark, service mark, trade name, and copyright agreements, and note renewal dates.
- Obtain an itemization of all pending patent applications.
- Determine annual patent renewal costs.
- Determine the current patent-related revenue stream.
- Document the patent application process. Have any potential patents not been applied for?
- List all trademark and service mark registrations and pending applications for registration. Verify that all affidavits of use and renewal applications have been filed and prosecution of all pending applications is current.
- List all unregistered trademarks and service marks used by the organization.
- Collect and catalog copies of all publications and check for unlisted trademarks and service marks, and proper notification.
- List all copyright registrations.
- List all registered designs.
- If the company has any information that provides a competitive advantage, verify that the information is marked as "confidential."
- Confirm that all employees have executed invention assignment and confidentiality agreements.
- Obtain copies of all licenses of intellectual property in which the company is the licensor or licensee.
- List all lawsuits pertaining to intellectual property in which the organization is a party.

Brands

- Review any branding strategy documents. Does the company have a long-term plan for brand support?
- Review budgeted and actual expenditures for customer support, marketing, and quality assurance related to branding.
- Determine what types of advertising and promotion are used.
- Ensure that the company has clear title to any branded names.
- Determine how well the brand is supported on the company website.
- Note the amount and trend of any legal fees needed to stop brand encroachment.

Risk Management

- Determine whether there is a risk management officer. What is this person's job description?
- Determine whether the company has an overall risk mitigation plan that it updates regularly.

- Review all corporate insurance, using a schedule from the company's insurance agency. If there is material pending litigation, determine the extent of insurance coverage and obtain insurance company confirmation. Note whether insurance terms are for "claims made" or "claims incurred," as well as the amounts of deductibles.
- Determine whether aggregate insurance amounts have been penetrated and whether there is a history of coming close to the aggregate totals.
- Determine whether there have been substantial premium adjustments in the past.
- Determine the extent to which the company self-insures its activities. Are there uninsured risks that the company does not appear to be aware of or is ignoring?

Capacity

- Determine the facility overhead cost required for minimum, standard, and maximum capacity.
- Ascertain the amount of capital replacements needed in the near future.
- Determine the periodic maintenance cost of existing equipment.
- Determine the maximum sustainable production capacity by production line.
- Estimate the cost of modifications needed to increase the capacity of each production line or facility.

Assets

- Verify bank reconciliations for all bank accounts harboring significant cash balances.
- Obtain current detail of accounts receivable (AR).
- Determine the days of receivables outstanding and the probable amount of bad debt. Review the allowance for doubtful accounts calculation.
- Obtain a list of all accounts and notes receivable from employees.
- Obtain a list of all inventory items, and discuss the obsolescence reserve. Determine the valuation method used.
- Obtain the current fixed asset listing as well as depreciation calculations. Audit the largest items to verify their existence.
- Appraise the value of the most expensive fixed assets.
- Obtain an itemized list of all assets that are not receivables or fixed assets.
- Ascertain the existence of any liens against company assets.
- Obtain any maintenance agreements on company equipment.
- Determine whether there is an upcoming need to replace assets.
- Discuss whether there are any plans to close, relocate, or expand any facilities.
- Itemize all capitalized research and development and/or software development expenses.
- Determine the value of any net operating loss carry forward assets.

Liabilities

- Review the current accounts payable (AP) listing.
- Obtain a list of all AP to employees.
- Review the terms of any lines of credit.
- Review the amount and terms of any other debt agreements. Review covenants in the debt agreements and determine if the company has breached the covenants in the past or is likely to do so in the near future.

- Look for unrecorded debt.
- Verify wage and tax remittances to all government entities and that there are no unpaid amounts.
- Review the sufficiency of accruals for wages, vacation time, legal expenses, insurance, property taxes, and commissions.
- Obtain copies of all unexpired purchasing commitments (purchase orders, etc.).
- Investigate any potential warranty, environmental, legal, and regulatory noncompliance issues.

Equity

- Obtain a shareholder list that notes the number of shares held and any special voting rights.
- Review all BoD resolutions authorizing the issuance of stock to ensure that all shares are validly issued.
- Review all convertible debt agreements to which the company or any subsidiary is a party. Note any restrictions on dividends, on incurring extra debt, and on issuing additional capital stock. Note any unusual consent or default provisions. Note the conversion trigger points.
- Review any disclosure documents used in the private placement of securities or loan applications during the preceding five years.
- Review all documents affecting ownership, voting, or rights to acquire the company's stock for required disclosure and significance to the purchase transactions, such as warrants, options, security holder agreements, registration rights agreements, shareholder rights, or poison pill plans.

Profitability

- Obtain audited financial statements for the last three years.
- Obtain monthly financial statements for the current year.
- Obtain copies of federal tax returns for the last three years.
- Determine profitability by product, customer, and segment.
- Determine what the revenues and profits per employee are.
- Determine what the direct materials expense as a percentage of revenue is.
- Determine the trend for revenues, costs, and profits for the past three years.
- Determine how many staff members are directly traceable to the servicing of specific customer accounts.
- Determine whether there are any delayed expenses. Has the customer avoided necessary maintenance expenditures or wage increases in order to boost profitability?
- Determine whether the company has capitalized a disproportionate amount of expenses.
- Obtain the budgets for the past three years. Does the company routinely achieve its budgets, or does it fall short?

Cash Flow

- Construct cash forecast for the next six months. Will the company spin off or absorb cash?
- Review the trend line of work capital for the past year. How is it changing in relation to total sales?

- Categorize working capital by segment, product line, and customer. What parts of the business are absorbing the most cash?
- Determine historical and projected capital expenditure requirements. Does the company have enough cash to pay for its capital investment needs?

Customers

- Determine how concentrated sales are among the top customers.
- Determine the distribution of sales among the various products and services.
- Determine the current sales backlog by customer.
- Determine the seasonality of sales. Are sales unusually subject to changes in the business cycle?
- Determine the financial condition of key customers. Does it appear that their businesses are sufficiently robust to continue supporting purchases from the company?
- Determine how long the company has had sales relationships with its key customers.
- Determine which new customers the company is actively pursuing and how much potential revenue and profit they represent.
- Determine how profitable each of the key customer accounts is. Do any customers require a disproportionate amount of servicing, or require special terms and conditions?
- Itemize any customer contracts that are coming up for renewal and likely changes to the key terms of those agreements.
- Determine whether there is a history of complaints from any customers. How profitable are the customers who appear to be the most dissatisfied?
- Obtain a list of all customers who have stopped doing business with the company in the last three years.

Sales Activity

- Determine the amount of ongoing maintenance revenue from standard products.
- Obtain copies of all outstanding proposals, bids, and offers pending award.
- Obtain copies of all existing contracts for products or services, including warranty and guarantee work.
- Determine what the sales strategy is (e.g. add customers, increase support, increase penetration into existing customer base, pricing, etc.).
- Determine how the company promotes its products and services (advertising, trade shows, etc.).
- Determine what the structure of the sales organization is. Are there independent sales representatives?
- Obtain the sales organization chart.
- Determine how many sales personnel are in each sales position.
- Determine what the sales force's geographic coverage is.
- Determine what the sales force's compensation, split by base pay and commission, is.
- Determine what the sales per salesperson was for the past year.
- Determine what the sales expense per salesperson for the past year was.
- Determine what the sales projection by product for the next 12 months is.

- Determine the category into which customers fall – end users, retailers, OEMs, wholesalers, and/or distributors.
- Determine how many customers there are for each product, industry, and geographic region.
- Determine what the average order size is.
- Determine whether the company has an Internet store. Does the site accept online payments and orders? What percentage of total sales comes through this medium?
- Determine what the structure of the technical support group is. How many people are in it, and what is their compensation?
- Determine whether the company uses e-mail for marketing notifications to customers.
- Determine what the proportions of sales by distribution channel are.
- Determine how many customers the company can potentially market its products to. What would be the volume by customer?
- Determine what the company's market share is. What is the trend?
- Determine whether there are new markets in which the products can be sold.

Product Development

- Determine which products are nearing the end of their useful lives and how much revenue is attached to them.
- Obtain a list of development projects in the product pipeline. What is the estimated remaining time and expense required to launch each one?
- Determine what attributes make the company's new products unique.
- Determine whether any products have been in the development pipeline for a long time and have no immediate prospects for product launch.
- Identify the key development personnel. What is their tenure and educational background?
- Determine whether the company primarily uses incremental product improvements or engages in major new product development projects.
- Determine how much money is invested annually in development. As a proportion of sales? How does this spending compare to that of competitors?
- Determine whether the company has a history of issuing inadequately engineered products that fail. Is this finding supported by warranty claim records?
- Determine whether there is a product development plan. Does it tend to target low-cost products or ones with special features, or is some other strategy used? How closely does the development team adhere to it?
- Determine whether the company uses target costing to achieve predetermined profitability targets.
- Determine whether it designs products that avoid constrained resources.

Production Process

- Does the company have a push or a pull manufacturing system?
- Does the company practice constraint management techniques?
- Does the company use work cells or continuous assembly lines?
- Is there an adequate industrial engineering staff? Does it have an ongoing plan for process improvement?

- What is the production area safety record? What types of problems have caused safety failures in the past?
- What issues have caused shipping delays in the past?
- What is the history of product rework, and why have rework problems arisen?

Information Technology

- What systems use third-party software and which ones use custom-built solutions? Are the third-party systems under maintenance contracts and are the most recent versions installed?
- To what degree have third-party systems been modified? Have they been so altered that they can no longer be upgraded?
- Are user computers monitored for unauthorized software installations?
- Are software copies secured and only released with proper authorization?
- What is the level of difficulty anticipated to integrate the company's databases into the buyer's systems?
- Are there adequate backup systems in place with off-site storage, both for the corporate-level databases and for individual computers?
- What is the level of security required for access to the company's servers?

Internet

- Does the company use the Internet for internal use as an interactive part of operations? What functions are used in this manner?
- Has the company's firewall ever been penetrated, and how sensitive is the information stored on the company network's publicly available segments?
- Does the company provide technical support information through its website?
- Are website usage statistics tracked? If so, how are they used for management decisions?
- In what way could operational costs decrease if the company's customers interacted with it through the Internet?

Legal Issues

- Obtain the articles of incorporation and bylaws. Review for the existence of preemptive rights, rights of first refusal, registration rights, and any other rights related to the issuance or registration of securities.
- Review the bylaws for any unusual provisions affecting shareholder rights or restrictions on ownership, transfer, or voting of shares.
- Obtain certificates of good standing for the company and all significant subsidiaries.
- Review the articles of incorporation and bylaws of each significant subsidiary. Determine if there are restrictions on dividends to the company. For each subsidiary, review the minutes of the BoD for matters requiring disclosure.
- Obtain a list of all states in which the company is qualified to do business and a list of those states in which it maintains significant operations. Determine if there is any state where the company is not qualified but should be qualified to do business.
- Obtain the minutes from all shareholder meetings for the past five years. Review for proper notice prior to meetings, the existence of a quorum, and proper voting procedures; verify that

stock issuances have been authorized; verify that insider transactions have been approved; verify that officers have been properly elected; verify that shares are properly approved and reserved for stock option and purchase plans.

■ Obtain the minutes of the executive committee and audit committee meetings for the past five years, as well as the minutes of any other special BoD committees. Review all documents.

■ Review all contracts that are important to operations. Also review any contracts with shareholders or officers. In particular, look for the following provisions:
  ■ Default or termination provisions
  ■ Restrictions on company action
  ■ Consent requirements
  ■ Termination provisions in employment contracts
  ■ Ownership of technology
  ■ Cancellation provisions in major supply and customer contracts
  ■ Unusual warranties or the absence of protective provisions

■ Obtain copies of all asset leases, and review for term, early payment, and bargain purchase clauses.

■ Obtain copies of all office space lease agreements and review for term and renewal provisions.

■ Review all related party transactions for the past three years.

■ Review the terms of any outbound or inbound royalty agreements.

■ Determine whether any company software (either used internally or resold) was obtained from another company. If so, what are the terms under which the code is licensed? Are there any associated royalty payments?

■ Review all legal invoices for the past two years.

■ Review all pending and threatened legal proceedings to which the company or any of its subsidiaries is a party. Describe principal parties, allegations, and relief sought. This includes any governmental or environmental proceedings. Obtain copies of existing consent decrees or significant settlement agreements relating to the company or its subsidiaries.

■ If the company is publicly held, obtain all periodic filings for the past five years, including the 10-K, 10-Q, 8-K, and Schedule 13D.

■ Review all annual and quarterly reports to shareholders.

■ Review the auditor's letter(s) to management concerning internal accounting controls and procedures, as well as any management response(s).

■ Review any reports of outside consultants or analysts concerning the company.

■ Research any press releases or articles about the company within the past year.

■ Review all related party transactions for the past three years.

■ Review the terms of any outbound or inbound royalty agreements.

■ Review title insurance for any significant land parcels owned by the company.

Regulatory Compliance

■ Review the company's correspondence with the SEC, any national exchange, and all applicable state securities commissions – other than routine transmittals – for the past five years. Determine if there are or were any enforcement or disciplinary actions or any ongoing investigations or suggestions of violations by any of these entities.

■ Review any correspondence during the past five years with the Environmental Protection Agency, Federal Trade Commission, Occupational Safety and Health Administration, Equal

Employment Opportunity Commission, and Internal Revenue Service. Determine if there are any ongoing investigations or suggestions of violations by any of these agencies.

- Review any required regulatory compliance and verify that necessary licenses and permits have been maintained, as well as ongoing filings and reports.
- Determine whether there is a General Service Administration schedule. If so, when does it come up for renewal?
- Obtain copies of the most recently filed EEO-1 and VETS-100 forms.
- Obtain copies of any affirmative action plans.
- Obtain copies of any open charges of discrimination, complaints, and related litigation, and any such cases that have been mitigated within the past five years.

Policies and Procedures

- Obtain the accounting policies and procedures manual.
- Review all key accounting policies to ensure that they comply with generally accepted accounting principles (GAAP).
- Obtain the standard offer letter format, the standard termination letter format, and the employment application form.
- Obtain the HR policies relating to sexual harassment, background investigations, and drug testing.

Purchase Transaction

- If the transaction involves the issuance of stock, are there sufficient authorized shares for the offering, including any conversion rights, taking into account any shares reserved for issuance pursuant to outstanding options, warrants, convertible securities, and employee benefit plans?

Red Flag Events

- Has an auditor resigned within the past three years?
- Is there evidence of continual changes in accounting methods?
- Are there unusually complex business arrangements that do not appear to have a business purpose?
- Is the company continually exceeding its loan covenant targets by very small amounts?
- Do any of the principals have criminal records?
- Have there recently been significant insider stock sales?
- Is the internal audit team subjected to significant scope restrictions?
- Are a large proportion of monthly sales completed during the last few days of each month?
- Has the company tried to sell itself in the past and failed?
- Has the company received major warnings from regulatory agencies?
- Does the company appear to manipulate reserve accounts in order to smooth or enhance its reported earnings?

TABLE OF CONTROLS – MERGERS AND ACQUISITIONS

Process: M&A

1. Perform a Comprehensive Due Diligence Process. Due diligence is the investigation or exercise of care that a reasonable business or person is expected to take before entering into an agreement or contract with another party, or an act done with a certain standard of care. It can be a legal obligation, but the term will more commonly apply to voluntary investigations.

2. Manage Risk. In an acquisition or merger, the goal is to minimize additional risk and maximize reward. One way to look at the risk of a business is to perform a financial risk assessment. This process highlights the areas of greatest risk across areas of the organization based on financial transaction materiality, subjectivity, frequency, and several other factors. Looking at the company through this lens can give the controller more insight about where to focus attention in his or her due diligence efforts. Weaknesses in the procedures and internal controls around high-risk areas indicate that proper financial management and reporting have not been occurring. Listen to these warning signs and investigate further. You might find additional unforeseen issues or opportunities that will add to your total understanding of the costs and benefits.

3. Ensure Consistency. A company with weak or insufficient controls is likely operating with inconsistent guidelines on how financial transactions and procedural matters are handled. In this climate, there's a greater chance that accounting mistakes and potential liability issues may impact the real cost of an acquisition or merger.

4. Identify the Potential for Fraud. When designed and executed properly, internal controls detect or prevent fraud before it can escalate into a serious problem. Review internal controls, particularly in the areas of order-to-cash and procure-to-pay, to ensure the numbers tie out properly.

5. Assess Tone-at-the-Top/Entity-Level Controls. Entity-Level controls are also known as tone-at-the-top controls and dictate the accepted behavioral patterns and integrity of the executive management team. At a company with strong entity-level controls, executives recognize and accept the fact that they're being held to the same standard as all staff are and that they are responsible for exemplifying the appropriate attitude being applied throughout the organization.

6. Evaluate Efficiency. Many public companies that expanded their internal control needs in the era of SOX have significantly overengineered their system. This is not surprising, because when new legislation goes into effect – and the definition of "good enough" is relatively unknown – it leads to overspending to compensate for unknown risk. Auditors can also push up the internal control counts over time in an effort to fully minimize their own liability.

7. Merge the Corporate Financial Cultures. The ability of two companies to merge cultures (rather than simply to consolidate assets) often predicts the success or failure of a merger or acquisition. You can help the two financial cultures merge smoothly by aligning the two companies' internal controls over financial reporting.

TABLE OF RISKS AND CONTROLS – MERGERS AND ACQUISITIONS

Process: M&A

Process Risk	Recommended Policies	Internal Controls	KPIs
1. Due diligence is incomplete. A key risk in the M&A process is an incomplete due diligence process caused by an unclear assignment of roles and responsibilities, and poor project management throughout the process.	■ Monthly Review of Operational Performance Metrics	1. Perform a Comprehensive Due Diligence Process 2. Ensure Consistency 3. Identify the Potential for Fraud 4. Assess Tone-at-the-Top/Entity-Level Controls 5. Evaluate Efficiency 6. Merge the Corporate Financial Cultures	■ Customer Retention Percentage ■ Employee Attrition Rate ■ System Conversion Percentage ■ System Adoption Percentage ■ Actual vs. Budget ■ Number of Outstanding M&A Issues
2. System integration does not occur. Another key risk is the lack of system integration after the M&A activity is completed. This creates the need for additional IT controls and can cause duplicate transactions and duplicate master file data.	■ Monthly Review of Operational Performance Metrics	1. Perform a Comprehensive Due Diligence Process 2. Ensure Consistency 5. Evaluate Efficiency	■ System Conversion Percentage ■ System Adoption Percentage
3. Business processes are not merged. To ensure that all businesses processes are properly mapped, the controller should consider developing a financial architecture for the fully merged company to ensure that all transactions are associated with the correct process and controls.	■ Monthly Review of Operational Performance Metrics	1. Perform a Comprehensive Due Diligence Process 2. Ensure Consistency 5. Evaluate Efficiency	■ Customer Retention Percentage ■ Employee Attrition Rate ■ System Conversion Percentage ■ System Adoption Percentage ■ Actual vs. Budget ■ Number of Outstanding M&A Issues

Process: M&A

Process Risk	Recommended Policies	Internal Controls	KPIs
4. **Employee matters are overlooked.** An often-overlooked procedure relates to ensuring that all employees have read the employee handbook and signed an acknowledgement form. Failure to do this can lead to liability concerns for the company in dealing with employee matters, which often come up after a merger or an acquisition has been completed.	■ HR Policies ■ Internal Controls Policy ■ Tone at the Top ■ Code of Conduct	1. Perform a Comprehensive Due Diligence Process 2. Ensure Consistency 4. Assess Tone-at-the-Top/Entity-Level Controls	■ Employee Attrition Rate
5. **The possibility of fraud.** Manipulation of invoices, purchase orders, and check writing is one of the largest sources of fraud and can often be overlooked due to the relatively small dollar amounts involved. But these small dollar amounts can accumulate quickly.	■ Internal Controls Policy ■ Tone at the Top ■ Code of Conduct	1. Perform a Comprehensive Due Diligence Process 3. Identify the Potential for Fraud	■ Number of Fraudulent Issues ■ Value of Fraudulent Issues ■ System Conversion Percentage ■ System Adoption Percentage ■ Actual vs. Budget ■ Number of Outstanding M&A Issues
6. **A double standard for tone at the top.** Organizations that tolerate a double standard – for example, where it is acceptable for executives but not staffers to reimburse themselves for personal expenses or use company resources for personal gain – leave themselves open to excessive risk and liability.	■ Tone at the Top ■ Code of Conduct	1. Perform a Comprehensive Due Diligence Process 4. Assess Tone-at-the-Top/Entity-Level Controls	■ Number of Issues Reported via the Ethics Hotline ■ Types of Issues Reported ■ Number of Employee Complaints

SECTION THREE

Internal Control Risk

 SECTION INTRODUCTION

The success of an internal control program is dependent upon ongoing management commitment as an operating requirement that is measured with the operating unit being held accountable.

As important as an internal control structure is to an organization, an effective system is not a guarantee that the organization will be successful. An effective internal control structure will keep the right people informed about the organization's progress (or lack of progress) in achieving its objectives, but it cannot turn a poor manager into a good one.

Internal controls cannot ensure success, or even survival. An internal control system is not an absolute assurance to management and the board about the organization's achievement of its objectives. It can only provide reasonable assurance due to the limitations inherent in all internal control systems.

For example, breakdowns in the internal control structure can occur due to simple error or mistake, as well as faulty judgments that could be made at any level of management. In addition, controls can be circumvented by collusion or by management override and a fraudulent payment.

Finally, the design of the internal control system is a function of the resources available, meaning that a cost-benefit analysis must be in the design of the system. The cost of payment controls should never exceed the benefits of the internal system. And the value of a good internal control system should always adequately reduce and help to mitigate risk for the corporate payment process.

CHAPTER EIGHT

Internal Control Program

 OVERVIEW

Internal controls are an integral part of an organization and are designed to provide reasonable assurance of achieving effective and efficient operations, reliability of financial reporting, and compliance with applicable laws and regulations. Internal controls include the plans, methods, and procedures used to meet missions, goals, and objectives. Internal controls also serve as the first line of defense in safeguarding assets and preventing and detecting errors and fraud. In short, internal controls help senior leaders and managers achieve desired business results.

Internal control is a system that is communicated and implemented across the organization and is usually the responsibility of the controller. Controllers and their staffs are in a unique position to see across all aspects of the operations they support. As such, they are responsible for monitoring the internal control environment and for providing guidance and consultation on internal control issues. Additionally, they have the responsibility to ensure that all financial accounts are reviewed for reasonableness and are reconciled to supporting transactions, and that asset verification is performed.

Controllers and financial management also have a fiduciary duty to report significant deviations from company policy in the areas of business ethics and financial reporting to the organization's CFO, chief audit executive (CAE), and senior management.

As previously noted, Digital Equipment Corporation, or DEC for short, (acquired by Compaq, which was in turn acquired by Hewlett Packard in 2001) recognized the value of these internal programs and created a quarterly monitoring process called balance sheet review. The program was initiated in the early 1980s and focused on the results of accounting reconciliations, and it was expanded to include other review components based on the feedback of executive finance and operational management.

The results of balance sheet reviews were presented quarterly to senior finance and operational management. Through this process, Digital integrated internal controls into business processes to ensure that business goals were accomplished and risk was properly identified and mitigated. The components of Digital's balance sheet review program were:

- Business operational overview
- Business plan update
- Status of prior internal audit findings
- Status of external audit management letter findings
- Results of CSA audits
- Corrective action plans and status
- Balance sheet account reconciliations
  - Account fluctuation analysis
  - Variance analysis
  - Action plans
- Metrics review

INTERNAL CONTROL PROCESS FLOW

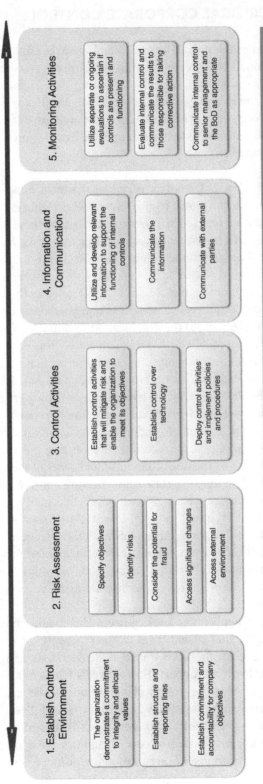

Internal Control

1. Establish Control Environment

- The organization demonstrates a commitment to integrity and ethical values
- Establish structure and reporting lines
- Establish commitment and accountability for company objectives

2. Risk Assessment

- Specify objectives
- Identify risks
- Consider the potential for fraud
- Access significant changes
- Access external environment

3. Control Activities

- Establish control activities that will mitigate risk and enable the organization to meet its objectives
- Establish control over technology
- Deploy control activities and implement policies and procedures

4. Information and Communication

- Utilize and develop relevant information to support the functioning of internal controls
- Communicate the information
- Communicate with external parties

5. Monitoring Activities

- Utilize separate or ongoing evaluations to ascertain if controls are present and functioning
- Evaluate internal control and communicate the results to those responsible for taking corrective action
- Communicate internal control to senior management and the BoD as appropriate

Internal Controls

Code of Conduct and Tone at the Top

THE THREE CRITICAL CORPORATE CONTROLS

The three most critical internal controls for any company can be established by corporate policies that should be "operationalized" into your company's business processes and monitored by the applicable internal control programs. The implementation of these controls set the foundation for good payment controls and risk mitigation. These controls are (1) segregation of duties (SoD), (2) systems access, and (3) delegation of authority (DoA). Many companies have implemented these controls as core controls but need to keep them updated by following some of the best practices that are recommended below.

1. **Segregation of Duties.** SoD control is one of the most important controls that your company can have. Adequate SoD reduces the likelihood that errors (intentional or unintentional) will remain undetected by providing for separate processing by different individuals at various stages of a transaction and for independent reviews of the work performed.

   The SoD control provides four primary benefits: (1) the risk of a deliberate fraud is mitigated as the collusion of two or more persons would be required in order to circumvent controls, (2) the risk of legitimate errors is mitigated as the likelihood of detection is increased, (3) the cost of corrective actions is mitigated as errors are generally detected earlier in their life cycle, and (4) the organization's reputation for integrity and quality is enhanced through a system of checks and balances.

   Although SoD is a basic, key internal control, it is often one of the most difficult to accomplish due to limited headcount, broadly defined responsibilities, and/or constantly changing responsibilities. Basically, the general duties to be segregated are planning/initiation, authorization, custody of assets, and recording or reporting of transactions. Additionally, control tasks such as review, audit, and reconciliation should not be performed by the same individual responsible for recording or reporting the transaction.

   Best Practice: One of the most common root causes of fraud is the lack of SoD controls, weak SoD controls, inappropriate compensating controls, or failure to update SoD controls when responsibilities change. As a best practice, many organizations review their SoD controls on a quarterly basis, and whenever staff turnover occurs, as part of their CSA process. As a result of this review, the applicable SoD controls are updated appropriately.

2. **System Access.** The principle of SoD is also critical in an information system environment, as it ensures the separation of different functions, such as transaction entry, online approval of transactions, master file initiation, master file maintenance, system access rights, and the review of transactions.

   In the context of application level controls, this means that one individual should only have access rights that permit them to enter, approve, or review transactions – but no combination of two for the same transaction. Therefore, assigning different security profiles to various individuals supports the principle of SoD. As an example, operational or process SoD within an AP department will determine the system access rights that should be granted for each associate based on roles and responsibilities.

   Best Practice: System access rights are reviewed on a periodic basis (usually monthly or quarterly) to ensure that system access capabilities are appropriate for current staff members and reflect any changes in responsibilities or movements to other departments.

3. **Delegation of Authority.** The last critical control for your company is the DoA policy and control. The purpose of the DoA control is to ensure the efficient operation of the company while maintaining fiscal integrity and adherence to policy. Accountability for the overall management of the property, assets, financial, and HR of the company rests with the CEO. In many cases "governance" of the DoA is the responsibility of the controller. Individuals that have been assigned authority under the terms of the DoA must safeguard company resources by establishing and maintaining internal controls that deter and detect any potential misuse of resources.

   Best Practice: Many companies assign levels of authority to the job grades or levels within the organization and apply workflow to streamline the approval process. If an individual is promoted or moves to another department, his or her level of authority is automatically updated in the employee master file.

THE COMMITTEE OF SPONSORING ORGANIZATIONS OF THE TREADWAY COMMISSION AND INTERNAL CONTROLS

COSO's *Internal Control – Integrated Framework* was first published in 1992 and gained wide acceptance following the financial control failures of the early 2000s. It is the most widely used framework in the United States and it is also widely used around the world.

The timeless concepts of the framework are that internal control is a process that is affected by people; that provides reasonable assurance; and that is geared to the achievement of objectives related to operations, compliance, and financial reporting.

Standards of Internal Control

The COSO framework is supported by standards of internal control. Internal controls must provide reasonable assurance that the operating unit will meet its objectives. The concept of reasonable assurance recognizes that the cost of a control normally will not exceed the benefits likely to be derived from instituting such control.

Internal control objectives are achieved to a great extent through the competence and integrity of personnel, the independence of their assigned function, their understanding of prescribed procedures, and – most importantly – the effectiveness of monitoring accepted risks.

Standards of internal control are developed to establish the foundation for the organization's internal control requirements for its operating units. The standards state the control requirements that are to be established and maintained by each operating unit. The standards support the organization's performance and customer satisfaction, ensuring the effectiveness of business cycles through the prevention, detection, and timely correction of defects.

The standards reduce risk, are a fraud prevention tool, support the CSA process, and support the monitoring process within a system of internal control. Standards of internal control support the new COSO framework as long as they are updated to reflect changes in the business environment. Lastly, standards of internal controls support the tone at the top of an organization and standards are synonymous with key controls.

Considerations for Setting an Internal Control Policy

Most controllers have the responsibility for establishing an internal control policy for their organizations. Below are some considerations to address when developing this policy:

- Internal controls must be applied within an operating unit in an effective and efficient manner and provide reasonable assurance that the operating unit will meet its objectives.
- Internal control objectives are achieved through the competence and integrity of personnel, the independence of their assigned function, their understanding of prescribed procedures, and the effectiveness of monitoring accepted risk.
- The effectiveness of an internal control system is dependent upon the following factors:
  1. The tone set by senior management is the most important aspect, contributing to the ongoing success of the internal control system.
  2. Managers and employees must understand the internal control system. Internal controls should be understood, supported, and promoted throughout the company.
  3. Continued appropriateness of the method of communication among employees is a key dependency. Impediments to necessary communication should be minimized.
  4. Adequate time and resources should be made available for the business operation to maintain and review internal controls.
- A control environment is composed of the following elements:
  1. Integrity and ethical values
  2. Commitment to competence
  3. BoD and audit committee
  4. Management's philosophy and operating style
  5. Organizational structure
  6. Assignment of authority and responsibility
  7. HR policies and procedures
- The overall control system must be geared to changes in risk within the business environment. In relation to any particular risk, there are four strategies to choose from (more than one may be used):
  1. Terminate the activity
  2. Transfer the risk to another party
  3. Reduce the risk by instituting the appropriate internal controls
  4. Accept the risk (where no further effective and efficient controls are possible)
- In summary, an internal control system supports the operating unit's objectives in the following categories:
  1. Effectiveness and efficiency of operations and resources
  2. Reliability of financial and operational reporting
  3. Compliance with policies, procedures, and applicable laws and regulations
  4. Safeguarding assets from fraud or waste

CONTROLLER'S TOOL 17 – ROLES AND RESPONSIBILITIES FOR INTERNAL CONTROLS

Introduction. Roles and responsibilities for internal controls may vary depending on the type and size of the organization as well as the industry. Roles and responsibilities are also impacted by a significant event that may require a renewed focus on the organization's internal control system. Examples of significant events include fraud, a serious internal or external audit weakness, a company merger, and the implementation or update of an ERP system. The chart was developed to reflect the roles and responsibilities for internal controls throughout the organization.

Role	Responsibilities
Employees	▪ Employees have responsibility for supporting the organization's internal control program. ▪ Employees have responsibility for supporting the organization's code of conduct and tone at the top.
BoD	▪ Management is accountable to the BoD, which provides governance, guidance, and oversight. ▪ Effective board members are objective, capable, and inquisitive. ▪ BoD members have knowledge of the entity's activities and environment, and commit the time necessary to fulfill their board responsibilities. ▪ Management may be in a position to override controls and to ignore or stifle communications from subordinates, enabling a dishonest management that intentionally misrepresents results to cover its tracks. A strong, active board – particularly when coupled with effective upward communications channels and capable financial, legal, and internal audit functions – is often best able to identify and correct such a problem.
Audit Committee	▪ BoDs and audit committees have responsibility for making sure the internal control system in the organization is adequate. ▪ This responsibility includes determining the extent to which internal controls are evaluated.
Executive Management of the Organization	▪ The CEO is ultimately responsible and should assume ownership of the system. ▪ More than any other individual, the chief executive sets the tone at the top that affects integrity and ethics and other factors of a positive control environment. ▪ Senior managers, in turn, assign responsibility for establishment of more specific internal control policies and procedures to personnel responsible for the unit's functions. ▪ In a smaller entity the influence of the chief executive, often a company owner, is usually more direct. In any event, in a cascading responsibility, a manager is effectively a chief executive of his or her sphere of responsibility. ▪ In a large company, the chief executive fulfills this duty by providing leadership and direction to senior managers and reviewing the way they're controlling the business. ▪ As an indication of management's responsibility, in the organization's annual financial report to the shareholders, top management at a publicly owned organization will include a statement indicating that management has established a system of internal control that management believes is effective. The statement may also provide specific details about the organization's internal control system. ▪ The primary responsibility for the development and maintenance of internal control rests with an organization's management. With increased significance placed on the control environment, the focus of internal control has changed from policies and procedures to an overriding philosophy and operating style within the organization. ▪ Emphasis on these intangible aspects highlights the importance of top management's involvement in the internal control system. If internal control is not a priority for management, then it will not be one for people in the organization either.

Role	Responsibilities
Controllers	■ Of particular significance are controllers and financial officers and their staffs, whose control activities cut across, as well as up and down, the operating and other units of an enterprise. ■ Controllers are usually responsible for the development and implementation of internal control programs for their companies. ■ They are required to ensure that all accounting practices impacting financial results are properly controlled.
Internal Controls Team **(Public Company Example)**	■ The **VP of internal controls**, along with the **internal controls team**, is responsible for implementing the requirements of SOX 404, by which the organization's internal controls are documented and evaluated. This requirement includes implementing the foundational direction for the organization's internal control program. Specific responsibilities of the internal controls team include those listed below. ■ **Project Management** ■ Act as primary liaison to impacted organizations and external service providers ■ Escalate project-wide issues to management and steering committee for resolution ■ **Tactical Project Focus** ■ Interact with controls and procedures owners ■ Ensure delivery of all tasks assigned to the specific work stream ■ Report to the internal control project manager to obtain scope approval ■ Assist with issue escalation and provide milestone progress updates ■ Responsible for day-to-day work effort in areas of ownership ■ Under the internal control project manager, complete assigned workload with designees from control and procedures owners ■ **Disclosure Committee, Audit Committee, and SEC Reporting (10-Q and 10-K)** ■ The VP of internal controls attends each disclosure committee meeting and presents significant controls issues that impact the organization's key controls. ■ The VP of internal controls attends each audit committee meeting, provides SOX 404 project updates, and presents significant control issues. ■ The VP of internal controls develops the response for the evaluation of internal controls for 10-Q and 10-K reports.
Assertion Team **(Public Company Example)**	■ As part of the structure for the SOX 404 project, and to establish the foundational structure control environment, **assertion teams** are established to represent each accounting cycle, process, and/or business area. On the assertion teams, there is a single point of contact for: ■ Controller teams ■ Process owner team ■ The assertion team is responsible for: ■ Providing input and sign-off on the scope of the SOX 404 project ■ Participating in workshops and providing access to subject matter experts (SMEs) ■ Completing assertion packages with the internal controls team ■ Approving deliverables ■ Providing input into testing effort during planning, execution, and results remediation stages ■ Addressing remediation actions ■ Accepting responsibility for ongoing maintenance of controls and documentation

Role	Responsibilities

SOX 404 Steering Committee (Public Company Example)	The **SOX 404 steering committee** has the following responsibilities:
	■ **Approval and Certification**
	  ■ The SOX Section 404 steering committee will provide written certification to support the organization's Section 404 assertion on internal controls on an annual basis. This effort is supported by the subcertification process at the detailed process-owner level and the deliverable acceptance in individual process areas.
	■ **Issue Resolution and Approval**
	  ■ The SOX 404 steering committee will review sensitive policies required for SOX 404 compliance, including SoD, DoA changes, and remediation and resolution of other enterprise-wide issues.
	■ **Leadership/Oversight**
	  ■ The SOX 404 steering committee will provide visible sponsorship of project and commitment of skilled resources from all represented areas.
	  ■ Steering committee members play an important role in reviewing and understanding the project scope, approach, and risks.

Internal Auditors	■ Internal auditors' responsibilities typically include ensuring the adequacy of the system of internal control, the reliability of data, and the efficient use of the organization's resources. ■ Internal auditors identify control problems and develop solutions for improving and strengthening internal controls. Internal auditors are concerned with the entire range of an organization's internal controls, including operational, financial, and compliance controls.
External Auditors	■ Internal control is also evaluated by the external auditors. ■ External auditors assess the effectiveness of internal control within an organization to plan the financial statement audit. ■ In contrast to internal auditors, external auditors focus primarily on controls that affect financial reporting. External auditors have a responsibility to report internal control weaknesses (as well as reportable conditions about internal control) to the audit committee of the BoD.

THE IMPACT OF SECTION 404 OF THE SARBANES–OXLEY ACT OF 2002 ON INTERNAL CONTROL PROGRAMS

Section 404 requires an annual report by management on the design and effectiveness of internal controls over financial reporting and an attestation by the company's auditors as to the accuracy of management's assessment. These requirements shouldn't be very challenging, provided a company is following the COSO framework or utilizing self-assessment programs. The balance sheet review process that was used by DEC is a good example of such a program, with an established schedule and management review component that:

■ Evaluated and tested internal controls over financial reporting using COSO to opine on effectiveness (broad and deep)
■ Based assessment on procedures that were sufficient to evaluate design and test operating effectiveness, believing that inquiry alone would not provide adequate basis for assessment
■ Required significant support from operations and controller organizations, as up to 70 percent of key controls can be outside of financial reporting

Management's responsibilities included:

- Evaluating design and effectiveness of internal controls over financial reporting
- Supporting evaluation with sufficient evidence, including documentation and test results
- Providing written assessment of the effectiveness of internal controls over financial reporting as of the end of the company's most recent fiscal year
- Maintaining evidential matter, including documentation, to provide reasonable support for its assessment and testing of both design and operating effectiveness

Two important definitions describing a control weakness include:

Significant deficiency: A control deficiency, or combination of control deficiencies, that adversely affects the company's ability to initiate, authorize, record, process, or report external financial data reliably in accordance with GAAP. A significant deficiency indicates that there is more than a remote likelihood of a misstatement of the company's annual or interim financial statements.

Material weakness: A significant deficiency, or combination of significant deficiencies, that results in more than a remote likelihood that a material misstatement of the annual or interim financial statements will not be prevented or detected.

CONTROLLER'S TOOL 18 – INTERNAL CONTROL BEST PRACTICES FOR PRIVATELY HELD COMPANIES

Introduction. Many privately held companies have implemented many of the internal control requirements mandated for public companies and follow the requirements for SOX Section 404. Although internal control programs are not a requirement for privately held companies, they have found that a controls program can reduce risk, prevent fraud, and support good business practices. Here are some examples:

- Maintains strong steering and disclosure committees
- Engages the external auditor early in the review of internal controls
- Develops organization-wide communications for every annual audit event
- Secures essential management buy-in for the identification of key stakeholders
- Balances internal control documentation efforts and uses automation where possible
- Ensures that company resources and process owners are engaged throughout the process
- Identifies and supports champions for keeping information current
- Develops livable, structured process for updating documentation to reflect organizational or system changes
- Ensures periodic reviews of the organization's internal control programs.

Taking a similar position on the need for internal controls within small- and medium-sized businesses in the private sector, Chief Executive Boards International posted a blog entry titled "8 Simple Internal Controls for Small Businesses" on October 22, 2008: "Here are eight simple and almost no-cost financial controls that could save you a lot of money:

1. **Approve checks.** If your travel schedule and work processes permit, signing your own checks is an excellent precaution.
2. **If you can't sign checks yourself, authorize ONE other person to sign checks in addition to yourself.** You can be the backup signer if he or she is unavailable. If someone else must have signature authority, make sure that person is someone different from the person who writes the checks and has access to the check stock.
3. **Keep check stock under lock and key.** Clever thieves can fabricate a check, even without your check stock. Don't make it easier than it needs to be.
4. **Approve invoices yourself.** This is a quick and easy process. Again, if someone else must approve invoices, make sure that person is different from the person writing or signing checks.
5. **Have the cancelled checks mailed to your home instead of the office.** This one is big. Open the envelope and just flip through the checks, verifying the vendors and signatures. Even if you only spend 10 seconds on this, shuffle the checks up so it looks like you rigorously examined them. Then take them to the office, to the person who does the bank reconciliations.
6. **Divide up processes for handling receipts and payments.** For example, different people should approve invoices, prepare checks, sign checks, and reconcile the checking account. Likewise, different people should be handling incoming cash and checks, posting payments, making deposits, and reconciling the checking account.
7. **If you take credit cards, the easiest fraud opportunity is for a person with access to the merchant account to give small credits to a card of their own or an accomplice.** Have your detailed merchant account statements reviewed by someone other than the person who enters the transactions, and watch for credits.
8. **Do background checks on all new employees.** People with credit problems will be a problem for you, as financial pressures drive desperate behavior. If they can't manage their own money, do you want them managing yours? A recent story of an employee theft revealed that the person had stolen from a prior employer as well – the new employer just failed to find that out due to lax hiring practices."[1]

CONTROLLER'S TOOL 19 – LEVERAGING INTERNAL CONTROL BASICS TO IMPLEMENT A CONTROL SELF-ASSESSMENT PROGRAM

Introduction. The Institute of Internal Auditors (IIA) defines CSA as a process through which internal control effectiveness is examined with the objective of providing reasonable assurance that all business objectives are met. The employees performing CSA work should be in the functional area being examined, as opposed to the upper-level managers who are responsible for the system of internal controls.

---

[1]Chief Executive Boards International (CEBI). (2008). 8 simple internal controls for small businesses (October 22; accessed July 31, 2020). https://www.chiefexecutiveboards.com/briefings/briefing078.htm.

These employees have a wealth of information about internal controls and fraud (if it exists). While internal (or independent) auditors can be involved with CSA initiatives, auditors do not "own" the process and do not make the assessments and evaluations.

The most common approaches to performing CSA activities are facilitated team meetings, CSA surveys, and a focus by management on a specific internal control or area of their business.

1. **A facilitated team meeting** is the most popular form of CSA. The facilitated sessions consist of 6–15 employees who are subject on a day-to-day basis to the internal controls being evaluated. A trained facilitator guides the meeting, and another individual records the activity.
2. **The survey approach** uses questionnaires to elicit data about controls, risks, and processes. It differs from traditional internal control questionnaires used by auditors because the operational employees (not the auditors) use the survey results to self-evaluate the controls or processes. At some companies, a survey approach may be used to evaluate "soft" controls. It may be used to evaluate the effectiveness of an ethics program that is considered an entity-level control.

The steps listed below support the self-assessment approach in a CSA program. Self-testing on a regular basis validates the effectiveness of control. This approach can also be used when management would like to review the controls of a specific process. Lastly, this approach can also be used in a workshop setting.

1. **Understand the operating unit or business process.** A key component of a CSA program is ensuring that the control points and responsibilities of the operating unit are understood.
2. **Determine the scope of the CSA initiative.**
3. **Ensure there is management commitment.** This is crucial to the ongoing support and success of the program. It is demonstrated by full management understanding of the value-added benefits of a CSA program.
4. **Develop a program that represents the operating unit or process, or select from the recommended standards of internal control**.
5. **Form a CSA team or work team.** Work teams and process teams, with the assistance of a facilitation team, can identify obstacles to overcome or strengths to be leveraged and agree upon appropriate action steps to improve the group's effectiveness. As an example, a process-based CSA team will focus on a process that may only entail one activity of a particular business unit or processes such as procure-to-pay and AP. Suitable candidates for the CSA team are:
   - Work teams that work together on a single business process that may cut across functional management boundaries
   - Work teams that are about to implement a new process or application system
   - Teams that are staff based, meaning that most of those who are part of the team are the individuals performing the work
   - Teams reflecting areas where basic day-to-day processes require improvement
6. **Plan and schedule the evaluation of internal controls.** Although an internal control program should be flexible in order to address the changing business environment,

a quarterly plan and schedule for the CSA program helps to work around peak periods of activity.

7. **Complete the evaluation of internal controls.**
8. **Develop deficiency findings and remediation activities.** A deficiency finding is a factual statement of a problem without judgment or conclusion that should be quantified where possible. Findings should address the root cause of the problem and identify what is really broken.
9. **Develop a corrective action plan.** A corrective action plan is an internal controls team and/or management plan that addresses the status of findings on an ongoing, scheduled basis. The CSA team is responsible for managing the implementation of the corrective action plan. The plan needs to include:
   ■ Finding reference
   ■ Corrective action
   ■ Owner of the individual corrective action (**Note:** An individual should own the corrective action plan to ensure accountability)
   ■ Commitment date
   ■ Status
   ■ Actual date the correction occurred
   ■ Recommendations for plan revision or retesting
   ■ Review of recommended corrective action
   ■ Attached supporting documentation as evidence of completion of the corrective action (e.g. process change, system access issues due to SoD issues corrected)
10. **Follow-up and retest the finding.** Corrected findings need to be verified by following up and retesting the issue by the review of audit trails, process changes, and sampling transactions after the correction took place.
11. **Management reporting and review.** Ongoing management review of internal-control program results demonstrates the commitment and strengthens the accountability of each organization in the operating unit.
12. **Conduct ongoing training.** Internal controls training is integral to the operating unit's understanding of internal controls components and requirements.
13. **Update standards of internal control (key controls).** Standards of internal control supporting the CSA process should be updated to reflect the results of corrective action plans.

INTERNAL CONTROLS AND FRAUD PREVENTION

Now that the internal control process has been defined, it's important to note that internal controls should never be considered static. Internal controls are a dynamic and fluid set of tools that change when the business, technology, and fraud environment changes in response to competition, industry practices, legislation, regulation, or current economic conditions. Sometimes internal controls need to be readjusted if a fraudster has been able to infiltrate a weakness in the process.

A controller and his or her staff constantly needs to ask what can go wrong and make the appropriate adjustments if a control weakness can be identified. A fraudster will always look for ways to find the weakness before anyone else and will take advantage in a case where weaknesses have not been properly addressed.

 ## THE FRAUD TRIANGLE

SAS No. 99 defines fraud as an intentional act that results in a material misstatement in financial statements. There are two types of fraud considered: misstatements arising from fraudulent financial reporting and misstatements arising from misappropriation of assets by the theft of assets or fraudulent expenditures. The standard describes the fraud triangle that was created by sociologist Donald Cressey.

Generally, all three fraud triangle conditions are present when fraud occurs. First, there is an incentive or pressure that provides a reason to commit fraud. Second, there is an opportunity for fraud to be perpetrated (e.g. absence of controls, ineffective controls, or the ability of management to override controls). Third, the individual committing the fraud possesses an attitude or thought process that enables rationalization of the fraud, as depicted in the diagram below.

Source: Association of Certified Fraud Examiners (ACFE); www.acfe.com.

 ## THE FIVE ELEMENTS OF FRAUD AND THE FRAUD DIAMOND

In his article entitled "AML Compliance: The 5 Elements of Fraud" (March 2, 2012), Dennis Lormel, former chief of the FBI's Financial Crimes Program, provides some new insights about fraud. He states:

"Although the various types of fraud contain different characteristics and warning signs, they are all contingent on five common elements:

■ Integrity
■ Opportunity
■ Incentive, motivation, or pressure
■ Rationalization or attitude
■ Capability

"The starting point is individual integrity. Does a person have the integrity to resist opportunity? If yes, fraud is an afterthought. If a person's integrity is compromised, it's usually because pressure and rationalization lead that individual to give into the enticement of opportunity. Opportunity is the driving factor. Without opportunity, a fraud scheme cannot succeed. Likewise, if an individual's integrity is influenced by pressure and rationalization, and the opportunity presents itself, unless the individual possesses the capacity to commit the fraud, the scheme will not succeed. The capacity represents the combination of being in a position to commit the fraudulent act(s) and having the skill sets necessary to carry the fraud off."[2]

Lormel also discusses the fraud diamond: "The fraud diamond was introduced by David T. Wolfe and Dana R. Hermanson in 2004. Basically, they added a fourth dimension to the fraud triangle. Their reasoning was that unless a fraudster possessed the capability to commit a fraud, opportunity, pressure, and rationalization by themselves were not enough to succeed. Capability required being in the right position at the right time and possessing the needed skill sets to perpetrate the fraud."

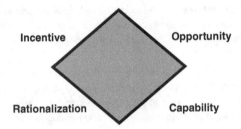

Source: ICS Risk Advisors.

DEFINITION AND EXAMPLES OF FRAUD

Fraud is a deliberate act (or failure to act) with the intention of obtaining an unauthorized benefit, either for oneself or for the institution, by using deception or false suggestions or suppression of truth or other unethical means, which are believed and relied upon by others.

Depriving another person or the institution of a benefit to which he/she/it is entitled by using any of the means described above also constitutes fraud. Examples of fraudulent acts include, but are not limited to, the following:

1. Embezzlement
2. Forgery or alteration of documents
3. Unauthorized alteration or manipulation of computer files
4. Fraudulent financial reporting
5. Misappropriation or misuse of the organization's resources (e.g. funds, supplies, equipment, facilities, services, inventory, and other assets)
6. Authorization or receipt of payment for goods not received or services not performed
7. Authorization or receipt of unearned wages or benefits
8. Conflict of interest or ethics violations

---

[2]Lormel, Dennis M. (2012). Fraud and money laundering: Can you think like a bad guy? DML Associates (February 23; accessed July 31, 2020). https://www.thefirma.org/files/conference/2013/Lormel-2.pdf.

TABLE OF CONTROLS – INTERNAL CONTROL PROGRAM

Process: Internal Control Program

---

1. Integrated Internal Controls Process. The organization's managers are responsible for integrating effective internal controls into all company operations. This responsibility includes identifying, assessing, and managing risks related to their business objectives. The resulting internal control activities must be monitored to verify that they are effective and working as intended.

2. Code of Conduct. All employees must comply with the company's code of conduct.

3. Adherence to Corporate Policy. The organization's statements of corporate policy must be adhered to by all operating units. Policies and procedures established within operating units must, at a minimum, meet and not be in conflict with the control requirements specified by corporate policy. Policies and procedures must be periodically reviewed and updated.

4. Accurate and Timely Financial Statements. The organization's financial statements must be prepared in conformity with US GAAP principles. Local country accounting principles, when different from US GAAP, are to be used only for local reporting. In addition, no false or intentionally misleading entries may be made in the company's accounting records.

5. Segregation of Duties. Adequate SoD, DoA, and control responsibilities must be established and maintained in all functional areas of the company. In general, custodial, processing/operating, and accounting responsibilities should be separated to promote independent review and evaluation of company operations. Where adequate segregation cannot be achieved, other compensating controls must be established and documented.

6. Internal Control Assertions. All representations and assertions regarding internal controls must be supported with the appropriate documentation.

7. Operating Unit Budgets. Costs and expenses of all operating units must be maintained under budgetary control. Comparisons of actual expenses to budgeted amounts must be performed on a regular basis, and all significant variances explained.

8. Operating Unit Internal Controls. All operating units must develop a system of internal controls to ensure that the assets and records of the company are adequately protected from loss, destruction, theft, alteration, and unauthorized access.

9. Critical Transactions. Critical transactions within the organization's business processes must be traceable, authorized, authenticated, have integrity, and be retained in accordance with established policy.

10. Retention of Business Records. The business records for the organization must be maintained and retained in accordance with established policy.

11. Sensitive and Confidential Information. The organization's network and information program, which states corporate policy on proprietary, confidential, and trade-secret information, must be adhered to. As a result, employees and contractors must refrain from unauthorized disclosure of sensitive or confidential information. Adequate security must also be maintained in disposing of this information.

12. Contract and Company Commitments Management and Approval. Contracts or documents that legally bind the organization or a subsidiary company to any obligation can execute by purchasing personnel (for agreements pertinent to their areas of responsibility) or individuals duly authorized under the organization's DoA policy. Legal should review and approve all contracts and legally binding documents. Right-to-audit clauses should be included in the contracts where appropriate.

13. Properly Managed Risk and Prevention of Fraud. Internal controls mitigate risk and are updated as the company's risk environment changes. Fraud flags are identified in a timely manner and fraud is detected and deterred.

TABLE OF RISKS AND CONTROLS – INTERNAL CONTROL PROGRAM

	Process: Internal Control Program		
Process Risk	**Recommended Policies**	**Internal Controls**	**KPIs**
1. The company has no SoD controls. SoD controls do not exist, resulting in unauthorized systems access and payments.	▪ SoD Policies and Self-Assessments	1. Integrated Internal Controls Process 5. SoD 6. Internal Control Assertions 13. Risk Is Properly Managed and Fraud Is Prevented	▪ Number of Outstanding SoD Issues ▪ Number of SoD Issues Mitigated ▪ Value of Outstanding SoD Issues
2. There is no implementation or monitoring of appropriate internal controls. Most risks can be mitigated with an appropriate system of internal control. Once a fraud risk assessment has been performed, the agency must identify the ongoing processes, controls, and other monitoring procedures that are needed to identify and/ or mitigate those risks.	▪ Internal Control Policy ▪ Self-Assessment Policy ▪ Tone at the Top ▪ Code of Conduct	1. Integrated Internal Controls Process 2. Code of Conduct 3. Adherence to Corporate Policy 5. SoD 6. Internal Control Assertions 8. Operating Unit Internal Controls 9. Critical Transactions 12. Contract and Company Commitment Management and Approval 13. Risk Is Properly Managed and Fraud Is Prevented	▪ Number of Fraudulent Issues ▪ Value of Fraudulent Issues ▪ Number of Outstanding Internal Control Issues
3. Proper authority and responsibility have not been assigned.	▪ DoA Policy	1. Integrated Internal Controls Process 2. Code of Conduct 3. Adherence to Corporate Policy 4. Financial Statements Are Accurate and Timely 5. SoD 6. Internal Control Assertions 8. Operating Unit Internal Controls 9. Critical Transactions 12. Contract and Company Commitment Management and Approval 13. Risk Is Properly Managed and Fraud Is Prevented	▪ Number of Fraudulent Issues ▪ Value of Fraudulent Issues ▪ Number of Outstanding Internal Control Issues

Process: Internal Control Program			
Process Risk	Recommended Policies	Internal Controls	KPIs
4. **Employee matters are overlooked.** An often-overlooked procedure relates to ensuring that all employees have read the employee handbook and signed the acknowledgement form. Failure to do this can lead to liability concerns for the company in dealing with employee matters, which often come up after a merger or an acquisition has been completed.	▪ HR Policies ▪ Internal Control Policy ▪ Tone at the Top ▪ Code of Conduct	1. Integrated Internal Control Process 2. Code of Conduct 3. Adherence to Corporate Policy 6. Internal Control Assertions 7. Operating Unit Budgets 8. Operating Unit Internal Controls 13. Risk Is Properly Managed and Fraud Is Prevented	▪ Employee Attrition Rate ▪ Number of Issues Reported via the Ethics Hotline ▪ Types of Issues Reported ▪ Number of Employee Complaints
5. **Fraud can occur.** Manipulation of invoices, purchase orders, and check writing are one of the largest sources of fraud and can often be overlooked due to relatively small dollar amounts. But these small dollar amounts can accumulate quickly.	▪ Internal Control Policy ▪ Tone at the Top ▪ Code of Conduct	1. Integrated Internal Controls Process 2. Code of Conduct 3. Adherence to Corporate Policy 6. Internal Control Assertions 7. Operating Unit Budgets 8. Operating Unit Internal Controls 13. Risk Is Properly Managed and Fraud Is Prevented	▪ Number of Fraudulent Issues ▪ Value of Fraudulent Issues ▪ Number of Outstanding Internal Control Issues
6. **Tone at the top sets a double standard.** Organizations that tolerate a double standard – for example, where it is acceptable for executives but not staffers to reimburse themselves for personal expenses or use company resources for personal gain – leave themselves open to excessive risk and liability.	▪ Tone at the Top ▪ Code of Conduct	1. Integrated Internal Controls Process 2. Code of Conduct 3. Adherence to Corporate Policy 6. Internal Control Assertions 7. Operating Unit Budgets 8. Operating Unit Internal Controls 13. Risk Is Properly Managed and Fraud Is Prevented	▪ Number of Issues Reported via the Ethics Hotline ▪ Types of Issues Reported ▪ Number of Employee Complaints

	Process: Internal Control Program		
Process Risk	**Recommended Policies**	**Internal Controls**	**KPIs**
7. **There is no independent audit committee or BoD.** Active oversight by the audit committee serves as a deterrent to management and employees engaging in fraudulent activity and helps management fulfill its responsibility. Active oversight by the audit committee helps to reinforce management's commitment to creating a culture with zero tolerance for fraud	■ Internal Audit Process ■ Audit Committee Charter	1. Integrated Internal Controls Process 2. Code of Conduct 3. Adherence to Corporate Policy	■ Number of Outstanding Internal Audit Issues ■ Number of Fraudulent Issues ■ Value of Fraudulent Issues ■ Number of Outstanding Internal Control Issues
8. **Financial statements are incorrect.** Financial statements are often misstated due to errors and manipulation.	■ Financial Close Process ■ Financial Close Approval Process	1. Integrated Internal Controls Process 2. Code of Conduct 3. Adherence to Corporate Policy 4. Financial Statements Are Accurate and Timely 5. SoD 6. Internal Control Assertions 8. Operating Unit Internal Controls 9. Critical Transactions 13. Risk Is Properly Managed and Fraud Is Prevented	■ Cycle Time to Close ■ Number of Post-close Adjustments ■ Number of Financial Statement Adjustments ■ Number of General Ledger Variances

SECTION FOUR

Compliance Risk

SECTION INTRODUCTION

According to *Corporate Compliance Principles*, developed by the National Center for Preventive Law, "A compliance program encompasses the set of operational methods that a company uses to ensure its activities adhere to legal requirements and broader company values. Designing effective compliance programs is an important corporate concern for two reasons. First, public harm and corporate injuries potentially resulting from corporate offenses and deviations from company values justify careful management of offense and misconduct risks. Second, under a number of recently developed legal standards – most notably the Federal Sentencing Guidelines for Organizations – firms with generally effective compliance programs can often significantly reduce or eliminate penalties for offenses that occur despite these programs."[1]

In general, compliance means conforming to a rule, such as a specification, policy, standard, or law. Regulatory compliance describes the goal that organizations aspire to achieve in their efforts to ensure that they are aware of and take steps to comply with relevant laws, policies, and regulations.

---

[1]Corporate compliance principles (n.d.). National Center for Preventive Law (accessed July 31, 2020). https://pdf4pro.com/amp/view/national-center-for-preventive-law-3536a.html.

CHAPTER NINE

Regulatory Compliance

 OVERVIEW

In recent years, both federal and state governments have increased enforcement activities as they relate to corporate conduct and compliance. Publicly traded companies and businesses that operate pursuant to a license, permit, statutory scheme, or government regulatory approval find themselves subject to higher governmental expectations. Companies that compete in industries of high government interest, such as health care and financial services, are particularly at risk and are increasingly targeted in both civil and criminal proceedings.

To avoid fines and reputational damage, employees, customers, and suppliers must be screened against specific government lists. Details for these screening requirements follow, under "Controller's Tool 20 – The Regulatory Compliance Toolkit."

REGULATORY COMPLIANCE PROCESS FLOW

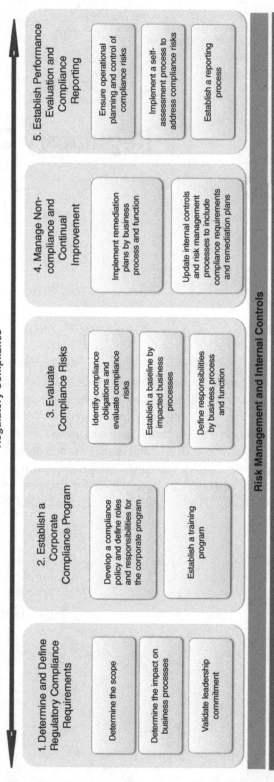

Regulatory Compliance

1. Determine and Define Regulatory Compliance Requirements

- Determine the scope
- Determine the impact on business processes
- Validate leadership commitment

2. Establish a Corporate Compliance Program

- Develop a compliance policy and define roles and responsibilities for the corporate program
- Establish a training program

3. Evaluate Compliance Risks

- Identify compliance obligations and evaluate compliance risks
- Establish a baseline by impacted business processes
- Define responsibilities by business process and function

4. Manage Non-compliance and Continual Improvement

- Implement remediation plans by business process and function
- Update internal controls and risk management processes to include compliance requirements and remediation plans

5. Establish Performance Evaluation and Compliance Reporting

- Ensure operational planning and control of compliance risks
- Implement a self-assessment process to address compliance risks
- Establish a reporting process

Risk Management and Internal Controls

Compliance Program

Code of Conduct and Tone at the Top

CONTROLLER'S TOOL 20 – REGULATORY COMPLIANCE TOOLKIT

Introduction. This toolkit is not all inclusive but does provide the most prevalent regulatory compliance requirements that a controller needs to consider. This toolkit also includes IRS, accounting, and auditing requirements. This compliance toolkit information is sorted by key regulatory compliance topics and provides information in the following manner:

- Compliance area and reference
- Specific industry focus
- Process areas impacted
- Summary

Controller's Regulatory Compliance Toolkit			
Compliance Area and Reference	**Specific Industry Focus**	**Process Areas Impacted**	**Summary**
Accountable T&E (Travel and Entertainment) Plans and Employee Expenses www.irs.gov	All industries	T&E	The IRS has several publications that provide guidance with respect to employee expenses and expense reimbursement. Publication 463 (*Travel, Entertainment, Gift, and Car Expenses*) is the primary document that provides information about the types of expenditures that are allowable, as well as record-keeping and reporting requirements. Section 11 of Publication 535 (*Business Expenses*) provides similar material. On the IRS website there are short documents that draw from Publication 463 as well as other IRS publications that provide overviews. These short documents are: ■ IRS Topic 305 (*Record Keeping*) ■ IRS Topic 510 (*Business Use of Car*) ■ IRS Topic 511 (*Business Travel Expenses*) ■ IRS Topic 512 (*Business Entertainment Expenses*) ■ IRS Topic 514 (*Employee Business Expenses*) The concept of an accountable plan is critical to the controlling and managing of employee expense reimbursements. An accountable plan must have three elements: ■ Expenses must have a business connection, and the connection and purpose must be documented. ■ Expense substantiation must be done within a reasonable period of time. ■ Excess reimbursement or allowances must be returned within a reasonable period of time.

Controller's Regulatory Compliance Toolkit			
Compliance Area and Reference	**Specific Industry Focus**	**Process Areas Impacted**	**Summary**
Anti–Money Laundering (AML) https://www.finra. org/rules-guidance/ key-topics/aml	All global companies	Payment processes	Firms must comply with the Bank Secrecy Act and its implementing regulations (AML rules). The purpose of the AML rules is to help detect and report suspicious activity, including the predicate offenses to money laundering and terrorist financing, such as securities fraud and market manipulation.

The Financial Industry Regulatory Authority (FINRA) reviews a firm's compliance with AML rules under FINRA Rule 3310, which sets forth minimum standards for a firm's written AML compliance program. The basic tenets of an AML compliance program under FINRA 3310 include the following:

- The program has to be approved in writing by a senior manager.
- It must be reasonably designed to ensure the firm detects and reports suspicious activity.
- It must be reasonably designed to achieve compliance with the AML rules, including, among others, having a risk-based customer identification program (CIP) that enables the firm to form a reasonable belief that it knows the true identity of its customers.
- It must be independently tested to ensure proper implementation of the program.
- Each FINRA member firm must submit contact information for its AML compliance officer through the FINRA Contact System (FCS).
- Ongoing training must be provided to appropriate personnel.

Controller's Regulatory Compliance Toolkit			
Compliance Area and Reference	**Specific Industry Focus**	**Process Areas Impacted**	**Summary**
Bureau of Industry and Security (BIS) http://www.bis.doc.gov	All industries	AR logistics	The US Department of Commerce's Bureau of Industry and Security, formerly known as the Bureau of Export Administration, is responsible for administering and enforcing export controls on US commercial products, software, and technology. BIS is also responsible for overseeing export controls on "dual-use" items that can be used in weapons of mass destruction applications, terrorist activities, or human rights abuses. In addition to enforcing the Export Administration regulations (EAR), BIS is responsible for issuing and administering several restricted party lists that apply to export and re-export transactions for which the agency has jurisdiction. These lists, which change frequently, include the following: ▪ Denied Persons List. This list includes the names of individuals and companies that have been denied export privileges by BIS, usually due to a violation of US export control laws. US persons and companies are generally prohibited from engaging in export transactions with parties named on the Denied Persons List. ▪ Entity List. This list identifies the names of companies, individuals, government agencies, and research institutions that trigger export and re-export license requirements. US companies need to ensure that the appropriate export licenses are in place before proceeding with transactions with parties on the Entity List. ▪ Unverified List. This list includes the names of foreign parties that BIS has been unable to conduct a pre-license check or post-shipment verification. Potential transactions with parties on the Unverified List constitute a red flag that must be addressed and resolved before proceeding with the export. Significant civil and criminal fines and other penalties can be imposed on persons or companies engaging in prohibited transactions with parties included on the Denied Persons and Entity Lists. Civil penalties can also be imposed on export transactions with such parties even if such activity occurred inadvertently.

Controller's Regulatory Compliance Toolkit			
Compliance Area and Reference	**Specific Industry Focus**	**Process Areas Impacted**	**Summary**
California's Safer Consumer Products Regulation https://dtsc.ca.gov	Manufacturing companies	Supply chain	California's Safer Consumer Products Regulation is part of that state's Green Chemistry Law and covers products that contain a "chemical of concern." Manufacturers, importers, assemblers, and retailers must notify the Department of Toxic Substance Control of potentially dangerous products and must determine how to limit exposure to them.
California's Transparency in Supply Chains Act https://oag.ca.gov/sites/all/files/agweb/pdfs/sb657/resource-guide.pdf	Retailers and manufacturers operating in California with more than $100M in sales	Supply chain	California's Transparency in Supply Chains Act seeks to eliminate human trafficking. Retailers and manufacturers operating in California with sales of more than $100M have to include statements on their website describing their "efforts to eradicate slavery and human trafficking from [their] direct supply chain for tangible goods offered for sale."
Dodd–Frank Act https://www.cftc.gov/LawRegulation/DoddFrankAct/index.htm	Public companies	Manufacturing	Dodd–Frank requires companies covered by the SEC's Exchange Act and that either manufacture or have "actual influence" over the manufacturing process to report if their product contains gold, tin, tantalum, tungsten, or other "conflict minerals." Conflict minerals are mined in the Democratic Republic of the Congo or other war zones, with the profits being used for continued fighting.
Environmental Protection Agency (EPA) https://www.epa.gov/laws-regulations/policy-guidance	Regulations are mandatory requirements that can apply to individuals, businesses, state and local governments, nonprofit institutions, and others	Risk management processes	The EPA has primary responsibility for enforcing many of the environmental statutes and regulations of the United States. As such, the agency is granted explicit enforcement authority in environmental statutes. Sometimes, however, that authority needs to be further refined or explained. In such cases, EPA may develop policies and write guidance. Policy documents represent EPA's interpretation or view of specific issues. Guidance documents are published to further clarify regulations and to assist in implementation of environmental regulations.

Controller's Regulatory Compliance Toolkit			
Compliance Area and Reference	**Specific Industry Focus**	**Process Areas Impacted**	**Summary**
EU's Regulation on Registration Evaluation, Authorisation and Restriction of Chemicals (REACH) https://www. chemsafetypro. com/Topics/EU/ REACH_Certificate_ of_Compliance_ REACH_ Declaration.html	If your product is a chemical product (substance or mixture), you need to ensure that every substance in it has been registered under REACH when the volume of that substance exceeds 1t/y = 1 tonne a year. A tonne is called a megagram or one million grams or one thousand kilograms. The best way to show compliance is to obtain a REACH registration number issued by the European Chemicals Agency (ECHA)	Companies making or selling products in the EU with a restricted chemical	REACH covers any chemicals in paint, clothing, electronic products, furniture, and so on that might be dangerous. Companies making or selling products in the EU with a restricted chemical need to show the ECHA that the product offered for sale is safe.
Fair and Accurate Credit Transactions Act of 2003 (FACT Act or FACTA) https://search financialsecurity .techtarget.com/ definition/FACTA	Companies dealing with consumers and medical information	Transactions related to consumers' medical information	The 2003 FACT Act, or FACTA (Pub. L. 108–159), is a US federal law passed by the United States Congress on November 22, 2003,[1] and signed by President George W. Bush on December 4, 2003,[2] as an amendment to the Fair Credit Reporting Act. The act allows consumers to request and obtain a free credit report once every 12 months from each of the three nationwide consumer credit reporting companies (Equifax, Experian, and TransUnion). In cooperation with the Federal Trade Commission, the three major credit reporting agencies set up the website AnnualCreditReport.com to provide free access to annual credit reports.[3] The act also contains provisions to help reduce identity theft, such as the ability for individuals to place alerts on their credit histories if identity theft is suspected, or if deploying overseas in the military, thereby making fraudulent applications for credit more difficult. Further, it requires secure disposal of consumer information.

Controller's Regulatory Compliance Toolkit			
Compliance Area and Reference	Specific Industry Focus	Process Areas Impacted	Summary
Federal Financial Institutions Examination Council (FFIEC) www.ffiec.gov	Financial institutions	Business continuity planning, development and acquisition, electronic banking, FedLine®, information security, IT audit, IT management, operations, outsourcing technology services, retail payment systems, supervision of technology service providers, and wholesale payment systems	The FFIEC is a five-member agency responsible for establishing consistent guidelines and uniform practices and principals for financial institutions. The member agencies include the Board of Governors of the Federal Reserve System (FRB), the Federal Deposit Insurance Corporation (FDIC), the National Credit Union Administration (NCUA), the Office of the Comptroller of the Currency (OCC), and the Office of Thrift Supervision (OTS). In 2004, the FFIEC updated its IT examination manual to account for the ever-quickening pace of changes and advancements in technology occurring at financial institutions and technology service providers. The result is the FFIEC *IT Examination Handbook*, a compilation of 12 booklets that can be updated individually as needed by the council.
Federal Risk and Authorization Management Program (FedRAMP) www.fedramp.gov	Federal agencies, cloud service providers	Cloud-based IT	FedRAMP is a government-wide program that provides a standardized approach to security assessment, authorization, and continuous monitoring for cloud products and services. FedRAMP enables agencies to rapidly adapt from old, insecure legacy IT to mission-enabling, secure, and cost-effective cloud-based IT. FedRAMP created and manages a core set of processes to ensure effective, repeatable cloud security for the government. FedRAMP has established a mature marketplace to increase utilization and familiarity with cloud services while facilitating collaboration across government through open exchanges of lessons learned, use cases, and tactical solutions.

Controller's Regulatory Compliance Toolkit			
Compliance Area and Reference	**Specific Industry Focus**	**Process Areas Impacted**	**Summary**
Financial Crimes Enforcement Network (FinCEN) www.fincen.gov	Financial institutions	Automated clearinghouse (ACH) transfers, wires, checks, and deposits	When the USA PATRIOT Act of 2001 was enacted, the act's Section 314(a) became a critical tool for investigating persons suspected of terrorism and/or money laundering. With FinCEN as the conduit, 314(a) enables law enforcement to solicit information from financial institutions related to such investigations through what is known as the FinCEN 314 list. The highly confidential and involved FinCEN compliance process depends upon the cooperation of three critical groups: 1. Federal, state, local, and foreign law enforcement agencies send FinCEN their requests for information regarding subjects suspected of terrorism or money laundering. 2. FinCEN reviews these requests and every two weeks sends its FinCEN list via a secure Internet site to financial institutions across the country. 3. Financial institutions must promptly search their entire customer database for any accounts maintained within the last 12 months and any transactions conducted within the last 6 months by named subjects on the FinCEN list.

Controller's Regulatory Compliance Toolkit			
Compliance Area and Reference	Specific Industry Focus	Process Areas Impacted	Summary
Foreign Corrupt Practices Act (FCPA) http://www.justice.gov/criminal/fraud/fcpa	All US companies	AR, procurement, AP, T&E, payroll	FCPA (originally passed in 1977), as amended, 15 U.S.C. §§ 78dd-1, et seq., was enacted for the purpose of making it unlawful for certain classes of persons and entities to make payments to foreign government officials to assist in obtaining or retaining business. Specifically, the anti-bribery provisions of FCPA prohibit the willful use of the mails or any means of instrumentality of interstate commerce corruptly in furtherance of any offer, payment, promise to pay, or authorization of the payment of money or anything of value to any person, while knowing that all or a portion of such money or thing of value will be offered, given, or promised, directly or indirectly, to a foreign official to influence the foreign official in his or her official capacity, induce the foreign official to do or omit to do an act in violation of his or her lawful duty, or to secure any improper advantage in order to assist in obtaining or retaining business for or with, or directing business to, any person. FCPA also requires companies whose securities are listed in the United States to meet its accounting provisions. (See 15 U.S.C. § 78m.) These accounting provisions, which were designed to operate in tandem with the anti-bribery provisions of the FCPA, require corporations covered by the provisions to (a) make and keep books and records that accurately and fairly reflect the transactions of the corporation, and (b) devise and maintain an adequate system of internal accounting controls.
Foreign Terrorist Organization (FTO) http://www.state.gov/j/ct/rls/other/des/123085.htm	All US industries	AR, procurement, AP, T&E, payroll	FTOs are foreign organizations that are designated by the secretary of state in accordance with Section 219 of the Immigration and Nationality Act (INA), as amended. FTO designations play a critical role in our fight against terrorism and are an effective means of curtailing support for terrorist activities and pressuring groups to get out of the terrorism business.

Controller's Regulatory Compliance Toolkit			
Compliance Area and Reference	**Specific Industry Focus**	**Process Areas Impacted**	**Summary**
EU's General Data Protection Regulation (GDPR) https://gdpr-info.eu	Although coming from the EU, the GDPR can also apply to businesses that are based outside the region; if a business in the United States, for instance, does business in the EU, then the GDPR can apply.	Processes that contain personal data	The EU"s GDPR can be considered the world's strongest set of data protection rules. It enhances how people can access information about themselves and places limits on what organizations can do with personal data. The full text of the GDPR is an unwieldy beast and contains 99 individual articles. The regulation exists as a framework for laws across the continent and replaces the previous 1995 Data Protection Directive. The GDPR's final form came about after more than four years of discussion and negotiations, and it was adopted by both the European Parliament and European Council in April 2016. The underpinning regulation and directive were published at the end of that month. The GDPR came into force on May 25, 2018. Countries within Europe were given the ability to make their own small changes to suit their own needs. Within the UK this flexibility led to the creation of the Data Protection Act (2018), which superseded the previous 1998 Data Protection Act.
Gramm–Leach–Bliley Act (GLBA) http://business.ftc.gov/privacy-and-security/gramm-leach-bliley-act	Per the GLBA, the term *financial institution* covers many parallel sectors, such as tax preparers, credit counselors, debt collectors, automobile dealers, and much more; in general, if a business collects and shares personal information about consumers to whom it extends or for whom it arranges credit, it has an obligation to follow GLBA	Transactions dealing with consumers' personal financial information	Three integral pieces of the 1999 GLBA focus on the information security of consumers' personal financial information. The Financial Privacy Rule, the Safeguards Rule, and the Pretexting Provisions together determine how financial institutions can collect this information and how they must ensure the security and confidentiality of it. To fulfill their GLBA compliance, all financial institutions must: ■ Provide notice to customers about its privacy requirements regarding their personal financial information (Financial Privacy). ■ Establish, implement, and maintain an information security program that secures and protects consumers' personal financial information from anticipated threats and/or unauthorized access (Safeguards). ■ Ensure that consumers' personal financial information is not being collected under false pretenses (Pretexting).

Controller's Regulatory Compliance Toolkit			
Compliance Area and Reference	**Specific Industry Focus**	**Process Areas Impacted**	**Summary**
Health and Insurance Portability and Accountability Act (HIPAA) http://www.hhs.gov/ocr/privacy	HIPAA applies to all health-care providers, health plans, health clearinghouses, and those entities that interact with them by exchanging protected health Information (PHI)	Transactions that contain patient or employee health information	On August 21, 1996, Congress passed the Health and Insurance Portability and Accountability Act, better known as HIPAA. Two primary outcomes of HIPAA are its Privacy Rule and its Security Rule, both of which work to protect patient health information. The goal of these uniform standards is to promote the secure flow of health information while at the same time supporting the highest level of patient care. The Privacy Rule identifies what patient information is to be protected. PHI includes data that identifies or could identify the patient, such as name, address, date of birth, or social security number. The Security Rule specifically protects PHI that is created, received, maintained, or transmitted electronically.
Know Your Customer (KYC) https://corpgov.law.harvard.edu/2016/02/07/fincen-know-your-customer-requirements	Financial institutions	Payment processes	KYC is the process of verifying the identity of customers. The objective of KYC guidelines is to prevent banks from being used by criminal elements for money laundering activities. It also enables banks to understand its customers and their financial dealings to serve them better and manage its risks prudently. KYC is the means of identifying and verifying the identity of the customer through independent and reliable sources of documents, data, or information for the purpose of verifying the identity of: ■ Individual customers. Banks obtain the customer's identity information, address, and a recent photograph. Similar information will also have to be provided for joint holders and mandate holders. ■ Nonindividual customers. Banks obtain identification data to verify the legal status of the entity, the operating address, the authorized signatories, and the beneficial owners. Information is also required on the nature of employment/business that the customer does or expects to undertake and the purpose of opening of the account with the bank. The KYC guidelines have been put in place by the Reserve Bank of India in the context of the recommendations made by the Financial Action Task Force (FATF) on AML standards and on Combating Financing of Terrorism (CFT). The Prevention of Money Laundering Act requires banks, financial institutions, and intermediaries to ensure that they follow certain minimum standards of KYC and AML.

Controller's Regulatory Compliance Toolkit

Compliance Area and Reference	Specific Industry Focus	Process Areas Impacted	Summary
Occupational Safety and Health Administration (OSHA) https://www.osha.gov/aboutosha	The OSH Act covers most private sector employers and their workers, in addition to some public sector employers and workers in the 50 states and certain territories and jurisdictions under federal authority; those jurisdictions include the District of Columbia, Puerto Rico, the Virgin Islands, American Samoa, Guam, the Northern Mariana Islands, Wake Island, Johnston Island, and the Outer Continental Shelf Lands as defined in the Outer Continental Shelf Lands Act	All US companies	With the Occupational Safety and Health Act of 1970, Congress created OSHA to ensure safe and healthful working conditions for working men and women by setting and enforcing standards and by providing training, outreach, education, and assistance. OSHA is part of the US Department of Labor. The administrator for OSHA is the assistant secretary of labor for occupational safety and health. OSHA's administrator answers to the secretary of labor, who is a member of the cabinet of the president of the United States.

Controller's Regulatory Compliance Toolkit

Compliance Area and Reference	Specific Industry Focus	Process Areas Impacted	Summary
Office of Foreign Asset Control (OFAC) http://www.treasury.gov/about/organizational-structure/offices/Pages/Office-of-Foreign-Assets-Control.aspx	All US industries	AR, procurement, AP, T&E, payroll	OFAC, part of the US Department of the Treasury, administers and enforces economic and trade sanctions based on US foreign policy and national security goals against targeted foreign countries and regimes, terrorists, international narcotics traffickers, those engaged in activities related to the proliferation of weapons of mass destruction, and other threats to the national security, foreign policy, or economy of the United States. OFAC acts under presidential national emergency powers, as well as authority granted by specific legislation, to impose controls on transactions and freeze assets under US jurisdiction. Many of the sanctions are based on United Nations and other international mandates, are multilateral in scope, and involve close cooperation with allied governments. Various sanctions programs administered by OFAC prohibit US citizens, permanent residents of the United States and US-based businesses, including US branches of foreign companies, from engaging in business or financial transactions with any party included on OFAC's Specially Designated Nationals List (SDN List). The SDN List, which contains thousands of names, includes individuals, banks, businesses, vessels, and other organizations that have been targeted and blocked by the US government for various policy reasons, such as terrorism, drug trafficking, and proliferation of weapons of mass destruction. Because of the ever-changing foreign policy landscape, OFAC frequently makes changes to the SDN List.

Controller's Regulatory Compliance Toolkit			
Compliance Area and Reference	**Specific Indus-try Focus**	**Process Areas Impacted**	**Summary**
Office of Inspector General (OIG) https://oig.hhs.gov	Hospitals, health-care systems, and health-care insurance companies	AR, patient billing	The mission of the OIG is to protect the integrity of Department of Health and Human Services (HHS) programs as well as the health and welfare of program beneficiaries. Since its 1976 establishment, OIG has been at the forefront of the nation's efforts to fight waste, fraud, and abuse in Medicare, Medicaid, and more than 300 other HHS programs.
			HHS's OIG is the largest inspector general's office in the federal government, with more than 1,700 employees dedicated to combating fraud, waste, and abuse and to improving the efficiency of HHS programs.
			A majority of OIG's resources goes towards the oversight of Medicare and Medicaid – programs that represent a significant part of the federal budget and that affect this country's most vulnerable citizens. OIG's oversight extends to programs under other HHS institutions, including the Centers for Disease Control and Prevention, the National Institutes of Health, and the Food and Drug Administration.
Regulation CC (Reg CC) http://www.federalreserve.gov/pubs/regcc/regcc.htm	Financial institutions	Deposits to financial institutions	In response to consumer complaints about lengthy deposit hold times, Congress passed the Expedited Funds Availability (EFA) Act in 1987, ushering in Regulation CC (Reg CC).
			Reg CC sets fair and uniform guidelines and required disclosures for how deposited funds are handled and credited to customers' accounts. It also gives financial institutions the right to delay availability in situations that pose a high risk of fraud.
			Subpart B of Regulation CC compliance deals specifically with funds availability and presents the most challenges for financial institutions. It stipulates by deposit type the amount of time that institutions can hold a deposit either under normal availability, or, if specific criteria are met, under an extension of normal availability.

Controller's Regulatory Compliance Toolkit			
Compliance Area and Reference	**Specific Industry Focus**	**Process Areas Impacted**	**Summary**
Regulation E (Reg E) http://www.fdic.gov/regulations/laws/rules/6500-3100.html	Financial institutions	All EFT transactions	Since 1978, when Congress passed the Electronic Fund Transfers Act (EFTA), better known as Regulation E (Reg E), financial institutions have been responsible for properly investigating consumer claims of electronic fund transfer (EFT) errors. Those investigations must follow very specific error-resolution procedures. At the time that Reg E was enacted, paper-based payments far outnumbered EFT payments. Today the exact opposite is true, with electronic payments representing over 66 percent of all payments. The rise in EFTs has been accompanied by a parallel rise in EFT error claims, making Reg E compliance that much more difficult for financial institutions to follow. Accurately complying with Reg E error resolution procedures requires financial institutions and their employees to recognize the following milestones and proceed accordingly with each claim: ■ When the official notice of a claim has occurred so that it can be investigated and resolved within the Reg E specified time period ■ When to issue provisional credit to the customer during an investigation ■ When to debit the customer's account if the investigation shows that no error occurred ■ When and how the customer should be notified throughout the investigation
Sarbanes–Oxley Act of 2002 (SOX) http://www.soxlaw.com www.sec.gov	All public companies	All financial transactions and processes	Congress reacted to corporate financial scandals, including those affecting Enron, Arthur Andersen, and WorldCom, by passing SOX. This act is designed to "protect investors by improving the accuracy and reliability of corporate disclosures made pursuant to the securities laws." SOX provides for new levels of auditor independence; personal accountability for CEOs and CFOs; additional accountability for corporate boards; increased criminal and civil penalties for securities violations; increased disclosure regarding executive compensation, insider trading, and financial statements; and certification of internal audit work by external auditors.

Controller's Regulatory Compliance Toolkit			
Compliance Area and Reference	**Specific Industry Focus**	**Process Areas Impacted**	**Summary**
Statement on Standards for Attestation Engagements 18 (SSAE 18) https://www. ssae-16.com/soc-1-report/the-ssae-18-audit-standard	All global service providers	Payroll processing; benefits providers; business process outsourcing (BPO) organizations; loan servicing organizations that process client data; data center, co-location/network monitoring services; software as a service (SaaS) providers; medical claims processors	SSAE 18 is a series of enhancements aimed to increase the usefulness and quality of system and organization controls (SOC) reports. It supersedes SSAE 16, and obviously the relic of audit reports, SAS 70. The changes made to the standard this time around will require companies to take more control and ownership of their own internal controls around the identification and classification of risk and appropriate management of third-party vendor relationships. These changes, while not overly burdensome, will help close the loop in key areas in which industry professionals noted gaps in many service organization reports. SSAE 18 is effective as of May 1, 2017, and if you have not made the necessary adjustments required, now is the time to find a quality provider to discuss the proper steps you need to take. All organizations are now required to issue their SOC report under the SSAE-18 standard in an SOC 1 report. The SOC 1 report produced will look and feel very similar to the one issued under SSAE 16, with just a couple of additional sections and controls to further enhance the content and quality, and thus, the ability for third parties to rely on it.
System for Award Management (SAM) https://www.sam.gov/SAM	Government contractors	Contractors and subcontractors	SAM is an official website of the US government. There is no cost to use SAM. This site can be used to: ▪ Register to do business with the US government ▪ Update or renew your entity registration ▪ Check status of an entity registration ▪ Search for entity registration and exclusion records
UK's Modern Slavery Act http://www.legislation.gov.uk/ukpga/2015/30/contents/enacted	Companies doing business in England and Wales with sales exceeding £36 million	Supply chain	The UK's Modern Slavery Act contains a transparency in supply chain provision that attempts to eliminate slavery. Companies doing business in England and Wales with sales exceeding £36 million have to include a description, on their websites, of their efforts to make sure slaves are not used in any part of their supply chain.

Controller's Regulatory Compliance Toolkit			
Compliance Area and Reference	**Specific Industry Focus**	**Process Areas Impacted**	**Summary**
US Sentencing Guidelines http://www.ussc.gov/guidelines/index.cfm	All US companies	All financial transactions	The US government appears to believe that a company's ethics and compliance culture are set by the very top levels of management, because US Sentencing Guidelines state: "High-level personnel and substantial authority personnel of the organization shall be knowledgeable about the content and operation of the compliance and ethics program . . . and shall promote an organizational culture that encourages ethical conduct and a commitment to compliance with the law." While the guidelines apply to all corporations, the larger the organization, the more formal the program should be, and the greater the penalty for failure to comply. Formal policies and procedures, and extensive communication programs, are expected of a large, publicly traded corporation. The expectations are not as extensive for a small business.
Washington State's Children's Safe Products Act (CSPA) https://ecology.wa.gov/Waste-Toxics/Reducing-toxic-chemicals/Childrens-Safe-Products-Act	Manufacturing companies	Supply chain	The CSPA limits the use of lead, cadmium, phthalates, and some flame retardants in children's products. It also requires manufacturers to report if their products contain chemicals of high concern to children.

TABLE OF CONTROLS – REGULATORY COMPLIANCE

Process: Regulatory Compliance

1. Assign a corporate compliance leader and committee. The compliance leader or officer has the ultimate responsibility for all regulatory compliance requirements for the company and ensures that business process owners are supporting the company. The compliance committee supports the implementation of all programs across the company with effective lines of communication.

2. Implement a compliance training and education program. Employees should attend compliance training on an annual basis, and more frequently when a new regulation is implemented.

3. Implement written policies, procedures, and standards of conduct. Policies and procedures are developed to support your compliance program across all business units.

4. Conduct internal monitoring and auditing. Noncompliant issues are reported and processes are updated. If a noncompliance issue is identified, due diligence is performed and the applicable business process is reviewed. Reports should indicate status for existing and new compliance requirements and should provide updates on all remediation issues and concerns. Business units should respond promptly to detected offenses and undertake corrective action.

5. Implement a regulatory compliance risk management program. The company's compliance program should be included with risk management initiatives to ensure that risk is properly identified and managed.

6. Stay compliant with current regulations. Stay updated on all regulatory compliance impacts and what they mean to your company and specific regions.

7. Implement compliance programs by business process. Ensure that business processes impacted have implemented compliance screening and compliance programs. As an example, the AP department should be screening suppliers against OFAC lists.

8. Balance regulatory compliance with the customer experience. Businesses should begin thinking holistically about compliance to proactively manage risks that could interfere with business growth – like massive fines and the devastating reputation fallout from a Target- or Equifax-caliber breach.

9. Implement an FCPA internal controls program. FCPA is a US law passed in 1977 that prohibits US firms and individuals from paying bribes to foreign officials in furtherance of a business deal. The FCPA places no minimum amount on a punishment for a bribery payment. The FPCA is enforced by the Department of Justice (DOJ) and the SEC.

10. Ensure HIPAA compliance. Broadly speaking, you will need to ensure proper measures are taken to protect the privacy and security of health data that is used, shared, and stored by your company. Your processes should include technical, physical, and administrative safeguards.

11. Ensure GDPR compliance. The GDPR has broad standards that can make compliance tricky to navigate. However, there are several key privacy and data protection requirements:

- Organizations must have consent from the subject to process their data.
- Collected data must be anonymized.
- Data must be safely handled for cross-border transfer.
- Certain companies must appoint a data protection officer to oversee compliance.

12. Screen new suppliers and customers. New suppliers and customers are screened against applicable OFAC, SDN, FCPA, and KYC listings. W-8s and W-9s are obtained for new suppliers and TIN matching is performed.

13. Comply with OSHA laws. Companies must comply with the General Duty Clause of the OSH Act, which requires employers to keep their workplaces free of serious recognized hazards.

14. Comply with EPA laws. The EPA's five most effective pieces of environmental legislation are the Clean Air Act, the Endangered Species Act, the Montreal Protocol, the Clean Water Act, and Reformation Plan No. 3 of 1970.

TABLE OF RISKS AND CONTROLS – REGULATORY COMPLIANCE

Process: Regulatory Compliance			
Process Risk	**Recommended Policies**	**Internal Controls**	**KPIs**
1. Company fines for violating regulatory compliance requirements. The company's noncompliance can result in severe penalties depending on the level of negligence. Fines can reach millions of dollars and some violations carry the risk of criminal charges and jail time.	■ Regulatory Compliance Policies ■ Regulatory Compliance Risk Management ■ Regulatory Compliance Audit Process ■ Regulatory Compliance Training Programs	1. Designation of a Corporate Compliance Leader and Committee 2. Implementation of a Compliance Education and Training Program 3. Implementation of Written Policies, Procedures, and Standards of Conduct 4. Conducting of Internal Monitoring and Auditing 5. Implementation of a Regulatory Compliance Risk Management Program 6. Compliance with Current Regulations 7. Implementation of Compliance Programs by Business Process 8. Balancing of Regulatory Compliance with the Customer Experience 9. Implementation of an FCPA Internal Controls Program 10. Compliance with HIPAA 11. Compliance with GDPR 12. Screening of New Suppliers and Customers 13. Compliance with OSHA Laws 14. Compliance with EPA Laws	■ Number of Noncompliance Incidences per Quarter (by Company and Business Unit) ■ Value of Company Fines ■ Value of Fines per Business Unit ■ Number of Corrective Action Plans

Process: Regulatory Compliance			
Process Risk	**Recommended Policies**	**Internal Controls**	**KPIs**
2. Damage to company's reputation. The company's reputation is damaged and there is a significant loss of revenue.	▪ Regulatory Compliance Policies ▪ Regulatory Compliance Risk Management ▪ Regulatory Compliance Audit Process ▪ Regulatory Compliance Training Programs	1. Designation of a Corporate Compliance Leader and Committee 2. Implementation of a Compliance Education and Training Program 3. Implementation of Written Policies, Procedures, and Standards of Conduct 4. Conducting of Internal Monitoring and Auditing 5. Implementation of a Regulatory Compliance Risk Management Program 6. Compliance with Current Regulations 7. Implementation of Compliance Programs by Business Process 8. Balancing of Regulatory Compliance with the Customer Experience 9. Implementation of an FCPA Internal Controls Program 10. Compliance with HIPAA 11. Compliance with GDPR 12. Screening of New Suppliers and Customers 13. Compliance with OSHA Laws 14. Compliance with EPA Laws	▪ Percentage Revenue Increase/Decrease

Process: Regulatory Compliance			
Process Risk	**Recommended Policies**	**Internal Controls**	**KPIs**
3. Environmental risk. The company may be damaging the environment due to noncompliance with environmental laws.	■ Regulatory Compliance Policies ■ Regulatory Compliance Risk Management ■ EPA Compliance Audit Process ■ EPA Compliance Training Programs	1. Designation of a Corporate Compliance Leader and Committee 2. Implementation of a Compliance Education and Training Program 3. Implementation of Written Policies, Procedures, and Standards of Conduct 4. Conducting of Internal Monitoring and Auditing 5. Implementation of a Regulatory Compliance Risk Management Program 6. Compliance with Current Regulations 7. Implementation of Compliance Programs by Business Process 8. Balancing of Regulatory Compliance with the Customer Experience 14. Compliance with EPA Laws	■ Number of Noncompliance Incidences per Quarter (by Company and Business Unit) ■ Value of Company Fines ■ Value of Fines per Business Unit ■ Number of Corrective Action Plans
4. Workplace and safety risk. The company may not be in compliance with the General Duty Clause of the OSH Act.	■ Regulatory Compliance Policies ■ Regulatory Compliance Risk Management ■ OSHA Compliance Audit Process ■ OSHA Compliance Training Programs	1. Designation of a Corporate Compliance Leader and Committee 2. Implementation of a Compliance Education and Training Program 3. Implementation of Written Policies, Procedures, and Standards of Conduct 4. Conducting of Internal Monitoring and Auditing 5. Implementation of a Regulatory Compliance Risk Management Program 6. Compliance with Current Regulations 7. Implementation of Compliance Programs by Business Process 13. Compliance with OSHA Laws	■ Number of Noncompliance Incidences per Quarter (by Company and Business Unit) ■ Value of Company Fines ■ Value of Fines per Business Unit ■ Number of Corrective Action Plans

Process: Regulatory Compliance			
Process Risk	**Recommended Policies**	**Internal Controls**	**KPIs**
5. Bribery and corrupt practices. The company may be violating FCPA.	■ Regulatory Compliance Policies ■ Regulatory Compliance Risk Management ■ FCPA Compliance Audit Process ■ FCPA Compliance Training Programs	1. Designation of a Corporate Compliance Leader and Committee 2. Implementation of a Compliance Education and Training Program 3. Implementation of Written Policies, Procedures, and Standards of Conduct 4. Conducting of Internal Monitoring and Auditing 5. Implementation of a Regulatory Compliance Risk Management Program 6. Compliance with Current Regulations 7. Implementation of Compliance Programs by Business Process 9. Implementation of an FCPA Internal Controls Program 12. Screening of New Suppliers and Customers	■ Number of Noncompliance Incidences per Quarter (By Company and Business Unit) ■ Value of Company Fines ■ Value of Fines per Business Unit ■ Number of Corrective Action Plans

2

SECTION FIVE

Payment Risk

SECTION INTRODUCTION

The Federal Reserve states that "The basic risks in payment, clearing, settlement, and recording systems may include credit risk, liquidity risk, operational risk, and legal risk."[1] Corporate payments are supported by many important and related functions. Controlling risk in corporate payments is dependent on managing risk in procurement, AP, hire-to-retire (H2R), order-to-cash (O2C), and AR, as well as in the initiation of the actual funds transfer. Risk management is a critical corporate function that needs to be addressed as an enterprise-wide focus.

This section focuses on all the processes and subprocesses that impact payment risk. Most controllers agree that their biggest concerns fall within the payment process and worry that payments are accurately made to suppliers and employees. Controllers also need to ensure that payments from customers are properly applied and accounted for.

CONTROLLER'S TOOL 21 – OVERVIEW OF BUSINESS PAYMENT PROCESSES, SUBPROCESSES, RISK IMPACTS, AND INDICATORS

Introduction. Risk may be introduced into corporate payments processes broadly throughout the corporation and is considered to be the largest area of risk. Corporate payments risk applies to the P2P, H2R, and O2C business processes. The payment risks and controls for each subprocess within each business process are addressed in the chapter that covers the process.

The following table identifies each business process, each applicable subprocess, the payee, impacts to the payments process, and the payment risk indicator. **Note:** The payment

---

[1]Federal Reserve (2017). Federal Reserve policy on payment system risk (as amended effective September 15, 2017) (p. 4; accessed December 8, 2019). https://www.federalreserve.gov/paymentsystems/files/psr_policy.pdf.

risk indicator is the impact of the risk that each subprocess has on the payments process and uses a "stoplight" indicator: red = high impact, yellow = medium impact, and green = low impact.

Table of Payment Business Processes, Subprocesses, Risk Impacts, and Indicators

Business Process	Subprocesses	Payee	Impact to the Payments Process	Payment Risk Indicator
Procure-to-Pay		1.0 Procurement		
1)	1.1 Supplier Selection and Management	Supplier	■ Suppliers are valid	●
1.3	1.2 Contract Management		■ Correct pricing and terms	●
1.3	1.3 Purchasing and Ordering		■ Approved supplier, correct pricing and terms per contract	●
1.3	1.4 Reporting, Metrics, and Analytics		■ Process is analyzed and anomalies are identified and remediated	●
1.3		2.0 Accounts Payable		
2.0	2.1 Supplier Master File	Supplier	■ Correct supplier data is recorded in the ERP system	●
2.0	2.2 Invoice Processing		■ Approved invoices are those that are matched with POs, package slips, or other related documents; such invoices are paid accurately, timely, within terms, and directed to the correct person and address	●
2.0	2.3 Payment Process		■ Supplier payments are accurate, timely, and reflect allowed discounts,	●
2.0	2.4 Accounting Processes		■ Accounting and financial reporting are accurate	○
2.0	2.5 Customer Service		■ Timely customer service is granted to both suppliers and internal customers	○
2.0	2.6 Reporting, Metrics, and Analytics		■ Process is analyzed and anomalies are identified and remediated	○

Business Process	Subprocesses	Payee	Impact to the Payments Process	Payment Risk Indicator
2.0	2.7 P-Cards		■ P-Cards are issued and used appropriately and per company policies	●
2.0			■ Process is analyzed and anomalies are identified and remediated	◐
2.0	2.8 Travel and Entertainment	Employee	■ Corporate credit cards are issued and used appropriately and per company policies	●
			■ Employee expenses are processed accurately and timely	●
			■ T&E expenses are reviewed for adherence to corporate policies; issues are reported and prompt remediation occurs	●
			■ Process is analyzed and anomalies are identified and remediated	●
Hire-to-Retire			**3.0 Human Resources**	
2.0	3.1 Human Resources Process	Employee	■ Employee data is accurate resulting in correct and nonfraudulent benefit, withholding, payment, and reporting processes	○
2)			**4.0 Payroll**	
	4.1 Payroll Processing Process	Employee	■ Payroll is processed using processing and data controls	●
	4.2 Payroll Payment Process		■ Payments are issued using correct and accurate employee and tax data; accounting and financial reporting are accurate	●
	4.3 Reporting, Metrics, and Analytics		■ Process is analyzed and anomalies are identified and remediated	◐

Business Process	Subprocesses	Payee	Impact to the Payments Process	Payment Risk Indicator
Order-to-Cash		5.0 Order-to-Cash		
3)	5.1 Sales	Customer	■ Controls are in place for the order-to-cash (O2C) process	◯
	5.2 Customer Master File		■ Customer data is validated, including performing KYC review	◯
	5.3 Credit Analysis		■ Customer is granted appropriate credit limits and terms	◯
	5.4 Order Fulfillment and Invoicing		■ Orders are fulfilled according to contract terms, and pricing and invoices are issued to the correct customers using accurate terms and pricing	◯
	5.5 Accounts Receivable and Collections		■ AR data is accurate and the GL is correctly stated and customer accounts are reviewed and prioritized to ensure payments within terms	●
	5.6 Cash Application and Management		■ Payments are applied to the correct customer account and AR is updated accordingly	●
	5.7 Order-to-Cash Reporting, Metrics, and Analytics		■ Process is analyzed and anomalies are identified and remediated	◯

CHAPTER 10

Procure-to-Pay

OVERVIEW

Although P2P does not necessarily refer directly to the application of technology to the purchasing process, it is most often used in relation to applications like e-procurement and ERP purchasing and payment modules. The P2P process is no longer viewed as a back-office function but as one of tremendous value, since the process can greatly impact an organization by providing opportunities for strategic sourcing, automation, improved controls, and business partnerships, which can greatly reduce risk and improve working capital.

This chapter will highlight the P2P business processes of procurement and AP, as well as their applicable subprocesses, as listed below. An overview, process flow, table of controls, and table of risks and controls will be provided for each subprocess.

Procure-to-Pay subprocesses included in this chapter

1.0 Procurement
    1.1 Supplier Selection and Management
    1.2 Contract Management
    1.3 Purchasing and Ordering
    1.4 Reporting, Metrics, and Analytics

2.0 Accounts Payable
    2.1 Supplier Master File
    2.2 Invoice Processing

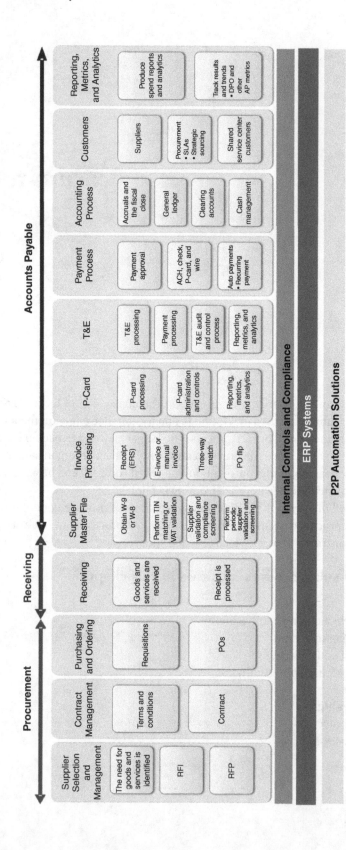

Procure-to-Pay Process Flow

1.0 PROCUREMENT

Procurement Process Overview

The Purchasing and Procurement Center defines procurement as "buying things."[1] The list below provides more detail for that definition. Procurement is the purchase of goods or services with the following criteria:

- Of the correct quality
- The appropriate quantity
- At the required time
- From the best supplier
- With optimum terms

Procurement Process Flow

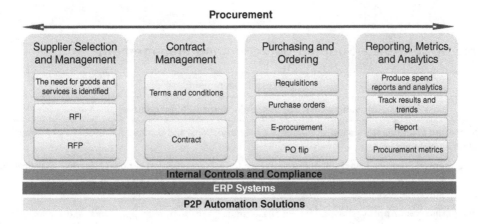

---

[1]Purchasing Insight (n.d.). The procurement process. Purchasing Insight website (accessed December 18, 2018). http://purchasinginsight.com/resources/the-procurement-process.

1.1 SUPPLIER SELECTION AND MANAGEMENT

Supplier Selection and Management Process Overview

The most effective suppliers are those who offer products or services that match – or exceed – the needs of your business. So when you are looking for suppliers, it's best to be sure of your business needs and what you want to achieve by buying, rather than simply paying for what suppliers want to sell you.

Supplier Selection and Management Process Flow

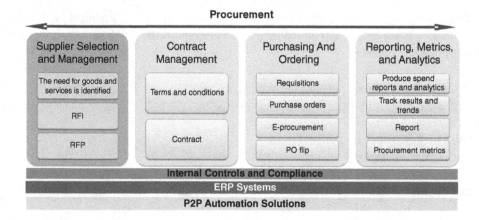

Table of Controls – Supplier Selection and Management

Process: Procurement
Subprocess: Supplier Selection and Management

1. Purchasing Strategies. Sourcing strategies, supplier selections, and contract negotiations processes should be developed and documented.

2. Documented Supplier Selection. There must be a formal, documented supplier selection, qualification, and evaluation process used based on criteria established by the team and approved by purchasing management/client sponsor(s).

3. Purchasing from Approved Suppliers. Purchases must be made from an approved vendor master file/list in accordance with local procedures. A formal process should be in place to approve purchases from suppliers not on the approved database on an exception basis. The supplier database must be reviewed, updated, and purged of inactive vendors (i.e. vendors with no activity for 18–24 months) at least annually. Suppliers should be added to the supplier list/database upon completion of the supplier selection process and financial review where applicable.

4. Global and Regional Contracts. Where global, regional, or geographic contracts are in place, all affected operating units will leverage that contract. Multinational contracts must contain export notification and control language.

5. Business Interruption Contingency Plans. Supplier and sourcing strategies must take into consideration contingency plans to address or minimize risk of business interruption. These plans should be regularly reviewed.

Process: Procurement
Subprocess: Supplier Selection and Management

6. Supplier Performance. Suppliers must be periodically monitored in accordance with company policy to ensure that actual performance meets your company's quality, delivery, product/technology, service and support, and cost expectations.

7. Supplier Master File Controls. Individuals not involved in the supplier selection, invoice, or payment processes must perform the actual update of approved supplier master/lists. Procurement personnel requesting supplier master updates must have the approval of their supervisor or his/her designee prior to submission of the supplier master update.

Table of Risks and Controls – Supplier Selection and Management

Process: Procurement			
Subprocess: Supplier Selection and Management			
Process Risk	**Recommended Policies**	**Internal Controls**	**KPIs**
1. Purchases from Unapproved Suppliers. A purchase may be made from an unapproved supplier, which can lead to higher prices, subpar quality, and/or unacceptable terms. Further, an unapproved supplier may not be a legitimate company.	■ Purchasing Policies ■ Supplier Selection Policies and Documentation ■ Business Rules for Initiating a Request for Proposal (RFP) and Request For Information (RFI)	1. Purchasing Strategies 2. Documented Supplier Selection 3. Purchasing from Approved Suppliers 4. Global and Regional Contracts 7. Supplier Master File Controls	■ Number of Active Suppliers in the Supplier Master File ■ Number and Percentage of One-Time Suppliers ■ Number and Percentage of Fraudulent Suppliers ■ Number and Percentage of Suppliers Under Contract
2. Underutilized Purchasing Power. Your company will not have sufficient information to conduct meaningful negotiations and utilize its full purchasing power and leverage the best supplier pricing available.	■ Supplier Selection Policies and Documentation ■ Business Rules for Implementing Global and Regional Contracts ■ Supplier Performance Management Criteria	2. Documented Supplier Selection 4. Global and Regional Contracts 6. Supplier Performance	■ Savings from Strategic Sourcing Initiatives ■ Supplier Service Level Agreements (SLAs)
3. Lack of Compliance Screening. Export control violations, related-party transactions, and/or conflict of interest situations may occur. The potential for errors and irregularities is substantially increased.	■ Supplier Selection Policies and Documentation ■ Business Rules for Implementing Global and Regional Contracts ■ Business Rules and SoD ■ Controls for Supplier Master File Updates	2. Documented Supplier Selection 3. Purchasing from Approved Suppliers 4. Global and Regional Contracts 7. Supplier Master File Controls	■ Number of Active Suppliers in the Supplier Master File ■ Number and Percentage of Supplier Onboarding Issues ■ Number and Percentage of Compliance Issues Identified ■ Value of Compliance Fines

Process: Procurement			
Subprocess: Supplier Selection and Management			
Process Risk	**Recommended Policies**	**Internal Controls**	**KPIs**
4. Quality and Pricing Issues. Goods and services purchased may not meet quality standards. Unauthorized prices or terms may be accepted.	■ Supplier Selection Policies and Documentation ■ Business Rules for Implementing Global and Regional Contracts ■ Business Rules and SoD ■ Controls for Supplier Master File Updates	2. Documented Supplier Selection 3. Purchasing from Approved Suppliers 4. Global and Regional Contracts 7. Supplier Master File Controls	■ Number of Active Suppliers in the Supplier Master File ■ Number and Percentage of Suppliers Under Contract ■ Value of Pricing Issues ■ Savings from Strategic Sourcing Initiatives
5. Records Management. Records may be misused or altered by unauthorized personnel to the detriment of the company and its suppliers.	■ Supplier Selection Policies and Documentation ■ Business Rules for Implementing Global and Regional Contracts	1. Purchasing Strategies 2. Documented Supplier Selection 3. Purchasing from Approved Suppliers 4. Global and Regional Contracts 7. Supplier Master File Controls	■ Number of Active Suppliers in the Supplier Master File ■ Number and Percentage of Suppliers Under Contract
6. Receipt of Goods and Services. Goods and services may be received early or late, resulting in business interruption or excessive levels of inventory.	■ Supplier Selection Polices and Documentation ■ Business Rules for Implementing Global and Regional Contracts ■ Business Rules and SoD ■ Controls for Supplier Master File Updates	3. Purchasing from Approved Suppliers 4. Global and Regional Contracts 7. Supplier Master File Controls	■ Number of Active Suppliers in the Supplier Master File ■ Number and Percentage of Suppliers Under Contract ■ Inventory Level Trends ■ Number and Value of Excessive Inventory by SKU Number
7. Lack of Strategic Sourcing. The company may lose the opportunity to revise the supplier base to better meet its needs.	■ Business Rules for Implementing Global and Regional Contracts ■ Supplier Performance Management Criteria	4. Global and Regional Contracts 6. Supplier Performance	■ Number of Active Suppliers in the Supplier Master File ■ Number and Percentage of Suppliers Under Contract ■ Savings from Strategic Sourcing Initiatives

1.2 CONTRACT MANAGEMENT

Contract Management Process Overview

Contract management includes negotiating the terms and conditions in contracts and ensuring compliance with any applicable regulations as well as documenting and agreeing on any changes that may arise during negotiations. Contract management is a strategic process that can result in large benefits in both operational efficiency and reducing risk.

A contract agreement is a document between two or more parties that outlines the responsibilities of each party and states what value or payment they will exchange for the performance of those obligations. Although a valid contract sometimes can be made verbally, the safest practice is to get terms in writing.

Contract Management Process Flow

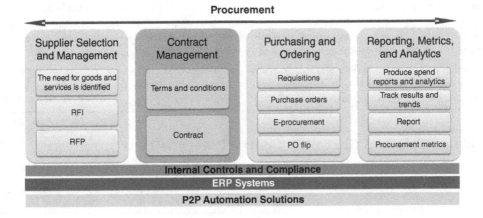

Table of Controls – Contract Management

Process: Procurement
Subprocess: Contract Management

1. Define the contract policy and approval process. Establish a signature approval process for all company commitments and contracts. Usually the legal department approves all contracts before implementation.

2. Define contract types and usage. A fixed-price contract is applicable for most standard materials, but not quite so relevant for procuring certain kinds of services. A cost-reimbursement plus percentage fee contract is far more difficult to administer than is a unit-price contract, but may be more appropriate in specific circumstances.

Process: Procurement

Subprocess: Contract Management

---

3. Define controls for pricing structures. A variety of contract-pricing mechanisms are used in procurement. Each structure has its advantages and disadvantages in different circumstances. The specific pricing alternatives considered are:

- Fixed price
- Unit price
- Target price
- Cost-reimbursement with incentive fees
- Cost-reimbursement with fixed or percentage fees.

4. Use approved company templates for contracts. Use an approved company template for all contracts.

5. Assign service level agreements for contracts. An Service Level Agreement (SLA) should also include a set of operating metrics that are reported on a monthly or quarterly basis. As an example, a good set of metrics for AP will include cost per invoice, days payable outstanding (DPO), invoices paid on time, outstanding credit balances, missed discounts, paid credits, and number of suppliers on the supplier master file.

6. Implement right-to-audit clauses. In the ever-evolving business of specialization and the desire for continued growth, many companies are utilizing third-party specialists to assist with various revenue streams. Using third parties can prove to be extremely beneficial in terms of cost and time savings, but they do come with added risks. Having a right-to-audit clause and acting on it annually will help mitigate those added risks.

7. Supplier management review process. To ensure that SLAs are reported and action is taken on potential issues, a supplier management review process establishes a schedule (monthly, quarterly, and annually) to formally review supplier performance.

Table of Risks and Controls – Contract Management

Process: Procurement

Subprocess: Contract Management

Process Risk	Recommended Policies	Internal Controls	KPIs
1. Unapproved and Fraudulent Suppliers. Contracts are initiated for fraudulent and unapproved suppliers without adhering to company policies.	■ Contract Policies and Procedures ■ DoA Policy	1. Define the Contract Policy and Approval Process 2. Define Contract Types and Usage 4. Use Approved Company Templates for Contracts.	■ Percentage Compliance with Contract Policy and Approval Process ■ Percentage of Correct Usage of Contract Types ■ Percentage Compliance with Company Templates
2. Pricing Issues. Pricing for goods and services is incorrect causing financial exposure to the company and incorrect payments to suppliers.	■ Pricing and Approval Policy ■ Contract Pricing Controls Self-Assessment	3. Define Controls for Pricing Structures	■ Number of Pricing Issues Found in Correct Reviews ■ Number of Pricing Issues by Supplier

Process: Procurement			
Subprocess: Contract Management			
Process Risk	Recommended Policies	Internal Controls	KPIs
3. Supplier performance is not tracked or reported in a timely manner and supplier issues are not identified nor corrected in a timely manner.	■ SLA Implementation Requirements ■ Supplier Management Reviews	5. Assign SLAs for Contracts. 7. Supplier Management Review Process	■ Percentage Suppliers Using SLAs ■ SLA Scorecard Results by Supplier
4. Performance of third parties cannot be reviewed or audited. Using third parties can prove to be extremely beneficial in terms of cost and time savings, but they do come with added operational and compliance risks.	■ Contract Policies and Procedures ■ Supplier Management Reviews	4. Use Approved Company Templates for Contracts. 6. Implement Right-To-Audit Clauses 7. Supplier Management Review Process	■ Percentage Compliance with Company Templates ■ Percentage Compliance with Right-to-Audit Clauses

1.3 PURCHASING AND ORDERING

Purchasing and Ordering Process Overview

Business owners usually designate purchase order (PO) authority or DoA to specific individuals in the business. Business owners, directors, and executive-level managers often allow operational managers to approve POs for their departments. POs for significant dollar amounts, such as several thousand dollars, are the only POs needing an executive's authorization. Business owners and executive managers delegate this ability to ensure that the company's business operations can continue without excessive oversight.

Purchasing and Ordering Process Flow

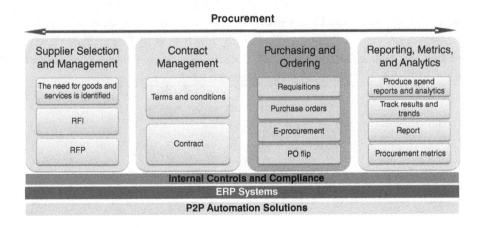

Table of Controls – Purchasing and Ordering

Process: Accounts Payable
Subprocess: Purchasing and Ordering

1. Segregation of Duties. All purchasing/ordering responsibilities must be segregated from AP payment, receiving, and accounting activities, and system access rights are granted appropriately.

2. Purchasing Procedures. Specific procedures will be used for the purchasing process (e.g. including on-site supplier warehouses, consortiums, etc.), including short- and long-term contract commitments. These procedures must be consistent with company policy. POs/transactions must include all pertinent information concerning formal commitments, including quantities, delivery means and requirements, payment terms and conditions, account distribution, and so on.

3. Systems Access Controls. All POs or access to input screens must be safeguarded and internal control procedures for processing and approval must be in place to prevent unauthorized use.

4. Purchase Price Negotiation. Finance will be involved in the purchase price negotiation processes for cost analysis (e.g. target costing), bidding, and industry cost benchmarking.

5. Conduct Prior to Vendor Selection Process. Any activity that may financially obligate the company, such as oral or written contracts, memorandums of understanding, and statements of intent must not be done prior to the completion of the selection process without proper approvals.

6. Order Audit Trail. All orders/transactions must be uniquely identifiable and traceable and periodically reviewed.

7. Invoice Processing. Supplier POs/transactions must instruct suppliers to forward their billings directly to AP using e-invoicing methods.

8. Purchase Order Distribution. POs/information must be made available to the receiving department for verification of incoming receipts and to the AP department for comparison with supplier billings. AP and receiving must be notified of changed or canceled POs on a timely basis.

9. Safeguarding Intellectual Property. Procedures governing the review and approval of contracts should address the safeguarding of company's intellectual property, including patents and trademarks.

10. Service Purchase Orders. A "not to exceed" limit and duration must be specified on each service PO.

11. Independence and Purchasing Ethics. Independence between purchasing agent/buyer and supplier must be maintained. This can be accomplished through periodic buyer rotation, or participation in corporate contracts, or use of commodity teams.

12. Requisitioning Procedures. Purchase requirements (e.g. POs, statements of work, contracts, etc.) must be initiated by the requesting department and be properly approved within the approver's limits before a purchase request is made. POs must not be split to get around approval limits.

13. Low-Value Requisitions. Authorization limits must be established for individuals making low-value purchases through special procurement processes (e.g. credit cards, catalogs, procurement cards, etc.).

14. Purchase Order Revisions. PO revisions for price or quantity that cause increases that exceed a buyer's approval level must be approved in compliance with company procedures.

Table of Risks and Controls – Purchasing and Ordering

Process: Procurement			
Subprocess: Purchasing and Ordering			
Process Risk	**Recommended Policies**	**Internal Controls**	**KPIs**
1. Purchase Order Inaccuracy. A PO may be: a. Unauthorized or improperly authorized b. Made from an unauthorized supplier c. Ordered and received by an unauthorized individual	■ PO Policies ■ SoD and Systems Access Business Rules	1. SoD 2. Purchasing Procedures 3. Systems Access Controls 4. Independence and Purchasing Ethics	■ Number of Non-PO Invoices Processed ■ Number of Fraudulent POs ■ Adherence to PO Policies
2. Import and Export Compliance Issues. Import and export control violations, related-party transactions, or conflict of interest situations may occur. The potential exists for errors and irregularities.	■ Compliance Screening and Review Policies (Office of Foreign Asset Control [OFAC], Office of Inspector General [IG], and Foreign Corrupt Practices Act [FCPA])	2. Purchasing Procedures	■ Number of Import and Export Issues Reported per Period ■ Amount of Compliance Fines Paid per Period
3. Unauthorized Purchases. Rather than being returned or refused, the following items may be received and ultimately paid for: a. Unordered goods or services b. Excessive quantities or incorrect items c. Canceled or duplicated orders	■ PO Policies ■ SoD and Systems Access Business Rules	1. SoD 2. Purchasing Procedures 3. Systems Access Controls 4. Independence and Purchasing Ethics	■ Number of Non-PO Invoices Processed ■ Number of Fraudulent POs ■ Adherence to PO Policies
4. Data Accuracy and Availability. Records may be lost or destroyed. Records may be misused or altered by unauthorized personnel to the detriment of the company and its suppliers. Data may not be available for external legal, tax, and audit purposes.	■ PO Policies ■ SoD and Systems Access Business Rules	1. SoD 2. Purchasing Procedures 3. Access Controls 4. Purchase Price Negotiation 5. Conduct Prior to Vendor Selection Process 6. Order Audit Trail 7. Invoice Processing 8. PO Distribution 11. Independence and Purchasing Ethics 14. PO Revisions	■ Adherence to PO Policies ■ Value of Clearing Account Variances ■ Value of Unmatched Invoices per Period

Process: Procurement			
Subprocess: Purchasing and Ordering			
Process Risk	**Recommended Policies**	**Internal Controls**	**KPIs**
5. Inaccurate Accounting. Goods and services may be received but not reported or reported inaccurately. Unrecorded liabilities and misstated inventory and cost of sales may occur.	■ SoD and Systems Access Business Rules	7. Invoice Processing 8. PO Distribution	■ Value of Clearing Account Variances ■ Value of Unmatched Invoices per Period ■ Value of Outstanding Accruals per Period ■ Gross and Net Inventory Cycle Count Variances ■ Value of Inventory Write-Offs
6. Quality of Goods and Services. Items and services purchased may not meet quality standards. Unauthorized prices or terms may be accepted.	■ PO Policies ■ SoD and Systems Access Business Rules	1. SoD 2. Purchasing Procedures 3. Access Controls 4. Purchase Price Negotiation 5. Conduct Prior to Vendor Selection Process 6. Order Audit Trail 7. Invoice Processing 8. PO Distribution 13. Low-Value Requisitions 14. PO Revisions	■ Value of Pricing Issues ■ Value of Clearing Account Variances ■ Value of Unmatched Invoices per Period
7. Duplicate Payments. Duplicate payments may occur, or payments may be made for the wrong amount or to unauthorized or nonexistent suppliers.	■ PO Policies ■ SoD and Systems Access Business Rules ■ Three-Way Match	1. SoD 2. Purchasing Procedures 3. Access Controls 4. Purchase Price Negotiation 5. Conduct Prior to Vendor Selection Process 6. Order Audit Trail 7. Invoice Processing 8. PO Distribution 10. Service POs 14. PO Revisions	■ Number and Value of Duplicate/Erroneous Payments Identified per Period ■ Number and Value of Duplicate/Erroneous Payments by Reason

Process: Procurement			
Subprocess: Purchasing and Ordering			
Process Risk	**Recommended Policies**	**Internal Controls**	**KPIs**
8. Incorrect Accounting. Purchases and/or payments may be recorded at the incorrect amount, to the wrong account, or in the wrong period.	■ PO Policies ■ Finance Close Cutoffs for Accruals ■ Three-Way Match	1. SoD 2. Purchasing Procedures 3. Access Controls 4. Purchase Price Negotiation 5. Conduct Prior to Vendor Selection Process 6. Order Audit Trail 7. Invoice Processing 8. PO Distribution 14. PO Revisions	■ Value of Clearing Account Variances ■ Value of Unmatched Invoices per Period ■ Value of Outstanding Accruals per Period ■ Unapproved Items in PO Workflow
9. Incorrect Payments. Payment may be made for goods or services never received.	■ PO Policies ■ Three-Way Match ■ Clearing Account Reconciliation Policies and Procedures	1. SoD 2. Purchasing Procedures 3. Access Controls 4. Purchase Price Negotiation 5. Conduct Prior to Vendor Selection Process 6. Order Audit Trail 7. Invoice Processing 8. PO Distribution 14. PO Revisions	■ Number and Value of Duplicate/Erroneous Payments Identified per Period ■ Number and Value of Duplicate/ Erroneous Payments by Reason
10. Unauthorized Receipts. A PO may be received by an unauthorized individual.	■ PO Policies ■ Three-Way Match ■ Clearing Account Reconciliation Policies and Procedures	1. SoD 2. Purchasing Procedures 3. Access Controls	■ Number and Value of Duplicate/Erroneous Payments Identified per Period ■ Number and Value of Duplicate/ Erroneous Payments by Reason
11. Loss of intellectual property.	■ Contract Management Policies ■ Nondisclosure Agreements	9. Safeguarding Intellectual Property	■ Value of Intellectual Property Loss

1.4 REPORTING, METRICS, AND ANALYTICS

Reporting, Metrics, and Analytics Overview

Metrics are used to drive improvements and help businesses focus their people and resources on what's important. The range of metrics that companies can employ vary from those that are mandatory – for legal, safety, or contractual purposes – to those that track increases in efficiency, reductions in complaints, greater profits, and better savings. Overall, metrics should reflect and support the various strategies for all aspects of the organization, including finance, marketing, competition, standards, and customer requirements and expectations. Metrics indicate the priorities of the company and provide a window on performance, ethos, and ambition.

Reporting, Metrics, and Analytics Process Flow

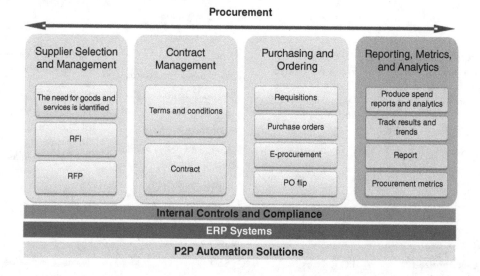

Table of Controls – Reporting, Metrics, and Analytics

Process: Procurement
Subprocess: Reporting, Metrics, and Analytics

1. **Visibility of Spending.** Spending results are tracked, analyzed, and reported to business stakeholders.

2. **Strategic Sourcing.** Strategic sourcing opportunities are identified to leverage suppliers and positively impact working capital. With few exceptions, Fortune 1000 organizations are burdened with an oversized base of suppliers. Given that the average Fortune 1000 company buys approximately 400–500 commodities and maintains a global supplier base of over 50,000 suppliers, there is an average of over 100 suppliers per commodity. This is clearly not optimal from procurement or AP standpoints. Those organizations that have successfully optimized their supply base have addressed the following challenges:

a. Senior management understands and supports the quantified impact that an aggressive strategic-sourcing program has on earnings per share.

Process: Procurement
Subprocess: Reporting, Metrics, and Analytics

b. The procurement organization has created the necessary systems to capture global spending and routinely quantifies the financial savings from sourcing projects.

c. Preferred supplier agreements are in place for 80% or more of the organization's common purchases.

d. The proper structure and/or incentives have been implemented to ensure that employees buy only from preferred suppliers and that there is compliance with negotiated prices.

3. Procurement Process Metrics. Metrics have been implemented to report procurement process results, identify process improvements, and address payment issues in a timely manner. Metrics should focus on cost, process efficiency, internal controls, and customer service impacts to the payments process.

4. Reporting Process. A reporting process has been developed so that the results of metrics and analytics are reported in a timely and consistent manner.

5. Diversity Spend. Opportunities for the increased use of diversity suppliers and spending activity have been identified and diversity spend is tracked.

Table of Risks and Controls – Reporting, Metrics, and Analytics

Process: Procurement			
Subprocess: Reporting, Metrics, and Analytics			
Process Risk	**Recommended Policies**	**Internal Controls**	**KPIs**
1. Spending Anomalies and Trends. Opportunities to address a spending issue for a specific supplier or commodity are not visible to the company, causing potential payment problems.	■ Spend Reporting Process	1. Visibility to Spending 2. Strategic Sourcing 3. Procurement Process Metrics	■ Strategic Sourcing Cost Savings ■ Unapproved Items in PO Workflow
2. Strategic Sourcing. Opportunities for strategic sourcing are not identified or acted upon. Strategic sourcing is an approach to supply chain management that formalizes the way that information is gathered and used so that an organization can leverage its consolidated purchasing power to find the best possible values in the marketplace.	■ Spend Reporting Process ■ Strategic Sourcing Program	1. Visibility to Spending 2. Strategic Sourcing 3. Procurement Process Metrics	■ Strategic Sourcing Cost Savings

Process: Procurement			
Subprocess: Reporting, Metrics, and Analytics			
Process Risk	**Recommended Policies**	**Internal Controls**	**KPIs**
3. Procurement Metrics. The results and impact of the procurement process upon the payment process are not reported or acted upon.	■ Procurement Metrics	3. Procurement Process Metrics	■ Number of Fraudulent POs ■ Number of Fraudulent Suppliers ■ Adherence to PO Policies ■ Cost per RFP ■ Cost per Contract ■ Cost per PO ■ Strategic Sourcing Cost Savings ■ PO Workflow Defects ■ Unapproved Items in PO Workflow ■ Non-PO Invoices
4. Procurement Reporting Process. Visibility to analytics and metrics is lost.	■ Procurement Reporting	1. Visibility to Spending 2. Strategic Sourcing 3. Procurement Process Metrics 4. Reporting Process Development	■ Number of Fraudulent POs ■ Number of Fraudulent Suppliers ■ Adherence to PO Policies ■ Cost per RFP ■ Cost per Contract ■ Cost per PO ■ Strategic Sourcing Cost Savings ■ PO Workflow Defects ■ Unapproved Items in PO Workflow ■ Non-PO Invoices
5. Action on High and Low Spend. There are no opportunities to address high- and low-spend suppliers, such as implementing a P-Card or implementing strategic sourcing to better leverage suppliers.	■ P-Card Policies and Procedures ■ Strategic Sourcing	1. Visibility to Spending 2. Strategic Sourcing 3. Procurement Process Metrics 4. Reporting Process Development	■ Number of P-Cards Implemented ■ Monthly Supplier Spending on P-Cards ■ Strategic Sourcing Cost Savings ■ Value of P-Card Rebates
6. Use of Diversity Suppliers. Opportunities for using diversity suppliers are not possible without procurement reporting and visibility.	■ Diversity Supplier Reporting and Programs	5. Diversity Spend Tracking	■ Percentage of Diversity Suppliers Used ■ Value of Spend for Diversity Suppliers

2.0 ACCOUNTS PAYABLE

Accounts Payable Process Overview

The integrity of AP results are directly influenced by the functions of securing and qualifying sources of supply; initiating requests for materials, equipment, merchandise, supplies, and services; obtaining information as to availability and pricing from approved suppliers; placing orders for goods or services; receiving and inspecting or otherwise accepting the material or merchandise; accounting for the proper amounts due to suppliers; and processing payments in a controlled and efficient manner. The goal of the AP process is to ensure that payments are made on time to the correct supplier for the correct amounts and that invoices are paid once and only once to the correct supplier using accurate and validated payment data.

The AP process consists of eight subprocesses. The risks, controls, and measurements of controls effectiveness will be explored in detail for each subprocess.

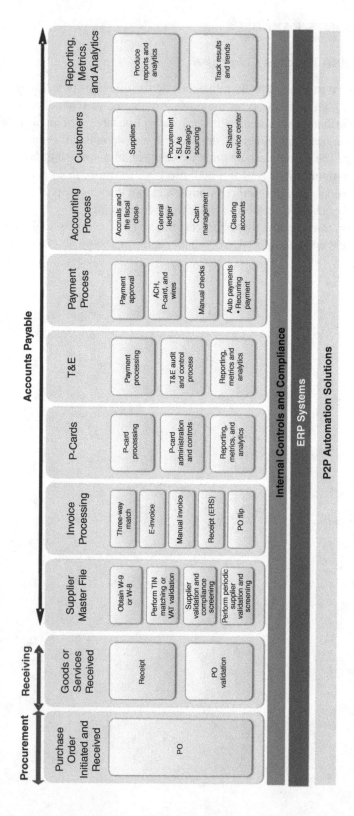

Accounts Payable Process Flow

2.1 SUPPLIER MASTER FILE

Supplier Master File Process Overview

The supplier master file is an integral part of the procurement and AP control environments. Responsibilities for the supplier master file include the set-up and maintenance process, which generally resides with the AP department.

A well-maintained supplier master file helps prevent failure of system controls, process inefficiencies, and inaccurate management reporting. Failure of system controls can result in duplicate and erroneous payments, missed earned discounts, uncashed checks, unapplied credits, tax reporting errors, pricing errors, and fraud.

Supplier Master File Process Flow

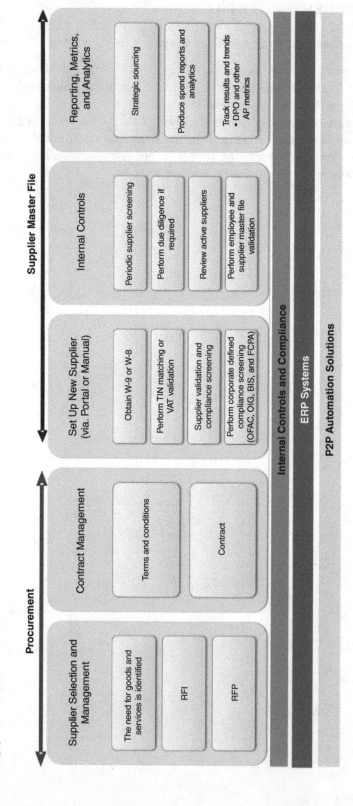

Table of Controls – Supplier Master File

Process: Accounts Payable
Subprocess: Supplier Master File

1. Implement segregation of duties controls. SoD controls are implemented to ensure that responsibilities for the supplier master file are separated from the invoice processing and payment processes.

2. Define ownership. Defining a data owner helps ensure accountability and responsibility for the accuracy and integrity of the supplier master file.

3. Implement system access controls. Many AP software packages have the ability to limit access to the supplier master file based on user IDs, passwords, and other controls. Password standards can be defined by password length, complexity, frequency of required change, and other restrictions. Access can be granted as read-only, or at a level that allows the user to change and update supplier master file data.

4. Establish clear supplier set-up procedures. The policies and procedures for supplier setup should be clearly documented. The use of a standard form or format will help ensure consistency and compliance with policies and procedures and naming conventions.

5. Implement supplier payment controls. Ensure that bank accounts for new suppliers are verified and are changed with proper authorization and additional verification. Establish an approval process for all payments that include wires, international payments, and large payments over a specific dollar amount (Example: >$250,000).

6. Implement a controls self-assessment process. A CSA process is implemented to check for duplicate and erroneous payments. Review the effectiveness of internal controls for this subprocess and review system-generated audit trails. Ensure that all issues are remediated in a timely manner to properly mitigate risk within the subprocess.

7. Enforce new supplier approval practices. Sufficient due diligence procedures should be in place that require review and evaluation of new supplier criteria (financial and operational) prior to accepting a new supplier.

8. Establish a supplier validation process. Ensure that new suppliers are compliance-checked with OFAC, BIS, the OIG, and FCPA lists as defined by the corporation. Other validation processes include obtaining a W-9 and completing TIN matching. Also, obtain a W-8 and perform value-added tax (VAT) verification. Also verify the supplier's address, phone number, and website.

9. Apply consistent naming conventions. One of the simplest way to help ensure accuracy and integrity of the supplier master file is to establish naming conventions and make sure that everyone responsible for data entry is adequately trained on entering and maintaining suppliers.

10. Enforce data validation. While many AP software packages contain data validation editing to help ensure the accuracy of data input to the system, a suggested best practice is to have a quality assurance function where someone separate from data entry review key data entry fields for accuracy prior to updating the supplier master file.

11. Remove old/unused suppliers from the system. It is considered a best practice to keep the supplier master file up to date. However, it is important to understand the limitations and requirement of the organization's AP system prior to deleting any suppliers, especially if the system links to archived transactional records. A best practice used by several Fortune 500 companies is to review and purge duplicate supplier records on an annual basis when there has been no activity for 18 months.

12. Retain the right records. Develop a record retention policy that is in compliance with federal, state, and local legal and regulatory requirements. Ensure that the supplier master file is in compliance with this policy.

13. Perform an employee and supplier master file cross-check. To ensure that employees are not posing as suppliers, run a cross-check on the employee and supplier master files. Check for name, address, TIN, EIN and SSN, contact information, and bank account data every six months to one year. Check to see if the employee's bank account has been changed on a frequent basis.

Table of Risks and Controls – Supplier Master File

Process: Accounts Payable			
Subprocess: Supplier Master File			
Process Risk	Recommended Policies	Internal Controls	KPIs
1. Failure to Follow SoD Processes. This may enable employees to set up a new supplier, pay that supplier, and cover their tracks with an accounting entry.	■ SoD ■ Data Ownership ■ System Access	1. Implement SoD Controls 2. Define Ownership 3. Engage System Access Controls	■ Number of SoD Reviews Performed ■ Number of SoD Conflicts Identified ■ Number of SoD Conflicts Mitigated ■ Number of Systems Access Reviews Performed ■ Number of Systems Access Issues Identified ■ Number of Systems Access Issues Mitigated
2. Incorrect Supplier Payments. Inappropriate, unauthorized, inaccurate, or duplicate payments to unauthorized suppliers.	■ Supplier Master File Setup ■ Payment Validation Controls ■ CSA Process	4. Establish Clear Supplier Set-Up Procedures 5. Implement Supplier Payment Controls 6. Implement a CSA Process	■ Number of Active Suppliers in the Supplier Master File ■ Number of Suppliers Paid Electronically ■ Number of Invoices Paid by Check, P-Card, Wire, and ACH ■ Number and Value of Payment Issues Stopped per Payment Run ■ Value of Payment Issues by Payment Type ■ Number of Controls Reviewed ■ Cycle Time for the Remediation of Control Issues
3. Unauthorized Access to Sensitive Information. An intentional or accidental update to the supplier master file, which could impact the safeguarding of assets and result in data corruption and/or violations of privacy.	■ System Access	7. Engage System Access Controls	■ Number of Systems Access Issues Identified ■ Number of Systems Access Issues Mitigated

Process: Accounts Payable			
Subprocess: Supplier Master File			
Process Risk	**Recommended Policies**	**Internal Controls**	**KPIs**
4. Supplier Master File Accuracy. Unauthorized or inaccurate or noncompliant supplier information in database, which could result in unauthorized payment to the supplier and significant fines.	▪ New Supplier Approval Process ▪ Supplier Set-Up Procedures ▪ Supplier Validation Process ▪ Supplier Payment Controls	4. Establish Clear Supplier Set-Up Procedures 5. Implement Supplier Payment Controls 7. Enforce New Supplier Approval Practices 8. Establish a Supplier Validation Process	▪ Number and Percentage of New Suppliers Established in the Supplier Master File ▪ Number of Active Suppliers in the Supplier Master File ▪ Number of Invalid Suppliers Identified ▪ Number of Suppliers Identified on Compliance Watch Lists ▪ Number of Suppliers Requiring Additional Due Diligence Verification ▪ Number of Suppliers Paid Electronically ▪ Number of Invoices Paid by Check, P-Card, Wire, and ACH ▪ Number and Value of Payment Issues Stopped per Payment Run ▪ Value of Payment Issues by Payment Type
5. Input of inaccurate information in ERP system. This may result in untimely payment to the supplier.	▪ New Supplier Approval Process ▪ Supplier Set-Up Procedures ▪ Supplier Naming Conventions ▪ Data Validation Process ▪ Supplier Master File Update Process ▪ Record Retention Process	4. Establish Clear Supplier Set-Up Procedures 7. Enforce New Supplier Approval Practices 10. Apply Consistent Naming Conventions 11. Enforce Data Validation 12. Remove Old/ Unused Suppliers from the System 13. Retain the Right Records	▪ Number and Percentage of New Suppliers Established in the Supplier Master File ▪ Number of Active Suppliers in the Supplier Master File ▪ Number of Inactive Suppliers (with No Activity in the Last 18 Months) ▪ Number of Suppliers With Invalid Data (Returned Checks, ACH notification of change [NOC], or Other Payment Issues) ▪ Number of Invalid Suppliers Identified ▪ Number of Suppliers Identified on Compliance Watch Lists ▪ Number of Suppliers Requiring Additional Due Diligence Verification

Process: Accounts Payable			
Subprocess: Supplier Master File			
Process Risk	**Recommended Policies**	**Internal Controls**	**KPIs**
6. Fraudulent Suppliers. Fictitious suppliers, scam suppliers, shell companies, or employees posing as suppliers.	■ SoD ■ Data Ownership ■ System Access ■ Employee and Supplier Master File Cross-Check	1. Implement SoD Controls 2. Define Ownership 7. Engage System Access Controls 14. Perform an Employee and Supplier Master File Cross-Check	■ Number of SoD Reviews Performed ■ Number of SoD Conflicts Identified ■ Number of SoD Conflicts Mitigated ■ Number of Systems Access Reviews Performed ■ Number of Systems Access Issues Identified ■ Number of Systems Access Issues Mitigated ■ Number of Employee and Supplier Master File Cross-Checks Performed ■ Number of Matches Identified and Remediated

2.2 INVOICE PROCESSING

Invoice Processing Process Overview

An invoice is a bill sent by a company or vendor that has sold a service or product to another company. The information contained on the invoice can vary based on the needs of the vendor, the type of transaction, and preferences of the purchasing company.

One of the problems with invoices, particularly paper invoices, is that they do not always contain consistent and validated supplier information. If your AP department is processing dozens of invoices at once, this can become difficult.

Invoice Processing Process Flow

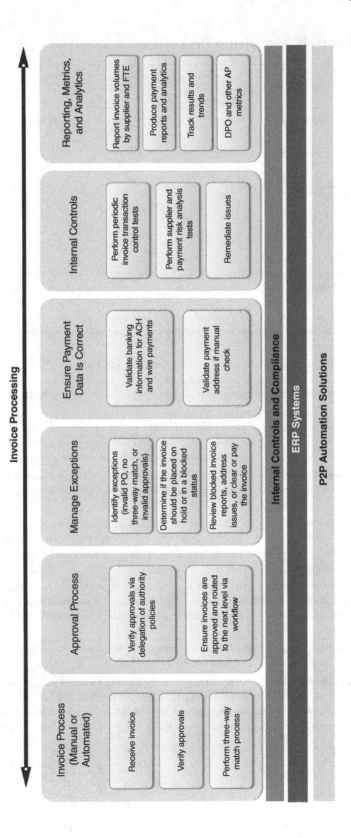

Table of Controls – Invoicing Processing

Process: Accounts Payable
Subprocess: Invoice Processing

1.Segregation of Duties. The AP invoice processing function must be segregated from the following functions:

a. Receiving (employees and warehouses)

b. Purchasing

c. Payment Processing

d. Audit and control

e. Vendor file maintenance

f. AP invoice approval

2. Invoice Accuracy. Prior to payment, the supplier's invoice must be reviewed for receipt of material or services, accuracy of price, quantity, currency, payment terms, and account classification and distribution. Any invoice with a discrepancy exceeding the tolerance limits or lacking reference information (e.g. price, quantity, etc.) must be resolved before payment is made. Discrepancy tolerance limits, if used, must be supported by a documented cost/benefit analysis, and must be approved and monitored by local operating and financial management.

4. Alternative Processes. If alternative processes are used, such as e-invoicing, pay on receipt, evaluated receipt settlement (ERS), or electronic data interchange (EDI), the procedures and contracts in place to ensure correct pricing and received quantities must be documented and approved by local operating and financial management.

5. Invoice Approval. Invoices for which a PO or receiving report does not exist (e.g. check requests, approved AP interfaces, e-invoicing processes, etc.) must be approved by authorized personnel in accordance with their approval per the corporate DoA policy with a workflow process.

6. Original Invoices. Original invoices should be used as the basis for payment using the invoice mechanisms identified in control number 4 in this table. Faxed invoices should not be used in the payment process.

7. Reason for Payment. The reason for payment must be fully explained by the payment request itself (e.g. invoice, check request if applicable), attached supporting documentation, or system documentation. This documentation must be reviewed before the request is approved for payment if e-invoicing and other system validations are not in place.

8. Duplicate Payments. A process must be in place to detect and prevent duplicate payments. Supporting documents for the payments must be originals and must be effectively canceled after payment to prevent accidental or intentional reuse. No payments should be based upon a statement unless the vendor has been preapproved for such.

9. Goods Receipt/Invoice Receipt (GR/IR). Aged, unmatched POs, receipts, and invoices must be periodically reviewed, investigated, and resolved.

10. Supplier Statements. Supplier statements must be regularly reviewed to resolve past due items and open credits in a timely manner. The currency used for statements and invoices should be consistent. Statements should be reconciled to vendors' accounts periodically to identify material issues. However, payments should never be issued directly from a statement without additional research and approvals.

Process: Accounts Payable
Subprocess: Invoice Processing

11. Reconciliations. The AP trial balance and associated clearing accounts noted in control number 8 should be reconciled (contents are known and status is current) with the general ledger (GL) each month. All differences must be resolved on a timely manner.

12. Debit Balance Accounts. AP should review debit balance accounts at least quarterly and request remittance on debit amounts outstanding for over 90 days.

13. Debit and Credit Memos. Debit and credit memos issued to supplier accounts must be documented, recorded, controlled, and approved by authorized personnel in accordance with their approval limits.

14. Debit and Credit Memo Audit Trails. Debit and credit memos must have a unique identifier (SAP assigned document number) and be traceable.

15. Established Suppliers. Prior to payment, AP must ensure the supplier is established on the approved vendor master file. Updating access to the vendor master file must be limited to appropriate personnel. Suppliers not on the approved vendor master file must be validated independent of the originating source.

16. Liability Accruals. Procedures and mechanisms must be in place to identify and capture all items and services that have been billed but not yet received and received but not yet billed.

17. Manual Check Request Procedure. Procedure governing check requests should be approved by management and updated regularly to reflect changes as determined by management. Any emergency checks or off-cycle payments should be processed on an exception basis and approved accordingly.

Table of Risks and Controls – Invoice Processing

Process: Accounts Payable			
Subprocess: Invoicing Processing			
Process Risk	Recommended Policies	Internal Controls	KPIs
1. Failure to Follow SoD Processes. This may enable an employee to set up a new supplier, pay that supplier, and cover their tracks with an accounting entry. Purchases may be stolen, lost, destroyed, or temporarily diverted, thus increasing the potential for errors and irregularities.	■ SoD	1. SoD Controls	■ Number of SoD Reviews Performed ■ Number of SoD Conflicts Identified ■ Number of SoD Conflicts Mitigated ■ Value and Number of Instances of Fraud

Process: Accounts Payable			
Subprocess: Invoicing Processing			
Process Risk	**Recommended Policies**	**Internal Controls**	**KPIs**
2. Proper Recording of Purchases. Purchases or services may be ordered and received by an unauthorized individual and not reported accurately. Additionally, purchases may be stolen, lost, destroyed, or temporarily diverted, thus increasing the potential for errors and irregularities.	■ SoD ■ Three-Way Match (PO, Receiving Document, and Invoice Are Matched for Pricing and Quantity)	1. SoD Controls 2. Invoice Accuracy 4. Alternative Processes 6. Original Invoice 7. Reason for Payment 12. Debit Balance Accounts 13. Debit and Credit Memos 14. Debit and Credit Memo Audit Trails 15. Established Suppliers 17. Check Request Procedure	■ Percentage of First Time Matches ■ Percentage of On-Time Payments
3. Quality and Inventory Issues. Rather than being returned or refused, the following goods or services may be received and ultimately paid for: ■ Unordered goods or services ■ Inventory that does not meet quality standards ■ Excessive quantities or incorrect items	■ SoD ■ Three-Way Match	1. SoD Controls 2. Invoice Accuracy 4. Alternative Processes 6. Original Invoice 7. Reason for Payment 15. Established Suppliers	■ Percentage of First Time Matches ■ Percentage of On-Time Payments ■ Percentage of Inventory Cycle Count Issues ■ Percentage of Inventory Quality Issues
4. Payment Issues. Payment may be made for goods or services not received and/or in advance of receipt. Payments to suppliers may be duplicated, incorrect, or fraudulent.	■ SoD ■ Three-Way Match ■ New Supplier Approval Process ■ Supplier Set-Up Procedures ■ Supplier Validation Process ■ Supplier Payment Controls	1. SoD Controls 2. Invoice Accuracy 4. Alternative Processes 6. Original Invoice 7. Reason for Payment 15. Established Suppliers 17. Check Request Procedure	■ Number of Invalid Suppliers Identified ■ Number of Invoices Paid by Check, P-Card, Wire and ACH ■ Number and Value of Payment Issues Stopped per Payment Run ■ Value of Payment Issues by Payment Type

Process: Accounts Payable			
Subprocess: Invoicing Processing			
Process Risk	**Recommended Policies**	**Internal Controls**	**KPIs**
5. Payment Data and Record Keeping. Records may be lost or destroyed. Records may be misused or altered to the detriment of the company or its suppliers.	▪ New Supplier Approval Process ▪ Supplier Set-Up Procedures ▪ Data Validation Process ▪ Record Retention Process	1. SoD Controls 2. Invoice Accuracy 4. Alternative Processes 6. Original Invoice 7. Reason for Payment 9. GR/IRs 10. Supplier Statements 11. Reconciliations 17. Check Request Procedure	▪ Number and Percentage of New Suppliers Established in the Supplier Master File ▪ Number of Active Suppliers in the Supplier Master File ▪ Number of Inactive Suppliers (With No Activity in the Last 18 Months) ▪ Number of Suppliers With Invalid Data (Returned Checks or Other Payment Issues) ▪ Number of Invalid Suppliers Identified ▪ Number of Suppliers Identified on Compliance "Watch Lists" ▪ Number of Suppliers Requiring Additional Due Diligence Verification
6. Misstatement of Financial Results. Financial statements, records, and operating reports may be misstated. Critical decisions may be based upon erroneous information resulting in the misstatement of financial results.	▪ Financial Closing Processes ▪ Accrual Business Rules	11. Reconciliations 12. Debit Balance Accounts 16. Liability Accruals	▪ Number and Value of Pre-Close and Post-Close Adjustments ▪ Number and Value of Monthly Accruals ▪ Number and Value of Outstanding Accruals by Reason

2.3 PAYMENT PROCESS

Payment Process Overview

Once invoices are approved for payment, the actual payment process commences, which leads to the exchange of funds between the purchasing company and its supplier. Personnel involved in the payment process must adhere to policies and procedures designed to ensure accurate, timely, and secure payments initiation using the appropriate payment method for each payment.

Payment Process Flow

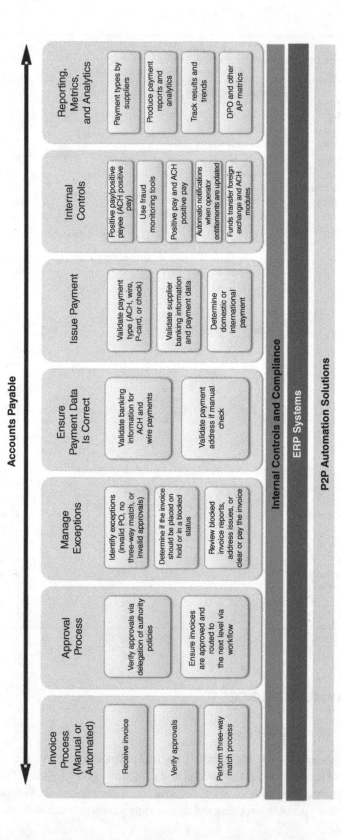

Table of Controls – Payment Process

Process: Accounts Payable
Subprocess: Payment Process

1. Segregation of Duties. The function of disbursing cash or its equivalent must be segregated from the following functions:

- Receiving
- Purchasing
- AP invoice processing
- Vendor file maintenance
- GL reconciliation
- AP invoice approval

2. Payment Reconciliations. All payments and other payment activities (as recorded on the payment register) must be traceable, uniquely identifiable, and reconciled (contents are known and status is current) with the GL and bank statements on a monthly basis.

3. Supporting Documentation. Requests for the preparation of checks, EFTs, and bank transfers must be supported by approved POs, receiving transactions, approved check requests, and/or original invoices. Such documentation will be provided to and reviewed by AP management prior to payment as specified in AP policies.

4. Payment Transaction Controls. Dual approval (secondary authorization) and transaction limits for various payment types, including funds transfer (wire), foreign exchange, and ACH. Token passcode is required for external funds movement.

5. Payment Approval Controls. Approved payments must be aged and made in accordance with company policy and within the agreed-upon supplier terms. Approval transaction limits established and permission groups employed to limit access to general ledger (GL) coding based on budget or location with cascading approval logic.

6. Supplier Discounts. All eligible supplier discounts should be taken whenever favorable to the company.

7. Bearer Checks. Checks must not be made payable to cash or bearer. Checks must not be made payable to the paying company or any of its subsidiaries; these payments will be resolved through the intercompany process.

8. Blank Check Storage. Blank checks must be safeguarded from destruction or unauthorized use through SoD controls. The supply of blank checks must be numerically controlled and regularly accounted for as issued, voided, or unused.

9. Voided and Canceled Checks. Spoiled and voided checks may be destroyed, provided the destruction is witnessed and documented by an additional individual. Canceled and cleared checks must be retained in accordance with company's record retention policy.

10. Bank Account Limits. Specific limits of signing authority for checks, promissory notes, and bank transfers must be established and approved according to an appropriate BoD's banking resolution and communicated to the disbursing entity and the appropriate bank(s).

11. Positive Pay and Positive Payee Controls. Checking accounts must be provided with "match pay" or "positive pay" controls that permit a preview of checks or ACH transactions presented to the bank for payment. If such controls are not practical, bank accounts must be subject to activity limits and dual signatory controls.

Process: Accounts Payable

Subprocess: Payment Process

---

12. Delegation of Authority Signatures. The signatures of authorized signers must be on file within the company and at the bank according to payment type and approval limits. Such signature authorities must be updated upon resignation or retirement of authorized signers.

13. Records Management. Documents or electronic data supporting expenditures must be safeguarded from loss or destruction and must be in a retrievable format. Such records must be retained and maintained in accordance with the company's record retention policy.

14. Check Delivery. All checks should be mailed. In those cases where this is not possible, prior arrangements should be made for check delivery. When the check is picked up in person, proper identification must be provided and delivery of the check must be documented via their signature.

15. Wire Transfers. Where practical, payments by wire transfer must be made only to preestablished bank accounts. Recurring wire payments should be established as repetitive payments within the wire transfer system. Nonrepetitive wires require independent review and approval. The preparation function must be segregated from the approval function.

16. Recording in Accounting Records. All payments must be recorded in the period payment was made. Expenses must be properly and accurately recorded in the accounting records during the period in which the liability was incurred.

17. Custody and Security of Check-Signing Equipment. Where check-signing equipment and facsimile signature plates or digitized signature images are utilized, the equipment and plates must be secured, and custody of the check-signing equipment and the signature plates or digitized signature image files must be segregated. In addition, a reconciliation (contents are known and status is current) should be made of checks written and checks authorized to the check-signing machine totals must be conducted as specified by policy and procedures.

18. Controls Monitoring Processes. Ability to track all invoices throughout their life cycle in the system. Automatic notifications when operator entitlements are updated in funds transfer, foreign exchange, and ACH modules.

19. Electronic Payment Controls. Monitor and reconcile accounts at least daily, including outbound ACH and wire transfers. Make sure your ACH payment procedures comply with ACH rules: verify routing numbers, secure Internet session (minimum 128-bit SSL encryption technology), and conduct annual security audit.

20. ACH Debits. Return unauthorized ACH debits no later than the opening of business on the second banking day following the settlement date of the original entry, or as required by current National Automated Clearing House Association (NACHA) rules.

21. ACH Positive Pay and Positive Payee. ACH Positive Pay is an online fraud mitigation service that allows you to manage ACH debits and credits posting to your business account via filters and blocks.

22. Changes to Bank Accounts. Bank details required are name of account, bank address, routing number, and bank account number. All bank details must be received in writing by post on company-headed paper signed by an appropriate person. Once received, and before these details are used to make any payment, they must be verified by making a telephone call to the supplier. Make sure you have a system of verification in place. This can include a callback to the payee to verify the data, comparison to independent market sources, verification to authorized signed documentation, and the like.

Table of Risks and Controls – Payment Process

Process: Accounts Payable			
Subprocess: Payment Process			
Process Risk	**Recommended Policies**	**Internal Controls**	**KPIs**
1. Failure to Follow SoD Processes. This may allow erroneous and fraudulent payments to invalid suppliers and other employees. Controls may be bypassed, allowing for the potential of theft or error.	■ SoD ■ Monthly Payment Reconciliation Process by Cash Accounting	1. SoD Controls 2. Payment Reconciliations	■ Number of SoD Reviews Performed ■ Number of SoD Conflicts Identified and Mitigated ■ Number and Value of Payment Issues and Errors Identified and Mitigated
2. Improper Recording of and Payment for Corporate Purchases. Purchases or services may be ordered and received by an unauthorized individual and not reported accurately. Additionally, purchases may be stolen, lost, destroyed, or temporarily diverted, thus increasing the potential for errors and irregularities.	■ SoD ■ Monthly Payment Reconciliation Process by Cash Accounting	1. SoD Controls 2. Payment Reconciliations 3. Supporting Documentation 4. Payment Transaction Controls 5. Payment Approval Controls	■ Value of Payment Issues by Payment Type ■ Number and Value of Payment Issues and Errors Identified and Mitigated
3. Diversion of Checks. Checks may be altered or may be stolen, resulting in financial harm and the misstatement of liabilities.	■ SoD ■ Check Controls and Security ■ Monthly Payment Reconciliation Process by Cash Accounting	1. SoD Controls 2. Payment Reconciliations 3. Supporting Documentation 4. Payment Transaction Controls 5. Payment Approval Controls 7. Bearer Checks 8. Blank Check Storage 9. Voided and Canceled Checks 10. Bank Account Limits 11. Positive Pay and Positive Payee Controls 12. DoA Signatures 14. Check Delivery 16. Recording in Accounting Records 17. Custody and Security of Check-Signing Equipment 18. Controls Monitoring Process	■ Percentage and Number of Invoices Paid by Check, P-Card, Wire, and ACH ■ Value of Payment Issues by Payment Type ■ Number and Value of Payment Issues and Errors Identified and Mitigated

Process: Accounts Payable			
Subprocess: Payment Process			
Process Risk	Recommended Policies	Internal Controls	KPIs
4. Diversion of Electronic Payments. Payment may be made for goods or services not received and/or in advance of receipt. Electronic payments may be altered or diverted, resulting in financial harm and the misstatement of liabilities.	■ SoD ■ Electronic Payment Controls ■ Monthly Payment Reconciliation Process by Cash Accounting ■ Supplier Master File and Payment Risk Analysis	1. SoD Controls 2. Payment Reconciliations 3. Supporting Documentation 4. Payment Transaction Controls 5. Payment Approval Controls 10. Bank Account Limits 11. ACH Positive Pay and Positive Payee Controls 12. DoA Signatures 15. Wire Transfers 16. Recording in Accounting Records 19. ACH Payment Controls 20. ACH Debits 21. ACH Positive Pay and Positive Payee 22. Changes to Bank Accounts	■ Percentage and Number of Invoices Paid by P-Card, Wire, and ACH ■ Value of Payment Issues by Payment Type ■ Number and Value of Payment Issues Stopped per Payment Run
5. Payment Data and Record Keeping. Records may be lost or destroyed. Records may be misused or altered to the detriment of the company or its suppliers.	■ Data Validation and Approval Processes ■ Record Retention Process	1. SoD Controls 2. Payment Reconciliations 3. Supporting Documentation 4. Payment Transaction Controls 5. Payment Approval Controls 10. Bank Account Limits 12. DoA Signatures	■ Number of Inactive Suppliers (with No Activity in the Last 18 Months) ■ Number of Suppliers With Invalid Data (Returned Checks or Other Payment Issues) ■ Number of Invalid Suppliers Identified ■ Number of Suppliers Identified on Compliance Watch Lists ■ Number of Suppliers Requiring Additional Due Diligence Verification

Process: Accounts Payable			
Subprocess: Payment Process			
Process Risk	**Recommended Policies**	**Internal Controls**	**KPIs**
6. Misstatement of Financial Results. Financial statements, records, and operating reports may be misstated. Critical decisions may be based upon erroneous information resulting in the misstatement of financial results.	▪ Financial Closing Processes ▪ Accrual Business Rules	2. Payment Reconciliations 3. Supporting Documentation 4. Payment Transaction Controls 5. Payment Approval Controls 10. Bank Account Limits	▪ Number and Value of Pre-Close and Post-Close Adjustments ▪ Number and Value of Monthly Accruals ▪ Number and Value of Outstanding Accruals by Reason

 ## 2.4 ACCOUNTING PROCESS

Accounting Process Overview

As stated in our introduction, the AP transaction has a tremendous impact on a corporation – particularly on the record-to-report (R2R), or closing process. I saw how attention to compliance and supplier onboarding establishes the right path for ensuring a correct payment. Now we'll review the controls required to support the AP accounting process that will set the foundation for an accurate and timely financial close, as listed below:

- Lag or latency of data related to payment status
- Un-normalized data (as reported by banks)
- Returned paper checks (e.g. bad addresses)
- Poor visibility or errors during the review process
- Unreconciled GL accounts

Accounting Process Flow

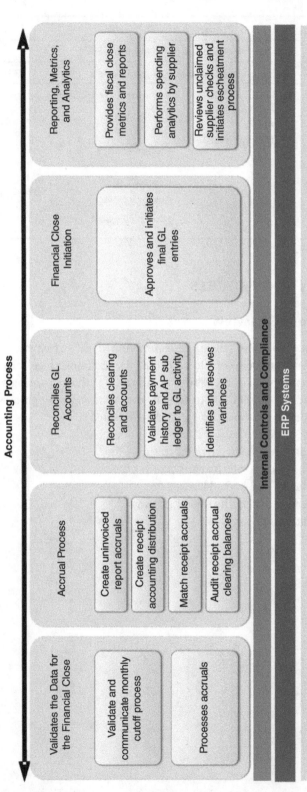

Table of Controls – Accounting Process

Process: Accounts Payable
Subprocess: Accounting Process

1. Trial Balance Report. Start the closing cycle with a trial balance report. Review the balances to identify any anomalies from what is expected. Review the transaction details for any accounts you are uncertain of and note any adjustments that need to be made and that accruals are correct.

2. Establish a Financial Closing Calendar with Defined Cutoffs. Establish a closing date by which all expenses and revenue must be posted. Communicate the closing date to everyone who has access to modify the ledger.

3. Establish a Financial Closing Checklist and Communication Process. The checklist should define the roles and responsibilities of all AP staff along with the business process owners that can impact the integrity of the process.

4. Adjusting Entries. Create the adjusting entries to recognize prepaid expenses, accrue outstanding invoices, relieve accruals that have been paid, and recognize depreciation and other amortizations. Post adjusting entries to correct the current balance of any ledger account that reflects expense postings in error.

5. Adjusted Trial Balance. Generate an adjusted trial balance report to review the final balances in the ledger. Verify that the trial balance matches on the debit and credit side. Verify that the balances are accurate, checking the account activity if needed. Trial balances will vary from the initial report due to the adjusting entries. This helps you identify any entries that posted incorrectly and need to be corrected prior to your approval process.

6. Complete Reconciliations. Reconcile the AP ledger to the subledger and any GI/IR clearing accounts on a monthly basis.

7. Reporting. Create reporting to show the final expense and payment activity for the period and year-to-date.

8. Escheatment Process. Escheatment is the process of identifying a check payment to a supplier that is considered abandoned and remitting the funds to the appropriate state if the supplier cannot be located or contacted. Once the check payment is deemed abandoned it becomes reportable to the state of the owner's last known address and is subject to be escheated.

Table of Risks and Controls – Accounting Process

Process: Accounts Payable			
Subprocess: Accounting Process			
Process Risk	Recommended Policies	Internal Controls	KPIs
1. Unreconciled General Ledger Accounts. Unreconciled GL accounts can cause delays and accuracy issues with the financial close, and fraudulent payment transactions can be undetected.	■ Financial Close Policies and Procedures ■ Monthly Payment Reconciliation Process	1. Trial Balance Report 2. Establish a Financial Closing Calendar with Defined Cutoffs 3. Establish a Financial Closing Checklist and Communication Process 4. Adjusting Entries 6. Complete Reconciliations	■ Number of GL Accounts Reconciled per Month ■ Value and Aging of Variances

Process: Accounts Payable			
Subprocess: Accounting Process			
Process Risk	**Recommended Policies**	**Internal Controls**	**KPIs**
2. Poor Visibility or Errors During the Review Process. The lack of financial close policies and procedures may cause errors to be undetected.	■ Financial Close Policies and Procedures ■ Monthly Payment Reconciliation Process by Cash Accounting	1. Trial Balance Report 2. Establish a Financial Closing Calendar with Defined Cutoffs 3. Establish a Financial Closing Checklist and Communication Process 4. Adjusting Entries 6. Complete Reconciliations	■ Number of GL Accounts Reconciled per Month ■ Value and Aging of Variances ■ Cycle Time to Complete the Close
3. Accruals. Accruals may be processed late, which may lead to incorrect financial data.	■ Financial Close Policies and Procedures ■ Monthly Payment Reconciliation Process by Cash Accounting	1. Trial Balance Report 2. Establish a Financial Closing Calendar with Defined Cutoffs 3. Establish a Financial Closing Checklist and Communication Process	■ Number of GL Accounts Reconciled per Month ■ Value and Aging of Variances ■ Cycle Time to Complete the Close ■ Number and Value of Adjusting Entries
4. Unclear and Undefined Roles and Responsibilities. Roles and responsibilities and expected results during the financial close are undefined, causing errors, duplication of efforts, and uncompleted tasks that impact the accurate creation of financial statements.	■ Financial Close Policies and Procedures ■ Financial Closing Calendar with Defined Cutoffs ■ Financial Closing Checklist and Communication Process	1. Trial Balance Report 2. Establish a Financial Closing Calendar with Defined Cutoffs 3. Establish a Financial Closing Checklist and Communication Process	■ Number of GL Accounts Reconciled per Month ■ Value and Aging of Variances ■ Cycle Time to Complete the Close ■ Number and Value of Adjusting Entries
5. Misstatement of Financial Results. Financial statements, records, and operating reports may be misstated. Critical decisions may be based upon erroneous information, resulting in the misstatement of financial results.	■ Financial Closing Policies and Procedures ■ Accrual Business Rules	1. Trial Balance Report 2. Establish a Financial Closing Calendar with Defined Cutoffs 3. Establish a Financial Closing Checklist and Communication Process 6. Complete Reconciliations	■ Number and Value of Pre-Close and Post-Close Adjustments ■ Number and Value of Monthly Accruals ■ Number and Value of Outstanding Accruals by Reason

Process: Accounts Payable			
Subprocess: Accounting Process			
Process Risk	Recommended Policies	Internal Controls	KPIs
6. Escheatment and Unclaimed Supplier Checks. Unclaimed supplier checks may not be properly identified and state escheatment rules may not be applied in a timely manner, leading to penalties or fees.	■ Escheatment Policies and Procedures	8. Escheatment Process	■ Number and Value of Unclaimed Supplier Payments ■ Number and Value of Escheatment Items by State

2.5 CUSTOMER SERVICE

Customer Service Process Overview

AP responds to a high volume of customer service inquiries through a supplier portal, supplier call center, or e-mail inquiries requesting information and resolving issues that prevent invoice payment. The customer service research process focuses on the review of outstanding invoices and determining the reason for nonpayment. Whenever possible, customer service determines the root cause of problems for long-term solutions.

Customer Service Process Flow

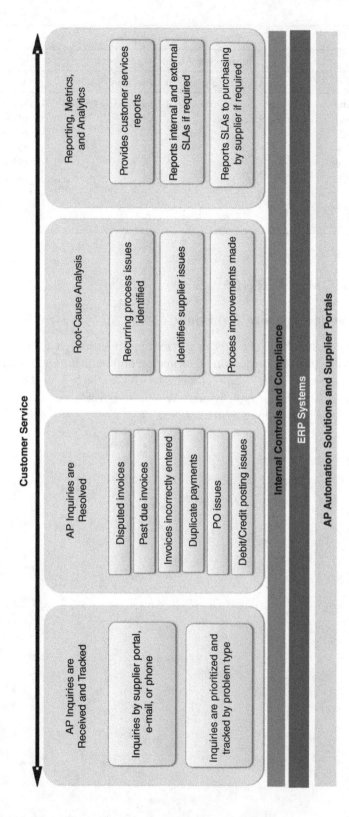

Table of Controls – Customer Service

Process: Accounts Payable
Subprocess: Customer Service

1. Customer Service Process for AP. Establish a customer service process. Prioritize, research, and resolve customer service inquiries for the AP process. Highlight and escalate significant process, supplier, and payment issues immediately.

2. Timely AP Inquiry Resolution. All inquiries should be resolved according to established metrics and internal and external SLAs with a focus on customer service and satisfaction.

3. Root-Cause Analysis and Process Improvements. Track and analyze the root causes of inquiries; report and implement process improvements.

4. Reporting, Metrics, and Analytics. Ensure that all required SLAs are reported and customer service process reports are communicated monthly.

5. AP Customer Service Performance. Establish a performance tracking process to ensure that AP customer service goals are met on a monthly basis and that all required internal and external SLA goals are archived.

Table of Risks and Controls – Customer Service

Process: Accounts Payable			
Subprocess: Customer Service			
Process Risk	Recommended Policies	Internal Controls	KPIs
1. Lack of Customer Service and the Untimely Resolution of Invoice and Payment Issues. Without a customer service process, AP process and supplier payment issues may be undetected for a significant period of time.	■ Customer Service Policies and Metrics	1. Establish a Customer Service Process for AP 2. Timely AP Inquiry Resolution 4. Reporting, Metrics, and Analytics 5. Track AP Customer Service Performance	■ Number and Type of Customer Service Inquiries (Internal and External) ■ Source of Customer Service Inquiries ■ Value and Percentage of Payment Issues Identified ■ Value and Percentage of Payment Issues Corrected ■ Payment Issues by Supplier ■ Cycle Time for Resolution ■ Adherence to Established SLAs

Process: Accounts Payable			
Subprocess: Customer Service			
Process Risk	**Recommended Policies**	**Internal Controls**	**KPIs**
2. AP Payment Process. AP payment process issues are not identified or resolved.	■ Customer Service Policies and Metrics	1. Establish a Customer Service Process for AP 2. Timely AP Inquiry Resolution 4. Reporting, Metrics, and Analytics 5. Track AP Customer Service Performance	■ Number and Type of Customer Service Inquiries (Internal and External) ■ Source of Customer Service Inquiries ■ Value and Percentage of Payment Issues Identified ■ Value and Percentage of Payment Issues Corrected ■ Payment Issues by Supplier ■ Cycle Time for Resolution ■ Adherence to Established SLAs
3. Insufficient Customer Satisfaction. Expectations and contracted payment requirements are not achieved, causing supplier satisfaction concerns.	■ Customer Service Policies and Metrics ■ Customer Satisfaction Survey Metrics	1. Establish a Customer Service Process for AP 2. Timely AP Inquiry Resolution 4. Reporting, Metrics, and Analytics 5. Track AP Customer Service Performance	■ Average Customer Service Ratings ■ Number and Type of Customer Service Inquiries (Internal and External) ■ Source of Customer Service Inquiries ■ Value and Percentage of Payment Issues Identified ■ Value and Percentage of Payment Issues Corrected ■ Payment Issues by Supplier ■ Cycle Time for Resolution ■ Adherence to Established SLAs
4. Reporting, Metrics, and Analytics. Results of the customer service process are not reported or tracked. Performance issues are not identified.	■ Customer Service Policies and Metrics ■ Customer Satisfaction Survey Metrics	1. Establish a Customer Service Process for AP 3. Root-Cause Analysis and Process Improvements 4. Reporting, Metrics, and Analytics 5. Track AP Customer Service Performance	■ Number and Type of Customer Service Inquiries (Internal and External) ■ Source of Customer Service Inquiries ■ Value and Percentage of Payment Issues Identified ■ Value and Percentage of Payment Issues Corrected ■ Payment Issues by Supplier ■ Cycle Time for Resolution ■ Adherence to Established SLAs

Process: Accounts Payable			
Subprocess: Customer Service			
Process Risk	**Recommended Policies**	**Internal Controls**	**KPIs**
5. AP Payment Process Impacts. Problems with the AP process causing incorrect payments are not identified and addressed in a timely manner.	■ Customer Service Policies and Metrics ■ Customer Satisfaction Survey Metrics ■ Root-Cause Analysis Reporting	1. Establish a Customer Service Process for AP 2. Timely AP Inquiry Resolution 4. Reporting, Metrics, and Analytics 5. Track AP Customer Service Performance	■ Number of AP Payment Process Impacts Identified ■ Number of AP Process Impacts Implemented ■ Number and Type of Customer Service Inquiries (Internal and External)

2.6 REPORTING, METRICS, AND ANALYTICS

According to a recent blog posting by SoftCo, in many cases the AP department does not get as much attention from an organization's CEO as other areas of a business do. It's not often the first area in a company that receives funding for improvement. With that said, it is clear that the performance of AP professionals definitely affects the working capital of the business and it is important to optimize that performance.

The AP team is responsible for saving money in the P2P cycle and developing relationships with suppliers. I have sifted through financial reports and spoken to members of the C-suite to find these seven key performance indicators that will pique your CEO's attention and allow them to easily visualize how AP impacts the organization as a whole.[2]

Seven KPIs for the AP process include:

1. Invoice Processing Time
2. Cost to Process an Invoice
3. Invoice Exception Rate
4. Discounts Captured vs. Offered
5. Number of Supplier Inquiries, Discrepancies and Disputes
6. Working Capital
7. The Rate of Incorrect Payments as a Percentage of Total Payment

[2]Duffy, James (2018). 7 key accounts payable metrics that matter to your CEO (September 8; accessed December 20, 2019). SoftCo blog. https://softco.com/blog/7-key-accounts-payable-metrics-that-matter-to-your-ceo.

Reporting, Metrics, and Analytics Process Flow

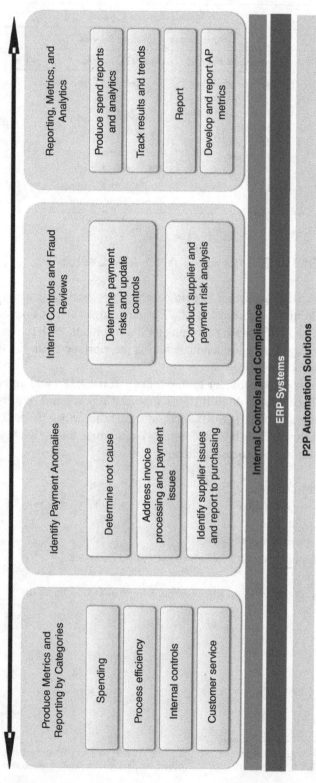

Reporting, Metrics, and Analytics

Table of Controls – Reporting, Metrics, and Analytics

Process: Accounts Payable
Subprocess: Reporting, Metrics, and Analytics

1. Visibility to Spending. Spending results are tracked, analyzed, and reported to business stakeholders.

2. AP Process Metrics. Implement metrics to report procurement process results, identify process improvements, and address payment issues in a timely manner. Metrics should focus on cost, process efficiency, internal controls, and customer service impacts to the payments process. Metrics should be organized by cost, process efficiency, internal controls, and customer service.

3. Develop a Reporting Process. Develop a reporting process so that the results of metrics and analytics are reported and acted upon in a predictable manner – at least monthly.

4. Root-Cause Analysis and Process Improvement Procedures. Identify opportunities to improve the process based on root-cause analysis of results, trends, and benchmarks.

Table of Risks and Controls – Reporting, Metrics, and Analytics

Process: Accounts Payable			
Subprocess: Reporting, Metrics, and Analytics			
Process Risk	Recommended Policies	Internal Controls	KPIs
1. Spending Anomalies and Trends. Opportunities to address a spending issue for a specific supplier or commodity are not visible to the company, causing potential payment problems.	■ Spend Reporting Process	1. Spending Visibility 2. AP Metrics 3. Develop a Reporting Process 4. Root-Cause Analysis and Process Improvement Procedures	■ Number and Percentage of Payment Issues Identified and Stopped ■ Value of Cost Savings Opportunities Identified in the AP Process
2. Strategic Sourcing. Opportunities for strategic sourcing are not identified nor acted open.	■ Spend Reporting Process ■ Strategic Sourcing Program	1. Spending Visibility 2. AP Metrics 3. Develop a Reporting Process 4. Root-Cause Analysis and Process Improvement Procedures	■ Strategic Sourcing Cost Savings

Process: Accounts Payable			
Subprocess: Reporting, Metrics, and Analytics			
Process Risk	Recommended Policies	Internal Controls	KPIs
3. AP Process Results Lack of Visibility. The results and impact of the AP process and resulting payments are not reported or acted upon and risks to the process are not identified or acted upon.	■ AP Metrics	2. AP Metrics 3. Develop a Reporting Process	■ Percentage and Number of Fraudulent Payments ■ Number of Fraudulent Suppliers ■ Percentage Adherence to AP Policies ■ Percentage of E-invoices Processed ■ Cost per Invoice ■ Cycle Time to Process an Invoice ■ Strategic Sourcing Cost Savings ■ PO Workflow Defects ■ Unapproved Items in PO Workflow ■ Non-PO Invoices
4. Action on Payment Anomalies. Opportunities to address or implement additional controls for payment anomalies are lost.	■ AP Metrics ■ AP Reporting	1. Spending Visibility 2. AP Metrics 3. Develop a Reporting Process 4. Root-Cause Analysis and Process Improvement Procedures	■ Percentage and Number of Fraudulent Payments ■ Number of Fraudulent Suppliers ■ Percentage Adherence to AP Policies ■ Percentage of E-invoices Processed ■ Cost per Invoice ■ Cycle Time to Process an Invoice ■ Strategic Sourcing Cost Savings ■ PO Workflow Defects ■ Unapproved Items in PO Workflow ■ Non-PO Invoices
5. AP Reporting Process. Analytics and metrics visibility are lost.	■ AP Metrics ■ AP Reporting	2. Accounts Payable Metrics 3. Develop a Reporting Process	■ Percentage and Number of Fraudulent Payments ■ Number of Fraudulent Suppliers ■ Percentage Adherence to AP Policies ■ Percentage of E-invoices Processed ■ Cost per Invoice ■ Cycle Time to Process an Invoice ■ Strategic Sourcing Cost Savings ■ PO Workflow Defects ■ Unapproved Items in PO Workflow ■ Non-PO Invoices

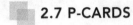

2.7 P-CARDS

P-Card Process Overview

According to the Professional Association for the Commercial Card and Payment Industry (NAPCP), P-Cards provide a means for streamlining the P2P process, allowing organizations to procure goods and services in a timely manner, reduce transaction costs, track expenses, take advantage of supplier discounts, reduce or redirect staff in the purchasing and/or AP departments, reduce or eliminate petty cash, and more. Originally, P-Cards were targeted for such low-value transactions as supplies and MRO (maintenance, repair, and operations), where their use eliminated POs and invoicing. Over the years, their use has expanded to higher-value transactions as the industry has grown and greater controls have been introduced.

Purchasing cards (P-Cards) or simply account numbers are issued to employees (i.e. cardholders) who are responsible for making purchases or payments on behalf of their employer; for example, cardholders can order and pay for office supplies via a supplier's website. Suppliers accept P-Cards for payment, utilizing the existing credit card infrastructure for payment processing. Transaction data is captured by a supplier's point-of-sale (POS) system and transmitted through the card network. The level of transmitted data depends on the supplier's process and technology systems; data levels include the following:

	Date	Supplier	Transaction Amount	Sales Tax	Customer-Defined Code	Line-Item Detail
Level 1 Standard	X	X	X			
Level 2 Variable Data	X	X	X	X	X	
Level 3 Detailed Data	X	X	X	X	X	X

P-Card Process Flow

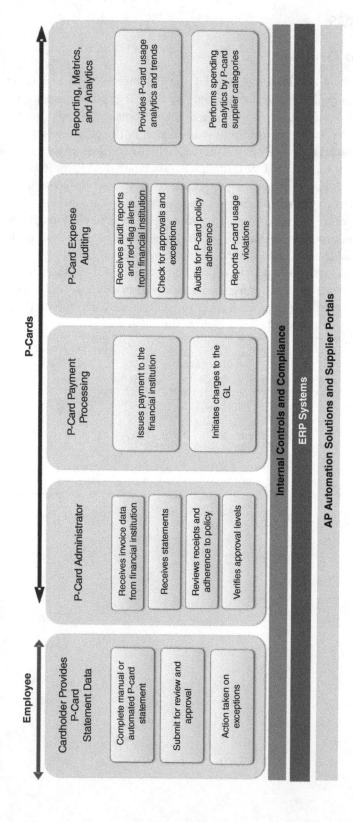

Table of Controls – P-Cards

Process: Accounts Payable

Subprocess: P-Cards

---

1. Segregation of Duties and System Access. Access to the card-issuance area and system access for P-Card activity is limited to employees of the organization. On a quarterly basis, the P-Card system access table is reviewed. The access table is reviewed to ensure that recent system access changes that result from employee changes in job responsibility are properly reflected. Reviewer checks for appropriate level of access based on the job function and appropriate SoD within the organization. The P-Card administrator only has access to reports from the financial institution. The function of processing and disbursing travel and expense claims must be segregated from the following functions:

- Receiving
- Purchasing
- AP invoice processing
- Vendor file maintenance
- GL reconciliation
- AP invoice approval

2. Cardholder Statements. The cardholder submits periodic statements with supporting documentation for each transaction according to P-Card policies and procedures to the P-Card administrator.

3. Management Responsibilities. Management with DoA is responsible for 100 percent audit of cardholder's statement and supporting documentation/receipts. Management DoA signature approval required on cardholder's statement (DoA applies to each transaction on the statement, not the statement total).

4. Review Spend Activity. Review of spend activity on credit card is conducted through an online recording and reporting system.

5. Statement Review Process. Every statement reviewed upon receipt:

- Date stamped with date received in AP
- Verified for appropriate management DoA

6. Statement Tracking. Track statements on P-card audit log:

- Used to monitor submission of statements
- Follow up on outstanding statements
- Document audit activity

7. P-Card Random Audit Process. A minimum of 10 percent of statements, with an average of 20–30 percent of random statements, must be audited sporadically to review the following:

- Supplier review – appropriateness of purchase
- Misuse of card – personal purchases
- Justification for unusual purchases and preapprovals if applicable

8. P-Card Targeted Audits. In addition to random audits, audits specific to cardholder and/or object account spend should include the following:

- Preferred supplier spending data on office supplies
- Charitable contributions
- Review 100 percent of statements for retail or restaurant spending to identify misuse or unusual purchases
- Credit card online reporting tool reports to assist with audit and review spend activity

9. P-Card Controls Monitoring. Monitor P-card audit tracking log – monitors tracking and audits performed by the program administrator.

10. Spending Level Reports. As an example, a company may receive an over $15K report that reflects any individual transaction over $15K, which should be reviewed to ensure that approval levels are correct. Review P-Card spending via reporting and metrics processes.

Process: Accounts Payable

Subprocess: P-Cards

---

11. Spending Limit Changes. Any temporary or permanent change spreadsheets or support must be approved by management who holds DoA with supporting reason for increase in limit.

12. Transaction Detail Report. Review volume by site to look for any unusual spending patterns.

13. Supplier Controls. Block suppliers from vouchering to a P-Card supplier. P-Card suppliers cannot also be paid via a check or ACH payment.

14. P-Card Management Review. Verify 100 percent of AP P-Card statements have supporting documentation and DoA approval on support.

15. Bank Payment Verification. The file feed is validated against statement from the issuing bank by the P-Card administrator.

16. P-Card Accruals. Review and analyze any accrued activity incurred but not included in the cycle-cut of the current month file.

17. Review Cardholder Listing. Conduct a cardholder listing and spending limit review to reassess limits and/or business need for card.

18. P-Card Cardholder Agreement. Ensure that all P-Card cardholders and their managers have signed a cardholder agreement that specifies requirements for the use of the card and clearly defines the responsibilities of the employee and manager. The cardholder agreement should also clearly define and specify the repercussions for both card abuse and misuse.

Table of Risks and Controls – P-Cards

Process: Accounts Payable

Subprocess: P-Cards

Process Risks	Recommended Policies	Internal Controls	KPIs
1. Improper SoD and System Access. The lack of good SoD and system access controls may result in incorrect payments and accounting data. Incorrect payments may be undetected for a lengthy period, and payments that are too high may be unrecoverable.	■ SoD Policy and Procedures ■ System Access Requirements and Review Process	1. SoD and Systems Access 4. Review Spend Activity 5. Statement Review Process 6. Statement Tracking 7. P-Card Random Audits 8. P-Card Targeted Audits 9. P-Card Controls Monitoring 10. Spending Level Reports 11. Spending Limit Changes 12. Transaction Detail Report 13. Supplier Controls 14. P-Card Management Reviews 17. Review Cardholder Listing 18. P-Card Cardholder Agreement	■ Number of SoD Reviews Performed ■ Number of SoD Conflicts Identified and Mitigated ■ Number and Value of P-Card Payment Issues and Errors Identified and Mitigated

Process: Accounts Payable			
Subprocess: P-Cards			
Process Risks	**Recommended Policies**	**Internal Controls**	**KPIs**
2. Violation of P-Card Policies. Policies may be violated, leading to duplicate, erroneous, or fraudulent payments to suppliers.	■ P-Card Policy ■ Approval Roles and Responsibilities	1. SoD and Systems Access 2. Cardholder Statements 3. Management Responsibilities 4. Review Spend Activity 5. Statement Review Process 6. Statement Tracking 7. P-Card Random Audits 8. P-Card Targeted Audits 9. P-Card Controls Monitoring 10. Spending Level Reports 11. Spending Limit Changes 12. Transaction Detail Report 13. Supplier Controls 14. P-Card Management Reviews 17. Review Cardholder Listing 18. P-Card Cardholder Agreement	■ Number and Percentage of P-Card Issues as Compared to Supplier Payments Issued ■ Number and Percentage of P-Card Violations ■ Number of P-Cards Issued ■ Number and Percentage of P-Card Privileges Revoked
3. Poor Visibility or Errors During the Review Process. The lack of a timely review process may cause errors to be undetected and incorrect payments to be made.	■ Criteria for the Audit and Review Process ■ Sample Size Reviews and Business Rules for Random and Targeted Audits	7. P-Card Random Audits 8. P-Card Targeted Audits 9. P-Card Controls Monitoring	■ Number and Percentage of P-Card Issues as Compared to Supplier Payments Issued ■ Number and Percentage of P-Card Violations ■ Number of P-Cards Issued ■ Number and Percentage of P-Card Privileges Revoked

Process: Accounts Payable			
Subprocess: P-Cards			
Process Risks	**Recommended Policies**	**Internal Controls**	**KPIs**
4. Unclear and Undefined Roles and Responsibilities. Unclear responsibilities for the cardholder and management may result in P-Card abuse and inappropriate payments.	■ P-Card Policy ■ Approval Roles and Responsibilities	1. SoD and Systems Access 3. Management Responsibilities 4. Review Spend Activity 5. Statement Review Process 6. Statement Tracking 7. P-Card Random Audits 8. P-Card Targeted Audits 9. P-Card Controls Monitoring 10. Spending Level Reports 11. Spending Limit Changes 12. Transaction Detail Report 13. Supplier Controls 14. P-Card Management Reviews 17. Review Cardholder Listing 18. P-Card Cardholder Agreement	■ Number and Percentage of P-Card Issues as Compared to Supplier Payments Issued ■ Number and Percentage of P-Card Violations ■ Number of P-Cards Issued ■ Number and Percentage of P-Card Privileges Revoked
5. Payment Activity Payment Errors. The lack of attention to the P-Card process may result in incorrect payments to the issuing financial institution and duplicate payments to suppliers.	■ P-Card Policy ■ Criteria for the Audit and Review Process ■ Sample Size Reviews and Business Rules for Random and Targeted Audits	1. SoD and Systems Access 2. Cardholder Statements 3. Management Responsibilities 4. Review Spend Activity 5. Statement Review Process 6. Statement Tracking 7. P-Card Random Audits 8. P-Card Targeted Audits 9. P-Card Controls Monitoring 10. Spending Level Reports 11. Spending Limit Changes 12. Transaction Detail Report 13. Supplier Controls 14. P-Card Management Reviews 15. Bank Payment Validation 17. Review Cardholder Listing 18. P-Card Cardholder Agreement	■ Number and Value of P-Card Payment Issues and Errors Identified and Mitigated

Process: Accounts Payable			
Subprocess: P-Cards			
Process Risks	**Recommended Policies**	**Internal Controls**	**KPIs**
6. Misstatement of Financial Results. Financial statements, records, and operating reports may be misstated. Critical decisions may be based upon erroneous information, resulting in the misstatement of financial results.	▪ P-Card Policy ▪ Month-End Cutoffs ▪ Approval Roles and Responsibilities	15. Bank Payment Validation 16. P-Card Accruals	▪ Number and Value of Pre-Close and Post-Close Adjustments

2.8 TRAVEL AND ENTERTAINMENT

Travel and Entertainment Process Overview

T&E expenses are incurred when an employee conducts business away from home or the company's offices. For example, if one must travel to another location to conduct a meeting with an important client, any lodging, meals, and transportation costs usually count as travel expenses. One may deduct travel expenses from one's taxable income, provided that they are in fact directly related to business

Travel and Entertainment Process Flow

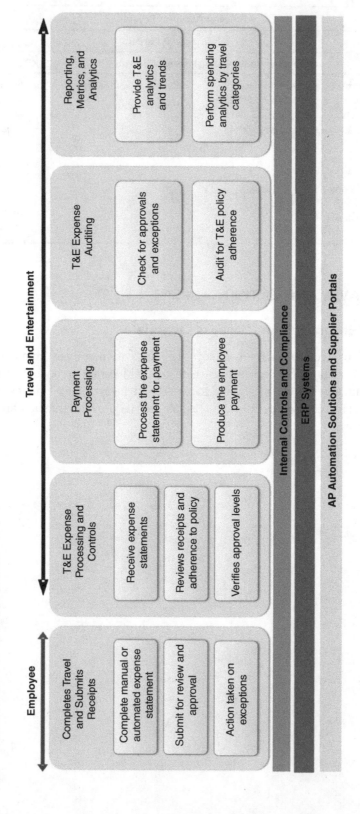

Table of Controls – Travel and Entertainment

Process: Accounts Payable

Subprocess: Travel and Entertainment

---

1. Corporate Travel and Entertainment Process Policy and Validation. Ensure company policy is well documented and communicated. Managers and employees must be aware of the policy and are aware of the repercussions when the policy is violated. T&E reimbursement requests are independently validated for compliance with company policy and accuracy. The policy should state the requirements for using a corporate travel agency for travel and define exceptions. Additionally, the policy should confirm the use of a corporate card for all T&E expenses. Training is conducted and updated at least annually.

2. Reimbursable Expenses. Reimbursed expenditures must be actual, necessary, reasonable, and consistent with the company's travel and expense policy. Expenditures that are excessive or outside of the corporate T&E policy should be investigated and reported. Severe incidents should be reported to the employee's vice president or similar level management. **All T&E expenses should be submitted in a timely manner as defined in the corporate policy.**

3. Audit and Review Process. There is a defined audit process of T&E expense statements.

4. Segregation of Duties and System Access. Access to card-issuing area and system access for T&E activity is limited to employees of the organization. On a quarterly basis, the T&E system access table is reviewed. The access table is reviewed to ensure that recent system access changes resulting from changes in job responsibility are properly reflected. The reviewer checks for appropriate level of access based on the job function and appropriate segregation of duties within the organization. The function of processing and disbursing travel and expense claims must be segregated from the following functions:

- Receiving
- Purchasing
- AP invoice processing
- Vendor file maintenance
- GL reconciliation
- AP invoice approval

5. Approval Process. T&E reimbursement requests must be reviewed and approved. Appropriate approval controls are in place to prevent unauthorized T&E transactions. Approval of T&E requests is based on the organizational hierarchy defined by the DoA policy. The employee's designated approver receives an e-mail notification of the pending approval. The approval/denial may be performed by replying to the e-mail, checking the appropriate box, or online within the T&E application itself. Approvers have the option of adding comments to their approvals. Each approver must execute specific approvals, unless he/she has delegated this to another approver. If delegation has been made, then the delegated approver must carry out the approval process. If approvers will be out of the office on leave or vacation they must delegate their authority, enabling the request to smoothly continue through the system.

6. Travel and Entertainment Transaction Processing. All T&E transactions are reviewed to ensure there are no duplicate transactions. Validated T&E reimbursement requests go through a field validation check before posting. The key fields include the following: cost center, project number, and employee number.

7. Travel and Entertainment Process Error Controls. T&E processing personnel reviews and corrects any errors and contacts the requestor's supervisor or supplier management, as necessary, to resolve the error. Additionally, the T&E processing supervisor reviews the transactions with an error status to ensure timely resolution. The errors are generally resolved by the following day.

8. Payment Authorization Levels. As an example, if the value of the T&E reimbursement request exceeds $1,500 for new T&E processors or $9,000 for second-level T&E processors, the request must be approved by the supervisor or manager. The supervisor can approve up to $10,000 and the manager up to $99,999.

9. Corporate Cardholder Agreement. Ensure that all corporate cardholders and their managers have signed a cardholder agreement that specifies requirements for the use of the card and clearly defines the responsibilities of the employee and manager. The cardholder agreement should also clearly define and specify the repercussions of both card abuse and misuse.

Table of Risks and Controls – Travel and Entertainment

Process: Accounts Payable			
Subprocess: Travel and Entertainment			
Process Risk	**Recommended Policies**	**Internal Controls**	**KPIs**
1. Improper SoD and System Access. The lack of good SoD and system access controls may result in incorrect payments and accounting data. Incorrect payments may be undetected for a lengthy period, and payments that are too high may be unrecoverable.	■ SoD Policy and Procedures ■ System Access Requirements and Review Process	3. Audit and Review Process 4. SoD and Systems Access	■ Number of SoD Reviews Performed ■ Number of SoD Conflicts Identified and Mitigated ■ Number and Value of T&E Payment Issues and Errors Identified and Mitigated
2. Violation of Corporate T&E Policies. Policies may be violated, leading to duplicate, erroneous, or fraudulent payments being issued to employees.	■ T&E Policy ■ Approval Roles and Responsibilities	1. Corporate T&E Policy and Validation 2. Reimbursable Expenses 3. Audit and Review Process 4. SoD and Systems Access 5. Approval Process 6. T&E Transaction Processing 7. T&E Error Controls 8. Payment Authorization Levels 9. Corporate Cardholder Agreement	■ Number and Percentage of T&E Issues as Compared to Total T&E Payments Issued ■ Number and Percentage of Corporate Card Violations ■ Number of Corporate Cards Issued ■ Number and Percentage of Corporate Card Privileges Revoked
3. Poor Visibility or Errors During the Review Process. The lack of a timely review process may cause errors to be undetected and incorrect payments to be made.	■ Criteria for the Audit and Review Process ■ 100 percent Audit ■ Sample Size Reviews	3. Audit and Review Process	■ Number and Percentage of T&E Issues as Compared to Total T&E Payments Issued ■ Number and Percentage of Corporate Card Violations ■ Number of Corporate Cards Issued ■ Number and Percentage of Corporate Card Privileges Revoked

Process: Accounts Payable			
Subprocess: Travel and Entertainment			
Process Risk	**Recommended Policies**	**Internal Controls**	**KPIs**
4. Unclear and Undefined Roles and Responsibilities. Unclear responsibilities for the cardholder and management may result in corporate card abuse and inappropriate payments.	■ T&E Policy ■ Approval Roles and Responsibilities	1. Corporate T&E Policy and Validation 2. Reimbursable Expenses 3. Audit and Review Process 4. SoD and Systems Access 5. Approval Process 6. T&E Transaction Processing 7. T&E Error Controls 8. Payment Authorization Levels 9. Corporate Cardholder Agreement	■ Number and Percentage of T&E Issues as Compared to Total T&E Payments Issued ■ Number and Percentage of Corporate Card Violations ■ Number of Corporate Cards Issued ■ Number and Percentage of Corporate Card Privileges Revoked
5. Misstatement of Financial Results. Financial statements, records, and operating reports may be misstated. Critical decisions may be based upon erroneous information resulting in the misstatement of financial results.	■ T&E Policy ■ Approval Roles and Responsibilities	1. Corporate T&E Policy and Validation 2. Reimbursable Expenses 3. Audit and Review Process 4. SoD 5. Approval Process 6. T&E Transaction Processing 7. T&E Error Controls 8. Payment Authorization Levels 9. Corporate Cardholder Agreement	■ Number and Value of Pre-Close and Post-Close Adjustments

CHAPTER ELEVEN

Hire-to-Retire

 ## OVERVIEW

H2R is an HR process that includes everything that needs to be done over the course of an employee's career with a company. The following are high-level process steps:

- **Human resources planning:** HR management planning, such as work design.
- **Recruiting:** Recruiting processes, such as relationship building, employer branding, job posting, job fairs, and interviewing.
- **Employee management:** Everything that is required to manage an employee, such as onboarding, performance management, training and development, and benefits and compensation processes.
- **Redeployment:** The processes related to an employee being redeployed, such as foreign work assignments.
- **Payroll:** The control and delivery of payroll.
- **Retirement:** The processes related to an employee leaving, such as exit interviews and retirement benefits.

Human Capital Management

Human capital management (HCM) is a term for managing people. According to Gartner, HCM is a "set of practices related to people resource management," specifically in the categories of workforce acquisition, management, and optimization. HCM is applicable to any organization, but it's especially important for companies with so-called knowledge workers, where the business's most critical asset is its people.

HCM is the complete series of business and systematic processes used for recruiting, managing, developing, and optimizing employees (as intangible assets) in order to maximize their business value.

HCM is considered to be essential for acquiring and retaining high-performing employees. HCM plays an essential role in helping the organization's HR department increase the overall productivity of employees. HCM functions are focused on hiring talented employees, providing orientation and onboarding best practices, training employees to best utilize their skills and talents, and retaining employees by providing job satisfaction and a well-defined career path.

Hire-to-Retire Process Flow

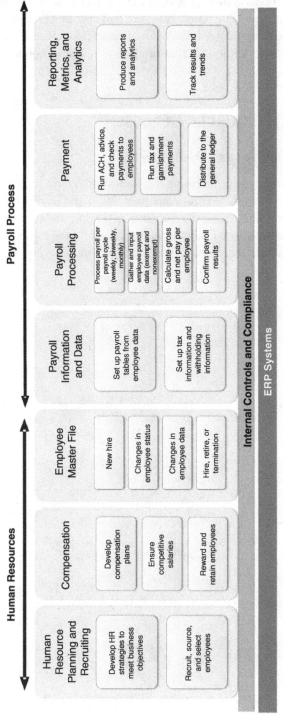

3.0 HUMAN RESOURCES

Human resources are the people who work in an organization. It is also the name of the department that exists to serve the needs of those people. In *The Human Resources Glossary*,[1] William R. Tracey defines human resources as "The people that staff and operate an organization. . .as contrasted with the financial and material resources of an organization." Human resources are the people who work for an organization in jobs that produce the products or services of the business or organization.

3.1 HUMAN RESOURCES PROCESS

Human Resources Process Overview

HR includes the activities involved in hiring employees and determining their proper classification and compensation; defining skills requirements; training and development; ensuring employee communications; providing employee services; reporting hours worked, attendance, and compensatory absence entitlements; maintaining all employee master data; and ensuring the confidentiality and physical security of personnel information.

---

[1]Tracey, William R. (2016). *The Human Resources Glossary: The Complete Desk Reference for HR Executives, Managers, and Practitioners.* CRC Press.

Human Resources Process Flow

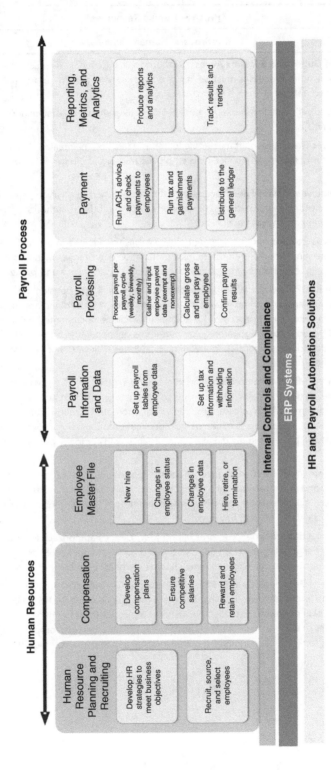

Table of Controls – Human Resources

Process: Human Resources
Subprocess: Human Resources

1. Segregation of Duties and Systems Access. Authorized change functions must be segregated from payroll payment functions. Processes must be in place to review and confirm appropriate levels of system access for authorized personnel.

2. Confidentiality. Confidentiality of payroll and HR information should be maintained and restricted to authorized personnel.

3. Employee Master File. A payment master file (database) must be maintained that includes all employees. The file must contain all information concerning employee master data, payments, void/reissues, and adjustments.

4. Security of Employee Master File. Processes must be established to physically secure and protect viewing access to master file information. Only properly documented and authorized changes related to payments and adjustments should be allowed.

5. Human Resources Policies. HR management must establish and maintain guidelines for the hiring, promotion, compensation, transfer, relocation, and termination of employees. The policies and guidelines should be clearly defined by HR management in the form of specific criteria and procedures.

6. Employee Benefits. Policies for all employee benefits, such as 401(k), pension, health and welfare, stock purchase and option plans, and compensated absences, must be reviewed and approved by executive management. Rules, criteria, and processes for all benefits must be documented and approved by senior management and the appropriate governing committees as defined in the benefit plan documentation. Senior management and the appropriate governing committees review additions, cessations, or an acquisition of any benefits plans.

7. Compensation. An effective compensation system will be in place for all employees, including base pay, monetary rewards (variable sales and nonsales pay programs), and nonmonetary rewards (awards and recognition programs). Effective compensation will be promoted through internal consistency, market competitiveness, and the recognition of individual contributions. Management must obtain proper authorization levels and pay in a timely manner in accordance with company policy for all changes to compensation.

8. Records Management. HR and company management, as required by each specific employee benefit plan, must properly and accurately maintain all compensation and benefit records. At a minimum, HR documentation must include properly executed employment data, new-hire forms, reviews and disciplinary actions, authorized classification, and pay rates.

9. Authorized Transactions. Formal processes, along with correctly authorized documentation, must be maintained to ensure that only authorized additions, deletions, or changes to employee information are allowed. Processes must be in place to ensure key payroll elements agree with HR documentation.

10. Administration of Employee Benefit Plans. Designated HR management must be responsible for the administration of the employee benefit plans. The plans must be administered in accordance with company policy and defined plan processes. Benefit payments to employees must be made in accordance with the terms and conditions of the plans and must be adequately documented and properly approved. Applicable federal and state reporting requirements and compliance testing must be completed.

Process: Human Resources

Subprocess: Human Resources

---

11. Employee Hiring Procedures. The goal of this control is to achieve headcount targets of the organization with top quality candidates. HR/staffing groups, along with the department manager, must ensure the following:

a. The hiring manager obtains appropriate approval for opening and contacts staffing to develop appropriate recruiting strategy.

b. Staffing identifies and screens appropriate candidates. All record keeping and hiring practices are documented and maintained.

c. Staffing will make reasonable opportunities for internal candidates to be considered; however, both internal and external recruiting may begin at the same time.

d. Staffing will identify adequate job descriptions with skill requirements and hiring criteria. These job descriptions can be used to measure and compare candidates' qualifications.

e. The hiring manager may extend an offer to the chosen candidate after appropriate approvals are obtained.

f. New employees receive an employee orientation and are exposed to an onboarding process.

12. Labor Arrangements. Processes will be in place to monitor employees' work environment to identify any hostile work situations. Reasonable steps will be taken to avoid work disputes.

13. Employee Termination/Resignation Procedures. HR must be promptly and formally notified of the termination or transfer of any employee or of payroll changes so that payroll records can be promptly adjusted. HR will establish the necessary processes to facilitate this notification. Upon notification of an employee's termination or resignation, the employee's supervisor will notify HR and must ensure that the following acts are completed:

a. All outstanding corporate credit card balances and loans/advances have been paid by employee.

b. All company credit cards, telephone cards, P-Cards, air travel cards) have been returned and destroyed.

c. Notification is made to the information services group to have all computer and telephone accounts cancelled.

d. All company property (such as computers, etc.), proprietary information, employee badges, security passes, and keys have been returned.

e. Notification is made to third-party vendors to eliminate any authority by the terminating employee to conduct company business (e.g. authority to sign checks, contracts, etc.).

14. Employee Transfers. Upon notification of employee's intent to transfer, the existing manager must ensure that the hiring manager is provided objective feedback regarding the employee's performance and work history.

15. Search Firm and Agency Agreements. Contracts are negotiated with specific terms and conditions that ensure effective use of company funds and protection against potential illegal acts on the part of the firms/agencies.

16. Equal Employment Opportunity/Diversity. Ensure that all aspects of employment meet varying governmental requirements at all levels.

Table of Risks and Controls – Human Resources

Process: Human Resources			
Subprocess: Human Resources			
Process Risk	Recommended Policies	Internal Controls	KPIs
1. **Improper SoD and System Access.** The lack of good SoD and system-access controls may result in incorrect employee payments and data required for the payroll process, withholdings, and employee benefits. Incorrect payments may be undetected for a lengthy period, and if the employee leaves the company before errors are detected, the company may not be able to recover funds not repaid by the employee. HR records are not subject to proper security procedures and confidential information may be accessed and/or disclosed to the detriment of the company and its employees.	■ SoD Policy and Procedures ■ System Access Requirements and Review Process ■ Employee Head-count Reporting	1. SoD and Systems Access 8. Records Management 9. Authorized Transactions	■ Number of SoD Reviews Performed ■ Number of SoD Conflicts Identified and Mitigated ■ Number and Value of Payroll Payment Issues and Errors Identified and Mitigated ■ Number of New Hires ■ Number of Transfers ■ Number of Terminations
2. **Violation of Hiring Practices.** Individuals may be employed who do not meet the company's hiring criteria resulting in an inadequate workforce in terms of numbers and/or quality. The company lacks a competitive talent pool; therefore, the company is unable to compete for business on an equal level with competitors. The company may not accurately account for the applicants or reflect applicants against specific staffing requirements.	■ HR Policies and Hiring Practices	11. Employee Hiring Practices 12. Labor Arrangements 15. Search Firm and Agency Agreements 16. Equal Opportunity/ Diversity	■ Number of Hiring Violations Identified

Process: Human Resources			
Subprocess: Human Resources			
Process Risk	**Recommended Policies**	**Internal Controls**	**KPIs**
3. Discrimination Issues. Employment decisions and practices may be discriminatory and/or not in compliance with governmental regulations, thus negatively impacting the company legally and financially.	■ HR Policies and Hiring Practices	11. Employee Hiring Practices 12. Labor Arrangements 15. Search Firm and Agency Agreements 16. Equal Opportunity/ Diversity	■ Number of Hiring and Discriminatory Issues Identified
4. Employee Data Inaccuracies. Management reports and employee earnings records may be inaccurate.	■ SoD Policy and Procedures ■ System Access Requirements and Review Process	1. SoD and Systems Access 8. Records Management 9. Authorized Transactions 11. Employee Termination/ Resignation Procedures 12. Employee Transfers	■ Number and Value of Payroll Payment Issues and Errors Identified and Mitigated
5. Employee Benefit Inaccuracies. Incorrect amounts may subsequently be disbursed to employees.	■ SoD Policy and Procedures ■ System Access Requirements and Review Process	6. Employee Benefits 8. Records Management 10. Administration of Employee Benefit Plans	■ Number and Value of Employee Benefit Issues Identified and Mitigated
6. Inaccurate Compensation Reporting. Accruals for benefits, such as 401(k), pension, compensated absences, and health and welfare, may be incorrectly calculated resulting in misstated liabilities.	■ SoD Policy and Procedures ■ System Access Requirements and Review Process	1. SoD and Systems Access 7. Compensation 8. Records Management 9. Authorized Transactions	■ Number and Value of Pre-Close and Post-Close Adjustments
7. Noncompliance with Regulatory Requirements. Laws and governmental regulations may be violated resulting in fines, penalties, lawsuits, or contingent liabilities. Violations, such as not having reviews or disciplinary actions, may result in employee relation issues as well.	■ SoD Policy and Procedures ■ System Access Requirements and Review Process	1. SoD and Systems Access 2. Confidentiality 3. Employee Master File 4. Security of the Employee Master 5. HR Policies 8. Records Management 9. Authorized Transactions 16. Equal Opportunity/ Diversity	■ Number of Regulatory Issues Identified and Mitigated

Process: Human Resources			
Subprocess: Human Resources			
Process Risk	Recommended Policies	Internal Controls	KPIs
8. Unauthorized Changes to Employee Records. Payroll and payroll tax accounts may be misstated. Unauthorized transactions may be processed, resulting in improper payments and/or payments to fictitious employees. Improper payments may not be detected and corrected.	■ SoD Policy and Procedures ■ System Access Requirements and Review Process ■ CSAs	1. SoD and Systems Access 8. Records Management 9. Authorized Transactions	■ Number of Unauthorized Employee Records Identified ■ Number of CSAs Performed
9. Inaccurate Financial Statements. Inaccurate information may be input into the GL, resulting in misstated financial statements.	■ SoD Policy and Procedures ■ System Access Requirements and Review Process	1. SoD and Systems Access 8. Records Management 9. Authorized Transactions 13. Employee Termination/ Resignation Procedures 14. Employee Transfers	■ Number and Value of Pre-Close and Post-Close Adjustments

4.0 PAYROLL

Payroll Process Overview

There are several important components of the payroll process. The processing of an employee's earned pay from gross to net amount must be done in a strict yet varying regulatory environment. The environment varies because the process is controlled by several entities on both the federal and state levels. A controller must be aware of the regulations that must be followed to ensure compliance, which will prevent audit exceptions that potentially result in penalties, fines, and interest.

Payroll includes the processes involved in preparing payroll payments in a controlled and accurate manner, which ensures accurate accounting for payroll costs, deductions, employee benefits, and other adjustments; distributing checks, initiating direct deposits, and issuing prepaid cards to employees; and ensuring the confidentiality and physical security of payroll and personnel information.

Payroll Process Flow

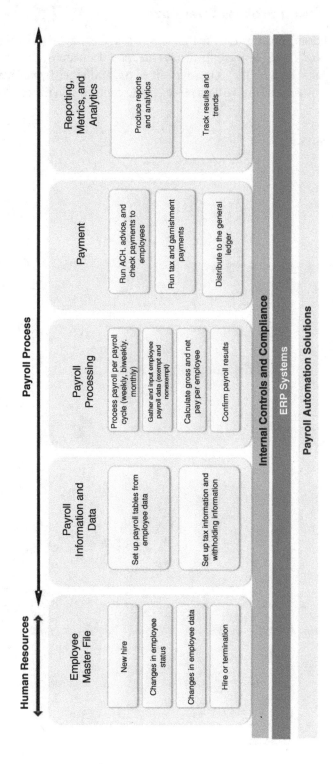

Payroll Process

Human Resources

Employee Master File	Payroll Information and Data	Payroll Processing	Payment	Reporting, Metrics, and Analytics
New hire	Set up payroll tables from employee data	Process payroll per payroll cycle (weekly, biweekly, monthly)	Run ACH. advice, and check payments to employees	Produce reports and analytics
Changes in employee status	Set up tax information and withholding information	Gather and input employee payroll data (exempt and nonexempt)	Run tax and garnishment payments	Track results and trends
Changes in employee data		Calculate gross and net pay per employee	Distribute to the general ledger	
Hire or termination		Confirm payroll results		

Internal Controls and Compliance

ERP Systems

Payroll Automation Solutions

4.1 PAYROLL PROCESSING PROCESS

Payroll Processing Process Overview

The payroll processing process refers to the steps required to pay employees each pay period and involves employees' hours worked, their pay rate, and deductions. Processing payroll ensures employees are paid based on their employment status and other Department of Labor requirements and that pay is based on the data reflected and controlled in the employee master file.

Payroll Processing Process Flow

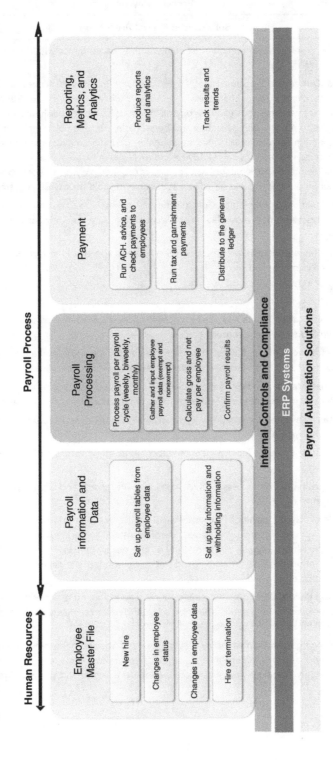

Table of Controls – Payroll Processing

Process: Payroll
Subprocess: Payroll Processing

1. **Employee Data.** Employee information must be managed in accordance with the company's safeguarding information guidelines.

2. **Segregation of Duties and System Access.** Payroll preparation responsibilities must be segregated from payroll authorization, check signing, check distribution responsibilities, and initiation and approval of ACH or other electronic payment methods used for payroll. Responsibilities for additions, deletions, and changes to information in the company's compensation and benefit administration systems must be segregated between the following in each set of activities: functional or operating management responsible for initiation and approval; HR personnel responsible for advice and review with respect to policy compliance as required; law department personnel responsible for legal review, as required; payroll and plans personnel responsible for transaction change processing; and payroll personnel responsible for payroll preparation.

3. **Controls Over Payment Source Data.** Controls must be maintained to ensure all payment source data is valid and properly input. Controls must also be established to ensure that only current, authorized payment source data is used.

4. **Payroll Process Reviews.** Payroll runs must be reviewed and approved for reasonableness and to confirm that all controls have been applied.

5. **Payroll Payment.** Salaries and wages must be paid by bank deposit, check, or prepaid card (if allowed) and supported by the company.

6. **Management Verification.** Managers must be able to verify the existence of employees charged to their units and that payroll charges are recorded correctly.

7. **Time and Attendance.** Time and attendance data input at the local site level into time-recording applications is reviewed and approved by authorized person(s).

8. **Processing Errors.** Manual review of any errors in the automated interface process to the payroll system are followed up on and reentered, using SoD entry and confirmation, on a timely basis.

9. **System Updates.** New hires, terminations, and transfers must be approved by authorized person(s) and accurately input in the system.

10. **Independent Contractors.** Independent contractors are properly vetted and approved. Background checks are conducted.

11. **Security of Payroll Records.** Access to employee payment records and source documents are restricted to authorized personnel.

12. **Reconciliation of Payroll Earnings Records.** Payrolls must be prepared from the payroll master file and the approved time-reporting records. Paychecks, payroll registers, and employee earnings records should be prepared from the same database of information. Where system constraints prohibit the use of the same database, a reconciliation (contents are known and status is current) of the payroll earnings records and the payroll register must be completed.

13. **Time-Reporting Records.** Department managers are responsible for ensuring that time-reporting records are authorized; comparing actual salary, benefits, and other payments to budgeted costs for reasonableness; and for approving exceptions.

14. **Payroll Withholdings and Garnishments.** Payroll withholdings and garnishments must be controlled to ensure the propriety of amounts, compliance with applicable governmental requirements, timely remittance to the appropriate entity, and timely reconciliation (contents are known and status is current) to the GL accounts.

Process: Payroll

Subprocess: Payroll Processing

15. Government/Regulatory Requirements. Annual summaries of employee wages and withholdings must be prepared and distributed to all employees in accordance with applicable governmental requirements. In addition, summaries of employee wages must be reconciled (contents are known and status is current) to payments made to the statutory government agencies.

16. Special Payments. All other/special payments processed by the payroll department (e.g. relocation, education, bonuses, advances, commissions, garnishments, adjustments, etc.) must be properly authorized independent of the payroll and HR processing departments, and approved and documented before payment and in accordance with applicable tax requirements.

17. Documentation of Payroll Procedures. Departmental processes should be clearly documented for all key payroll functions and cutoff procedures.

18. Expense Distribution. Payroll expenses must be complete and accurately distributed to the appropriate department or cost center.

19. Approved Time-Reporting Records. Employees must, where required by local laws, submit on a timely basis approved time-reporting and attendance records before payroll processing is performed. The payroll department will establish the necessary processes to facilitate notification to the employee's manager of actual time submitted.

Table of Risks and Controls – Payroll Processing

Process: Payroll

Subprocess: Payroll Processing

Process Risk	Recommended Policies	Internal Controls	KPIs
1. Improper SoD and System Access. The lack of good SoD and system access controls may result in incorrect employee payments and data required for the payroll process, withholdings, and employee benefits. Incorrect payments may be undetected for a lengthy period. Unauthorized payments may be made and funds may be misappropriated, and may be unrecoverable if the employee leaves the company before the error is identified.	■ SoD Policy and Procedures ■ System Access Requirements and Review Process	1. Employee Data 2. SoD and System Access 3. Controls Over Source Data 9. System Updates 11. Security of Payroll Records	■ Number of SoD Reviews Performed ■ Number of SoD Conflicts Identified and Mitigated ■ Number and Value of Payroll Payment Issues and Errors Identified and Mitigated

Process: Payroll			
Subprocess: Payroll Processing			
Process Risk	Recommended Policies	Internal Controls	KPIs
2. **Security and Access to the Payroll Department.** Inadequate security over the payroll department and its records may result in: a. Destruction or loss of employee payment records, including the payment master file b. Unauthorized review and/or disclosure of confidential payroll information c. The processing of unauthorized changes to the payment master file, which in turn may result in the following: i. Misappropriation of company assets ii. Misstatement of accruals, such as pensions	■ HR Policies and Hiring Practices	1. Employee Data 2. SoD and System Access 3. Controls Over Source Data 11. Security of Payroll Records	■ Number of SoD Reviews Performed ■ Number of SoD Conflicts Identified and Mitigated ■ Number and Value of Payroll Payment Issues and Errors Identified and Mitigated
3. **Unapproved Time and Attendance Records.** Unapproved time and attendance records may impact the accuracy and timeliness of employee payroll payments, and may reflect more working hours than the employee deserves, leading to undeserved pay.	■ Payment Reconciliation Process ■ Self-Assessment Process ■ Management Reviews	6. Management Verification 7. Time and Attendance 13. Time-Reporting Records 19. Approved Time-Reporting Records	■ Number and Value of Payroll Payment Issues and Errors Identified and Mitigated

Process: Payroll			
Subprocess: Payroll Processing			
Process Risk	**Recommended Policies**	**Internal Controls**	**KPIs**
4. Inconsistent Payroll Process. The lack of payroll procedures may impact the accuracy and timeliness of employee payroll payments.	■ Payroll Process Documentation ■ Payment Reconciliation Process ■ Self-Assessment Process	8. Processing Errors 12. Reconciliation of Payroll Earnings Records 17. Documentation of Payroll Procedures 18. Expense Distribution	■ Number and Value of Payroll Payment Issues and Errors Identified and Mitigated
5. Classification of Contractors. Contractors may be inaccurately classified and paid as employees.	■ HR Policies and Hiring Practices ■ Headcount Reporting	10. Independent Contractors	■ Number and Value of Payroll Payment Issues and Errors Identified and Mitigated
6. Risk of Fines for Noncompliance. Noncompliance and/or calculation errors may result in fines and penalties being assessed by state, local, and federal government agencies.	■ Payment Reconciliation Process ■ Self-Assessment Process	15. Government/ Regulatory Requirements	■ Number and Value of Fines Incurred
7. Employee Data Inaccuracies. Management reports and employee payment records may be inaccurate.	■ SoD Policy and Procedures ■ System Access Requirements and Review Process	1. Employee Data 2. SoD and System Access 3. Controls Over Source Data 9. System Updates 11. Security of Payroll Records	■ Number and Value of Payroll Payment Issues and Errors Identified and Mitigated
8. Withholding Errors. Detailed withholdings and payments may not agree with the recorded withholdings and payments, which will require considerable time, resources, and money to resolve.	■ Payment Reconciliation Process	8. Processing Errors 12. Reconciliation of Payroll Earnings Records 17. Documentation of Payroll Procedures	■ Number and Value of Payroll Payment Issues and Errors Identified and Mitigated
9. Payroll Exceptions. Detailed withholdings and payments may not agree with the recorded withholdings and payments, which will require considerable time, resources, and money to resolve.	■ Payroll Process Documentation ■ Payment Reconciliation Process ■ Self-Assessment Process	11. Payroll Withholdings and Garnishments 16. Special Payments	■ Number and Value of Payroll Exceptions Identified ■ Number of Special Payments Paid Per Period

Process: Payroll			
Subprocess: Payroll Processing			
Process Risk	**Recommended Policies**	**Internal Controls**	**KPIs**
10. Unauthorized Changes to Employee Records. Payroll and payroll tax accounts may be misstated. Unauthorized transactions may be processed, resulting in improper payments and/or payments to fictitious employees. Improper payments may not be detected and corrected.	▪ SoD Policy and Procedures ▪ System Access Requirements and Review Process ▪ CSAs	1. SoD and Systems Access 8. Records Management 9. Authorized Transactions	▪ Number of Unauthorized Employee Records Identified. ▪ Number of CSAs Performed
11. Payroll Reconciliation and Reporting. Detailed withholdings and payments may not agree with the recorded withholdings and payments.	▪ Payroll Reconciliation Process ▪ Self-Assessment Process	8. Processing Errors 12. Reconciliation of Payroll Earnings Records 17. Documentation of Payroll Procedures 18. Expense Distribution	▪ Cost to Process Payroll Results ▪ Cycle Time for Each Payroll Process
12. Inaccurate Financial Statements. Inaccurate information may be input into the GL, resulting in misstated financial statements.	▪ Financial Close Process ▪ SoD Policy and Procedures ▪ System Access Requirements ▪ Payroll Reconciliation Process	8. Processing Errors 12. Reconciliation of Payroll Earnings Records 17. Documentation of Payroll Procedures 18. Expense Distribution	▪ Number and Value of Pre-Close and Post-Close Adjustments for the Payroll Process

4.2 PAYROLL PAYMENT PROCESS

Payroll Payment Process Overview

Payroll in the sense of employee payments plays a major role in a company for these reasons:

- From an accounting perspective, payroll is crucial because payroll and payroll taxes considerably affect the net income of most companies and because they are subject to laws and regulations (e.g. in the United States, payroll is subject to federal, state, and local regulations).
- From an HR viewpoint, the payroll department is critical because employees are sensitive to payroll errors and irregularities: good employee morale requires payroll to be paid timely and accurately. The primary mission of the payroll department is to ensure that all employees are paid accurately and timely with the correct withholdings and deductions, and that the withholdings and deductions are remitted in a timely manner.

Payroll Payment Process Flow

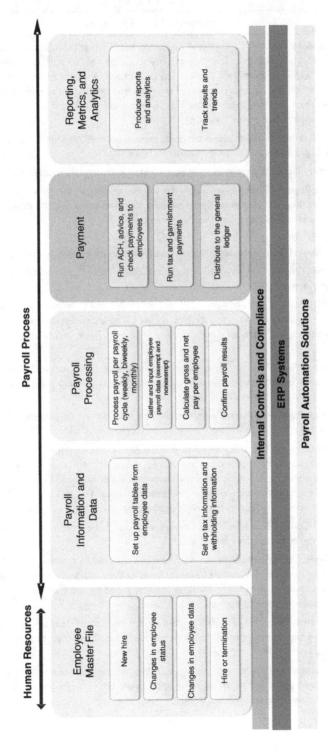

Table of Controls – Payroll Payment

Process: Payroll
Subprocess: Payroll Payment

1. Payroll Payment Bank Accounts. For payroll payments, management should use an imprest or zero balance bank account when available. The imprest system is a form of financial accounting system. The most common imprest system is the petty cash system. The base characteristic of an imprest system is that a fixed amount is reserved, which after a certain period of time or when circumstances require because money was spent will be replenished. This replenishment will come from another account source (e.g. petty cash will be replenished by cashing a check drawn on a bank account).

2. Account Reconciliations. All payroll bank accounts and GL payment accounts must be reconciled (contents are known and status is current) on a monthly basis.

3. Payroll Payments. All payroll payments must be traceable and uniquely identifiable.

4. Security of Blank Payroll Checks. Blank check stock used, identifying the company or its financial institutions, must be safeguarded, and accessed by more than one employee. All payroll checks must be periodically accounted for as being issued, voided, or unused.

5. Voided Check Procedures. Spoiled, voided, and/or canceled checks must be accounted for, destroyed or clearly stamped void, and kept protected in a process conducted by more than one employee.

6. Security of Payroll Checks. Signed payroll checks and direct deposit advices must be secured until distributed to employees.

7. Segregation of Duties and System Access. Payroll check signatories must be individuals having no payroll authorization or preparation responsibilities, access to the unused checks, or check distribution responsibilities. Persons responsible for the distribution of payroll checks must not approve time cards or special payments.

8. Approval of Payroll Records. Completed payroll registers, journal reports, and requests for payroll account reimbursement (or similar documents to support the amounts being paid) must be reviewed and approved by appropriate management in a timely manner.

9. Issuance of Payroll Payments. Formal authorization procedures must be established and adhered to in the signing of payroll checks.

10. Custody and Security of Check Signing Equipment. Where check signing equipment and facsimile signature plates or digitized signature images are utilized, the equipment and plates must be secured, and custody of the check signing equipment and the signature plates or digitized signature image files must be segregated. In addition, a weekly reconciliation (contents are known and status is current) should be made of checks written and checks authorized to the check signing machine totals.

11. Payroll Payment Control Function. Payroll must review distribution of payments to ensure that payments are not made to nonexistent employees.

12. Unclaimed Wages. Unclaimed wages not disbursed in a reasonable time frame, and after a reasonable attempt to redirect funds to employees, are to be returned to the company. Unclaimed wages must be remitted to the appropriate government authorities when required by law. Payments of unclaimed wages should be made only upon proper employee identification.

13. Nonwage Payments. Payments processed by the payroll department that are not related to wages earned (e.g. special recognition, commissions, etc.) must be included in the employee payment file and distributed following normal distribution channels.

14. Bank Account Limits. Specific limits of signing authority for checks, promissory notes, and bank transfers must be established and approved according to an appropriate BoD's banking resolution and communicated to the disbursing entity and the appropriate bank(s).

Process: Payroll

Subprocess: Payroll Payment

15. Positive Pay and Positive Payee Controls. Checking accounts must be provided with match-pay or positive-pay controls that permit a preview of checks presented to the bank for payment. If such controls are not practical, bank accounts must be subject to activity limits and dual signatory controls.

16. Check Delivery. All checks should be mailed. In cases where this is not possible, prior arrangements should be made for check delivery. When the check is picked up in person, proper identification must be provided and delivery of the check must be documented via the payee's signature.

17. Recording in Accounting Records. All payments must be recorded in the period that the payment was made. Expenses must be properly and accurately recorded in accounting records during the period in which the liability was incurred.

18. Custody and Security of Check Signing Equipment. Where check signing equipment and facsimile signature plates or digitized signature images are utilized, the equipment and plates must be secured, and custody of the check signing equipment and the signature plates or digitized signature image files must be segregated. In addition, a reconciliation (contents are known and status is current) should be made of checks written and checks authorized to the check signing machine totals.

19. ACH Payment Controls. Monitor and reconcile accounts at least daily, including outbound ACH and wire transfers. Make sure your ACH payment procedures comply with ACH rules: verify routing numbers, secure Internet session (minimum 128-bit SSL encryption technology), and conduct annual security audit.

20. ACH Debits. Return unauthorized ACH debits no later than the opening of business on the second banking day following the settlement date of the original entry, or as required by current NACHA rules.

21. ACH Positive Pay and Positive Payee ACH Positive Pay. This is an online fraud mitigation service that allows you to manage ACH debits and credits posting to your business account via filters and blocks.

Table of Risks and Controls – Payroll Payment

Process: Payroll

Subprocess: Payroll Payment

Process Risk	Recommended Policies	Internal Controls	KPIs
1. Improper SoD and System Access. The lack of good SoD and system access controls may result in incorrect employee payments and data required for the payroll process, withholdings, and employee benefits. Incorrect payments may be undetected for a lengthy period. Unauthorized payments may be made, funds may be misappropriated, and payments that are more than they should be may be unrecoverable.	■ SoD Policy and Procedures ■ System Access Requirements and Review Process	3. Payroll Payments 7. SoD and Systems Access 14. Bank Account Limits	■ Number of SoD Reviews Performed ■ Number of SoD Conflicts Identified and Mitigated ■ Number and Value of Payroll Payment Issues and Errors Identified and Mitigated

Process: Payroll			
Subprocess: Payroll Payment			
Process Risk	**Recommended Policies**	**Internal Controls**	**KPIs**
2. Security and Access to the Payroll Department. Inadequate security for the payroll department and its records may result in: a. Destruction or loss of employee payment records, including the payment master file b. Unauthorized review and/or disclosure of confidential payroll information c. The processing of unauthorized changes to the payment master file, which in turn may result in the following: i. Misappropriation of company assets ii. Misstatement of accruals, such as pensions	■ SoD Policy and Procedures ■ System Access Requirements and Review Process	3. Payroll Payments 7. SoD and Systems Access 8. Approval of Payroll Records	■ Number of SoD Reviews Performed ■ Number of SoD Conflicts Identified and Mitigated ■ Number and Value of Payroll Payment Issues and Errors Identified and Mitigated
3. Payroll Bank Accounts. Special bank accounts should be used for payroll payments for accounting, reporting and visibility to the payroll process. All bank accounts should be reconciled on a monthly basis.	■ Cash Accounting Reconciliation Processes	1. Payroll Payment Bank Accounts 2. Account Reconciliations 3. Payroll Payments 8. Approval of Payroll Records 14. Bank Account Limits	■ Value of Variances Reported in Payroll Bank Accounts ■ Aging of Variances Reported in Payroll Bank Accounts

Process: Payroll			
Subprocess: Payroll Payment			
Process Risk	**Recommended Policies**	**Internal Controls**	**KPIs**
4. Payroll Check Fraud. The lack of control over check payments may impact the accuracy and timeliness of employee payments and allow a fraudulent payment to go undetected. All voided checks should be properly reconciled.	■ Cash Accounting Reconciliation Processes	3. Payroll Payments 4. Security of Blank Payroll Checks 5. Voided Check Procedures 6. Security of Payroll Checks 8. Approval of Payroll Records 9. Issuance of Payroll Payments 10. Custody and Security of Check Signing Equipment 11. Payroll Control Function 14. Bank Account Limits 15. Positive Pay and Positive Payee Controls 16. Check Delivery 17. Recording in Accounting Records 18. Custody and Security of Check Signing Equipment	■ Value of Variances Reported in Payroll Bank Accounts ■ Aging of Variances Reported in Payroll Bank Accounts
5. ACH Payment Fraud. The lack of control over ACH payments may impact the accuracy and timeliness of employee payments and allow a fraudulent payment to go undetected.	■ Cash Accounting Reconciliation Processes	3. Payroll Payments 19. ACH Payment Controls 20. ACH Debits 21. ACH Positive Pay and Positive Payee ACH Positive Pay	■ Value of Variances Reported in Payroll Bank Accounts ■ Aging of Variances Reported in Payroll Bank Accounts
6. Employee Data Inaccuracies. Management reports and employee payment records may be inaccurate.	■ SoD Policy and Procedures ■ System Access Requirements and Review Process	7. SoD and Systems Access 11. Payroll Control Function	■ Number and Value of Payroll Payment Issues and Errors Identified and Mitigated
7. Payroll Exceptions. Detailed withholdings and payments may not agree to the recorded withholdings and payments, which will require considerable time, resources and money to resolve.	■ Payroll Exception Handling Process	11. Payroll Payment Control Function 13. Nonwage Payments	■ Number and Value of Payroll Payment Issues and Errors Identified and Mitigated ■ Number and Value of Payroll Exception Payments

Process: Payroll			
Subprocess: Payroll Payment			
Process Risk	**Recommended Policies**	**Internal Controls**	**KPIs**
8. Payroll Reconciliation and Reporting. Detailed withholdings and payments may not agree to the recorded withholdings and payments, which will require considerable time, resources and money to resolve.	■ Payroll Reconciliation Procedures	11. Payroll Control Function 17. Recording in Accounting Records	■ Number and Value of Payroll Payment Issues and Errors Identified and Mitigated ■ Number and Value of Payroll Exception Payments
9. Unclaimed Wages. Unclaimed wages may not be identified. Unclaimed paychecks are a special kind of unclaimed property. If you are sitting on unclaimed paychecks, you (the employer) are legally bound by state law to return any un-cashed paychecks to the state where the person last worked. You can be fined or penalized if you don't return the check, even if the person can't be found.	■ Unclaimed Wage Procedures	11. Payroll Control Function 12. Unclaimed Wages	■ Number and Value of Unclaimed Wages (By State)
10. Inaccurate Financial Statements. Inaccurate information may be input into the GL, resulting in misstated financial statements.	■ Financial Close Process ■ SoD Policy and Procedures ■ System Access Requirements and Review Process ■ Payroll Reconciliation Process	11. Payroll Control Function 17. Recording in Accounting Records	■ Number and Value of Pre-Close and Post-Close Adjustments

 ## 4.3 REPORTING, METRICS, AND ANALYTICS

Reporting, Metrics, and Analytics Process Overview

Payroll metrics measure your payroll process. Metrics are numeric indicators of how well your payroll process is doing. Every business uses different payroll metrics. You should use payroll KPIs that meet your business's needs. Below are suggestions for payroll metrics that might help your business.

Reporting, Metrics, and Analytics Process Flow

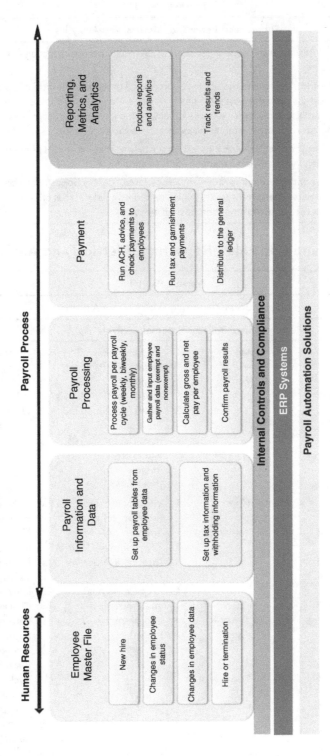

Table of Controls – Reporting, Metrics, and Analytics

Process: Payroll
Subprocess: Reporting, Metrics, and Analytics

1. Visibility of Payroll Results and Payment Trends. Payroll results are tracked, analyzed, and reported to business stakeholders.

2. Payroll Process Metrics. Implement metrics to report payroll process results, identify process improvements, and address payment issues in a timely manner. Metrics should focus on cost, process efficiency, internal controls, and customer services impacts to the payments process. Metrics should be organized by cost, process efficiency, internal customers and customer service.

3. Develop a Reporting Process. Develop a reporting process so that the results of metrics and analytics are reported and acted upon in a predictable manner – at least monthly.

4. Root-Cause Analysis and Process Improvement Procedures. Identify opportunities to improve the process based on root-cause analysis of results, trends, and benchmarks. Focus on how to resolve employee payment issues, reduce cost, and implement process efficiencies.

Table of Risks and Controls – Reporting, Metrics, and Analytics

Process: Payroll			
Subprocess: Reporting, Metrics, and Analytics			
Process Risk	Recommended Policies	Internal Controls	KPIs
1. Payroll Process Anomalies and Trends. Opportunities to address payroll process payment problems may result in inaccurate employee payments and significant HR issues.	■ Payroll Reporting Process ■ Payroll Metrics	1. Visibility of Payroll Results and Payment Trends 2. Payroll Process Metrics 3. Develop a Reporting Process 4. Root-Cause Analysis and Process Improvement Procedures	■ Number and Percentage of Payroll Issues Identified and Stopped ■ Value of Cost Savings Opportunities Identified in the Payroll Process
2. Lack of Visibility of Payroll Process Results. The results and impact of the payroll process and resulting employee payments are not reported or acted upon and risks to the process are not identified nor acted upon. Key process issues may be undetected for a significant period of time.	■ Payroll Reporting Process ■ Payroll Metrics	1. Visibility of Payroll Results and Payment Trends 2. Payroll Process Metrics 3. Develop a Reporting Process 4. Root-Cause Analysis and Process Improvement Procedures	■ Percentage and Number of Fraudulent Payments ■ Number of Fraudulent Employees ■ Percentage Adherence to Payroll Policies ■ Percentage of Manual Checks Issued ■ Percentage of ACH Payments Issued ■ Percentage of Nonwage Payments Issued ■ Cycle Time to Process a Payroll Transaction ■ Unapproved Items in Time and Attendance Records in Workflow ■ Value and Aging of Unclaimed Wages

Process: Payroll			
Subprocess: Reporting, Metrics, and Analytics			
Process Risk	**Recommended Policies**	**Internal Controls**	**KPIs**
3. Payroll Reporting Process. Visibility of analytics and metrics is lost. KPIs may be undetected for a significant period of time, increasing costs of payroll processing.	■ Payroll Reporting Process ■ Payroll Metrics	1. Visibility of Payroll Results and Payment Trends 2. Payroll Process Metrics 3. Develop a Reporting Process 4. Root-Cause Analysis and Process Improvement Procedures	■ Percentage and Number of Fraudulent Payments ■ Number of Fraudulent Employees ■ Percentage Adherence to Payroll Policies ■ Percentage of Manual Checks Issued ■ Percentage of ACH Payments Issued ■ Percentage of Non-wage Payments Issued ■ Cycle Time to Process a Payroll Transaction ■ Unapproved Items in Time and Attendance Records in Workflow ■ Value and Aging of Unclaimed Wages
4. Action on Payment Anomalies. Opportunities to address or implement additional controls for payment anomalies are not identified.	■ Payroll Reporting Process ■ Payroll Metrics	1. Visibility of Payroll Results and Payment Trends 2. Payroll Process Metrics 3. Develop a Reporting Process 4. Root-Cause Analysis and Process Improvement Procedures	■ Percentage and Number of Fraudulent Payments ■ Number of Fraudulent Employees ■ Percentage Adherence to Payroll Policies ■ Percentage of Manual Checks Issued ■ Percentage of ACH Payments Issued ■ Percentage of Non-wage Payments Issued ■ Cycle Time to Process a Payroll Transaction ■ Unapproved Items in Time and Attendance Records in Workflow ■ Value and Aging of Unclaimed Wages

CHAPTER TWELVE

Order-to-Cash

 OVERVIEW

O2C and AR are important business processes within a corporation. O2C is a process that includes everything that needs to be done when a customer places an order with a company. AR is one of a series of accounting transactions dealing with the billing of a customer for goods and services received and is foundational to the O2C process

In most business entities the AR function is accomplished by generating an invoice and mailing or electronically delivering it to the customer, who in turn must pay it within an established timeframe called credit or payment terms. Terms of payment are established in the customer contract.

 5.0 ORDER-TO-CASH

The diagram below provides an overview of the O2C process.

Order-to-Cash Process Flow

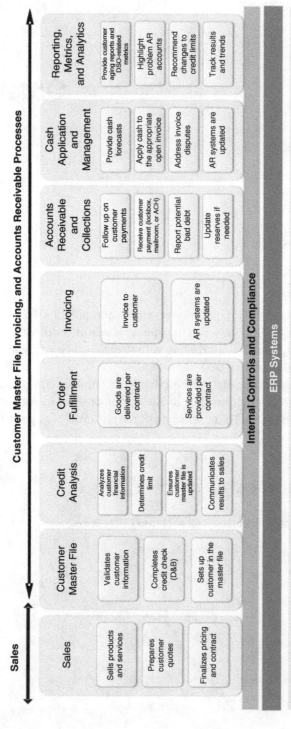

 **5.1 SALES**

Sales Process Overview

A sales process is a set of repeatable steps that a sales person takes to take a prospective buyer from the early stage of awareness to a closed sale. Simply put, it is a potential customer's journey from realizing they have a need for a product or service to making an actual purchase. And since the sales process is a journey for a prospect, it is a road map for a sales person.

Typically a sales process consists of five to seven steps, as reflected in the process flow diagram below: prospecting, preparation, approach, presentation, handling objections, closing, and follow-up.

Sales Process Flow

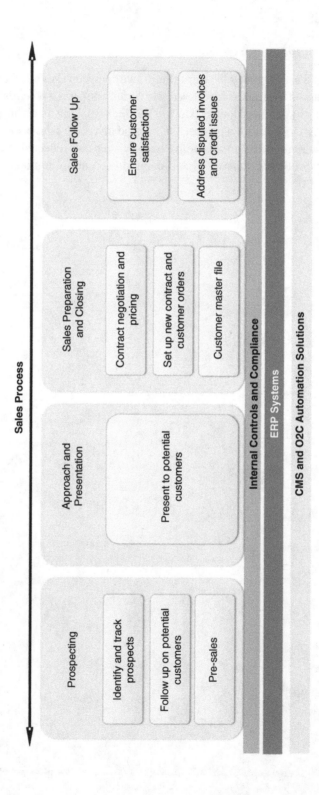

Table of Controls – Sales

Process: Order-to-Cash

Subprocess: Sales

1. Sales Contracts. Sales contracts must be standardized, clearly written, and supportable, with the terms of the sale completely documented. The contracts should be financially and operationally sound (achievable) and strategically aligned. Authorization to draft, modify, approve, and sign contracts must be clearly defined in accordance with company policy. Legal counsel and business development must review contracts where appropriate to assure that the organization is entering into a correct and suitable contract and that it is not assuming liability for the negligence, errors, or omissions of another party.

2. Sales Contract Review and Administration. All sales contracts must be reviewed for product/service availability and administrative, financial, and performance feasibility and communicated to those responsible for implementation and follow up (e.g. pricing, terms and conditions, onboarding, implementation, etc.). All sales contracts must be filed, readily accessible, and safeguarded appropriately using a manual or automated contract management system. Compliance reviews must be performed periodically so potential losses are recognized. Oral/side agreements in lieu of a sales contract are not authorized.

3. Pricing Controls. Pricing controls are needed to ensure all international contracts include detailed pricing and monetary conversion schedules. Changes to contract terms must be communicated to all impacted operational organizations.

4. Third-Party Contracts. The process for the receipt of information to validate or support contractual pricing procedures from third parties must be properly documented.

5. Termination of Contracts. Standard and consistent terminology, approved by legal counsel, should be used in contracts.

6. International Contracts. For international contracts, all international policies, tax laws, and jurisdictional guidelines will be followed.

7. Contract Renewals. Contract renewal discussions should occur with customers in advance of the contract expiration date. A process should exist to ensure all contracts are current.

8. Pricing Policy. A documented pricing policy as well as specific pricing actions must be approved by global business unit and local business unit management and reviewed with pricing and business development for administrative feasibility. Local legal staff must review for compliance with local pricing regulations and global pricing strategies (price discrimination, parallel trade, etc.). Pricing strategies must be consistent in determining global market prices and preestablished minimum margin targets for all products. Agreement must be obtained from executive management if a decision is made to forego such minimums when the overall contract maintains certain margin minimums. Where relevant, pricing must be viewed along with promotional programs, terms and conditions, and the like to ensure the overall offering to the customer is appropriate. Terms and conditions included in a contract will be supportable in the billing systems or through the contract billing organization.

9. Pricing Strategies. Pricing strategies must be consistent in determining global market prices and preestablished minimum margin targets for all products. Where relevant, pricing must be viewed along with promotional programs, terms and conditions, and the like to ensure the overall offering to the customer is appropriate. Pricing strategy will be developed by the following organizations:

a. Marketing will determine individual product pricing ("established pricing"), ensuring competitive positioning and adherence to applicable minimum margins

b. Promotional pricing will be reviewed and approved by both marketing and business units

c. Custom (special) pricing for individual contracts determined by business units, within predetermined minimum margin targets

d. Legal/regulatory staff will be responsible for reviewing/approving any guide and/or contract changes prior to sending to customer

Process: Order-to-Cash
Subprocess: Sales

10. Discounts. A price must be set for each product with a clear set of price discounts established for each customer or well-defined customer group. Authorization and processes to establish or change pricing must be clearly defined with appropriate segregation of duties. Those responsible for the price list should collectively review material list price moves and decide on material pricing actions regularly. Where pricing is dependent on meeting volume commitments, the local legal staff must be consulted.

11. Domestic Pricing. Domestic pricing must be consistent with local tax laws. International pricing – exit pricing to foreign trade customers (export to trade), transfer pricing to foreign subsidiaries (export to subsidiaries), and the like – must comply with domestic and international tax guidelines as well as the organization's policy.

12. Payment Terms. Standard payment terms by operating unit by country must be extended to customers or classes of customers. Exceptions to standard payment terms must only be made in concert with individual customer pricing decisions, including compliance with local laws, and impact to the operating unit global pricing strategy. Changes or exceptions to standard terms require approval in accordance with policy.

13. Special Bid Pricing. Where special bid pricing is practiced, local legal counsel should be consulted to ensure local laws and regulations sanction the practice and to ensure appropriate records of such pricing are generated and maintained. Any special pricing developed needs to:

a. Follow appropriate evaluation within the business units
b. Adhere to customer-specific (predetermined) minimum margin targets; and
c. Use an appropriate financial model and cost elements that have been reviewed and approved by Finance.

14. Sales goal structure. Sales goal structure must not encourage end-of-period discounts, which should be limited in use. Up-front bonuses/credits to customers should be limited in use. Selling of the most profitable products should be encouraged. Selling at established prices, versus special pricing beyond thresholds, should be encouraged.

15. Nonstandard contractual pricing. Nonstandard contractual pricing and discounting should be avoided where possible. Where this is required (e.g. global accounts, major accounts, etc.), there must be business development and legal review. Appropriate administrative processes must be established.

16. Special Pricing. Special pricing should have direct linkage to compensation, in that any pricing deviation from established pricing should have a direct impact to a sales representative's commission.

17. Customer-Specific Pricing. Customer-specific pricing must follow an approval process within each operating unit (e.g. sales, finance, legal, and unit management) depending on the existence of predetermined variables that may result in potentially adverse terms and conditions.

Table of Risks and Controls – Sales

	Process: Order-to-Cash		
	Subprocess: Sales		
Process Risk	Recommended Policies	Internal Controls	KPIs
1. **Nonadherence to Customer Contracts.** Lost, incorrectly recorded, and/or misappropriated sales contracts may not be identified and corrected in a timely manner. Customer dissatisfaction and the assessment of fines and/or penalties may result. The company may be operating under an expired contract.	■ Sales Contract Policies ■ Sales Contract Review and Administration	1. Sales Contracts 2. Sales Contract Review and Administration 3. Pricing Controls 4. Third-Party Contracts 5. Termination of Contracts 6. International Contracts 7. Contract Renewal	■ Customer Satisfaction Ratings ■ Customer Contract Accuracy Percentage ■ Percentage of Billing Errors ■ Billing Accuracy Percentage ■ Percentage of Pricing Errors ■ Days Sales Outstanding (DSO)
2. **Company Liability.** The company could be held responsible for the negligence, errors, or omissions of another party, resulting in financial loss to its shareholders. If the contract is not consistent regarding liability provisions, it can be unenforceable.	■ Sales Contract Policies ■ Sales Contract Review and Administration	1. Sales Contracts 2. Sales Contract Review and Administration 3. Pricing Controls 4. Third-Party Contracts 5. Termination of Contracts 6. International Contracts 7. Contract Renewal 14. Sales Goal Structure	■ Customer Satisfaction Ratings ■ Number of Cases Reported ■ Percentage of Billing Errors ■ Billing Accuracy Percentage ■ Percentage of Pricing Errors ■ DSO
3. **Inability to Deliver Product or Service.** Inability to deliver product or service will result in customer service issues and damage to the company's reputation. Financial losses may occur.	■ Sales Contract Policies ■ Sales Contract Review and Administration	1. Sales Contracts 2. Sales Contract Review and Administration 3. Pricing Controls 4. Third-Party Contracts 5. Termination of Contracts 6. International Contracts 7. Contract Renewal 14. Sales Goal Structure	■ Customer Satisfaction Ratings ■ Product Delivery Cycle Time ■ DSO
4. **Noncompliance with Legally Binding Contractual Terms and Conditions.** Contract noncompliance and the inability to deliver product or service will result in customer service issues and damage to the company's reputation. Financial losses may occur.	■ Sales Contract Policies ■ Sales Contract Review and Administration	1. Sales Contracts 2. Sales Contract Review and Administration 3. Pricing Controls 4. Third-Party Contracts 5. Termination of Contracts 6. International Contracts 7. Contract Renewal	■ Customer Satisfaction Ratings ■ Customer Contract Accuracy Percentage ■ Percentage of Billing Errors ■ Billing Accuracy Percentage ■ Percentage of Pricing Errors ■ DSO

Process: Order-to-Cash			
Subprocess: Sales			
Process Risk	**Recommended Policies**	**Internal Controls**	**KPIs**
5. Underreported or Inflated Revenue. Contract and pricing issues impact revenue reporting accuracy.	■ Pricing Policy ■ Customer Invoice and Pricing Reviews	8. Pricing Policy 9. Pricing Strategy 10. Discounts 11. Domestic Pricing 12. Payment Terms 13. Special Bid Pricing 16. Special Pricing 17. Customer-Specific Pricing	■ Number and Value of Revenue Account Adjustments per Period
6. Misstated Internal Management Reporting and Forecasting. Contract and pricing issues impact internal reporting and revenue forecasting accuracy.	■ Sales Contract Policies ■ Sales Contract Review and Administration ■ Pricing Policy ■ Customer Invoice and Pricing Reviews	1. Sales Contracts 2. Sales Contract Review and Administration 3. Pricing Controls 4. Third-Party Contracts 5. Termination of Contracts 6. International Contracts 7. Contract Renewal 14. Sales Goal Structure	■ Number and Value of Revenue Account Adjustments per Period
7. Delayed Payment. Payment may be delayed due to contract inaccuracies and issues.	■ Sales Contract Policies ■ Sales Contract Review and Administration ■ Pricing Policy ■ Customer Invoice and Pricing Reviews	8. Pricing Policy 9. Pricing Strategy 10. Discounts 11. Domestic Pricing 12. Payment Terms 13. Special Bid Pricing 16. Special Pricing 17. Customer-Specific Pricing	■ Customer Satisfaction Ratings ■ Customer Contract Accuracy Percentage ■ Percentage of Billing Errors ■ Billing Accuracy Percentage ■ Percentage of Pricing Errors ■ DSO ■ Collection Effectiveness Index (CEI)
8. Inaccurate Customer Pricing. Inaccurate customer pricing will impact revenue and the accuracy of customer invoices and revenue reporting.	■ Sales Contract Policies ■ Sales Contract Review and Administration ■ Pricing Policy ■ Customer Invoice and Pricing Reviews	8. Pricing Policy 9. Pricing Strategy 10. Discounts 11. Domestic Pricing 12. Payment Terms 13. Special Bid Pricing 14. Sales Goal Structure 16. Special Pricing 17. Customer-Specific Pricing	■ Customer Satisfaction Ratings ■ Customer Contract Accuracy Percentage ■ Percentage of Billing Errors ■ Billing Accuracy Percentage ■ Percentage of Pricing Errors ■ DSO ■ CEI

Process: Order-to-Cash			
Subprocess: Sales			
Process Risk	Recommended Policies	Internal Controls	KPIs
9. Customer Satisfaction Issues. Inability to deliver product or service will result in customer service issues and damage to the company's reputation. Financial losses may occur.	∎ Sales Contract Policies ∎ Sales Contract Review and Administration ∎ Pricing Policy ∎ Customer Invoice and Pricing Reviews	8. Pricing Policy 9. Pricing Strategy 10. Discounts 11. Domestic Pricing 12. Payment Terms 13. Special Bid Pricing 14. Sales goal structure must not encourage end-of-period discounts 16. Special Pricing 17. Customer-Specific Pricing	∎ Customer Satisfaction Ratings ∎ DSO

5.2 CUSTOMER MASTER FILE

Customer Master File Process Overview

The customer master file is used to maintain information in the accounting database that is unique to each customer. Correct data will ensure that customer information is accurate and that payments are accurately applied. In fact, customer data is an essential element of a strong risk-management foundation. The credit risk manager needs to understand with precision the entity to which the firm is exposed. Customer identity is vital to compliance with KYC guidelines and AML regulations. Operational risk management, focusing as it does on errors and fraud, is undermined by customer data that is stale or incorrect.

Examples of the information contained in the master file are:

- Customer name
- Customer identification number
- Customer address
- Contact name and phone number
- Sales representative name
- Customer tax identification number
- Customer credit limit
- Customer credit score
- Customer payment terms
- Customer ship-via settings
- Past due notification flag
- Monthly statement flag
- Taxable flag
- Tax exempt ID number

Customer Master File Process Flow

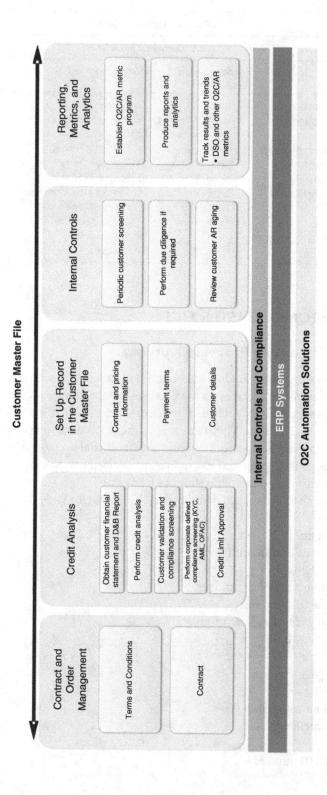

Table of Controls – Customer Master File

Process: Order-to-Cash
Subprocess: Customer Master File

1. **SoD and Systems Access.** Control of the customer master file is established to ensure that the file is safeguarded, records cannot be altered, and fictitious customers are not set up for the purpose of diverting product or services.

2. **Customer Data Safeguards.** Customer and product/service master data must be accurate, with the appropriate safeguards to ensure the data is secured and protected from unauthorized access.

3. **Customer Master File Compliance.** A critical challenge in onboarding a prospective customer is accurate identification of parties (obligors, beneficial owners, etc.) This is foundational for KYC and other due diligence and for effective Bank Secrecy Act compliance. Regulators have formalized this process by requiring the implementation of customer identification programs (a statutory requirement under the PATRIOT Act) and have included both identification and hierarchy management in single-counterparty credit limits (SCCL) rules. False transaction alert positives and undetected negatives that may arise from misidentification of a customer undermine compliance and suspicious activity report (SAR) filing processes.

4. **Credit Review.** All new customers must go through appropriate credit reviews/financial approvals prior to installation of service and/or execution of sales contracts.

5. **Order and Contract Evidence.** A business customer's request for service is evidenced by a signed agreement. In cases where a customer's contract has expired, service will be provided on a month-to-month basis in accordance with company policy.

6. **Order Capture.** The service order must be obtained from the customer and submitted in a timely manner to an authorized agent of the corporation via company-approved order submission guidelines. The service order must meet standards of accuracy and completeness before it can be processed. Orders must be fully edited before they are released to production and/or shipping, as appropriate.

7. **Contract and Pricing Verification.** Verification that a valid contract exists must be performed prior to fulfilling a service order. Any order subject to contract pricing must have pricing attached prior to entry of the order to a billing system.

Table of Risks and Controls – Customer Master File

Process: Order-to-Cash			
Subprocess: Customer Master File			
Process Risk	Recommended Policies	Internal Controls	KPIs
1. SoD issues. Such issues may enable an employee to set up a fictitious customer and divert products and services to that customer.	■ SoD ■ Data Ownership ■ Systems Access	1. SoD and Systems Access 2. Customer Data Safeguards 3. Customer Master File Compliance	■ Number of SoD Reviews Performed ■ Number of SoD Conflicts Identified ■ Number of SoD Conflicts Mitigated ■ Number of Systems Access Reviews Performed ■ Number of Systems Access Issues Identified ■ Number of Systems Access Issues Mitigated

Process: Order-to-Cash			
Subprocess: Customer Master File			
Process Risk	**Recommended Policies**	**Internal Controls**	**KPIs**
2. Lack of Credit Worthiness. If a credit review is not conducted there is a significant credit risk that a client may not satisfy the company's credit extension criteria, which may result in incorrect AR balances and costly collection efforts. Invalid customers are reflected in the customer master file.	■ Credit Reviews	4. Credit Review 5. Order Capture	■ Number of Credit Reviews Performed ■ Number of Changes to Credit Limits ■ Number of Customer Accounts Denied Credit
3. Incorrect Customer Invoicing and AR Balances. Inappropriate and inaccurate customer balances with credit checks result in inaccurate AR balances.	■ SoD ■ Data Ownership ■ Systems Access ■ CSA	1. SoD and Systems Access 2. Customer Data Safeguards 3. Customer Master File Compliance 4. Credit Review	■ Number of Active Customers in the Customer Master File ■ Number of Customers Submitting Payments Electronically ■ Number of Controls Reviewed ■ Cycle Time for the Remediation of Control Issues
4. Inappropriate Access to Sensitive Information. Intentional or accidental update to the customer master file could impact safeguarding of assets and cause data corruption.	■ Systems Access	1. SoD and Systems Access 2. Customer Data Safeguards 3. Customer Master File Compliance.	■ Number of Systems Access Issues Identified ■ Number of Systems Access Issues Mitigated
5. Customer Master Compliance. Compliance requirements, such as KYC and SCCL, are not adhered to, which may result in significant fines.	■ Compliance Reviews ■ CSA	1. SoD and Systems Access 2. Customer Data Safeguards 3. Customer Master File Compliance	■ Number of Active Customers in the Customer Master File ■ Number of Customers Submitting Payments Electronically ■ Number of Controls Reviewed ■ Cycle Time for the Remediation of Control Issues ■ Value of Compliance Fines ■ Cost of Compliance Remediation

Process: Order-to-Cash			
Subprocess: Customer Master File			
Process Risk	**Recommended Policies**	**Internal Controls**	**KPIs**
6. Inaccurate ERP Information. Inaccurately input information in ERP system may result in untimely payment to the supplier.	■ SoD ■ Data Ownership ■ Systems Access ■ CSA	1. SoD and Systems Access 2. Customer Data Safeguards 3. Customer Master File Compliance	■ Number of Active Customers in the Customer Master File ■ Number of Customers Submitting Payments Electronically ■ Number of Controls Reviewed ■ Cycle Time for the Remediation of Control Issues
7. Lack of Valid Customer Orders and Contracts. If a customer record is established without a valid contract or order, this situation could result in fraud or the diversion of products and services.	■ Customer Master Policies and Procedures ■ Order/Contract Validation ■ CSA	5. Order and Contract Evidence 6. Order Capture 7. Contract and Pricing Verification	■ Number of Active Customers in the Customer Master File ■ Number of Customers Submitting Payments Electronically ■ Number of Controls Reviewed ■ Cycle Time for the Remediation of Control Issues

5.3   CREDIT ANALYSIS

Credit Analysis Process Overview

The credit analysis process is intended to help a company evaluate the risks of allowing customers to defer payments for goods and services to a later date. The risk is that payment for those goods or services may be late or may not be collected. If a customer pays late on a regular basis, a credit hold or reduction in the credit line may be initiated.

There are a number of ways to evaluate a customer's credit. Credit books, such as Dun & Bradstreet (D&B), are available for large, established companies. Other references are Hoovers and www.sec.gov. Bank references, financial statements, and payment history with other companies allowing credit are all sources of information available to help evaluate the risk of granting credit to a given customer.

A potential customer's credit rating or financial health and history are then used to determine payment terms. Terms may include a certain amount of cash paid up front with the remainder to be paid at a later date. Payment may be deferred for 10, 20, or 30 days depending on the customer's credit rating. Many customers pay their suppliers using 45-day payment terms. Discounts may be granted for early payment. In some instances actual payment may be deferred until a service contract has been completely fulfilled or until a transaction involving multiple shipments over time is complete.

Credit Analysis Process Flow

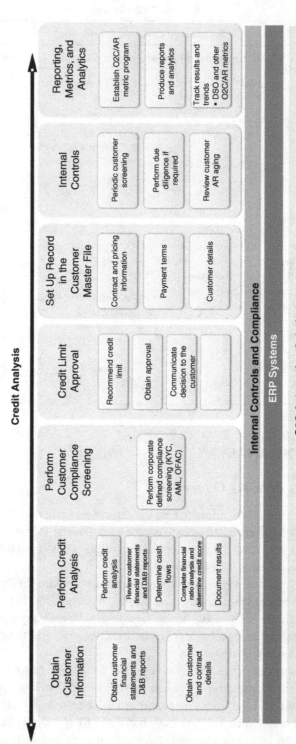

Table of Controls – Credit Analysis

Process: Order-to-Cash
Subprocess: Credit Analysis

1. **SoD and Systems Access.** Individuals with system capability to make entries in the AR subsidiary ledger (e.g. cash application, account write-offs, sales concessions, and sales discounts) must not have system capability to invoice customers, issue credit memos, or adjust the GL. If this separation is not possible, compensating controls must be documented, implemented, and followed.

2. **Credit Policies and Procedures.** Formal, written credit procedures (e.g. establishment of credit terms, reserves for bad debt, promissory notes, direct loans, and indemnified transactions) should be established and implemented by credit and collections and approved in accordance with company policy. All credit policies must follow the Fair Credit Reporting Act, Equal Credit Opportunity Act, and state-required guidelines as applicable.

3. **Credit Limits.** Credit limits must be established for each business customer that is granted credit. Credit limits must be recorded in an information system so that customers are routinely monitored to verify that their usage level remains within established credit limits.

4. **Credit Limit Approval.** A review of approved credit limits and the current receivable balance must be made before additional orders are accepted for a customer. Credit management approval is required before credit is extended in excess of approved limits. When extended credit is granted, a timeline should be established with criteria for an extension/reduction process when the period expires or criteria are not met.

5. **Proof of Credit Analysis.** Established business customer credit limits must be documented, filed, and reviewed for adequacy at least annually. Where appropriate, adjustments to credit limits must be made in accordance with approved departmental policies/procedures. Business customer credit history must be maintained. Any change in ownership or entity assignment or requests for additional orders or increases of usage beyond the customer's assigned credit limit requires approval of credit management. Actual customer credit experience must be compared to assumptions in predictive model to ensure actual results are aligned with expectations.

6. **Customer Payment Terms.** Contract, tariff, or the book guide defines standard business customer payment terms. Exceptions to standard terms of sale require credit management approval and may also require approval of other levels of management.

7. **Credit Administration.** Credit administration must be independent of the order entry, billing, GL, and sales functions.

8. **Customer Refunds.** Where refunds are not handled as credits, a process must be established to ensure the account is current. Cash refunds should be initiated by the credit management office, authorized by unit controller (or delegate), paid by AP, and reconciled by the accounting department.

9. **Payment Terms.** Deviation from standard payment terms requires prior credit management approval.

10. **Disputes.** Guidelines must be developed and monitored for dispute detection, tracing, and resolution. Criteria and approval for concession must be developed and monitored.

11. **Confidential Information.** All information exchanged for credit purposes must be held strictly confidential, remain within credit management, and must be used for credit purposes only.

12. **Metrics and Reporting.** Metrics must be established and monitored to measure average time to process and number of items greater than the defined interval.

13. **Credit Management.** Credit management is responsible for the tracking and monitoring of all customer surety held.

14. **Customer Deductions.** Customer deductions (debit memos) are created by the billing department, approved by Finance, and applied by the appropriate Finance function.

Table of Risks and Controls – Credit Analysis

Process: Order-to-Cash			
Subprocess: Credit Analysis			
Process Risk	**Recommended Policies**	**Internal Controls**	**KPIs**
1. SoD and Systems Access Violations. Improper system access rights could result in unapproved changes to AR accounts.	■ Credit Policies and Procedures	1. SoD and Systems Access	■ Number of SoD Reviews Performed ■ Number of SoD Conflicts Identified ■ Number of SoD Conflicts Mitigated ■ Number of Systems Access Reviews Performed ■ Number of Systems Access Issues Identified ■ Number of Systems Access Issues Mitigated
2. Inconsistent and/or Inadequate Credit Review May Be Completed. Product or service may be sold to an unauthorized customer or to an unacceptable credit risk, resulting in uncollectible accounts.	■ Credit Policies and Procedures	2. Credit Policies and Procedures 3. Credit Limits 4. Credit Limit Approval 5. Proof of Credit Analysis 6. Customer Payment Terms 7. Credit Administration 13. Credit Management	■ Number of Credit Reviews Performed ■ Number of Changes to Credit Limits ■ Number of Customer Accounts Denied Credit ■ DSO ■ CEI
3. Lost Revenue. Revenue may be lost due to poor credit decisions.	■ Credit Policies and Procedures	2. Credit Policies and Procedures 3. Credit Limits 4. Credit Limit Approval 5. Proof of Credit Analysis 6. Customer Payment Terms 7. Credit Administration 13. Credit Management	■ Number of Credit Reviews Performed ■ Number of Changes to Credit Limits ■ Number of Customer Accounts Denied Credit ■ DSO ■ CEI
4. Increase in Cost of Collections. Product or service may be sold to an unauthorized customer or to an unacceptable credit risk, resulting in uncollectible accounts.	■ Credit Policies and Procedures ■ AR Reporting and Metrics Program	2. Credit Policies and Procedures 3. Credit Limits 4. Credit Limit Approval 5. Proof of Credit Analysis 6. Customer Payment Terms 7. Credit Administration 13. Credit Management	■ CEI

Process: Order-to-Cash			
Subprocess: Credit Analysis			
5. Uncollectable AR Accounts. Products and services may be sold to an unauthorized customer or to an unacceptable credit risk, resulting in uncollectible accounts	■ Credit Policies and Procedures ■ AR Reporting and Metrics Program	2. Credit Policies and Procedures 3. Credit Limits 4. Credit Limit Approval 5. Proof of Credit Analysis 6. Customer Payment Terms 7. Credit Administration 13. Credit Management	■ AR Aging ■ Value of Write-offs per Period
6. Intentional Alteration of Receivable Records/Invoices Could Occur. AR records could be altered to hide a fraudulent transaction. Credit analysis results could be falsified and confidential information could be shared inappropriately.	■ Credit Policies and Procedures ■ AR Reporting and Metrics Program ■ CSA	1. SoD and Systems Access	■ Number of SoD Reviews Performed ■ Number of SoD Conflicts Identified ■ Number of SoD Conflicts Mitigated ■ Number of Systems Access Reviews Performed ■ Number of Systems Access Issues Identified ■ Number of Systems Access Issues Mitigated
7. Customer Refunds. Company funds may be disbursed to customers with past-due balances or with inadequate surety.	■ Customer Refund Policies and Procedures ■ AR Reporting and Metrics Program	8. Customer Refunds	■ Value of Customer Refunds per Period ■ Customer Refunds Issues by Reason
8. Misstated Internal Management Reporting and Forecasting. Improper credit analysis can impact internal reporting and revenue forecasting accuracy.	■ Credit Policies and Procedures ■ AR Reporting and Metrics Program ■ CSA	2. Credit Policies and Procedures 3. Credit Limits 4. Credit Limit Approval 5. Proof of Credit Analysis 6. Customer Payment Terms 7. Credit Administration 12. Metrics and Reporting 13. Credit Management	■ Number of Management Adjustments per Period ■ Cash-Flow Forecast and Reporting Accuracy
9. Customer Satisfaction Issues. Due to inaccurate credit analysis, the inability to deliver product or service will result in customer service issues and damage to the company's reputation. Financial losses may occur.	■ Customer Satisfaction Surveys	2. Credit Policies and Procedures 3. Credit Limits 4. Credit Limit Approval 5. Proof of Credit Analysis 6. Customer Payment Terms 7. Credit Administration 10. Disputes 12. Metrics and Reporting 13. Credit Management 14. Customer Deductions	■ Average Customer Satisfaction Rating

5.4 ORDER FULFILLMENT AND INVOICING

Order Fulfillment and Invoicing Process Overview

Broadly defined, the term *order fulfillment* refers to everything a company does between receiving an order from a customer (the point-of-sale) and placing the product in the customer's hands. Unless you actively participate in the fulfilment process, you're probably not fully aware of what a successful delivery requires and how companies manage to accomplish this task.

Order fulfilment can be quite complex and varies widely for different kinds of businesses. For example, a fast-food restaurant can receive an order, place the requested food items in a bag, and deliver them to the customer within 60 seconds. Other industries might not be quite as fast. Furniture manufacturers, for instance, often wait until having an actual order from a customer before they actually begin making a product. This means it can take several weeks until the final product arrives at the client's door.

Order Fulfillment and Invoicing Process Flow

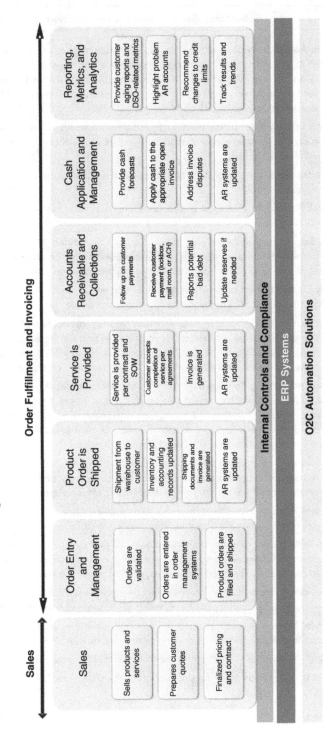

Order Fulfillment and Invoicing

Sales

Sales
- Sells products and services
- Prepares customer quotes
- Finalized pricing and contract

Order Entry and Management
- Orders are validated
- Orders are entered in order management systems
- Product orders are filled and shipped

Product Order is Shipped
- Shipment from warehouse to customer
- Inventory and accounting records updated
- Shipping documents and invoice are generated
- AR systems are updated

Service is Provided
- Service is provided per contract and SOW
- Customer accepts completion of service per agreements
- Invoice is generated
- AR systems are updated

Accounts Receivable and Collections
- Follow up on customer payments
- Receive customer payment (lockbox, mail room, or ACH)
- Reports potential bad debt
- Update reserves if needed

Cash Application and Management
- Provide cash forecasts
- Apply cash to the appropriate open invoice
- Address invoice disputes
- AR systems are updated

Reporting, Metrics, and Analytics
- Provide customer aging reports and DSO-related metrics
- Highlight problem AR accounts
- Recommend changes to credit limits
- Track results and trends

Internal Controls and Compliance

ERP Systems

O2C Automation Solutions

Table of Controls – Order Fulfillment and Invoicing

Process: Order-to-Cash
Subprocess: Order Fulfillment and Invoicing

1. SoD and Systems Access. Individuals with system capability to make entries in the AR subsidiary ledger (e.g. cash application, account write-offs, sales concessions, and sales discounts) must not have system capability to invoice customers, issue credit memos, or adjust the GL. The billing function must be independent of the service delivery and AR functions. If this separation is not possible, compensating controls must be documented, implemented, and followed.

2. Accounting. Accounting for sales transactions is a financial responsibility and must not be delegated to other functional areas. Local financial/operational management must ensure invoice preparation is adequately controlled and maintained.

3. Nonstandard Transactions. Unusual or nonstandard sales transactions should be reviewed by Finance to determine proper revenue recognition.

4. Revenue Reversal. Revenue reversal must be recognized for any billing credit adjustments to previously invoiced revenue (including rebates, etc.).

5. Right of Return. Sales with a substantial right of return should be avoided. However, should such sales occur, appropriate reserves should be established and revenue should not be recognized until the sales can be reviewed by a designated level of Finance to determine the timing for revenue recognition.

6. Contract Review. Contracts must be periodically reviewed to ensure terms and conditions are being met with respect to product/service provided, revenue recognition, and billing.

7. Reserves. Appropriate reserves should be established to cover estimated service outages, customer returns, or other customer allowances. These reserves must be periodically reviewed for adequacy. An appropriate reserve must be established for approved pricing reductions and associated outstanding claims. Nonstandard price protection terms must be approved in accordance with company policy.

8. Deferred Revenue Accounting Policies. Deferred revenue, accruals, clearing accounts, and deferred asset accounts must be reviewed and reconciled on a timely basis to ensure the accounts are current, complete, and accurate, and supported by the appropriate documentation. A procedure must be established to ensure amounts billed have in fact been earned. Where revenue has been deferred, a process must be established to ensure the deferred revenue is relieved when it is earned.

9. Billing Business Rules. All billing transactions must be prepared in a timely manner on the basis of authorized master file data and supporting documentation, service delivery, and acceptance criteria. All invoices must be prenumbered where the integrity of sequencing is not computer controlled.

10. Unbilled Accounts. Where accruals have been made for unbilled AR, a procedure must be established to ensure that when subsequent billings are generated, revenue is not recorded twice.

11. Cash Advances. A procedure must be established to ensure that cash advances received from customers are accrued to the extent that they have not been earned. When cash advances have been earned, revenue should be recognized and the liability for cash advances received should be relieved.

12. Accuracy of Invoices. Invoices must accurately reflect the services provided or goods shipped. Invoices, both manual and computer generated, should be reviewed for accuracy during the audit process.

13. Accurate Billing of Taxes. Sales, use, and/or VATs must be billed in accordance with local laws. Where tax is not billed, supporting documentation is required to support the customer's tax-exempt status.

14. Customer Pricing. All customers' pricing must match contract-negotiated rates.

15. Partial Shipments. Where a customer does not accept partial shipments, billing should be in agreement with the customer's PO.

Process: Order-to-Cash
Subprocess: Order Fulfillment and Invoicing

16. Invoice Distribution. Invoices must be sent directly to the customer. E-invoicing processes will provide additional controls and will expedite the payment and cash application process. If any adjustments are made outside of billing process (such as contractual adjustments), adjustments must be sent to AR to ensure adjusted invoice is reflected in the AR system. Blank invoice and credit memo stock must be safeguarded.

17. Billing Exceptions. All billing exceptions, such as no-charge invoices/line items, billing price overrides, credits and adjustments, and change orders must be approved in accordance with company policy.

18. Promotional Programs. Credits and adjustments associated with promotional programs, billing issues, and discounts of products must be only processed when the dispute has been investigated, proper documentation has been prepared, and authorization has been obtained from appropriate sales and finance groups depending on the nature of the adjustment. All discrepancies (e.g. unmatched documents) must be resolved in a timely manner. Credit memos must be prepared for all credits.

19. Credit Memos. Credit memo transactions must be numerically controlled and they should be accounted for, with their value properly accrued. Credit memos must be prenumbered where the integrity of sequencing is not computer controlled.

20. Billing Validations. Reviews will be conducted every processing period to include the items below. Appropriate and documented audit processes will be adhered to. All validation and auditing practices will be thoroughly documented. Invoices must accurately reflect the correct tariff or contractual pricing. All pricing/taxing must be audited and certified before moving to production and a process must exist to verify that pricing matches the legal source document (contract/tariff).

    a. Invoice to data feeds validation
    b. Account ID validation
    c. Pricing accuracy validation
    d. Contractual commitments compliance

21. Customer Inquiries. Inquiries pertaining to prior months' invoices will be documented and tracked. Periodic updates to the account team will be sent in a timely manner and will include complete information necessary for the account team to fully understand the issue.

22. Reporting. Reports identifying the number of invoices generated should be compared to the appropriate source to ensure invoices are generated for all customers. Edit/exception reports that identify invoices that do not print should be reviewed and investigated.

23. Third-Party Billing. Reconcile charges received from vendors to charges applied to customer accounts. Differences are investigated and reviewed.

Table of Risks and Controls – Order Fulfillment and Invoicing

Process: Order-to-Cash			
Subprocess: Order Fulfillment and Invoicing			
Process Risk	**Recommended Policies**	**Internal Controls**	**KPIs**
1. Incorrect Shipments. Shipments may be made to incorrect or unauthorized customers or to incorrect customer locations. Incorrect equipment or quantity of equipment may be shipped, or equipment may be shipped early, late, or in violation of export control and/or customs requirements.	▪ Order Fulfillment Processes and Controls	1. SoD and Systems Access 2. Accounting 3. Nonstandard Transactions 4. Revenue Reversal 5. Right of Return 6. Contract Review 14. Customer Pricing 15. Partial Shipments	▪ Average Customer Satisfaction Rating ▪ Percentage and Value of Inventory Control Issues
2. SoD and Systems Access. Intentional errors or misappropriation of assets could occur.	▪ SoD and Systems Access Controls	1. SoD and Systems Access	▪ Number of SoD Reviews Performed ▪ Number of SoD Conflicts Identified ▪ Number of SoD Conflicts Mitigated ▪ Number of Systems Access Reviews Performed ▪ Number of Systems Access Issues Identified ▪ Number of Systems Access Issues Mitigated
3. Incorrect Customer Billings. Equipment may have been shipped but not billed or recorded.	▪ Order Fulfillment Processes and Controls	9. Billing Business Rules 10. Unbilled Accounts 11. Cash Advances 12. Accuracy of Invoices 13. Accurate Billing of Taxes 16. Invoice Distribution 17. Billing Exceptions 18. Promotional Programs 19. Credit Memos 20. Billing Validations 21. Customer Inquiries 22. Reporting 23. Third-Party Billing	▪ Percentage and Value of Revenue Reversals ▪ CEI ▪ AR Aging ▪ Value of Write-offs per Period

Process: Order-to-Cash			
Subprocess: Order Fulfillment and Invoicing			
Process Risk	Recommended Policies	Internal Controls	KPIs
4. Accountability for Lost Customer Shipments. Customer shipments may be lost, misplaced, or misappropriated. The company may not recover for equipment lost by the carrier. Accountability over equipment shipped may be lost.	■ Order Fulfillment Processes and Controls ■ Logistics and Shipping Controls	4. Revenue Reversal 5. Right of Return	■ Percentage and Value of Revenue Reversals ■ CEI ■ AR Aging ■ Value of Write-offs per Period ■ Average Customer Satisfaction Rating
5. Unbilled Shipments. Unbilled and/or misappropriated shipments may not be identified.	■ Order Fulfillment Processes and Controls ■ Logistics and Shipping Controls	9. Billing Business Rules 10. Unbilled Accounts 11. Cash Advances 12. Accuracy of Invoices 13. Accurate Billing of Taxes 16. Invoice Distribution 17. Billing Exceptions 18. Promotional Programs 19. Credit Memos 20. Billing Validations 21. Customer Inquiries 22. Reporting 23. Third-Party Billing	■ Percentage and Value of Inventory Control Issues ■ Percentage and Value of Revenue Reversals ■ CEI ■ AR Aging ■ Value of Write-offs per Period ■ Average Customer Satisfaction Rating
6. Orders Not Shipped. Equipment that has been authorized for shipment may not have been shipped.	■ Order Fulfillment Processes and Controls ■ Logistics and Shipping Controls	9. Billing Business Rules 10. Unbilled Accounts 11. Cash Advances 12. Accuracy of Invoices 13. Accurate Billing of Taxes 16. Invoice Distribution 17. Billing Exceptions 18. Promotional Programs 19. Credit Memos 20. Billing Validations 21. Customer Inquiries 22. Reporting 23. Third-Party Billing	■ Percentage and Value of Inventory Control Issues ■ Percentage and Value of Revenue Reversals ■ CEI ■ AR Aging ■ Value of Write-offs per Period ■ Average Customer Satisfaction Rating

Process: Order-to-Cash			
Subprocess: Order Fulfillment and Invoicing			
Process Risk	**Recommended Policies**	**Internal Controls**	**KPIs**
7. Uncollectable AR Accounts. Products and services may be sold to an unauthorized customer or to an unacceptable credit risk, resulting in uncollectible accounts	■ Credit and Collection Procedures ■ AR Aging ■ Customer Segmentation	2. Accounting 3. Nonstandard Transactions 4. Revenue Reversal 5. Right of Return 6. Contract Review 14. Customer Pricing 15. Partial Shipments 22. Reporting	■ AR Aging by Customer ■ CEI ■ DSO
8. Intentional Alteration of Receivable Records/ Invoices Could Occur. AR records could be altered to hide a fraudulent transaction. Credit analysis results could be falsified and confidential information could be shared inappropriately.	■ SoD and Systems Access Controls	1. SoD and Systems Access	■ Number of SoD Reviews Performed ■ Number of SoD Conflicts Identified ■ Number of SoD Conflicts Mitigated ■ Number of Systems Access Reviews Performed ■ Number of Systems Access Issues Identified ■ Number of Systems Access Issues Mitigated
9. Customer Refunds. Company funds may be disbursed to customers with past-due balances or with inadequate surety.	■ Customer Refund Procedures	2. Accounting 3. Nonstandard Transactions 4. Revenue Reversal 5. Right of Return 6. Contract Review 14. Customer Pricing 15. Partial Shipments 22. Reporting	■ Average Customer Satisfaction Rating ■ AR Aging by Customer ■ CEI ■ DSO
10. Misstated Internal Management Reporting and Forecasting. Improper credit analysis can impact internal reporting and revenue forecasting accuracy.	■ Financial Closing Procedures and Cutoffs	2. Accounting 3. Nonstandard Transactions 4. Revenue Reversal 5. Right of Return 6. Contract Review 14. Customer Pricing 15. Partial Shipments 22. Reporting	■ Number and Value of Pre-Close and Post-Close Adjustments to the GL

Process: Order-to-Cash			
Subprocess: Order Fulfillment and Invoicing			
Process Risk	**Recommended Policies**	**Internal Controls**	**KPIs**
11. Delayed Payment. Payment may be delayed due to contract inaccuracies and issues.	■ Credit and Collection Procedures ■ Customer Segmentation	2. Accounting 3. Nonstandard Transactions 4. Revenue Reversal 5. Right of Return 6. Contract Review 14. Customer Pricing 15. Partial Shipments 22. Reporting	■ AR Aging by Customer ■ CEI ■ DSO
12. Accounting for Backorders. Backorders or lost sales orders may not be identified and resolved on a timely basis.	■ Customer Service Surveys	2. Accounting 3. Nonstandard Transactions 4. Revenue Reversal 5. Right of Return 6. Contract Review 14. Customer Pricing 15. Partial Shipments 22. Reporting	■ Average Customer Satisfaction Rating ■ AR Aging by Customer ■ CEI ■ DSO
13. Customer Satisfaction Issues. Due to inaccurate credit analysis, the inability to deliver product or service will result in customer service issues and damage to the company's reputation. Financial losses may occur.	■ Customer Service Surveys	21. Customer Inquiries 22. Reporting	■ Average Customer Satisfaction Rating ■ AR Aging by Customer
14. Incorrect Accounting and Financial Records. Revenues and related cost of sales may be recorded in the wrong accounting period, as complete and accurate information may not be forwarded to accounting/billing.	■ Financial Closing Procedures and Cutoffs	9. Billing Business Rules 10. Unbilled Accounts 11. Cash Advances 12. Accuracy of Invoices 13. Accurate Billing of Taxes 16. Invoice Distribution 17. Billing Exceptions 18. Promotional Programs 19. Credit Memos 20. Billing Validations 21. Customer Inquiries 22. Reporting	■ Number and Value of Pre-Close and Post-Close Entries to the GL

5.5 ACCOUNTS RECEIVABLE AND COLLECTIONS

Accounts Receivable and Collections Process Overview

AR represents a company's efforts to generate revenue by providing goods or services to customers who are then allowed to make payments at a later date. Not all customers are able or willing to pay cash when making orders. Allowing payments on credit opens the market to more customers and expands a company's ability to generate revenue and thus improve and maintain a healthy cash flow. Lastly, it is an accounting requirement that all invoices generated are properly accounted for in an AR account with the company's GL. Other accounts associated with the AR process are bad-debt reserves and clearing accounts.

Granting credit and allowing customers to defer payment to a later time expands the available market to a company's services and products. Though there are risks inherent to credit, and there are costs to managing and adequately controlling AR, the benefits can offset the risks.

Accounts Receivable and Collections Process Flow

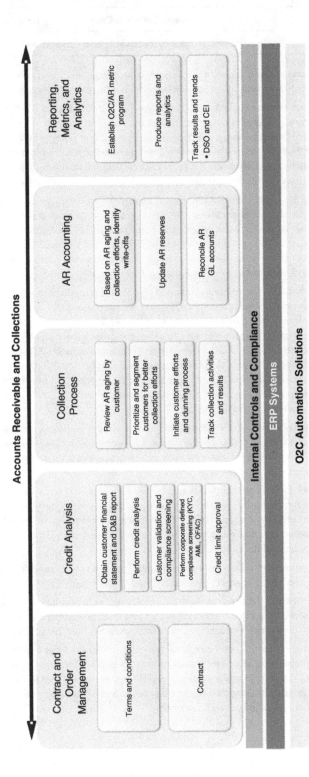

Table of Controls – Accounts Receivable and Collections

Process: Order-to-Cash
Subprocess: Accounts Receivable and Collections

1. SoD. The AR function must be separate from credit, collections, billing, and vendor payable functions. Posting to the GL should be made by persons independent of the posting of AR subsidiary ledger detail.

2. AR Subledger Input and Reconciliation. Input to the detailed AR subsidiary ledger must be based upon valid customer billing records and remittances. Procedures must be established to ensure the accurate and timely recording of billings, remittances, billing adjustments, and posting of receipts. The detailed AR subsidiary ledger must be reconciled (contents are known and status is current) to the GL monthly and any differences researched and resolved. The reconciliation detailed supporting documentation must be approved in accordance with the organization's policy.

3. AR Aging Review. An aging of the AR detail must be reviewed monthly by operating unit management for any unusual or seriously delinquent items. The aging must be accurate and not distorted by customer liabilities (e.g. customer advances, security deposits, notes receivables, milestone payments, or unapplied cash or credits). Unusual or delinquent items should be documented and addressed. Aging of AR should not be altered. Operating unit financial management, in accordance with company policy, must approve any changes to the aging of a specific invoice, billing adjustment, or cash applied.

4. AR Management Process. The operating unit and Finance must implement a consistent system of management reporting and review to assist in managing the AR balance. An aging of the AR detail must be reviewed monthly by operating unit management for any unusual or delinquent items. The aging must be accurate and not distorted by customer liabilities (e.g. customer advances, down payments, milestone payments, and unapplied cash or credits). Internal reporting should include DSO, aging of accounts, listing of delinquent accounts, potential write-offs, adequacy of collection efforts, dispute tracking, and the like. Internal reports should agree with or reconcile to external reporting, and financial metrics should be calculated in accordance with financial reporting policy. Ratio analysis (DSO, AR turnover, AR aging, etc.) should be periodically prepared and reviewed.

5. Valuation Reserve. Using the organization's policy as a minimum guideline, a valuation reserve must be established by Finance to record receivables at their net realizable value. Consistent with the organization's policy, valuation reserves must be reviewed by Finance at least quarterly for adequacy and reasonableness with adjustments made to the reserves as required.

6. Customer Disputes. Resolution of a disputed customer's receivable balance as well as contractual adjustments must be documented via a credit memo. Customer concerns (billing/shipping complaints, service problems, etc.) must be logged in the customer's account history, investigated, and resolved in a timely manner. Discrepancies related to billed amounts should be investigated and considered in the calculation of the allowance of doubtful accounts.

7. Protection of AR Information. Detailed AR information must be safeguarded from loss, destruction, and unauthorized access, and be maintained in accordance with the company's record retention policy.

8. Employee AR Policies and Procedures. AR from employees, including travel advances, must be maintained independently from the customer AR ledger and must be reviewed and reconciled on a monthly basis. A procedure to settle employee accounts prior to termination must be established and enforced.

9. Collection Policies and Procedures. Formal, written collection procedures must be developed and implemented by each operating unit that controls AR balances. These procedures, which define collection as well as the frequency of contact and reporting, must be appropriately reviewed and approved and should comply with relevant policy. Credit and collections processes and procedures must follow the Fair Debt Collection Practices Act and state required guidelines.

Process: Order-to-Cash

Subprocess: Accounts Receivable and Collections

10. Collection Process. The collection department must review the customer's outstanding balances (both debits and credits) regularly and initiate collection efforts on all accounts outstanding. Collection efforts must be adequately documented and easily retrievable in the customer credit files.

11. Customer Write-offs. Customer account write-offs must be adequately documented and approved. The approval should be in accordance with company policy (unless local procedure is more restrictive).

12. Customer Payment Policies and Procedures. Credit cards, checks, EFT, and EDI receipts must be considered to be cash, and the same standards associated with cash receipts must be followed.

13. Customer Check Payments. All customer remittances should be directed to a lockbox or remote deposit capture (RDC) should be used. RDC is a system that allows a customer to scan checks remotely and transmit the check images to a bank for deposit, usually via an encrypted Internet connection. When the bank receives a check image from the customer, it posts the deposit to the customer's account and makes the funds available based upon the customer's particular availability schedule. Banks typically offer RDC to business customers rather than to individuals. Lastly, all checks must be restrictively endorsed for deposit only and secured immediately upon receipt or becoming negotiable (e.g. post-dated checks).

14. Accounting for Customer Payments. Cash receipts received by the company or its designated agents will be deposited in the appropriate bank accounts each banking day. Daily bank receipts should be compared with system-posted receipts and reconciled daily. Daily deposit balances should be compared to G/L and subledger balances periodically by someone independent from the cash posting function.

15. Employee Receivables. There is a formal, documented process to record and track employee receivables. Employee receivables are treated like customer receivables.

Table of Risks and Controls – Accounts Receivable and Collections

Process: Order-to-Cash			
Subprocess: Accounts Receivable and Collections			
Process Risk	**Recommended Policies**	**Internal Controls**	**KPIs**
1. SoD and Systems Access. Intentional errors or misappropriation of assets could occur. Examples include: ■ Sales are invoiced but not recorded. Upon receipt, cash is misappropriated. ■ Cash receipts are incorrectly applied to customer accounts and/or are misappropriated or diverted.	■ SoD and Systems Access Controls	1. SoD 2. AR Subledger Input and Reconciliation	■ Number of SoD Reviews Performed ■ Number of SoD Conflicts Identified ■ Number of SoD Conflicts Mitigated ■ Number of Systems Access Reviews Performed ■ Number of Systems Access Issues Identified ■ Number of Systems Access Issues Mitigated

Process: Order-to-Cash			
Subprocess: Accounts Receivable and Collections			
Process Risk	Recommended Policies	Internal Controls	KPIs
2. Poor AR Management. Errors and omissions, poor receivable management practices, and inappropriate concentration of risk may not be detected and corrected on a timely basis.	■ AR Processes and Reporting	1. SoD 2. AR Subledger Input and Reconciliation 3. AR Aging Review 4. AR Management Process	■ AR Aging by Customer ■ CEI ■ DSO
3. Security of AR Data. Loss, destruction, or alteration of AR records may result in the inability to collect outstanding balances. Unauthorized use of customer receivable information could adversely affect the company's competitive position or reputation and cause the firm to be liable for misrepresentation.	■ SoD and Systems Access Controls	1. SoD 2. AR Subledger Input and Reconciliation 7. Protection of AR Information	■ Customer Master Accuracy Percentage ■ AR Data Accuracy Percentage ■ Number of SoD Reviews Performed ■ Number of SoD Conflicts Identified ■ Number of SoD Conflicts Mitigated ■ Number of Systems Access Reviews Performed ■ Number of Systems Access Issues Identified ■ Number of Systems Access Issues Mitigated
4. AR Accounting Errors. Outstanding AR balances are not properly stated in the GL. The subsidiary ledger may be inaccurate as invoices and/or cash receipts may not be recorded, may be incorrectly recorded, or may be recorded in the wrong accounting period. Errors in either the general or subsidiary ledgers may not be identified and corrected on a timely basis.	■ Financial Closing Procedures and Cutoffs	2. AR Subledger Input and Reconciliation 4. AR Management Process 14. Accounting for Customer Payments	■ Value of AR Account Reconciliation Variances ■ Number and Value of Pre-Close and Post-Close Entries to the GL

Process: Order-to-Cash			
Subprocess: Accounts Receivable and Collections			
Process Risk	**Recommended Policies**	**Internal Controls**	**KPIs**
5. Inefficient Collection Focus. Inefficient collection activities may occur, and/or incorrect aging may result in delinquent customer remittances or the write-off of delinquent accounts.	■ Credit and Collection Procedures ■ Customer Segmentation	9. Collection Policies and Procedures 10. Collection Process 12. Customer Payment Policies and Procedures	■ AR Aging by Customer ■ CEI ■ DSO
6. Misstatement of Valuation Reserves. The AR valuation reserves may be incorrectly calculated. Net receivables and the related financial statements may be misstated. The AR/long-term lease receivable valuation reserves may be incorrectly calculated. Net receivables and the related financial statements may be misstated.	■ Financial Closing Procedures and Cutoffs	2. AR Subledger Input and Reconciliation 4. AR Management Process 5. Valuation Reserves 7. Protection of AR Information 11. Customer Write-offs 14. Accounting for Customer Payments	■ AR Aging by Customer ■ CEI ■ DSO ■ Value of AR Account Reconciliation Variances ■ Number and Value of Pre-Close and Post-Close Entries to the GL
7. Inaccurate AR Adjustments. Adjustments processed may not reflect good business practices, or adjustment errors may not be detected.	■ Financial Closing Procedures and Cutoffs	2. AR Subledger Input and Reconciliation 4. AR Management Process 7. Protection of AR Information 11. Customer Write-offs 14. Accounting for Customer Payments	■ Value of AR Account Reconciliation Variances ■ Number and Value of Pre-Close and Post-Close Entries to the GL
8. Incorrect AR Write-offs. Collectible AR may be written off, and/or cash receipts may be misappropriated.	■ Credit and Collection Procedures ■ Customer Segmentation ■ Financial Closing Procedures and Cutoffs	2. AR Subledger Input and Reconciliation 4. AR Management Process 7. Protection of AR Information 11. Customer Write-offs 14. Accounting for Customer Payments	■ Value of AR Account Reconciliation Variances ■ Number and Value of Pre-Close and Post-Close Entries to the GL

Process: Order-to-Cash			
Subprocess: Accounts Receivable and Collections			
Process Risk	**Recommended Policies**	**Internal Controls**	**KPIs**
9. Intentional Alteration of Receivable Records/Invoices Could Occur. AR records could be altered to hide a fraudulent transaction. Credit analysis results could be falsified and confidential information could be shared inappropriately.	■ SoD and Systems Access Controls	2. AR Subledger Input and Reconciliation 4. AR Management Process 7. Protection of AR Information 11. Customer Write-offs 14. Accounting for Customer Payments	■ Customer Master Accuracy Percentage ■ AR Data Accuracy Percentage ■ Number of SoD Reviews Performed ■ Number of SoD Conflicts Identified ■ Number of SoD Conflicts Mitigated ■ Number of Systems Access Reviews Performed ■ Number of Systems Access Issues Identified ■ Number of Systems Access Issues Mitigated
10. Customer Refunds. Company funds may be disbursed to customers with past due balances or with inadequate surety.	■ AR Processes and Reporting	4. AR Management Process 5. Customer Disputes	■ Value and Number of Customer Refunds Issued ■ Percentage of Customer Refunds Compared to AR Subledger Balance
11. Misstated Internal Management Reporting and Forecasting. Improper credit analysis can impact internal reporting and revenue forecasting accuracy.	■ Credit and Collection Procedures ■ Customer Segmentation ■ Financial Closing Procedures and Cutoffs	2. AR Subledger Input and Reconciliation 4. AR Management Process 14. Accounting for Customer Payments	■ Value of AR Account Reconciliation Variances ■ Number and Value of Pre-Close and Post-Close Entries to the GL
12. Delayed Payment. Payment may be delayed due to contract inaccuracies and issues.	■ Credit and Collection Procedures ■ Customer Segmentation ■ Financial Closing Procedures and Cutoffs	9. Collection Policies and Procedures 10. Collection Process 12. Customer Payment Policies and Procedures	■ AR Aging by Customer ■ CEI ■ DSO

Process: Order-to-Cash			
Subprocess: Accounts Receivable and Collections			
Process Risk	**Recommended Policies**	**Internal Controls**	**KPIs**
13. Customer Satisfaction Issues. Due to inaccurate credit analysis, the inability to deliver product or service will result in customer service issues and damage to the company's reputation. Financial losses may occur.	■ Customer Satisfaction Surveys	9. Collection Policies and Procedures 10. Collection Process 12. Customer Payment Policies and Procedures	■ AR Aging by Customer ■ CEI ■ DSO ■ Value and Percentage of Disputed Invoices ■ Average Customer Satisfaction Rating
14. Employee Receivables. Receivables may not be collected from terminated employees.	■ Employee Receivable Policies and Procedures	15. Employee Receivables	■ AR Aging by Employee ■ CEI ■ DSO
15. Incorrect Accounting and Financial Records. Revenues and related cost of sales may be recorded in the wrong accounting period, as complete and accurate information may not be forwarded to accounting/billing.	■ Financial Closing Procedures and Cutoffs	2. AR Subledger Input and Reconciliation 14. Accounting for Customer Payments	■ Value of AR Account Reconciliation Variances ■ Number and Value of Pre-Close and Post-Close Entries to the GL

5.6 CASH APPLICATION AND MANAGEMENT

Cash Application and Management Process Overview

Cash application and management is one of the most important components of any AR process. At the highest level, there are two ways that cash application and management is done: manually or automated. A manual process involves a cash application specialist going through payments and associated remittance and matching the payment amounts with their associated invoices. The cash application specialist will look at the customer name or invoice number on the payment, find the associated remittance, and post it to the outstanding AR invoice in his/her company's ERP. An automated cash application process goes through the same process but is able to match payment and remittance at a must faster speed. As the cash application process has grown more and more complex many companies have moved to an automated process, since reducing staff workload to reduce costs and work burnout and cash application becomes more important.

Automation of cash application has allowed companies to eliminate routine tasks in the process. A centralized archive can be set up for storing all remittances. Robotic process automation (RPA) can retrieve remittances from web portals, receive e-mails, and extract the remittance information. From there, remittances from all sources can be put in a centralized archive, eliminating the issue facing cash application teams that work with multiple sources of remittance information. RPA can also automate the matching. Whether a company decides to automate one part of the cash application process or the entire process, automation can lead to faster cash application, more accurate AR aging, and a lower DSO.

Cash Application and Management Process Flow

Cash Application and Management

Receive Customer Payments	Payment Remittance Details	Apply Payments	Accounting and Reporting
Wire	ACH remittance details	Automated application to customer account and ERP system	Updated customer account and AR aging
ACH	Manual remittance details	Manual application using remittance details	Update O2C and AR Metrics
Card			
EDI/Corporate trade exchange (CTX)			

Internal Controls and Compliance

ERP Systems

Cash Application Automation Solutions

Table of Controls – Cash Application and Management

Process: Order-to-Cash
Subprocess: Cash Application and Management

1. Customer Payments. Credit cards, checks, EFT, and EDI receipts must be considered to be cash, and the same standards associated with cash receipts must be followed.

2. Customer Remittances. All customer remittances paid by check must be directed to a lockbox. All manual checks must be restrictively endorsed for deposit only and secured immediately upon receipt or becoming negotiable (e.g. post-dated checks).

3. Deposits. Cash receipts received by the company or its designated agents will be deposited in the appropriate bank accounts each banking day. Daily bank receipts should be compared with system posted receipts and reconciled daily. Daily deposit balances should be compared to GL and subledger balances periodically by someone independent from the cash posting function.

4. SoD and Systems Access. Control and responsibility for receiving and depositing cash must be assigned to an individual, group, or third party who is not responsible for the items listed below. Summary listing of receipts should be forwarded to persons independent of remittance processing and responsible for posting AR detail. Where practical, all customers should be encouraged to remit payments directly to depository accounts or other automated payment systems at the organization's established banking facilities or third-party payment processors. All cash receipt posting files should be posted to subsidiary ledgers within 24 hours.

SoD and Systems Access controls need to be strictly followed to ensure the following:

a. Recording to the AR subsidiary ledger is assigned to the applicable staff members to ensure that correct accounting transactions are processed to support an accurate and timely financial closing process.
b. Recording to the GL is assigned to the applicable staff members to ensure that incorrect and fraudulent transactions cannot occur.
c. Collecting receivables responsibilities are assigned to authorized staff members to ensure that funds are not diverted.
d. Authorizing bad debt write-offs responsibilities are appropriately assigned.
e. Responsibilities for authorizing credit memos, discounts, allowances, and customer returns are properly assigned to avoid SoD conflicts and the potential of fraudulent transactions.
f. Responsibilities for preparing billing documents are properly assigned.
g. Reconciling to bank statements is assigned to cash accounting staff members.
h. Sending monthly statements to customers is assigned to avoid SoD conflicts.
i. Comparing cash receipts journals to deposit advices is the responsibility of cash accounting staff members.

5. Depository Accounts. Where practical, all customers should be encouraged to remit payments directly to depository accounts or other automated payment systems at established company banking facilities or third-party payment processors.

6. Posting. All cash receipt posting files should be posted to subsidiary ledgers within 24 hours.

7. Application of Customer Remittances. All remittances must be applied to the specific customer account level within 72 hours. Remittances lacking documentation to support posting to an invoice within 72 hours should be placed "on account" to ensure that receipts are viewable on a succeeding customer statement. Remittances lacking customer or invoice information should be held in suspense until sufficient documentation is received to support posting. Unless otherwise approved by the customer, payments must be applied to specific invoices. Monthly customer remittance cutoff procedures must be established and enforced. Adequate controls must be established to control such remittances during the period for which they are on site.

8. Cutoff Procedures. Monthly customer remittance cutoff procedures must be established and enforced.

Process: Order-to-Cash
Subprocess: Cash Application and Management

9. Miscellaneous Remittances. All customer remittances received on site should be directed to a designated financial institution or third-party processor. Adequate controls must be established to control such remittances during the period for which they are on site.

10. Checks with Insufficient Funds. Controls should be in place to ensure that insufficient fund and returned items are reversed timely to reflect the chargeback within the receivables system.

Table of Risks and Controls – Cash Application and Management

Process: Order-to-Cash (O2C)			
Subprocess: Cash Application and Management			
Process Risk	**Recommended Policies**	**Internal Controls**	**KPIs**
1. SoD and Systems Access. Unauthorized use of customer receivable information could adversely impact the company's competitive position or reputation and cause the firm to be liable for misrepresentation.	■ SoD and Systems Access Controls	4. SoD and Systems Access	■ Number of SoD Reviews Performed ■ Number of SoD Conflicts Identified ■ Number of SoD Conflicts Mitigated ■ Number of Systems Access Reviews Performed ■ Number of Systems Access Issues Identified ■ Number of Systems Access Issues Mitigated
2. Misappropriation or Loss of Customer Payments. Cash receipts may be lost and/or misappropriated. Cash receipts may be incorrectly applied to customer accounts and/or may be misappropriated or diverted. Lost, incorrectly recorded, and/or misappropriated cash receipts may not be identified and corrected timely.	■ SoD and Systems Access Controls ■ AR Metrics and Reporting	1. Customer Payments 2. Customer Remittances 3. Deposits 4. SoD and Systems Access 5. Depository Accounts 6. Posting 7. Application of Customer Remittances 8. Cutoff Procedures 9. Miscellaneous Remittances 10. Checks with Insufficient Funds	■ AR Aging by Customer ■ CEI ■ DSO ■ First-Time Customer Payment Match ■ Number and Value of Cash Application Issues ■ Cycle Time to Remediate a Customer Payment Issue ■ Value of AR Fraud Instances ■ Average Customer Satisfaction Rating

Process: Order-to-Cash (O2C)			
Subprocess: Cash Application and Management			
Process Risk	**Recommended Policies**	**Internal Controls**	**KPIs**
3. Cash-Flow Impacts by Lack of Visibility to Cash Receipts. Cash flow may not be reported correctly or maximized.	▪ AR Metrics and Reporting	1. Customer Payments 2. Customer Remittances 3. Deposits 4. SoD and Systems Access 5. Depository Accounts 6. Posting 7. Application of Customer Remittances 8. Cutoff Procedures 9. Miscellaneous Remittances 10. Checks with Insufficient Funds	▪ Cash-Flow Reporting Accuracy Percentage ▪ Variance and Trend Analysis for Cash-Flow Reporting Changes to Working Capital Reporting
4. Security of AR Data. Loss, destruction, or alteration of AR records may result in the inability to collect outstanding balances. Unauthorized use of customer receivable information could adversely impact the company's competitive position or reputation and cause the firm to be liable for misrepresentation.	▪ SoD and Systems Access Controls	4. SoD and Systems Access	▪ Number of SoD Reviews Performed ▪ Number of SoD Conflicts Identified ▪ Number of SoD Conflicts Mitigated ▪ Number of Systems Access Reviews Performed ▪ Number of Systems Access Issues Identified ▪ Number of Systems Access Issues Mitigated
5. Account Balance and Reporting of AR Aging. The receivable balance and/or aging of receivables included in internal receivable management reporting may not be accurate.	▪ AR Metrics and Reporting ▪ Credit and Collection Procedures ▪ Customer Segmentation	1. Customer Payments 2. Customer Remittances 3. Deposits 4. SoD and Systems Access 5. Depository Accounts 6. Posting 7. Application of Customer Remittances 8. Cutoff Procedures 9. Miscellaneous Remittances 10. Checks with Insufficient Funds	▪ AR Aging by Customer ▪ CEI ▪ DSO

Process: Order-to-Cash (O2C)			
Subprocess: Cash Application and Management			
Process Risk	**Recommended Policies**	**Internal Controls**	**KPIs**
6. Inefficient Collection Focus. Inefficient collection activities may occur, and/or incorrect aging may result in delinquent customer remittances or the write-off of delinquent accounts	■ AR Metrics and Reporting ■ Credit and Collection Procedures ■ Customer Segmentation	1. Customer Payments 2. Customer Remittances 3. Deposits 4. SoD and Systems Access 5. Depository Accounts 6. Posting 7. Application of Customer Remittances 8. Cutoff Procedures 9. Miscellaneous Remittances 10. Checks with Insufficient Funds	■ AR Aging by Customer ■ CEI ■ DSO
7. Misstatement of Valuation Reserves. The AR valuation reserves may be incorrectly calculated. Net receivables and the related financial statements may be misstated. The AR/long-term lease receivable valuation reserves may be incorrectly calculated. Net receivables and the related financial statements may be misstated.	■ AR Metrics and Reporting ■ Credit and Collection Procedures ■ Customer Segmentation	1. Customer Payments 2. Customer Remittances 3. Deposits 4. SoD and Systems Access 5. Depository Accounts 6. Posting 7. Application of Customer Remittances 8. Cutoff Procedures 9. Miscellaneous Remittances 10. Checks with Insufficient Funds	■ AR Aging by Customer ■ CEI ■ DSO ■ Value of AR Account Reconciliation Variances ■ Number and Value of Pre-Close and Post-Close Entries to the GL
8. Inaccurate AR Adjustments. Adjustments processed may not reflect good business practices, or adjustment errors may not be detected.	■ AR Metrics and Reporting ■ Credit and Collection Procedures ■ Customer Segmentation	1. Customer Payments 2. Customer Remittances 3. Deposits 4. SoD and Systems Access 5. Depository Accounts 6. Posting 7. Application of Customer Remittances 8. Cutoff Procedures 9. Miscellaneous Remittances 10. Checks with Insufficient Funds	■ AR Aging by Customer ■ CEI ■ DSO ■ Value of AR Account Reconciliation Variances ■ Number and Value of Pre-Close and Post-Close Entries to the GL

Process: Order-to-Cash (O2C)			
Subprocess: Cash Application and Management			
Process Risk	**Recommended Policies**	**Internal Controls**	**KPIs**
9. Incorrect AR Write-offs. Collectible AR may be written off, and/or cash receipts may be misappropriated.	■ AR Metrics and Reporting ■ Credit and Collection Procedures ■ Customer Segmentation	1. Customer Payments 2. Customer Remittances 3. Deposits 4. SoD and Systems Access 5. Depository Accounts 6. Posting 7. Application of Customer Remittances 8. Cutoff Procedures 9. Miscellaneous Remittances 10. Checks with Insufficient Funds	■ AR Aging by Customer ■ CEI ■ DSO ■ Value of AR Account Reconciliation Variances ■ Number and Value of Pre-Close and Post-Close Entries to the GL
10. Misstated Internal Management Reporting and Forecasting. Improper credit analysis can impact internal reporting and revenue forecasting accuracy.	■ Financial Closing Procedures and Cutoffs	1. Customer Payments 2. Customer Remittances 3. Deposits 4. SoD and Systems Access 5. Depository Accounts 6. Posting 7. Application of Customer Remittances 8. Cutoff Procedures 9. Miscellaneous Remittances 10. Checks with Insufficient Funds	■ AR Aging by Customer ■ CEI ■ DSO ■ Value of AR Account Reconciliation Variances ■ Number and Value of Pre-Close and Post-Close Entries to the GL
11. Customer Satisfaction Issues. Customer dissatisfaction could result if order fulfillment fails to correctly apply cash payments.	■ Customer Satisfaction Surveys	1. Customer Payments 2. Customer Remittances 3. Deposits 4. SoD and Systems Access 5. Depository Accounts 6. Posting 7. Application of Customer Remittances 8. Cutoff Procedures 9. Miscellaneous Remittances 10. Checks with Insufficient Funds	■ Average Customer Satisfaction Rating

Process: Order-to-Cash (O2C)			
Subprocess: Cash Application and Management			
Process Risk	**Recommended Policies**	**Internal Controls**	**KPIs**
12. Incorrect Accounting and Financial Records. Revenues and related cost of sales may be recorded in the wrong accounting period, as complete and accurate information may not be forwarded to accounting/billing.	■ Financial Closing Procedures and Cutoffs	1. Customer Payments 2. Customer Remittances 3. Deposits 4. SoD and Systems Access 5. Depository Accounts 6. Posting 7. Application of Customer Remittances 8. Cutoff Procedures 9. Miscellaneous Remittances 10. Checks with Insufficient Funds	■ Cash Application Accuracy Percentage ■ AR Aging by Customer ■ CEI ■ DSO ■ Value of AR Account Reconciliation Variances ■ Number and Value of Pre-Close and Post-Close Entries to the GL

5.7 REPORTING, METRICS, AND ANALYTICS

Reporting, Metrics, and Analytics Process Overview

O2C is often challenged by siloed operations and inefficient processes. Analytical application and intelligent systems can help reduce consumer fraud, identify anomalies in the processes, predict risk, and much more. I have outlined some possible use cases below to improve and optimize your O2C process using advanced analytics.

Receivable Analytics

Today most financial transactions are done on credit for almost every purchase for B2B customers. AR is the most critical function for an organization to use well. The AR staff's competence and judgment will help the organization to receive money for its sold goods and services. This requires the AR group to be proactive in knowing whom to give credit to and when to start the credit recovery process. Advanced analytics can help go beyond the standard AR aging report. Using advanced analytics, AR personnel can predict payments at risk, judge the likelihood of recovery of long overdue payments, and identify customers who are at risk of potentially not paying.

Detecting Accounts Receivable Fraud

Advanced analytics can build models that identify attributes or patterns that can identify fraud. For example, anomaly detection can detect a sudden drift in historical customer payment pattern. Customer profiling can assist in determining potential fraudsters by matching attributes with known fraudsters' attributes. Text mining can help discover the customer's sentiments towards the product/service.

Reporting, Metrics, and Analytics Process Flow

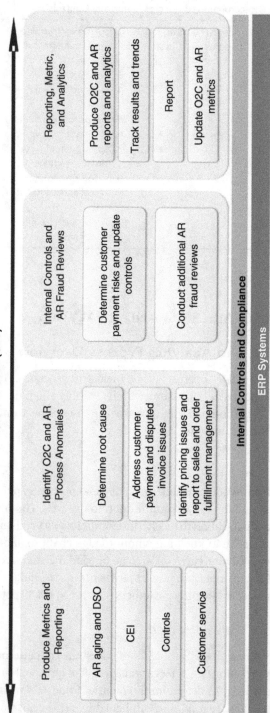

Table of Controls – Reporting, Metrics, and Analytics

Process: Order-to-Cash
Subprocess: Reporting, Metrics and Analytics

1. Visibility to the Results of the O2C and Customer Payment Trends. O2C process results are tracked, analyzed, and reported to business stakeholders.

2. O2C Process Metrics. Implement metrics to report procurement process results, identify process improvements, and address payment issues in a timely manner. Metrics should focus on cost, process efficiency, internal controls, and customer service's impacts to the payments process. Metrics should be organized by cost, process efficiency, internal customers, and customer service.

3. Develop a Reporting Process. Develop a reporting process so that the results of metrics and analytics are reported and acted upon in a predictable manner – at least monthly.

4. Root-Cause Analysis and Process Improvement Procedures. Identify opportunities to improve the process based on root-cause analysis of results, trends, and benchmarks. Focus on how to resolve employee payment issues, reduce cost, and implement process efficiencies.

Table of Risks and Controls – Reporting, Metrics, and Analytics

Process: Order-to-Cash			
Subprocess: Reporting, Metrics, and Analytics			
Process Risk	**Recommended Policies**	**Internal Controls**	**KPIs**
1. O2C Process Anomalies and Customer Payment Trends. Failure to address O2C payment problems may result in inaccurate billing and the application of customer payments, causing significant customer service issues and incorrect financial information. Process improvement opportunities are not identified or acted upon.	▪ O2C Reporting Process ▪ O2C Metrics	1. Visibility of the Results of O2C and Customer Payment Trends 2. O2C Process Metrics 3. Develop a Reporting Process 4. Root-Cause Analysis and Process Improvement Procedures	▪ Number and Percentage of O2C Issues Identified and Remediated ▪ Value of Cost Savings Opportunities Identified in the O2C Process

Process: Order-to-Cash			
Subprocess: Reporting, Metrics, and Analytics			
Process Risk	**Recommended Policies**	**Internal Controls**	**KPIs**
2. Lack of Visibility of O2C Process Results. The results and impact of the O2C process and the customer payment process are not reported or acted upon and risks to the process are not identified or acted upon. Key process issues may be undetected for a significant period of time. Uncollectible accounts are not properly stated and bad-debt reserves may not be accurate.	■ O2C Reporting Process ■ O2C Metrics	1. Visibility of the Results of the O2C and Customer Payment Trends 2. O2C Process Metrics 3. Develop a Reporting Process 4. Root-Cause Analysis and Process Improvement Procedures	■ DSO ■ CEI ■ AR Aging ■ Value of AR Write-offs ■ Unapplied Cash
3. O2C Reporting Process. Visibility of analytics and metrics is lost. Key process issues may be undetected for a significant period of time.	■ O2C Reporting Process ■ O2C Metrics	1. Visibility of the Results of the O2C and Customer Payment Trends 2. O2C Process Metrics 3. Develop a Reporting Process 4. Root-Cause Analysis and Process Improvement Procedures	■ DSO ■ CEI ■ AR Aging ■ Value of AR Write-offs ■ Cycle Time to Apply Cash ■ First-Time Customer Payment Matches ■ Unapplied Cash
4. Action on Customer Payment Anomalies. Opportunities to address or implement additional controls for payment anomalies and possible AR fraud are missed.	■ O2C Reporting Process ■ O2C Metrics	1. Visibility of the Results of the O2C and Customer Payment Trends 2. O2C Process Metrics 3. Develop a Reporting Process 4. Root-Cause Analysis and Process Improvement Procedures	■ DSO ■ CEI ■ AR Aging ■ Cycle Time to Apply Cash ■ First-Time Customer Payment Matches ■ Value of AR Write-offs ■ Unapplied Cash

PART THREE

SECTION SIX

Financial Operations Risk

SECTION INTRODUCTION

This section focuses on financial operations risk, which includes the record-to-report (R2R) process, budgets and forecasts, the supply chain process and inventory control, the treasury and cash management process, shared services and business process outsourcing (BPO), and data validation, analytics, metrics, and benchmarking.

CHAPTER THIRTEEN

Record-to-Report

 OVERVIEW

Controllers and corporate financial departments often find themselves in the eye of today's market whirlwinds with both internal and external reporting requirements to fulfill. Timely, accurate, and consistent data is always of critical importance: operational and strategic decisions are based upon it and precise planning depends upon it.

Statutory, regulatory, and compliance requirements add yet another layer of complexity. Global organizations are required to support reporting with multiple accounting standards, and new legislation requires new systems. The information age has created a class of investors and shareholders who expect fast and easy access to the data created by current business activities.

The record-to-report (R2R) process is composed of four major process steps, which are listed below and depicted in the process flowchart in the next section.

1. **Transaction accumulation and reconciliation:** All company transactions must be recorded and processed per accepted accounting principles. The accuracy of the financial data in this process step sets the stage for the rest of the R2R process.
2. **Subledger close:** During this process finance and accounting teams are required to complete all postings to the GL. The number of GLs, the complexity of a company's chart of accounts, and the number of cost or profit centers will determine the time it takes to complete this process.
3. **Corporate close and consolidation:** The corporate close and consolidation process includes collecting, validating, and mapping financial transactions across functions, departments, and geographies within the organization.
4. **Analysis and reporting:** During this step various reports, such as balance sheets and income statements, are developed using appropriate accounting principles and regulatory requirements.

RECORD-TO-REPORT PROCESS FLOW

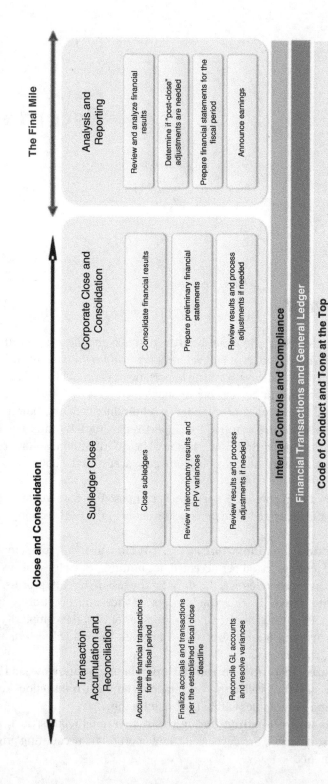

CONTROLLER'S TOOL 22 – MONTHLY CLOSING BEST PRACTICES

Introduction. The accounting process and financial closing process can differ slightly from one business to another based on variances in the chart of accounts, revenue and expense recognition, and cost center breakdown. Despite these differences, the overall monthly closing process should follow the same standards to ensure consistent, timely, and accurate reporting. This tool recommends the best practices for the closing process.

Monthly Closing Best Practices

1. Closing Date. Establish a closing date by which all expenses and revenue must be posted. Communicate the closing date to everyone who has access to modify the ledger. Close the books for the month as of the date communicated, prohibiting any further changes to the ledger for the period.

2. Trial Balance Report. Start the closing cycle with a trial balance report. Review the balances to identify any anomalies from what is expected. Review the transaction details for any accounts you are uncertain of and note any adjustments that need to be made.

3. Adjusting Entries. Create the adjusting entries to recognize prepaid expenses, accrue outstanding invoices, relieve accruals that have been paid, and recognize depreciation and other amortizations. Post adjusting entries to correct the current balance of any ledger account that reflects expense postings in error.

4. Adjusted Trial Balance. Generate an adjusted trial balance report to review the final balances in the ledger. Verify that the trial balance on the debit and the credit side match. Verify that the balances are accurate, checking the account activity if needed. Trial balances will vary from the initial report due to the adjusting entries. This helps you to identify any entries that posted incorrectly.

5. Reporting. Create reporting to show the final expense activity for the period and year to date. Include documentation of the balance sheet, income statement, and depreciation schedules. Save copies of the entire set of journal entries posted, along with the documentation supporting their necessity for audit purposes.

 ## CONTROLLER'S TOOL 23 – 15 BEST PRACTICES TO SIMPLIFY YOUR FINANCIAL CLOSE

Introduction. There are many factors that place the spotlight on the financial closing process. This process is usually led by a team of individuals in the corporate finance and accounting department, which is managed by the corporate controller. The complexity of the process is driven by the nature of the company (private, public, or nonprofit) and type of industry. Complexity can impact the closing process and the time it takes to deliver the final financial statements; however, the best practices recommended in this tool can help to simplify the process.

15 Best Practices to Simplify Your Financial Close

1. Review unused accounts in the general ledger and minimize accounting data. Minimize accounting data in the core GL by limiting code segments to subledgers. This is a somewhat overlooked opportunity to improve the close process, since keeping the GL relatively simple accelerates data roll-ups while pushing problem resolution into payables, receivables, and other departments that are closer to transactions.

2. Document your closing process. Involve the whole organization in understanding the goals and schedule for the close using checklists, project plans, and good communication. Ensure that roles and responsibilities are documented and well communicated.

3. Cross-train your accounting staff. Cross-training and documentation of all closing processes can be very beneficial, especially when there is the unexpected absence of a critical associate.

4. Establish a closing date. Establish a closing date by which all expenses and revenue must be posted. Communicate the closing date to everyone who has access to modifying the ledger. Close the books as of the date communicated, prohibiting any further changes to the ledger during the close.

5. Move to a monthly soft close process. Transition from a monthly hard close to soft monthly closes and quarterly hard closes. This change allows companies to reduce investigation levels and rely on accruals and estimates during soft closes.

6. Identify routine work and move it out of the closing crunch. Identify routine work and move it out of the closing crunch. Move recurring allocations and accruals out of the closing process. This alleviates the task of posting journal entries during the close and adding additional tasks to the process.

7. Use the trial balance report. Generate an adjusted trial balance report to review the final balances in the ledger. Verify that the trial balance matches on the debit and credit side. Verify that the balances are accurate, checking the account activity if needed.

8. Manage the financial close like a project. Implement a schedule for posting closing entries with duties assigned to specific individuals. Ensure that everyone knows the deadlines and what is needed to meet the deadline. The schedule should be maintained on the company's network and updated by the responsible person as tasks are completed, enabling management to review the status of the closing process throughout the cycle and take action in a timely manner.

9. Complete standard allocations in advance of close. Use a standard allocation system with a true-up when something goes out of the established tolerance. This approach moves the standard allocation process out of the financial close and can speed up cycle time.

10. Use adjusting entries, accruals, and estimates to shorten the close. Using a "not invoice and not received" report, which is based on POs, this approach supports the accrual process, since companies are better able to accrue for all received product and services using accurate data.

Create the adjusting entries to recognize prepaid expenses, accrue outstanding invoices, relieve accruals that have been paid, and recognize depreciation and other amortizations. Post adjusting entries to correct the current balance of any ledger account that reflects expense postings in error.

11. Minimize and automate journal entries during the closing process. Reduce the manual journal entry process. If some journal entries need to be created manually, use an upload process with built-in checks and balances. Consider the use of recurring entries and estimates that can streamline the closing process.

12. Use standard templates for the reporting process. Use standard templates for recurring reports. This makes month-end closing much faster, since it streamlines the reporting process. Report writers can streamline and make reports consistent and substantially reduce data entry and the need for reconciliations. Lastly, consider the audiences for your reports and create executive level reports with the ability to drill down to obtain additional information.

13. Develop partnerships across departments to resolve recurring cross-functional issues. Following each close, an "obstacles to close" or "postmortem" report is distributed across the organization. This report provides visibility of cross-functional issues and identifies areas for process improvement.

14. Develop and monitor close performance metrics. Implement and monitor closing metrics as suggested in this toolkit. Gathering metrics and publishing the results can lead to changes in behavior and supports adherence to deadlines and critical paths, and avoidance of bottlenecks.

15. Continuously improve your closing process. By constantly looking at ways to improve the financial close, the process can become less cumbersome and easier to manage. If the close is treated like a project, these improvements should be identified and tracked to ensure implementation.

FRAUD WITHIN THE RECORD-TO-REPORT PROCESS

Within the R2R process, controllers are often concerned about financial statement fraud, which is commonly referred to as "cooking the books." Financial statement fraud involves deliberately overstating assets, revenues, and profits and/or understating liabilities, expenses, and losses. A business that engages in cooking the books stands to lose a tremendous amount of money when penalties and fines, legal costs, the loss of investor confidence, and reputational damage are taken into account.

CONTROLLER'S TOOL 24 – GENERAL FINANCIAL STATEMENT FRAUD RED FLAGS

Introduction. When an auditor, internal controls expert, fraud investigator, or forensic accountant investigates financial statement fraud, he or she looks for red flags or accounting warning signs. A good controller should also be aware of these flags. General red flags that indicate suspect business accounting practices are provided in this tool.

General Financial Statement Fraud Red Flags

1. Aggressive revenue recognition practices, such as recognizing revenue in earlier periods than when the product was sold or the service was delivered.

2. Unusually high revenues and low expenses at period end that cannot be attributed to seasonality.

3. Significant growth in inventory that does not correlate with growth in sales.

4. Improper capitalization or accounting treatment of expenses in excess of industry norms.

5. Reported earnings that are positive and growing but operating cash flow that is declining.

6. Growth in revenues that is far greater than growth in other companies in the same industry or peer group.

7. Gross margin or operating margins out of line with peer companies.

8. Extensive use of off–balance sheet entities that are not considered standard in the industry.

9. Sudden increases in gross margin or cash flow as compared with the company's prior performance and with industry averages.

10. Unusual increases in the book value of assets, such as inventory and receivables.

11. Disclosure notes so complex that it is impossible to determine the actual nature of the transaction.

12. AP invoices that go unrecorded in the company's financial books and accruals that are not properly booked.

13. Loans to executives or other related parties that are written off.

14. Pressure on accounting personnel to complete financial statements in an unusually short time period, as reflected by approval date of financial statements.

15. Unusually long business cycles.

16. Rapid expansion into new product lines.

17. Limited collateral available.

18. A significant investment in an industry or product line noted for rapid change by the entity.

19. Poor interpersonal relationships among executives.

20. Heavy dependence on one or a few products, customers, or suppliers by the entity.

21. Declining demand for products.

22. Key executives feeling undue family, peer, or community pressure to succeed.

23. Adverse political, social, or environmental impact.

CONTROLLER'S TOOL 25 – FRAUD RED FLAGS FOR LENDERS AND INVESTORS

Introduction. The National Commission on Fraudulent Financial Reporting conducted a survey in 1987 and identified the following 10 common financial statement fraud flags, which are still applicable today. The table below is organized from the viewpoints of lenders and investors, but it can also be applied internally or when evaluating a supplier. The fraud red flags are presented in order of importance.

	Fraud Red Flags for Lenders and Investors	
Rank	Lenders	Investors
1.	There is dishonest or unethical management.	There is dishonest or unethical management.
2.	There are frequent changes of legal counsel, auditors, or external board members.	There has been a breakdown in accounting and control systems as reflected by the late issuing of financial statements or a qualified report.
3.	Management is dominated by one person (or a small group) and there is no effective oversight board or committee.	The entity has been suspended or delisted from a stock exchange.
4.	The entity has been suspended or delisted from a stock exchange.	Management's reputation in the business community is poor.
5.	The entity is unable to generate cash flows from operations but reports earnings and earnings growth.	Management is dominated by one person (or a small group) and there is no effective oversight board or committee.
6.	The entity has continual problems with regulatory agencies.	There are frequent changes of legal counsel, auditors, or external board members.
7.	There is a high turnover rate of key top management, specifically financial executives.	Internal or external factors raise substantial doubt about the entity's ability to continue as a going concern.
8.	Internal or external factors raise substantial doubt about the entity's ability to continue as a going concern.	There are continual problems with regulatory agencies.
9.	Management's reputation in the business community is poor.	Important matters not previously disclosed by management are identified.
10.	There is a reluctance to provide investors/bankers with needed data.	The entity is unable to generate cash flows from operations but reports earnings and earnings growth.

TABLE OF CONTROLS – RECORD-TO-REPORT

Process: Record-to-Report

1. Policy and Procedures. Accounting policies and procedures must be developed and documented in accordance with US GAAP and corporate policy. These policies and procedures must be followed regardless of materiality. A current version of the above-mentioned policies and procedures should be readily available in all company locations.

2. Policy Changes. New accounting policies or changes to existing policies should be properly researched, reviewed, documented, and communicated on a timely basis. The controller must authorize all changes in accounting policies. Local finance management may also develop tailored policies and procedures. Those conflicting with corporate policy must be approved in writing by the corporate controller.

3. Journal Entries. Journal entries must be accurately entered into the GL within the correct accounting period. Processes should be in place to ensure the accuracy of journal entry postings to the GL.

4. Documented Journal Entries. All manual GL journal entries must be documented, reviewed, and approved by financial supervision. A process should also be in place to identify manual journal entries so that it may be determined if any were omitted or duplicated.

5. Standardized Journal Entries. Standardized (i.e. system calculated and posted) GL journal entries must be utilized whenever possible. When the journal entry is established, the process for calculation must be reviewed, approved, and documented by local financial management. A process should also be in place to identify standardized journal entries so that it may be determined if any were omitted, duplicated, or have unreasonable values.

6. Nonstandard Transactions. Policies must be established to review and approve the accounting treatment of GL journal entries that do not occur on a regular basis.

7. Contra-Asset Accounts. Contra-asset accounts should be utilized where necessary to maintain both proper asset valuation and detailed accounting records (e.g. receivables, inventory, and property).

8. Monthly Accruals. On a monthly basis, an accrual must be made of all known liabilities that have not been processed for payment or recorded in the accounting records, as determined by corporate policy. A quarterly review and evaluation should be conducted at the operating unit reporting level to determine if any existing contingent liabilities should be recorded in accordance with US GAAP requirements.

9. Asset Account Reviews. All noncurrent asset accounts should be reviewed at least annually to ensure values do not exceed the lower of cost or market value. All current asset accounts should be reviewed at least quarterly to ensure that values do not exceed the lower of cost or market value.

10. Journal Entry Processing. Controls must be established to ensure all journal entries have been processed and posted once they have been input into the system. Transaction error registers should be generated and significant discrepancies resolved prior to period close.

11. Reporting Schedules and Cutoffs. Adherence to monthly, quarterly, and annual closing and reporting schedules and cutoffs must be strict and consistent.

12. GL Reconciliations. GL balances must be reconciled (contents are known and status is current) to the subsidiary ledgers or other supporting records on a timely basis. Any differences must be promptly resolved and recorded, generally by the next monthly reporting interval. All unexplained differences, however, must be reported to appropriate financial management as soon as discovered, even if not yet resolved.

13. Suspense Account Transactions. Clearing and suspense account transactions, including the transfer of expense, income, or capital, must be resolved on a timely basis. Proper recognition of income or expense for these accounts must be made on at least a quarterly basis, and on a monthly basis where possible.

14. GL Adjustments. Consolidation, reclassification, and other adjustments to GL balances must be adequately explained and documented. Such adjustments must be approved by the appropriate controller/manager or authorized designee.

15. Financial Report Preparation. Procedures and responsibilities must be established and maintained to ensure timely and accurate preparation, review, and approval of external financial reports, including reports to governmental and regulatory bodies. These procedures must also ensure that such reports comply with the established requirements for financial information and related disclosures.

16. Access to Accounting and Finance Records. Access to documents and information systems must be safeguarded and access granted only on the principle of "need to know."

17. Records Management. Accounting and financial records must be complete, well organized, and retained in accordance with corporate policy on records management and tax requirements. Sufficient records must be kept in a secure but accessible environment to accurately and completely support all nonfixed assets and all liabilities.

18. Financial Results. Only authorized individuals must be given the responsibility to discuss financial results with individuals outside of the company.

19. Financial Reporting Requirements. All operating units must comply with the current financial reporting requirements established by the corporate controller.

20. Legal Financial Reporting Requirements. Adherence to all legal reporting requirements (e.g. tax returns, statutory audits, etc.) must be strict and consistent.

21. Financial Statement Translation. Foreign financial statements must be translated in accordance with U.S. GAAP and corporate policy.

22. GL Accounts Definitions. Current definitions must be documented and maintained for all ledger accounts.

23. GL Account Owners. Lists of ledger account owners must be kept current and cost center managers shall have responsibility for the accuracy of the account balance.

24. Actual-to-Forecast Comparisons. Comparisons and explanations of actual financial information to forecast information must be routinely completed according to established policies and procedures; all significant variances must be researched and reflected in revised estimates/plans as appropriate in a timely way. Uniformly defined (same methodology) balance sheet performance measures must be established and actual performance measured against forecast on a monthly basis.

25. Related Party Transactions. Related party transactions should be reported in accordance with GAAP.

26. Double Taxation. The company may be subjected to double taxation due to adjustments made by the taxing authorities.

27. Penalties. The company may be subjected to penalties or fines by the taxing authorities.

28. Pricing Method. The organization uses the specified pricing method that best fits the circumstances of each category of transactions, according to the OECD (Organisation for Economic Co-operation and Development) guidelines and the laws and regulations of the United States and other jurisdictions in which the organization operates. When no specified method is applicable, another method is used that best approximates arm's length conditions.

29. Responsibilities. The standard transfer pricing method for each category of international transactions must be reviewed by the corporate tax department and approved by the treasurer and controller.

30. Transaction Processing. All intercompany transactions must be processed in accordance with written corporate policy.

31. Required Information. Intercompany suppliers must provide to their trading partners appropriate, relevant, and accurate information on all products or service billing transactions. At a minimum, valid charge number, description, receiving party information, supplier contact information, and billed value should be provided on all nonfinished product or service billing transactions. The information supplied must be sufficient to allow account reconciliations to be performed.

32. Transaction Recording. All intercompany transactions must be recorded in the same accounting period by both parties.

33. On-Time Payments. All intercompany receivables/payables must be paid at specified terms and conditions.

34. Management Reviews. Intercompany account imbalances must be reported to corporate and local management monthly for review.

35. Account Reconciliations. Intercompany imbalances must be reconciled (contents are known and status is current) and aged monthly. Reconciling items and items in dispute must be resolved within 60 days. The operating unit with the receivable balance will be assumed to have the correct balance unless the operating unit with the payable balance can demonstrate proof of delivery.

36. GL Reconciliations. Subsidiary (detail) ledgers supporting related party accounts should be reconciled (contents are known and status is current) to the corresponding GL control accounts monthly.

37. Minimum Billing Amount. Intercompany transactions must be above the minimum amount defined in company policy. An example of such a policy is that intercompany billings will occur only if they are greater than $10,000, unless the transaction affects cost of sales or is legally required to be billed.

TABLE OF RISKS AND CONTROLS – RECORD-TO-REPORT

Process: Record-to-Report Process			
Process Risk	**Recommended Policies**	**Internal Controls**	**KPIs**
1. **SEC and other governmental reporting requirements and/or loan restrictions may be violated.** Exposure to shareholder litigation increases substantially due to improper reporting.	■ Financial Close Checklist ■ Financial Close Policies and Procedures	1. Policies and Procedures 2. Policy Changes 3. Journal Entries 4. Documented Journal Entries 5. Standardized Journal Entries 6. Nonstandard Transactions 7. Contra-Asset Accounts 8. Monthly Accruals 9. Asset Account Reviews 10. Journal Entry Processing 11. Reporting Schedules and Cutoffs 12. GL Reconciliations 13. Suspense Account Transactions 14. GL Adjustments 15. Financial Report Preparation 16. Access to Accounting and Finance Records 17. Records Management 18. Financial Results 19. Financial Reporting Requirements 20. Legal Financial Reporting Requirements 21. Financial Statement Translation 22. GL Account Definitions 23. GL Account Owners 24. Actual-to-Forecast Comparisons 25. Related Party Transactions 26. Double Taxation 27. Penalties 28. Pricing Methods 29. Responsibilities 30. Transaction Processing 31. Transaction Reporting 32. Required Information 33. On-Time Payments 34. Management Reviews 35. Account Reconciliations 36. GL Reconciliations 37. Monthly Billing Amount	■ Number of Adjustments After Cutoffs ■ Number of Post-Close Entries ■ Number of Management Adjustments ■ Days to Close ■ Number of Financial Statement Corrections (Restatements)

Process: Record-to-Report Process			
Process Risk	Recommended Policies	Internal Controls	KPIs
2. **Reports may not be accurate, and critical decisions may be based upon erroneous information.** The financial records and financial statements may be misstated.	■ Financial Close Checklist ■ Financial Close Policies and Procedures	1. Policies and Procedures 2. Policy Changes 3. Journal Entries 4. Documented Journal Entries 5. Standardized Journal Entries 6. Nonstandard Transactions 7. Contra-Asset Accounts 8. Monthly Accruals 9. Asset Account Reviews 10. Journal Entry Processing 11. Reporting Schedules and Cutoffs 12. GL Reconciliations 13. Suspense Account Transactions 14. GL Adjustments 15. Financial Report Preparation 16. Access to Accounting and Finance Records 17. Records Management 18. Financial Results 19. Financial Reporting Requirements 20. Legal Financial Reporting Requirements 21. Financial Statement Translation 22. GL Account Definitions 23. GL Account Owners 24. Actual-to-Forecast Comparisons 25. Related Party Transactions 26. Double Taxation 27. Penalties 28. Pricing Methods 29. Responsibilities 30. Transaction Processing 31. Transaction Reporting 32. Required Information 33. On-Time Payments 34. Management Reviews 35. Account Reconciliations 36. GL Reconciliations 37. Monthly Billing Amount	■ Number of Adjustments After Cutoffs ■ Number of Post-Close Entries ■ Number of Management Adjustments ■ Days to Close ■ Number of Financial Statement Corrections (Restatements)

Process: Record-to-Report Process			
Process Risk	**Recommended Policies**	**Internal Controls**	**KPIs**
3. Cash flows may not be maximized, as projected receipts may not be accurate. Unanticipated currency purchases may be required or excess financing incurred.	■ Financial Close Checklist ■ Financial Close Policies and Procedures ■ Cash Management Policies	1. Policies and Procedures 2. Policy Changes 3. Journal Entries 4. Documented Journal Entries 5. Standardized Journal Entries 6. Nonstandard Transactions 7. Contra-Asset Accounts 8. Monthly Accruals 9. Asset Account Reviews 10. Journal Entry Processing 11. Reporting Schedules and Cutoffs 12. GL Reconciliations 13. Suspense Account Transactions 14. GL Adjustments 15. Financial Report Preparation	■ Amount of Cash Account Variances ■ Types and Numbers of Cash Forecasting Issues
4. Intercompany transactions are incorrect. Intercompany transactions are incorrectly reported and reconciled, causing discrepancies in both intercompany AP and AR.	■ Intercompany Policies and Procedures	30. Transaction Processing 31. Transaction Reporting 32. Required Information 33. On-Time Payments 34. Management Reviews 35. Account Reconciliations 36. GL Reconciliations 37. Monthly Billing Amount	■ Amount of Intercompany Variances ■ Purchase Price Variance (PPV) Trends
5. Transactions are recorded incorrectly. Transactions may result in inefficient use of company resources. Transactions may result in undesirable legal and/or tax implications.	■ Account Reconciliation Policies and Procedures ■ Financial Close Checklist	1. Policies and Procedures 2. Policy Changes 3. Journal Entries 4. Documented Journal Entries 5. Standardized Journal Entries 6. Nonstandard Transactions 7. Contra-Asset Accounts 8. Monthly Accruals 9. Asset Account Reviews 10. Journal Entry Processing 11. Reporting Schedules and Cutoffs 12. GL Reconciliations 13. Suspense Account Transactions 14. GL Adjustments 15. Financial Report Preparation 30. Transaction Processing 31. Transaction Reporting	■ Number of Adjustments After Cutoffs ■ Number of Post-Close Entries ■ Number of Management Adjustments ■ Number of GL Accounts with Variances ■ Days to Close ■ Number of Financial Statement Corrections (Restatements)

Process: Record-to-Report Process			
Process Risk	Recommended Policies	Internal Controls	KPIs
6. **There is a lack of adherence to company policies and procedures.** Policies and procedures may not be properly or consistently applied by or between the organization's operating units. The risk of error in the accumulation and reporting of financial information is increased.	■ Financial Close Checklist ■ Financial Close Policies and Procedures	1. Policies and Procedures 2. Policy Changes	■ Number of Adjustments After Cutoffs ■ Number of Post-Close Entries ■ Number of Management Adjustments ■ Number of GL Accounts with Variances ■ Days to Close ■ Number of Financial Statement Corrections (Restatements)
7. **Journal entries may be incorrectly prepared.** Entries may be duplicated, omitted, or made for the purposes of misstating account balances to conceal irregularities or shortages.	■ Financial Close Checklist ■ Financial Close Policies and Procedures ■ Journal Entry Approval Limits	3. Journal Entries 4. Documented Journal Entries 5. Standardized Journal Entries 6. Nonstandard Transactions	■ Number of Adjustments After Cutoffs ■ Number of Post-Close Entries ■ Number of Management Adjustments ■ Number of GL Accounts with Variances ■ Days to Close ■ Number of Financial Statement Corrections (Restatements)

Process: Record-to-Report Process			
Process Risk	**Recommended Policies**	**Internal Controls**	**KPIs**
8. **Accountability over recorded transactions may not be maintained.** Records may be destroyed or altered. This may result in the inability to prepare accurate and reliable financial statements. The company may be exposed to litigation due to inadequate record maintenance.	■ Financial Close Checklist ■ Financial Close Policies and Procedures	15. Financial Report Preparation 16. Access to Accounting and Finance Records 17. Records Management	■ Number of Adjustments After Cutoffs ■ Number of Post-Close Entries ■ Number of Management Adjustments ■ Number of GL Accounts with Variances ■ Days to Close ■ Number of Financial Statement Corrections (Restatements)
9. **Confidential and proprietary information may be reviewed and disclosed by unauthorized individuals.** The organization's competitive position and reputation may be adversely affected.	■ Financial Close Checklist ■ Financial Close Workflow Approval Process ■ Financial Close Policies and Procedures	16. Access to Accounting and Finance Records	■ Number of Ethics Violations Reported via Hotline
10. **Amounts could be accrued for expenses that are not likely to occur in order to generate "funding" sources for future periods.**	■ Account Reconciliation Policies and Procedures ■ Financial Close Checklist	8. Monthly Accruals 11. Reporting Schedules and Cutoffs	■ Trend Analysis of Accruals ■ Amount of AP Clearing Account Variances ■ Number of Open POs ■ Amounts of Open POs

Process: Record-to-Report Process			
Process Risk	**Recommended Policies**	**Internal Controls**	**KPIs**
11. **Financial information required for budgeting, forecasting, or analysis may not be available.**	■ Budget and Forecast Policies and Procedures	24 Actual-to-Forecast Comparisons	■ Variance Amount – Budgets to Actuals ■ Variance Amount – Forecast to Actuals
12. **Errors and omissions in physical safeguarding, authorization, and transaction processing may go undetected and uncor- rected.** Financial statements and records may be prepared inaccurately or untimely.	■ Financial Close Checklist ■ Financial Close Workflow Approval Process ■ Financial Close Policies and Procedures	1. Policies and Procedures 2. Policy Changes 3. Journal Entries 4. Documented Journal Entries 5. Standardized Journal Entries 6. Nonstandard Transactions 7. Contra-Asset Accounts 8. Monthly Accruals 9. Asset Account Reviews 10. Journal Entry Processing 11. Reporting Schedules and Cutoffs 12. GL Reconciliations 13. Suspense Account Transactions 14. GL Adjustments 15. Financial Report Preparation 30. Transaction Processing 31. Transaction Reporting	■ Number of Adjustments After Cutoffs ■ Number of Post- Close Entries ■ Number of Management Adjustments ■ Number of GL Accounts with Variances ■ Days to Close ■ Number of Financial Statement Corrections (Restatements)

CHAPTER FOURTEEN

Budgets, Forecasts, and Capital Budgeting

 OVERVIEW – BUDGETS AND FORECASTS

Budgeting is a key responsibility for controllers and their staff. The controller's organization "controls" access to corporate funds. In many situations, professionals in the controller's organization must approve expenditures according to the organization's delegation of authority policy. Controllers typically are part of the organization lead by an organization-wide or divisional CFO. In smaller companies and organizations, the roles of controller and CFO may be combined into one position.

BUDGETS, FORECASTS, AND CAPITAL BUDGETING PROCESS FLOW

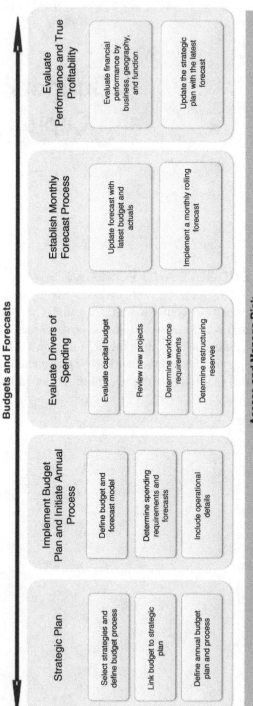

Budgets and Forecasts

Strategic Plan
- Select strategies and define budget process
- Link budget to strategic plan
- Define annual budget plan and process

Implement Budget Plan and Initiate Annual Process
- Define budget and forecast model
- Determine spending requirements and forecasts
- Include operational details

Evaluate Drivers of Spending
- Evaluate capital budget
- Review new projects
- Determine workforce requirements
- Determine restructuring reserves

Establish Monthly Forecast Process
- Update forecast with latest budget and actuals
- Implement a monthly rolling forecast

Evaluate Performance and True Profitability
- Evaluate financial performance by business, geography, and function
- Update the strategic plan with the latest forecast

Assess and Manage Risk

Link Budgets and Forecasts to the Strategic Plan

FINANCIAL STATEMENT ANALYSIS

Financial statement analysis is a basic form of financial forecasting. Companies often compare several financial statements during a specific time period to determine if any trends exist relating to the company's financial information. Trends may include increases or decreases in revenue sales, cost of goods sold, and business expenses listed on the company's income statement. Companies can also use financial ratios to break down their balance sheets and determine how well they are generating economic value through the use of assets. Ratios indicate how well the company can meet short-term financial obligations, generate profit from the sale of individual goods or services, generate capital from assets, and other specific information.

THE PURPOSE OF BUDGETING

According to PricewaterhouseCoopers (PwC), company and business unit budgets give financial expression to strategy, motivate managers to achieve commonly understood targets, and provide a coherent framework for the analysis of results. Historically spreadsheets have been used as the main budgeting tool. However, they have a number of weaknesses when used for budgeting, including reconciliation problems arising from complex links across many sheets and workbooks, and inflexibility of reporting structures. Many organizations of all sizes have moved towards automating their budget processes.

In order to make effective decisions and coordinate the decisions and actions of the various departments, a business needs to have a plan for its operations. Planning the financial operations of a business is called budgeting. A budget is a written financial plan of a business for a specific period of time expressed in dollars. Each area of a business's operations typically has a separate budget.

For example, a business might have an advertising budget, a capital budget, a purchasing budget, a sales budget, a manufacturing budget, a research and development budget, and a cash budget. New and ongoing projects would each have a detailed budget. Each budget would then be compiled into a master budget for the operations of the entire company.

A business that does not have a budget or a plan will make decisions that do not contribute to the profitability of the business because managers will lack a clear idea of the goals of the business. A budget serves five main purposes:

1. Communication
2. Coordination
3. Planning
4. Control
5. Evaluation

The budget process is usually initiated after the completion and approval of the organization's strategic planning process.

CONTROLLER'S TOOL 26 – TYPES OF BUDGETING

Introduction. An organization cannot use only one type of budget to accommodate all its operations. Therefore, it chooses from among the following budget types:

Fixed Budget. The fixed budget, often called a static budget, is not subject to change or alteration during the budget period. A company "fixes" budgets in at least two circumstances:

1. The cost of a budgeted activity shows little or no change when the volume of production fluctuates within an expected range of values. For example, in a manufacturing company a 10 percent increase in production may have little or no impact on administrative expenses.
2. The volume of production remains steady or follows a tight, preset schedule during the budget period. A company may fix its production volume in response to an all-inclusive contract, or it may produce stock goods.

Variable, or Flexible, Budget. The variable, or flexible, budget is called a dynamic budget. It is an effective evaluative tool for a company that frequently experiences variations in sales volume that strongly affect the level of production. In these circumstances a company initially constructs a series of budgets for a range of production volumes that it can reasonably and profitably meet.

Continuous Budget. The continuous budget adds a new period (month) to the budget as the current period comes to a close. Under the fiscal year approach, the budget year becomes shorter as the year progresses. However, the continuous method forces managers to review and assess budget estimates for a never-ending 12-month cycle.

Operating Budget. The operating budget gathers the projected results of the operating decisions made by a company to exploit available business opportunities. In the final analysis, the operating budget presents a projected (pro forma) income statement, which displays how much money the company expects to make. This net income demonstrates the degree to which management is able to respond to the market in supplying the right product at an attractive price, with a profit to the company.

The operating budget consists of a number of parts that detail the company's plans on how to capture revenues, provide adequate supply, control costs, and organize the labor force. These parts are the sales budget, production budget, direct materials budget, direct labor budget, factory overhead budget, selling and administrative expense budget, and pro forma income statement.

Financial Budget. The operating budget and the financial budget are the two main components of a company's master budget. The financial budget consists of the capital expenditure budget, the cash budget, and the budgeted balance sheet. Much of the information in the financial budget is drawn from the operating budget, and then all of the information is consolidated into the master budget.

Consolidated Budget. The consolidated budget aggregates all business activities into one comprehensive plan. It is not a single document, but the compilation of many interrelated budgets, which together summarize an organization's business activities for the coming year. Standardization of the process facilitates comparison and aggregation even of mixed products and industries.

Preparation of the consolidated budget is a sequential process that starts with the sales budget. The sales budget predicts the number of units a company expects to sell. From this information, a company determines how many units it must produce. Subsequently, it calculates how much it will spend to produce the required number of units. Finally, it aggregates the foregoing to estimate its profitability.

CONTROLLER'S TOOL 27 – THE BUDGETING PROCESS

Introduction. The corporate budgeting, forecasting, and reporting process presents a challenge to most companies, regardless of size or industry. Budgeting is often seen as burdensome and time consuming. Yet budgeting is also a crucial element of financial management, which in turn is a huge contributor to a company's overall success or failure

There are several approaches and methodologies for developing the organization's budget. The approach will depend on the size and complexity of the organization and the controller's prior experience with the budgeting process.

Key point: The budgeting process applies to organizations of all types and industries of all types. Many organizations have developed a standard budget process and template that fits the needs of their companies.

Step 1: Determining the Flow of Information

A company gathers the data necessary to compile a budget in one of two ways:

1. It centralizes the process and has senior management establish the company's priorities and projections.
2. It directs individual work units and departments to assemble the information on their own.

The former is referred to as "top-down budgeting," the latter as "bottom-up budgeting."

In general, budgets that are constructed from the bottom up are preferable, if only for the reason that individual workers and units know more about their departments than central management. On the other hand, bottom-up budgeting requires more time to execute and is difficult to manage since all departments and divisions need to complete their budgets for approval and consolidation at the corporate level. There may be several iterations of the budget using this approach, since changes may be needed after the consolidated budgets are reviewed and the results are either too high or too low.

Step 2: Organizing Your Budget Process

The budget process is driven by the way your organization is organized. The budget process can be organized by function, product division, project, facility, region, country, or division.

- If the company's geographic operations are separate profit centers (sometimes called "accountability centers"), then it may choose to budget by region.
- If the company is organized based on traditional functions – for instance, there's a separate sales department that handles all products in all regions, a separate manufacturing department that handles all products in all regions, and a separate distribution department for all products in all regions – then it may budget along these lines. The sales department, in this situation, would be referred to as a revenue center, while the manufacturing and distribution divisions would be considered cost centers.

Key Point: Budget processes can be driven by an organization's organizational or financial hierarchy, as established within its ERP system.

Step 3: Gathering Historical Data

After a company decides how it will organize the budget process, it turns its attention to gathering historical performance information. The first place to look for historical performance data is the company's financial statements: its balance sheet, income statement, and cash flow statement. Another source is the company's financial ratio data.

Key Point: Many organizations start with the actual results from prior years to establish a so-called run rate for the budget process.

1. **Gathering Sales Information**

   When it comes to gathering historical sales data, your company ought to know its past performance based on:
   - Product lines
   - Regions
   - Customers

2. **Gathering Expense Information**

   When it comes to gathering historical expense data, your organization should know its past performance that is reflective of actual spending based on:
   - **Direct Costs.** This includes raw materials, labor, and inventory costs.
   - **Indirect Costs.** This includes selling, research and development, and general and administrative expenses.
   - **Fixed Costs.** This includes many of the indirect costs of doing business, such as rent and depreciation, which are part of general and administrative (G&A) expenses.
   - **Variable Costs.** This includes many of the direct costs of doing business, such as raw materials, energy, and labor costs, as well as taxes, which are also considered a variable expense.

Step 4: Making Projections

The forth step in the budgeting process is for the company to project its performance for the coming year. Establishing budget projections can be as simple or as complicated a task as your company makes it.

Some companies rely on incremental budgeting, in which forecasts are directly tied to past performance and are therefore easy to prepare. Others rely on zero-based budgeting, in which forecasts have nothing to do with past performance and are therefore more difficult to prepare. And still others rely on a hybrid approach.

1. **Incremental Budgeting**
   - Incremental budget projections are the easiest to prepare; all you need to know is what the company spent or made in the previous year. Then you tack on whatever percentage increase or decrease you think is appropriate. This approach can also be described as adding a percentage to the organization's current run rate.
   - The incremental approach is the least-precise method for preparing a budget. Often companies that rely on incremental budgets repeat past mistakes, such as continuing to overspend.

2. **Zero-Based Budgeting**

Zero-based budgeting is the antithesis of the incremental approach. Made popular in the 1970s, zero-based budgets operate on the premise that the amount a company budgeted for a line item in one year has little to do with what it should be budgeting in future years. While more accurate than incremental budgets, zero-based budgets require tremendous amounts of information. As a result, this process is time-consuming and expensive.

3. **Hybrid Method**

Many organizations rely on a hybrid approach to budgeting, in which projections are based in part on past performance. However, current industry trends and macroeconomic forces are also considered as part of the equation.

Step 5: Determining the Break-Even Point

The break-even point is the level of sales where the organization neither makes money nor loses money. It is the level of sales where the gross profit is the same as the fixed costs.

 CONTROLLER'S TOOL 28 – BUDGET PROCESS BEST PRACTICES

1. **Make the budget process part of the corporate culture.** Excellent business management requires excellent financial management, which in turn requires a company-wide commitment to excellence in budgeting, forecasting, and reporting. Most companies acknowledge the importance of corporate planning and claim to be actively participating in ongoing planning. But in reality senior management may be engaged in strategic planning, with finance running the budgeting show and department managers viewing the annual planning process as an unwelcome chore.

2. **Align the strategic and operating plans.** Controllers can help translate strategic goals into specific departmental plans and related expense drivers, such as headcount and equipment. By translating their strategic goals into operational plans, and by tracking and measuring performance against plan, leading companies are able to make meaningful progress in achieving their objectives.

3. **Start the budget process at the top and bottom.** An important ingredient in successful budgeting and forecasting lies in an organization's ability to plan from the bottom up and to meet top-down strategic objectives. Some companies establish top-down targets and then turn the annual budget process over to finance, with a mandate to meet the numbers.

   Other companies require detailed bottom-up planning and then plug the total company numbers at the top so that the plan meets strategic targets. Neither of these approaches reflects a commitment to planning excellence. Instead, leading companies provide a top-down perspective on strategic goals, objectives, and expectations through initial guidance from senior management. Next department managers build a plan from the bottom up, showing how they intend to meet those goals. This process will often require frequent iterations for the top-down and bottom-up approaches to meet.

The result is a plan that:

- Is supported by department managers, because they helped create it and will be rewarded for meeting it. There is a greater sense of ownership and commitment to the budget process and its results.
- Is supported by senior management, because operational goals are aligned with the strategic goals.
- Is supported by finance, because they added value to a productive, collaborative effort, rather than demanding participation in an exercise with little added value.

4. **Drive collaboration between functions.** Not only should strategic and operating plans be aligned, but plans between functional areas should also be linked. Best practices include direct involvement from line-of-business managers and a collaborative approach to budgeting and forecasting. In addition to understanding strategic goals, department managers also need to know what other functions are planning. For example, in a company that is planning a new product rollout, manufacturing needs to ramp up production, marketing needs to produce new collateral, and sales needs to add new headcount. But the marketing plan should also include programs timed to support the new sales representatives. The facilities department needs to plan for new headcount, equipment, and product storage.

   This collaborative planning can be accomplished through an iterative process that provides managers with the opportunity to forecast and share different scenarios with each other. Controllers can play a key role in facilitating the coordination of plans across the company.

5. **Adapt to changing business conditions.** The next important steps are evaluating actual progress against budget and reforecasting in response to changing business conditions. All businesses, particularly those in flux, are better served by a planning process that can quickly adapt to changes in the company or in the market.

   The key elements of such a process include:

   a. **Frequent Reforecasting.** Especially in fast-moving, quickly growing businesses with multiple market pressures, forecasting may be needed on a monthly or even biweekly basis. Ongoing reforecasting will help managers to continually answer critical questions such as, "What did we expect?", "How are we doing against our plan?", and even more importantly, "How should we adapt our plans as a result?"

   b. **Rolling Forecasts.** A company engaged in ongoing rolling forecasts is always looking forward to the immediate or near-term future. The forecast time frame should extend out two to eight quarters, depending on the volatility of the business. Planning should be an ongoing process with frequent opportunities for managers to view the latest internal and external data on how the organization is doing. They should be able to make alterations to their plans based on new information.

6. **Model business drivers.** An important feature of a so-called best practice budget or forecast is that it is based on a model with formulas that are tied to fundamental business drivers. Simply importing and manipulating actual results does not reflect the underlying cause and effect relationships in a business. Building modeling into plans provides a way to ensure appropriate consistency across functions. It also provides a way to promote planning coordination between functions. For example, future sales forecasts can be tied to the marketing expenditure needed to generate the necessary number of leads.

7. **Manage content that is material to the organization.** A focus on material content in budgeting will free managers from unnecessary detail, enabling them to produce better plans. While supporting detail can provide audit trail and insight into managers' thinking, more detail does not necessarily make for a better plan. According to a Hackett Group study of planning best practices, the fewer the number of line items, the better the planning practices. Hackett found that world-class companies average 15–40 line items in their budgets, compared to highly inefficient companies that average 2,000 line items.

   Managing material content means that a company pays attention to whatever has a real and significant impact on expenses, revenues, capital, and cash flow. This company will:

   - **Avoid false precision.** A complex model might not have any more precision than a simpler model. More detail and intricate calculations can lure managers into the trap of thinking their plan is therefore more accurate.
   - **Monitor volatile – not stable – accounts.** Efforts are best spent on fluid expenses, such as headcount and compensation.
   - **Aggregate accounts.** The budget does not need to reflect the same level of detail as the GL. Even if the GL has 15 different travel accounts, managers should provide the total travel budget.

8. **Focus on a timely and accurate budget process.** Many organizations have an inefficient and inflexible planning process, at the center of which is the annual budget. These companies' time-consuming distribution and consolidation processes practically guarantee that the plan data is irrelevant before it is even shared. And plans based on stale data and assumptions are of no value. According to the Hackett Group, the average annual planning and budgeting process is three to five months long. A plan that takes this long to prepare is out of date by the time it is completed. The Hackett Group reports that world-class organizations, on the other hand, spend less than two months preparing the annual plan.

9. **Budget for major projects.** Even though IT includes technology projects in its budget, it's important to consider the impact on other departments that may be required to support the project effort. It's also critical to ensure that the funding is agreed upon before the project is initiated and that the stakeholder is defined.

10. **Establish a budget owner and tracking process.** Lastly, a budget owner needs to be assigned to implement the process and track actual results on a monthly and quarterly process. Many organizations not only tie the budget process to strategic planning, they operationalize the process by including a budget review with the monthly financial closing process. These organizations track the components listed below, and explanations for established dollar or percentage variances must be included.

    - Actuals
    - Forecast
    - Budget

11. **Perform variance analysis.** Once a budget is established, one of the main financial tasks for the operations or support manager is to explain variances between actual performance and the budget. All types of companies will require managers to review and explain any variances on the budget variance report.

Format for the Budget Variance Report

Budget variance reports, sometimes known as monthly operating reports or departmental reports, are created from the GL system and have rows of statistics, revenues, and expenses. The titles will be listed in a column down the left side (or sometimes in the middle) of the report.

Across the top are column titles for actual results, along with budget, budget variance, percent variance, and sometimes last year. It is common to have both current period (month) and year-to-date information, abbreviated YTD.

The body of the report will contain the numbers associated with row and column titles. For instance, most departments will have a line for supplies. A simple row may show:

Actual	Budget	Variance	Percent
$900.00	$1,000.00	$100.00	10%

This shows that although $1,000 was budgeted, only $900 was spent, leaving a variance of $100, which is 10 percent. The percent is computed by dividing the variance by the *budget*, not the actual amount.

The variance is referred to as a positive or *favorable* variance, since it is better that actual be lower than budget for expenses. When expenses are greater than the budget, it is known as a negative or unfavorable variance. Report formats and terminology vary by company, so consult your finance department for specifics.

MOVING YOUR FINANCE FUNCTION TO DYNAMIC BUDGETING AND PLANNING

To be competitive in today's volatile business conditions, controllers must help to lead their companies beyond the traditional budgeting and planning cycles. In a recent Accenture study, two-thirds of respondents reported that their planning accuracy had decreased due to economic volatility. Just 10 percent said they were "fully satisfied" with their current planning capabilities. Along similar lines, Ventana research reveals that a mere 9 percent of companies react to major change in a well-coordinated manner.

Dynamic Budgeting and Planning

Clearly, alternatives are needed to the traditional time-consuming and poorly performing budget ritual. Budgeting and planning must evolve from a once-a-year exercise into a dynamic and continuously adjustable process.

This can be achieved by utilizing analytics-based modeling capabilities. Such technology enables scenario planning – the posing of what-if events that could significantly alter budget assumptions, and then testing practical solutions.

Such a dynamic model features so-called input dials that are adjusted as needed, providing a built-in capability for rapid response and adjustment.

In contrast, traditional planning and budgeting tend to rely heavily on historical data that's unlikely to be relevant to future developments. To meet this challenge, more companies are moving towards a rolling-quarters planning process to replace the year-to-year model.

Improving Quality and Speed

Most companies still utilize desktop spreadsheets as their principal budgeting and planning tools. Dedicated planning software can not only improve the quality of budgeting and planning but also improve their efficiency and speed.

With new Web-based solutions, data is held in a centralized database or budget model that can be securely shared across company units. This replaces the cumbersome e-mailing of spreadsheets back and forth between numerous stakeholders. As it's gathered, data can be updated virtually in real time.

Of course, the effectiveness of the analytic tools depends on the quality of the data that is gathered, validated, and consolidated – ranging from market share of competitors to customer repurchase intent.

The gathering of such data requires a high degree of coordination, starting early in the planning process, between the finance function and operational business units.

CONTROLLER'S TOOL 29 – TYPES OF FINANCIAL FORECASTING MODELS

Introduction. There are several types of financial forecasting models that controllers should be aware of when developing a forecasting process for their organizations.

Types of Financial Forecasting Models

Macroeconomic Financial Models. Macroeconomic financial models are usually based on econometric analysis, built by government departments, universities, or economic consulting firms, and used to forecast the economy of a country. Macroeconomic models are used to analyze the effect of government policy decisions on variables such as foreign exchange rates, interest rates, disposable income, and the gross national product (GNP).

Industry Financial Models. Industry models are usually econometric-based models of specific industries or economic sectors. Industry models are often similar to macroeconomic models and are typically used by industry associations or industry research analysts to forecast KPIs within the industry in question.

Corporate Financial Models. Corporate financial models are built to model the total operations of a company and are often perceived to be critical in the strategic planning of business operations in large corporations and startup companies alike. Almost all corporate financial models are built in Excel, although specialized financial modeling software is increasingly being used, especially in large corporations, to ensure standardization and accuracy of multiple financial models or to comply with spreadsheet management requirements imposed by SOX.

Deterministic Financial Models. In a deterministic model, a financial analyst enters a set of input data into a spreadsheet and programs the spreadsheet to perform a series of mathematical calculations, which displays an output result.

Most deterministic financial models are built by performing an analysis on historical data to derive the relationship between key forecast variables. In a corporate context, historical accounting relationships are often used to forecast key revenue and cost variables.

Most deterministic models use one or two dimensional sensitivity analysis tables built into the model to analyze the question of risk and uncertainty in the model's output results. Each sensitivity analysis table allows a financial analyst to perform a what-if analysis on one or two variables at a time. The advantages of sensitivity tables are their simplicity and the ease of integrating them into existing deterministic financial models that have already been built.

Multiple sensitivity analysis tables can be combined in a scenario manager. The scenario manager is useful when there are interdependencies between the changing variables, as financial analysts can configure and change multiple variables in each scenario.

In certain scenarios, multiple regression analysis is used to determine the mathematical relationship between multiple variables in a deterministic financial model, and such analysis is termed *econometric analysis*.

The deterministic model is probably the most common type of financial model used in business and finance today. Most financial forecasting models used for revenue management, cost management, and project financing are primarily deterministic-based financial models.

Simulation-Based Financial Models. While a deterministic financial model is normally structured in such a way that a single-point estimate is used for each input variable, simulation-based financial models work by entering the likely distribution of key inputs defined by the mean, variance, and type of distribution.

Simulation models use these range of inputs to recalculate the defined mathematical equation in the financial model through a few hundred iterations, normally 500 or more. The results of the analysis will produce the likely distribution of the result, therefore providing an indication of the expected range of results instead of a single-point estimate.

Where risk is a dominant factor in the financial modeling scenario being analyzed, a reliable estimation of the likely range of results is often more useful than a single-point estimate. Simulation-based financial models therefore allow a financial analyst to model the question of risk and uncertainty using a higher level of granularity.

Specialized Financial Models. Specialized financial models are narrower in scope and essentially sophisticated calculators built to address a specific business problem or financial computation. Cost management models, marginal contribution analysis models, and option pricing models are examples of specialized financial models.

CONTROLLER'S TOOL 30 – THE FORECASTING PROCESS FOR SMALL BUSINESSES

Introduction. In the article "Financial Forecasting Tools," Osmond Vitez of Demand Media states, "Small businesses often use a variety of tools and techniques for measuring performance and forecasting future financial returns. Financial forecasting is the business function responsible for analyzing current internal business information, external economic information and processing these items through a financial calculation. Financial calculations determine the profitability of business expansion or new business opportunities. Smaller or home-based businesses may not use financial forecasting tools as frequently as larger business organizations." The types of financial forecasting tools utilized by small businesses and discussed by Vitez are:[1]

Net Present Value

The net present value calculation estimates future cash inflows from expanded business or new business opportunities and discounts these dollar amounts back to today's dollar value. The discount rate is usually a predetermined rate of return percentage that a company wishes to achieve on new business opportunities. A baseline percentage is usually 10 percent or 12 percent, which is commonly seen as the rate of return earned by investing money in the stock market. The sum of discounted cash inflows is compared with the initial cash outflow used to expand operations or begin new business opportunities. If the future cash inflows are higher than the initial cash outflow, the opportunity is usually seen as a good investment.

Cost of Capital

A cost of capital financial forecast usually compares the interest rates companies must pay on debt or equity financing to the return on current or future business operations. The weighted average cost of capital and capital asset pricing model are two basic forecasting tools used to compare financing interest rates. These financial forecasting tools usually rely on the market cost of debt, equity-prime interest rate, or similar interest rates to determine if the company should use external financing when accepting new business opportunities.

 TABLE OF CONTROLS – BUDGETS AND FORECASTS

Process: Budgets and Forecasts

---

1. **Budget Process Linkage to the Strategic Plan.** The company needs to have both a strategic plan and a budget. The strategic plan lays out the direction and goals of the business and guidelines for actions to achieve those goals, while the budget looks at the money needed to support achieving those goals. Budgeting is only one part of the strategic planning process.

2. **Ability to Benchmark Budgets**. Budgets should be designed to be used as a benchmark against which results are measured.

3. **Expense Approval.** All expenditures must be approved under budgetary procedures and controls. This means that they must be prepared by using the organization's hierarchical structure and adapted as needed to accommodate changes in funding and anticipated expenditures.

4. **Budget Revisions**. Any change in funding must be presented in the organization's budget. Whether staffing levels will be modified or new contracts awarded, determining what impact the additional anticipated expenditures will have on the budget becomes increasingly difficult, because the same cost allocation methodologies used in practice must be applied to planned expenditures.

5. **Record of Budget Assumptions and Calculations**. As budgets are developed and subsequently modified, it is imperative that staff keep adequate records of the assumptions and calculations used.

---

[1]Vitez, Osmond (n.d.). Financial forecasting tools. CHRON. (Accessed July 31, 2020) https://smallbusiness.chron.com/financial-forecasting-tools-4583.html.

6. **Budget Variance Analysis.** Variances can occur for a variety of reasons, including benign factors such as timing issues related to contractor and supplier payments. In other cases, the variance may be indicative of cost allocation issues, a material accounting error, or even fraud.

7. **Budget Review Process**. An example of a way to corroborate financial representation is to verify revenue and review historical budgets and actual results. If actual results have previously averaged 10 percent below budget and the current year results were 20 percent over budget, obtain information supporting this exception in performance. Some areas to examine would include changes in budget format or process, purchases or new additions of new product lines, changes in industry, and changes in business. Confirm revenue figures by reviewing shipping records and sales data.

8. **Actual to Forecast Comparisons**. Comparisons and explanations of actual financial information to forecast information must be routinely completed according to established policies and procedures; all significant variances must be researched and reflected in revised estimates/plans as appropriate in a timely way. Uniformly defined (same methodology) balance sheet performance measures must be established and actual performance measured against forecast on a monthly basis.

TABLE OF RISK AND CONTROLS – BUDGETS AND FORECASTS

Process: Budgets and Forecasts			
Process Risk	**Recommended Policies**	**Internal Controls**	**KPIs**
1. **The budget is not linked to the strategic plan.** Company objectives will be compromised and not achieved.	■ Strategic Plan ■ Budget Process	1. Budget Process Linkage to the Strategic Plan	■ Percentage Budget Variance ■ Percentage Strategic Goals Achieved
2. **Budget discrepancies are not reported.** This could result in the misalignment of company funds or fraud.	■ Budget Process ■ Budget Results Tracking	4. Budget Revisions 6. Budget Variance Analysis 7. Budget Review Process 8. Actual-to-Forecast Comparisons	■ Percentage Budget Variance
3. **There is a lack of visibility for budget results.** There is an inability to benchmark and analyze results, actuals, and spending trends. Poor financial decisions can be made.	■ Budget Process ■ Budget Results Tracking	4. Budget Revisions 6. Budget Variance Analysis 7. Budget Review Process 8. Actual-to-Forecast Comparisons	■ Percentage Budget Variance
4. **There are no expense approvals**. Overspending and fraud can occur without defined management approvals.	■ Budget Process ■ Budget Results Tracking	3. Expense Approval	■ Percentage Budget Variance ■ Value of Unapproved Expenditures

Process: Budgets and Forecasts			
Process Risk	**Recommended Policies**	**Internal Controls**	**KPIs**
5. **Budget revisions are not approved.** Without approval, overspending and fraud can occur, which will adversely impact company funds.	■ Budget Process	3. Expense Approval 4. Budget Revisions 6. Budget Variance Analysis 7. Budget Review Process 8. Actual-to-Forecast Comparisons	■ Percentage Budget Variance
6. **Budget assumptions and calculations are not documented.**	■ Budget Process	5. Record of Budget Assumptions and Calculations	■ Percentage Budget Variance ■ Percentage Strategic Goals Achieved
7. **Budget variances are not visible.** When variances are not made visible, rogue spending or fraud can occur. This also indicates a potential lack of management of company funds.	■ Budget Process ■ Budget Results Tracking	4. Budget Revisions 6. Budget Variance Analysis 7. Budget Review Process 8. Actual-to-Forecast Comparisons	■ Percentage Budget Variance ■ Value of Unapproved Expenditures

OVERVIEW – CAPITAL BUDGET AND FIXED ASSETS

The capital budget is the result of the capital planning process. The capital budget includes planned outlays for long-lived assets that are expected to generate income or support business operations over a number of years.

Capital budgeting is the process that a business uses to determine which proposed fixed-asset purchases it should accept and which should be declined. This process is used to create a quantitative view of each proposed fixed asset investment, thereby giving a rational basis for making a judgment.

DEVELOPING THE CAPITAL BUDGET

The controller has an active role in the capital budget and fixed assets budget process. The controller is usually responsible for driving the capital approval and review process and may establish a review board described as follows.

To formalize the capital review and approval process, private and public companies utilize the review board approach to formalize the process and to ensure that all capital requests are consolidated and reviewed within the same venue.

Capital budgeting has many aspects. It includes searching for new and more profitable investment proposals, investigating engineering and marketing considerations to predict the consequences of accepting an investment, and conducting economic analysis to determine the profit potential of an investment proposal. The basic features of capital budgeting decisions are:

1. Current funds are exchanged for future benefits.
2. There is an investment in long-term activities.
3. The future benefits will accrue to the firm over a series of years.

Some organizations may have a capital planning committee that reviews and approves all requests for capital. The committee always meets on an annual basis in tandem with the budgeting process. The committee also meets throughout the fiscal year on a quarterly basis to review the results of capital expenditures. The capital planning process begins with two primary questions:

1. What do we need?
2. Why do we need it?

CONTROLLER'S TOOL 31 – CONTROLLER'S AREAS OF RESPONSIBILITY FOR THE CAPITAL BUDGET AND FIXED ASSETS

Introduction. This tool outlines the areas of a controller's responsibility for the capital budget and fixed asset management processes.

Controller's Areas of Responsibility for the Capital Budget and Fixed Assets

- Establish a procedure for the planning and control of fixed assets.
- Establish the criteria for the approval process.
- Review approval limits to ensure that the company's DoA policy is followed.
- Establish a review and approval process.
- Review projected return rates.
- Ensure that capital expenditures reflect the organization's strategic plan and that the funds are available to pay for the expenditures.
- Review economic alternatives to asset purchases, such as leasing, renting, or buying the item from another supplier.
- Establish a reporting system that informs managers about the cost of maintenance, idle time, productivity, and actual costs versus budget.
- Implement a depreciation policy for all types of equipment for book and tax purposes.
- Maintain property records that identify all assets, describe their locations, track transfers, and account for depreciation.
- Ensure that proper insurance coverage is maintained for the fixed assets.
- Develop internal controls to ensure that fixed assets are physically counted on a regular basis.

CONTROLLER'S TOOL 32 – ALTERNATIVE METHODS FOR CAPITAL BUDGETING

Introduction. This tool suggests methods for the decision-making process to finalize a capital budget.

Alternative Methods for Capital Budgeting

- **Internal Rate of Return (IRR).** The discount rate at which net present value of the project becomes zero. Higher IRR should be preferred.

- **Profitability Index (PI).** The ratio of present value of future cash flows of a project to initial investment required for the project.

- **Payback Period** measures the time in which the initial cash flow is returned by the project. Cash flows are not discounted. Lower payback period is preferred.

- **Net Present Value (NPV).** NPV is equal to initial cash outflow less sum of discounted cash inflows. Higher NPV is preferred and an investment is only viable if its NPV is positive. Using NPV as a measure, capital budgeting involves selecting those projects that increase the value of the organization because they have a positive NPV. The timing and growth rate of the incoming cash flow is important only to the extent of its impact on NPV. Using NPV as the criterion by which to select projects assumes efficient capital markets so that the firm has access to whatever capital is needed to pursue the positive NPV projects. In situations where this is not the case, there may be capital rationing and the capital budgeting process becomes more complex.

- **Accounting Rate of Return (ARR).** The profitability of the project calculated as projected total net income divided by initial or average investment. Net income is not discounted.

- **Real Options Analysis.** Real options analysis has become important, as option pricing models have gotten more sophisticated. Discounted cash flow methods essentially value projects as if they were risky bonds, with the promised cash flows known. But managers will have many choices about how to increase future cash inflows or decrease future cash outflows. In other words, managers get to manage the projects – not simply accept or reject them. Real options analysis tries to value the choices – the option value – that the managers will have in the future and adds these values to the NPV.

- **Ranked Projects.** The real value of capital budgeting is to rank projects. Most organizations have many projects that could potentially be financially rewarding. Once it has been determined that a particular project has exceeded its hurdle, it should be ranked against peer projects (e.g. highest PI to lowest PI). The highest-ranking projects should be implemented until the budgeted capital has been expended.

- **Funding Sources.** When a corporation determines its capital budget, it must acquire said funds. Three methods are generally available to publicly traded corporations: corporate bonds, preferred stock, and common stock. The ideal mix of those funding sources is determined by the financial managers of the firm and is related to the amount of financial risk that the corporation is willing to undertake. Corporate bonds entail the lowest financial risk and therefore generally have the lowest interest rate. Preferred stock has no financial risk, but dividends – including all in arrears – must be paid to the preferred stockholders before any cash disbursements can be made to common stockholders.

TABLE OF CONTROLS – CAPITAL BUDGET AND FIXED ASSETS

Process: Capital Budget and Fixed Assets

1. Capital Budget Process. Capital budgeting, along with investment appraisal, is the planning process used to determine whether an organization's long-term investments – such as new machinery, replacement of machinery, new plants, new products, and research development projects – are worth the funding of cash through the firm's capitalization structure. Capital budgeting helps a company to understand the various risks involved in an investment opportunity and how these risks affect the returns of the company.

2. Prioritization of Funds for Projects. Capital budgeting is most involved in ranking projects and raising funds when long-term investment is taken into account. It helps the company to estimate which investment option would yield the best possible return.

3. Control of Fixed Assets. The responsibilities for custody and approval of movements and transfers of fixed assets must be separated from accounting duties.

4. Control of Fixed Asset Records. Records of fixed assets must be maintained in the company's chart of accounts and they must:

■ Detail depreciation, depletion, or amortization
■ Describe the physical location of the assets in sufficient detail to facilitate
  ■ Conducting physical inventories
  ■ Define custodianship

Asset records must be transferred from incomplete construction to the property, plant, and equipment accounts as soon as the asset is obtained and placed into operation.

■ Appropriations and deletions must be closed out on a timely basis.
■ An initial inventory must be made of new plant facilities when transferred to the property, plant, and equipment account.

5. Control of Assets in the Custody of a Third Party. Assets that are in the custody of a third party must be identified and written acknowledgment of the custody should be obtained from the custodian. Clearly defined associate and third-party contracts are suitable forms of acknowledgment.

6. Inventory and Reconciliation of Capital Assets. All capitalized assets must be verified and reconciled to the fixed-asset accounting records by personnel independent of asset custody at least every fiscal year. The verification process must be endorsed by controllers and internal audit when the process is other than by physical count (e.g. sampling).

■ Thorough investigation of discrepancies must be conducted by employees independent of asset custody.
■ Adjustments to the fixed-asset accounting records must be timely and must be approved in accordance with the DoA policy.

7. Assets Not in Use. Assets that are no longer in use must be periodically identified and decisions on their disposal or further utilization must then be made.

1. Proposals to sell, retire, transfer, or otherwise dispose of assets must be documented and approved in accordance with the DoA policy.

2. Authorizations must accurately describe the asset, its location, and the reason for its disposal or transfer.

3. Where appropriate, bids must be solicited for assets to be sold, consistent with internal control requirements.

8. Sale, Liquidation, or Disposal of Assets. Sale, liquidation, or other disposal of a business segment must only be implemented after appropriate reviews, endorsements, and approvals in accordance with the DoA policy. Procedures must be implemented and evaluations of reserves must be conducted by qualified personnel in a consistent manner per the corporate appraisal schedule.

TABLE OF RISKS AND CONTROLS – CAPITAL BUDGET AND FIXED ASSETS

Process: Capital Budget and Fixed Assets			
Process Risk	**Recommended Policies**	**Internal Controls**	**KPIs**
1. **Poor investments on capital projects are made.** Investments are made on the lack of decision-making criteria.	■ Capital Budget Process ■ Investment and Project Approval Process	1. Capital Budget Process 2. Prioritization of Funds for Projects or Disposal of Assets	■ Percentage Variance of Actuals to Capital Budgets ■ ROI on Capital Investments
2. **Capital investments are made that are unapproved and not prioritized.** Company funds may be used for the wrong capital projects.	■ Capital Budget Process ■ Investment and Project Approval Process	1. Capital Budget Process 2. Prioritization of Funds for Projects	■ Percentage Variance of Actuals to Capital Budgets ■ ROI on Capital Investments
3. **Fixed assets are not tracked or correctly reported.** Assets are incorrectly categorized, resulting in incorrect depreciation and balance sheet misstatement.	■ Fixed-Asset Inventory and Reconciliation Process	3. Control of Fixed Assets 4. Control of Fixed Asset Records 5. Control of Assets in the Custody of a Third Party 6. Inventory and Reconciliation of Capital Assets 7. Assets Not in Use 8. Sale, Liquidation, or Disposal of Assets	■ Percentage Accuracy of Fixed-Asset Inventories ■ Amount of Fixed Asset Write-offs
4. **Fixed assets are not controlled.** This could result in the theft or loss of company property.	■ Fixed-Asset Inventory and Reconciliation Process	3. Control of Fixed Assets 4. Control of Fixed Asset Records 5. Control of Assets in the Custody of a Third Party 6. Inventory and Reconciliation of Capital Assets 7. Assets Not in Use 8. Sale, Liquidation, or Disposal of Assets	■ Percentage Accuracy of Fixed-Asset Inventories ■ Amount of Fixed Asset Write-offs

Process: Capital Budget and Fixed Assets			
Process Risk	**Recommended Policies**	**Internal Controls**	**KPIs**
6. There are no controls for fixed assets held by a third party. This could result in the theft or loss of company property.	■ Fixed-Asset Inventory and Reconciliation Process	5. Control of Assets in the Custody of a Third Party	■ Percentage Accuracy of Fixed-Asset Inventories ■ Amount of Fixed-Asset Write-offs
8. There is no reconciliation of capital assets. Impaired assets are not reported or disposed of in a timely manner.	■ Fixed-Asset Inventory and Reconciliation Process	6. Inventory and Reconciliation of Capital Assets	■ Percentage Accuracy of Fixed-Asset Inventories ■ Amount of Fixed Asset Write-offs
9. Assets may be improperly sold, liquidated, or disposed of. The accounting for this process is incorrect, resulting in financial misstatements.	■ Fixed-Asset Inventory and Reconciliation Process	6. Inventory and Reconciliation of Capital Assets 7. Assets Not in Use 8. Sale, Liquidation, or Disposal of Assets	■ Percentage Accuracy of Fixed-Asset Inventories ■ Amount of Fixed Asset Write-offs

CHAPTER FIFTEEN

Supply Chain Management and Inventory Control

 OVERVIEW

The supply chain business process includes manufacturing, warehousing, transportation, customer service, demand planning, supply planning, and supply chain management. It is made up of the people, activities, information, and resources involved in moving a product from its supplier to customers. Some organizations include procurement in their supply chain organization. Others include procurement in the finance organization. The structure of the supply chain organization is dependent upon the industry, and the size and complexity of the company. Some companies will not have a supply chain organization if their revenue is only based on services and not product.

In a global company, the finished goods inventory is held at many locations and distribution centers, and managed by third parties. A lot of inventory would also be in the pipeline in transportation, besides the inventory with distributors and retail stocking points. Since any loss of inventory anywhere in the supply chain would result in loss of value, effective control of inventory and visibility of inventory gains importance as a key factor of the supply chain management function.

SUPPLY CHAIN MANAGEMENT AND INVENTORY CONTROL PROCESS FLOW

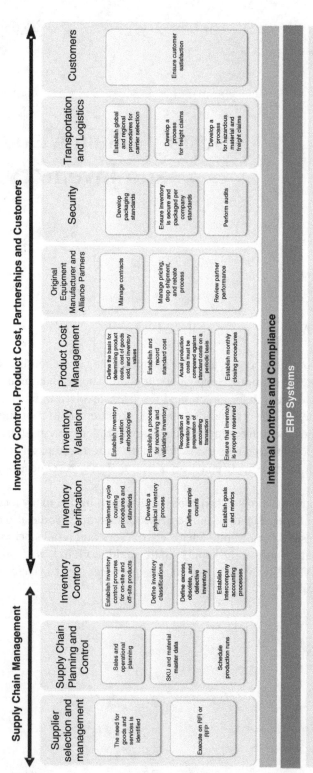

Supply Chain Management

Inventory Control, Product Cost, Partnerships and Customers

Supplier selection and management
- The need for goods and services is identified
- Execute on RFI or RFP

Supply Chain Planning and Control
- Sales and operational planning
- SKU and material master data
- Schedule production runs

Inventory Control
- Establish inventory control procures for on-site and off-site products
- Define inventory classifications
- Define excess, obsolete, and defective inventory
- Establish intercompany accounting processes

Inventory Verification
- Implement cycle counting procedures and standards
- Develop a physical inventory process
- Define sample counts
- Establish goals and metrics

Inventory Valuation
- Establish inventory valuation methodologies
- Establish a process for receiving and validating inventory
- Recognition of inventory and preparation of accounting transaction
- Ensure that inventory is properly reserved

Product Cost Management
- Define the basis for determining product costs, cost of goods sold, and inventory values
- Establish and record standard cost
- Actual production costs must be compared against standard costs on a periodic basis
- Establish monthly closing procedures

Original Equipment Manufacturer and Alliance Partners
- Manage contracts
- Manage pricing, drop shipment, and rebate process
- Review partner performance

Security
- Develop packaging standards
- Ensure inventory is secure and packaged per company standards
- Perform audits

Transportation and Logistics
- Establish global and regional procedures for carrier selection
- Develop a process for freight claims
- Develop a process for hazardous material and freight claims

Customers
- Ensure customer satisfaction

Internal Controls and Compliance

ERP Systems

Supply Chain and Inventory Control Automation

THE ROLE OF THE CONTROLLER

Controllers are connected to most, if not all, of the key business processes within the organization. Controllers provide the stewardship and accountability systems that ensure the organization is conducting its business in an appropriate, ethical manner.

Controllers and their staffs should also provide the information, analysis, and advice that enable the organization's operational management to perform effectively. This means understanding the impacts that the supply chain can have upon the accounting processes for the organization.

SUPPLY CHAIN FINANCE

According to PwC, today's executives are actively looking at supply chain finance (SCF) options in order to lower their overall financial supply chain costs.

SCF is defined as the use of financing and risk mitigation practices and techniques to optimize the management of the working capital and liquidity invested in supply chain processes and transactions. SCF is typically applied to open-account trade and is triggered by supply chain events. SCF is actually a range of techniques built around finance for global and domestic open-account trade complementing classical trade finance.

There is great interest in SCF using blockchain technology, but only a handful of corporations (examples below) have taken action.

IBM has teamed with companies in China and India to implement new blockchain-based solutions. IBM has also partnered with the Danish logistics company Maersk Line to develop a new solution to digitize its cross-border supply chain process. In addition, the financial services sector of iPhone manufacturer Foxconn of Taiwan has partnered with Chinese online lender Dianrong to launch Chained Finance.

CONTROLLER'S TOOL 33 – BLOCKCHAIN FEATURES THAT ENABLE SUPPLY CHAIN FINANCING

Feature	Description
Security and Reputation	Securely keep track of the creation and modification time of a document.
Title Transfer	Property whose ownership is controlled via the blockchain.
Chain of Possession (Provenance)	Physical products with a digital "passport" that proves authenticity and origin.
Smart Contract	A blockchain transaction will read and write data within the blockchain's distributed ledger.
Irrevocability/Immutability (Time Stamping Reflecting the Historical Audit Trail of All Transactions)	Irrevocable trail of all the transactions that have ever been made, which can prevent hacking or fraud.
Ownership and Uniqueness of Separately Held Documents	A feature made possible by smart contracts.
Confidentiality	Confidential transactions do not disclose the value of a transaction but allow the network to validate that inputs and outputs balance.

INVENTORY TYPES

Merchandising Companies

Inventories are assets items for sale in the ordinary course of business or goods that will be used or consumed in the production of goods to be sold. The investment in inventories is frequently the largest current asset of merchandising and manufacturing businesses. Therefore, the description and measurement of inventory require careful attention.

A merchandising company ordinarily purchases its merchandise in a form ready for sale. It reports the cost assigned to unsold units left on hand as merchandise inventory. Only one inventory account, merchandise inventory, appears in the financial statements.

Manufacturing Companies

Manufacturing companies produce goods that may be sold to merchandising companies as well as directly to customers. Manufacturing companies normally have three inventory accounts. These are:

- Raw materials
- Work in process
- Finished goods

These three inventory accounts are briefly explained below:

Raw Materials

The cost assigned to goods and materials on hand but not yet placed into production is reported as raw materials inventory. Examples include the wood to make a baseball bat and the steel to make a car. These materials can be traced directly to the end product.

Work in Process

Some units are not completely processed at any point in a continuous process. The cost of the raw material on which production has been started but not completed, plus the direct labor cost applied specifically to this material and a ratable share of manufacturing overhead costs, constitute the work in process inventory.

Finished Goods

The costs identified with the completed but unsold units on hand at the end of the fiscal period are reported as finished goods inventory.

 INVENTORY MANAGEMENT

Inventory management is a very important function that determines the health of the supply chain and impacts the financial health of the balance sheet. Every organization constantly strives to maintain optimum inventory levels to be able to ship customer orders on-time and to avoid over- or under-inventory levels that impact financial results.

Inventory is always dynamic. Inventory management requires constant and careful evaluation of external and internal factors and control through planning and review. Most organizations have a separate department or a job function called inventory planners that continuously monitor, control, and review inventory and interface with production, procurement, and finance departments.

Inventory management essentially deals with balancing inventory levels. Inventory is categorized into two types based on the demand pattern, which creates the need for inventory. The two types of demand for inventories are (1) independent demand, and (2) dependent demand.

1. **Independent Demand.** An item is classified as being independent demand when the demand for such an item is not dependent upon the demand for another item.
   - Finished goods items, which are ordered by external customers or manufactured for stock and sale, are called independent demand items.
   - Independent demands for inventories are based on confirmed customer orders, forecasts, estimates, and past historical data.
2. **Dependent Demand.** If the demand for inventory of an item is dependent upon another item, such demands are categorized as dependent demand. Raw materials and component inventories are dependent upon the demand for finished goods and hence can be called dependent demand inventories. This differentiation is necessary because the inventory management systems and process are different for each category.

While finished goods inventories are characterized as independent demand, they are managed with a sales order process and supply chain management processes that are based on sales forecasts. The dependent demand for raw materials and components to manufacture the finished goods is managed through material resources planning (MRP) or ERP using models such as just-in-time (JIT), Kanban, and others. MRP as well as ERP planning depends upon the finished goods sales process as the starting point for further action.

Just-in-Time

Managers at Toyota developed the JIT production and inventory control system. In a JIT process, materials are purchased and units are produced only as needed to meet actual customer demand.

When companies use a JIT manufacturing and inventory control system, they purchase materials and produce units only as needed to meet actual customer demand. In JIT manufacturing systems, inventories are reduced to the minimum and in some cases are zero.

The JIT approach can be used in both manufacturing and merchandising companies. It has the most profound effects, however, on the operations of manufacturing companies, which maintain three classes of inventories: raw material, work in process, and finished goods.

Kanban

Kanban is based on the lean manufacturing principle of "pull," or demand-based, replenishment and goods creation. For most organizations, this means driving production and replenishment based on customer demand and exceptions from the forecast. Instead of using a forecast to drive all production and supplier orders, the forecast is used to identify major spikes or declines in usage that are typically caused by product introductions and phaseouts, along with promotions and new customer wins. In a pull system, consumption information from the manufacturer is sent to the supplier (or supplying work station) to replenish material that has been consumed, replacing the inventory as it is used.

Managing Raw Material

Managing raw material inventories is far more complicated than managing finished goods inventory. It involves analyzing and co-coordinating delivery capacity, lead times, and delivery schedules of all raw material suppliers, coupled with the logistical processes and transit time-lines involved in transportation and warehousing of raw materials before they are ready to be supplied to the production shop floor. Raw material management also involves periodic review of the inventory holding and inventory counting and audits, followed by detailed analysis of the resulting reports, leading to financial and management decisions.

 ## INVENTORY COSTING METHODS

First In–First Out versus Last In–First Out Accounting

Two popular inventory accounting methods are first in–first out (FIFO) and last in–first out (LIFO) accounting. FIFO regards the first unit that arrived in inventory as the first one to be sold. LIFO considers the last unit arriving in inventory as the first one to be sold. The method that a controller selects can have a significant effect on net income and book value, and in turn on taxation. Using LIFO accounting for inventory, a company generally reports lower net income and lower book value, due to the effects of inflation.

Standard Cost Accounting

Standard cost accounting uses ratios called efficiencies that compare the labor and materials actually used to produce a good with those that the same goods would have required under "standard" conditions. Standard methods continue to emphasize labor efficiency even though that resource now constitutes a (very) small part of cost in most cases.

 ## TRENDS IN INVENTORY MANAGEMENT

The latest trend in all industries has been to outsource inventory management functions to third-party service providers. Companies outsource both raw material and finished goods inventory,

In the case of finished goods inventory, and depending upon the supply chain design, there may be multiple stocking points at national, regional, and state levels. In such an event, each of the warehouses may use a different service provider to manage operations. The inventory will be managed in the company's system as well as in the service provider's system. Inventory management and control becomes a critical function, especially in such situations where multiple locations and multiple service providers are involved.

Third-Party Logistics Inventory Management

To ensure inventory control is maintained across all locations, the following processes will provide additional controls, visibility, and risk reduction:

1. **Establish and outline operations process for service providers.** Develop procedures detailing warehouse operational processes, warehouse inventory system processes, and documentation requirements.
2. **Establish inventory visibility at each location through reporting.** Draw up a list of reports and data for all locations and ensure they are mailed to a central desk in the inventory team for daily review. The inventory team leader should analyze daily reports of all locations, highlight any issues, and define action plans to resolve them.
3. **Initiate daily cycle counting procedures.**
4. **Wall-to-wall physical inventory.** A physical inventory or wall-to-wall count should be conducted every 6 to 12 months. The criteria for this process depend upon the volume of transactions as well as value of transactions at each location. Controllers should also consider the frequency of inventory adjustments and write-offs when defining a specific physical inventory process.
5. **Reconcile inventory.** Inventory reconciliation involves reconciling physical inventory at the site with the system inventory at the third-party logistics (3PL) site and then reconciling 3PL system stocks with the company's system stock.
6. **Visit major sites.** Being present during physical stock audits on quarterly or half yearly basis is very important.

About Logistics

Logistics plays an important role in the post-procurement function of delivery of raw material from the supplier to the point of production and finished goods management from the point of dispatch from the factory to the point of delivery to the customer.

The flow of goods flows through a network of transportation by road, rail, air, or ship and intermediary warehouses to hold inventories before moving to the forward locations. The entire activity involves multitier suppliers, agents, and agencies, including freight forwarders, packers, customs departments, distributors, and logistics service providers.

Supply chain design in an organization would detail, plan, and strategize the procurement strategy and the manufacturing location selection; design and develop distribution network and strategy for finished goods; and so on. Logistics planning would deal with procurement logistics, finished goods distribution, sales order fulfillment and inventory management, and the like.

Reverse Logistics

As supply chain strategies and activities are evolving and partnering changes in business models, the focus and activities are not restricted to management of raw materials and finished goods from point of origin from the suppliers to plants and further on to the end customers.

Reverse logistics (as the name denotes) deals with the planning, process, and flow of finished goods inventory, packaging materials, and parts of finished product back from the end customer to the product company as sales returns or warranty returns or unsold inventory with trading partners. Reverse logistics planning further recaptures value from these materials as much as possible by way of salvaging, repair, refurbishing, and recycling.

OTHER PROCESSES RELEVANT TO THE SUPPLY CHAIN BUSINESS PROCESS

Bill of Materials

A bill of materials (BoM) is a list of the parts or components that are required to build a product. The BoM provides the manufacturer's part number (MPN) and the quantity needed for each component.

At its most complex, a BoM is a multilevel document that provides build data for multiple subassemblies (products within products) and includes for each item the part number, approved manufacturers list (AML), mechanical characteristics, and a whole range of component descriptors. It may also include attached reference files, such as part specifications, CAD files, and schematics.

Originally used internally within a company, the BoM served as a way to track product changes and maintain an accurate list of required components. As manufacturing has become increasingly distributed, however, the BoM has taken on even greater importance.

According to the International Electronics Manufacturing Initiative, BoM errors typically fall within three categories:

1. Completeness
2. Consistency
3. Correctness

Completeness. Incomplete data is the most common BoM defect. Critical pieces of information that are often omitted, including quantity, part description, reference designation, and AML.

Consistency. Information in the BoM sometimes conflicts with information provided in engineering drawings and design files. For example, quantities may not match – there may be 10 locations for a particular component indicated on a board, while the BoM only specifies 9. Another consistency problem is format. The format of the BoM, even though it is from the same customer, can change from one transmission to the next, making it difficult to match and confirm data. Language is another stumbling block, because it too can vary from BoM to BoM.

Correctness. Incorrect data is a serious problem. Common errors include invalid manufacturer or supplier information, obsolete data, and incorrect part numbers (i.e. the MPN given does not match the description of the part, or the MPN is not recognized by the manufacturer/supplier). Additional errors can result from receipt of information in hard-copy format, which requires manual reentry of data, an error-prone and time-consuming task.

Item Master File

The item master file is where inventory item records are set up and policies for the selling, replenishment, manufacturing, and warehousing, as well as user-defined information about each item, is maintained.

Master Production Schedule

A master production schedule (MPS) is the plan that outlines individual commodities to be produced in each time period covering such areas as production, staffing, and inventory. It is usually linked to manufacturing where the plan indicates product demand. The MPS quantifies significant processes, parts, and other resources in order to optimize production, to identify bottlenecks, and to anticipate needs and completed goods. Since an MPS drives manufacturing activity, its accuracy and viability dramatically affect profitability.

The benefits of an MPS are:

1. Gives production, planning, purchasing, and management the information to plan and control manufacturing
2. Supports the operational budget by linking overall business planning and forecasting to detail operations
3. Supports the sales process by the ability to make legitimate delivery commitments to warehouses and customers
4. Increases the efficiency and accuracy of a company's manufacturing process

Material Requirements Planning

Material requirements planning (MRP) is a production planning and inventory control system used to manage manufacturing processes.

An MRP system is intended to achieve the following objectives:

1. Ensure materials are available for production and products are available for delivery to customers.
2. Maintain the lowest possible material and product levels in storage.
3. Plan manufacturing activities, delivery schedules, and purchasing activities.

CONTROLLER'S TOOL 34 – SUPPLY CHAIN PERFORMANCE METRICS

Introduction. It's a well-known axiom that an organization's success or failure rides on the effectiveness of its supply chain. Companies spend a great deal of time analyzing their supply chains to improve efficiency and visibility while attempting to minimize cost and risk. This tool suggests a series of metrics for the supply chain process to measure performance.

Table of Metrics

Procurement Cost per Order. The total cost of all business functions involved in procurement orders, including planning, purchasing, inventory control, traffic, receiving, incoming inspection, and salvage.

Time to Market. The actual elapsed time from design to launch of a product.

Transportation Efficiency. A comparison of budget to actual costs for all transportation costs.

Warehouse Efficiency. A comparison of actual labor to standard labor for warehouse tasks, or the actual number of units versus standard units.

Perfect Order Measurement. The percentage of orders that are error free.

Perfect orders = ((Total orders - Error orders) / Total orders) x 100

Cash-to-Cash Cycle Time. The number of days between paying for materials and getting paid for product.

Cash-to-Cash cycle time = Materials payment date - Customer order payment date

Customer Order Cycle Time. Measures how long it takes to deliver a customer order after the PO is received.

Customer order cycle time = Actual delivery date - PO creation date

Fill Rate. The percentage of a customer's order that is filled on the first shipment. This can be represented as the percentage of items, SKUs, or order value that is included with the first shipment.

Supply Chain Cycle Time. Supply chain cycle time indicates the overall efficiency of the supply chain. Short cycles make for a more efficient and agile supply chain. Analysis of this critical metric can help recognize pain points or competitive advantages.

Inventory Days of Supply. Inventory DOS is the number of days it would take to run out of supply if it were not replenished.

Inventory DOS = Inventory on hand / Average daily usage

Freight Bill Accuracy. The percentage of freight bills that are error free.

(Error-free freight bills / Total freight bills) x 100

Freight Cost per Unit. Usually measured as the cost of freight per item or SKU.

Freight cost per unit = Total freight cost / Number of items

Inventory Turnover. The number of times that a company's inventory cycles per year.

Inventory turnover = Cost of goods sold / Average inventory

Average Payment Period for Production Materials. The average time from receipt of materials and payment for those materials.

Average payment period for production materials = (Materials payables / Total cost of materials) x Days in period

On-Time Shipping Rate. The percentage of items, SKUs, or order value that arrives on or before the requested ship date. The on-time shipping metric is used in determining customer satisfaction. A high rate indicates an efficient supply chain.

On-time shipping rate = (Number of on-time items / Total items) x 100

Inventory Turnover Ratio. ITR helps to measure the number of times we sell or turn our average inventory kept in the warehouse. It measures the number of opportunities to earn profit that we experience each year from our working capital invested in the inventory.

ITR = Cost of goods / Average inventory investment

Turn-Earn Index. TEI helps us to combine the gross margin and turnover.

Days of Supply. DOS is the most common KPI used by managers in measuring supply chain efficiency. It is calculated by dividing the average inventory on hand (as value) by the average monthly demand (as value) and then multiplying it by 30, when measuring on a monthly basis.

Inventory Velocity. IV is the percentage of inventory that we project will be consumed within the next period. It helps managers to understand how well the inventory on hand matches demand. It is calculated by dividing the opening stock by the sales forecast of the following period.

TABLE OF CONTROLS – SUPPLY CHAIN MANAGEMENT AND INVENTORY CONTROL

Process: Supply Chain Management and Inventory Control

---

1. Segregation of Duties. The inventory control process must have the following SoD:

- Segregation of manufacturing and custodial responsibilities from accounting activities.
- Segregation of the supervision and verification of the physical existence of inventory from the performance of the actual count.
- Shipping function independent of the physical inventory count, order entry, billing, AR, and GL functions.

2. Physical Security and Access for Warehouses and Production Facilities. Corporate physical security requirements are in place for warehouse and production facilities. Inventory must be safeguarded from unauthorized access by the establishment of physical or other compensating controls.

3. Corporate Policies and Procedures. Policies and procedures exist to provide guidance on business practices, promote corporate consistency, and clarify roles, responsibilities, and accountability within transportation and logistics. Documented policies and procedures defining the roles and responsibilities of all functions must exist and be reviewed at least annually. A formal process must be used to identify problems and improvement opportunities and to implement solutions and improvements.

4. Protection of Inventory from Deterioration and Damage. Inventory must be protected against physical deterioration and damage.

5. General Ledger Reconciliation. Results from physical inventory verification procedures must be reconciled (contents are known and status is current) with the financial inventory records. The appropriate adjustments must be documented, approved, and made according to policies and procedures. In turn, these records must be reconciled to the GL.

6. Monthly Closing Procedures. Costs incurred by the manufacturing unit must be fully and accurately distributed to inventory, cost of goods sold, or approved special accounts (special items of cost, research and development, etc.) on a regular (monthly) basis. To facilitate this, consistent, documented monthly closing procedures must be developed in conjunction with operational and financial management to ensure proper cutoffs in manufacturing, systems, and financial processes. GL account balances must be reconciled (contents are known and status is current) monthly to supporting item level detail; significant adjustments must be approved by the appropriate level of financial and operational management.

7. Process for the Elimination of Intercompany Profit in Inventory. Inventory received from other company locations must be recorded by source and monitored to provide necessary support for the periodic elimination of intercompany profit.

8. Sales and Operations Planning. Sales (or demand) forecasts must be prepared and approved through a formal sales and operations planning process. These forecasts must be at a meaningful level to allow for production and inventory planning, development of production schedules, detailed material and labor requirements, and financial planning in accordance with balanced scorecard requirements. Changes in the formal plan must be approved through the sales and operations planning process by the appropriate level of management.

9. Scheduled Orders and Production Runs. Products must be manufactured or ordered according to a schedule (e.g. a master schedule) or a material requirements plan developed from the approved sales (or demand) and operations plan. The schedule or material requirements plan must be achievable based on available labor, materials, and capacity.

10. Allocation Model. Profitability analysis, channel demand forecasting, and the global management of inventory must be integrated into the product allocation decisions of managers.

11. Material Master Data. Formal master data change control procedures must exist and be followed. All product and item or material master data must be reviewed at least annually and updated. Bills of material and routings must be established and updated to reflect current product specifications and manufacturing processes.

Process: Supply Chain Management and Inventory Control

---

12. Scrap/Waste. Operating and financial management must establish procedures and approval limits for the disposal of scrap/waste. Scrap/waste must be accumulated, safeguarded, monitored, and reported on a timely basis to the financial organization and operating management. Scrap/waste must be reprocessed or disposed of by persons independent of custodial responsibilities on a timely basis. Disposal of scrap/waste to noncompany entities should be done through competitive bidding.

13. In-Transit Inventory. Inventory in transit between organizations must be reconciled (contents are known and status is current) and aged according to local written policies and procedures. Reconciling items and items in dispute must be resolved according to the guidelines set by local written policies and procedures after expected delivery. It is assumed the unit sending the inventory will have the correct balance unless the receiving unit can demonstrate it was a shipping error.

14. Product Return Procedures. Returned product should be received against a notice of the return from a customer or distribution and must be entered into inventory records. Cost of goods manufactured (e.g. product bill) or interdivisional billings must reflect adjustments for returned inventory. Returned product must be kept segregated from regular inventory unless returned to stock immediately. Disposition or restocking of all other returns (return to stock, remanufacture, or scrap) should be made within a reasonable amount of time.

15. Existence and Maintenance of Inventory Records. Inventory records must be maintained to safeguard inventory and provide current information on inventory quantities available. On a periodic basis (at least annually), the quantities in the inventory records must be reconciled (contents are known and status is current) with the physical quantities through either cycle counting or physical inventories. Required adjustments must be made to the physical and financial inventory records on a timely basis to reflect actual quantities. Follow-up investigation and corrective action must be taken in a timely fashion on any differences.

16. Off-Site Inventory. Company inventory stored or processed at off-site locations (e.g. at noncompany distribution, supplier, or vendor facilities or in the possession of sales, engineering, or other personnel) is subject to the same standards of internal control as any other inventory. Inventory quantities at off-site locations must be reconciled (contents are known and status is current) quarterly to statements provided by the custodian. All unexplained negative inventory variances must be reported to company immediately. Follow-up investigation and corrective action must be taken in a timely fashion on any differences.

17. Supplier-Owned Consignment Inventory Located at the Company. Supplier-owned inventory on consignment at company facilities is subject to the same standards of internal control as any other inventory. Inventory on consignment must be identified and reconciled (contents are known and status is current) with supplier records on a quarterly basis with follow-up investigation and corrective action taken in a timely fashion on any differences. Supplier-owned consignment inventory must be excluded from company's financial records and should *not* be reported to the corporate risk management/insurance department for inclusion in insurable asset calculations, as it is the owner's responsibility to insure the inventory.

18. Excess, Obsolete, and Defective Inventory. On a periodic basis, management must review inventory. Inventory specifically identified as excess, obsolete, or defective must be disposed of by sale, scrap, returns to the vendor, or other suitable means in a prompt and timely manner. Inventory identified as potentially excess and obsolete must be reserved in compliance with the company's inventory policy.

19. Receipts and Issuance of Inventory. Receipts and inventory issued must be identified, accurately costed, and accounted for in a timely manner.

20. Physical Inventory Procedures. Where perpetual inventory records are not verified through cycle counting or statistical sampling procedures, the existence of inventory must be verified through an annual physical inventory conducted with appropriate procedures as stated in the authorized corporate policy to ensure the accuracy of the count.

21. Cycle Counting Procedures. Where cycle counting is required, cycle counting procedures must meet the minimum requirements specified in corporate policy.

Process: Supply Chain Management and Inventory Control

22. Statistical Sampling Procedures. Statistical sampling procedures must be approved by the company controller prior to implementation.

23. Receiving – Recognition of Inventory and Corresponding Liability. Inventory and the corresponding liability must be recorded in the accounting records upon legal transfer of title. An estimate of known inventory in transit for which title has legally transferred to company must be completed and required adjustments to inventory balances made monthly.

24. Inventory Valuation. As an example, inventory must be valued at the lower of cost (i.e. full acquisition cost plus any import, transportation, etc., or manufactured cost) or market (i.e. net realizable value).

25. Inventory Reserves. The reserves must be reviewed for adequacy and reasonableness according to corporate policy and adjusted accordingly.

26. Documented Cost Accounting Procedures and System. Documented cost accounting procedures must exist and describe, at a minimum, the methodologies used to determine product costs, total cost of goods manufactured (e.g. product bill), and inventory values. A cost accounting system must be maintained that accurately accumulates and identifies manufacturing costs in an appropriate manner (e.g. by cost center or product) and provides adequate information to analyze standard and actual manufacturing costs and variances.

27. Annual Establishment of Item Level Standard Costs. Accurate item level standard costs must be established or revised in accordance with established policies and procedures through the joint efforts of supply chain. Manufacturing management is responsible for the accuracy and approval of standard costs and must ensure standard costs are developed for all items in the item master or planned for production and is based on information in the relevant company database.

28. Bills of Materials. A single identifiable BoM used for manufacturing, planning, purchasing, and costing must exist for each manufactured product or subassembly. Site BoMs are extensions from corporate and engineering BoMs and can be different from site to site. It is the engineering department's responsibility to make changes with input from the operating unit and site product cost analysts.

29. Material and Labor Transactions. Issues of material and labor into production and receipts of items out of production must be controlled by appropriate transaction accountability. Monthly cutoff procedures must be coordinated with the financial organization.

30. Labor and Overhead Distribution. Labor and overhead costs must be completely distributed to products on a rational and consistent basis. Such activity drivers as current operational conditions, production rates, and capacity utilization must support cost distributions. Significant changes in allocation methodologies must be reviewed and approved by the appropriate level of operating and financial management.

31. Variance Analysis and Disposition. Actual production costs must be compared against standard costs on a periodic basis. All variances must be reported to management and significant variances must be investigated with appropriate action taken in a timely manner. Variances must be allocated to cost of goods sold and inventory in a way that reflects the proportion of sales quantities to inventory levels.

32. Selection of Transportation Carriers. All 3PL providers and carriers must be selected in accordance with the respective regional carrier selection process and procedures.

33. Contract Administration. The company has contracts established with transportation carriers and those contracts are current and complete and contain adequate protection clauses. Agreements with third-party providers include metrics and recourse, including financial liability, for goods damaged while in their possession.

34. Regional Location Management and Policies and Procedures. Regional policies and procedures have been developed, documented, and implemented relative to transportation and logistics regional contract administration. Agreements with third-party providers include metrics and recourse, including financial liability, for goods damaged while in their possession.

Process: Supply Chain Management and Inventory Control

---

35. Freight Claims. All eligible freight claims are filed, processed on time, communicated to appropriate support and control groups, and paid timely. The corporate transportation department monitors regional compliance with related procedures and works with the regions to establish action.

36. Hazardous Materials Management. The corporate transportation department has an adequate program for hazardous materials awareness, training, and enforcement. All 3PL providers understand and follow the standards for damaged goods. Compliance with these standards are included as part of the company's audit of logistics providers.

37. Selection and Monitoring of Logistics and Transportation Carriers. All 3PL providers and carriers have been selected in accordance with the respective regional carrier selection process and procedures. 3PL providers understand and comply with the company's inventory classification process and procedures.

38. Policies and Procedures for Damaged Product. Policies and procedures have been developed and implemented to resolve products damaged at a 3PL provider's site.

39. Damaged Goods. Damaged goods process includes criteria to determine cost-benefit analysis to retest and/or repackage damaged goods and timelines to redirect damaged goods to alternate flows.

40. Authorized Shipments. Proper written authorization with an appropriate business need is required for all products shipped from company premises.

41. Accounting for Shipments. Sales orders or shipping authorizations must be accounted for on a periodic basis by someone independent of the order processing and shipping functions. This will include ensuring all product shipments have been billed and are accurately reflected in the inventory records.

42. Documented Shipments. Accurate documentation that meets legal and contractual requirements must be prepared for all shipments.

43. Shipping Records. Shipping documents must be prenumbered where the integrity of sequencing is not computer controlled. Missing documents must be investigated.

44. Product Transfers. Evidence of shipment, such as a signed bill of lading, must be obtained from the carrier to establish the physical and legal transfer of products. Such documents must always reflect the actual date of shipment.

45. Quantity and Product Verification. A person independent of the shipping function must verify the types and quantities of products to be shipped on at least a test basis. Some form of validation of quantity/type should be obtained from carrier.

46. Warehouse Layout and Access. The shipping department must be physically segregated from the production and receiving facilities, as dictated by good business practices. Returned product must be segregated from inventory available for sale. Admittance to the shipping area must be restricted to authorized personnel only.

47. Sales Cutoff. There will be no deviations from the company's sales cutoff policy.

48. Blank Shipping Forms. Blank shipping authorizations, numerically controlled shipping documents, and bills of lading must be safeguarded from unauthorized access and use.

49. Customer Complaints. Customer correspondence (billing and shipping complaints, service problems, etc.) must be investigated and resolved in a timely manner.

50. Drop Shipments. Locations involved with domestic and international drop shipments must have documented procedures that are enforced.

TABLE OF RISKS AND CONTROLS – SUPPLY CHAIN MANAGEMENT AND INVENTORY CONTROL

Process: Supply Chain Management and Inventory Control			
Process Risk	**Recommended Policies**	**Internal Controls**	**KPIs**
1. **Lack of Segregation of Duties and Systems Control.** Lack of SoD control may lead to theft and the manipulation of the company's data to cancel a fraudulent activity.	▪ SoD Policies and Procedures	1. SoD	▪ Number of SoD Conflicts ▪ Number of Internal Control Issues
2. **Company Resources.** Company resources may not be used efficiently or effectively, resulting in excessive cost and/ or inability of the manufacturing unit to achieve its business objectives.	▪ MRP	8. Sales and Operations Planning 9. Scheduled Orders and Production Runs 10. Allocation Model	▪ Cost per Supply Chain Employee ▪ Employee Salaries as a Percentage of Revenue
3. **Delivery Against Production Plan.** The ability to deliver against the agreed upon production plan may be adversely impacted or achieved at excessive cost. Unauthorized products or quantities in excess of acceptable levels may be produced. Inadequate supply of components or parts inventories could result in interruption of production. Plant capacity may be underutilized or inadequate to meet specified customer requirements or service levels. Labor may be used in an inefficient manner.	▪ Production Plans	8. Sales and Operations Planning 9. Scheduled Orders and Production Runs 10. Allocation Model	▪ Perfect Order Measurement ▪ Fill Rate ▪ Supply Chain Cycle Time ▪ Average Payment Period for Production Materials ▪ DOS ▪ IV ▪ Inventory DOS

Process: Supply Chain Management and Inventory Control			
Process Risk	**Recommended Policies**	**Internal Controls**	**KPIs**
4. Errors and Omissions. Errors and omissions in transaction processing or poor physical safeguarding practices may result in inventory that is lost, stolen, destroyed, or temporarily diverted. Incorrect production may be reported, which masks waste, shortages, or thefts.	■ Cycle Count Procedures ■ Physical Inventory Procedures ■ Inventory Control Procedures ■ Month-End Close ■ GL Reconciliation	1. SoD 5. GL Reconciliation 6. Monthly Closing Procedures 20. Physical Inventory Procedures 21. Cycle Counting Procedures 22. Statistical Sampling Procedures 23. Receiving – Recognition of Inventory and Corresponding Liability 24. Inventory Valuation 25. Inventory Reserves 47. Sales Cutoff	■ Perfect Order Measurement ■ Fill Rate ■ Supply Chain Cycle Time ■ Average Payment Period for Production Materials ■ DOS ■ IV ■ Inventory DOS
5. Inaccurate Data. Critical decisions may be based upon financial statements, records, or manufacturing reports that are inaccurate.	■ Cycle Count Procedures ■ Physical Inventory Procedures ■ Inventory Control Procedures ■ Month-End Close ■ GL Reconciliation	5. GL Reconciliation 6. Monthly Closing Procedures 11. Material Master Data 20. Physical Inventory Procedures 21. Cycle Counting Procedures 22. Statistical Sampling Procedures 23. Receiving – Recognition of Inventory and Corresponding Liability 24. Inventory Valuation 25. Inventory Reserves 47. Sales Cutoff	■ Cash-to-Cash Cycle Time ■ Customer Order Cycle Time
5. Incorrect Scrap Sales. Scrap sales may be recorded incorrectly or not at all, sold at an inappropriate price, or sold to an unacceptable credit risk.	■ Procedures for Scrap Sales and Returns	12. Scrap and Waste Procedures	■ Amount of Scrap Inventory on Hand ■ Scrap Inventory Turnover
6. Scrap/Returns Issues. Scrap or returns may be stolen. Scrap may be sold at an inappropriate price or to an unacceptable credit risk.	■ Procedures for Scrap Sales and Returns	12. Scrap and Waste Procedures 14. Product Return Procedures	■ Amount of Scrap Inventory on Hand ■ Scrap Inventory Turnover ■ Returned Orders

Process: Supply Chain Management and Inventory Control			
Process Risk	**Recommended Policies**	**Internal Controls**	**KPIs**
7. **Financial Loss.** The organization may be unnecessarily exposed to financial loss from damage to inventory and inability to meet future customer demand.	■ SoD Policies ■ Warehouse Security Policies	5. GL Reconciliations 6. Monthly Closing Procedures	■ Supply Chain Department Cost as a Percentage of Revenue ■ Value of Inventory Write-offs per Period ■ TEI
8. **Quality.** The quality of items transferred or shipped may be unacceptable, resulting in excessive returns or rework and customer dissatisfaction.	■ Cycle Count Procedures ■ Physical Inventory Procedures ■ Inventory Control Procedures ■ Month-End Close ■ GL Reconciliation	4. Protection of Inventory from Deterioration and Damage 14. Product Return Procedures 18. Excess, Obsolete, and Defective Inventory	■ Percentage of Order Defectives ■ Percentage of Customer Returns Compared to Total Sales ■ Value of Inventory with a Quality Block
9. **Product Costs and Cost of Goods Sold.** Individual product costs, total cost of goods manufactured (e.g. product bill), and inventories may be misstated in financial statements, records, and manufacturing reports. Critical decisions on product pricing, product line investment or discontinuance, and factory sourcing and loading may be based upon inaccurate information.	■ Cost Accounting Standards	4. Protection of Inventory from Deterioration and Damage 5. GL Reconciliations 6. Monthly Closing Procedures 11. Material Master Data 20. Physical Inventory Procedures 21. Cycle Counting Procedures 22. Statistical Sampling Procedures 23. Receiving – Recognition of Inventory and Corresponding Liability 24. Inventory Valuation 25. Inventory Reserves 26. Documented Cost Accounting Procedures and System 27. Annual Establishment of Item Level Standard Costs 28. BoM 31. Variance Analysis and Distribution 47. Sales Cutoff	■ Value of Inventory by Type ■ Value of Inventory Reserve per Period ■ Value of Inventory Write-offs per Period

Process: Supply Chain Management and Inventory Control			
Process Risk	**Recommended Policies**	**Internal Controls**	**KPIs**
10. Improper Value of Inventory. Inventory may be improperly valued due to inadequate cutoffs or inaccurate compilations.	■ Cost Accounting Standards ■ Inventory Validation Processes	5. GL reconciliations 6. Monthly Closing Procedures 11. Material Master Data 31. Variance Analysis and Disposition 24. Inventory Valuation 25. Inventory Reserves 26. Documented Cost Accounting Procedures and System 27. Annual Establishment of Item Level Standard Costs 28. BoM 31. Variance Analysis and Disposition	■ Value of Inventory by Type ■ Value of Inventory Reserve per Period ■ Value of Inventory Write-offs per Period ■ ITR
11. Inaccurate Count of Inventory. Counts may be improperly recorded or omitted. Potential for errors and irregularities is substantially increased.	■ Cycle Count Procedures ■ Physical Inventory Procedures ■ Inventory Control Procedures ■ Month-End Close ■ GL Reconciliation	5. GL Reconciliation 6. Monthly Closing Procedures 13. In-Transit Inventory 15. Existence and Maintenance of Inventory Records 16. Off-Site Inventory 17. Supplier-Owner Consignment Inventory Located at Company 18. Excess, Obsolete, and Defective Inventory 20. Physical Inventory Procedures 21. Cycle Counting Procedures 22. Statistical Sampling Procedures 45. Quantity and Product Verification 46. Warehouse Layout	■ Value of Inventory by Type ■ Value of Inventory Reserve per Period ■ Value of Inventory Write-offs per Period ■ ITR ■ Cycle Count Results ■ Physical Inventory (Gross and Net) ■ Results (Gross and Net)

Process: Supply Chain Management and Inventory Control			
Process Risk	**Recommended Policies**	**Internal Controls**	**KPIs**
12. Incorrect Adjustments. Incorrect book-to-physical adjustments could result in inaccurate inventory valuations and misstatements in operating income.	■ Cycle Count Procedures ■ Physical Inventory Procedures ■ Inventory Control Procedures ■ Month-End Close ■ GL Reconciliation	5. GL Reconciliation 6. Monthly Closing Procedures 20. Physical Inventory Procedures 21. Cycle Counting Procedures 22. Statistical Sampling Procedures	■ Value of Inventory by Type ■ Value of Inventory Reserve per Period ■ Value of Inventory Write-offs per Period ■ ITR ■ Cycle Count Results ■ Physical Inventory (Gross and Net) ■ Results (Gross and Net)
13. Inadequate Review Procedures. If review procedures are inadequate, appropriate corrective actions for inventory management and recording may not be initiated in a timely manner.	■ Self-Assessment and Audit Processes	5. GL Reconciliation 6. Monthly Closing Procedures 20. Physical Inventory Procedures 21. Cycle Counting Procedures 22. Statistical Sampling Procedures	■ Value of Inventory by Type ■ Value of Inventory Reserve per Period ■ Value of Inventory Write-offs per Period ■ ITR ■ Cycle Count Results ■ Physical Inventory (Gross and Net) ■ Results (Gross and Net)
14. Customer Service and Satisfaction. Customer service may be negatively impacted if physical inventories do not match accounting and product handling records. Customer satisfaction may suffer because product cannot be delivered due to damage or other delays in delivery.	■ Customer Satisfaction Surveys	14. Product Return Procedures 45. Quantity and Product Verification 49. Customer Complaints	■ Customer Order Cycle Time ■ Cash-to-Cash Cycle Time ■ Perfect Order Measurement ■ On-Time Shipping Rate ■ Days Sales Outstanding (DSO)

Process: Supply Chain Management and Inventory Control			
Process Risk	**Recommended Policies**	**Internal Controls**	**KPIs**
15. Misstated Financial Statements. Individual product costs, total cost of goods manufactured (e.g. product bill), and inventories may be misstated in financial statements, records, and manufacturing reports. Critical decisions on product pricing, product line investment or discontinuance, and factory sourcing and loading may be based upon inaccurate information	■ Cycle Count Procedures ■ Physical Inventory Procedures ■ Inventory Control Procedures ■ Month-End Close ■ GL Reconciliation	5. GL Reconciliations 6. Monthly Closing Procedures 11. Material Master Data 20. Physical Inventory Procedures 21. Cycle Counting Procedures 22. Statistical Sampling Procedures 23. Receiving – Recognition of Inventory and Corresponding Liability 24. Inventory Valuation 25. Inventory Reserves 47. Sales Cutoff	■ Value of Inventory by Type ■ Value of Inventory Reserve per Period ■ Value of Inventory Write-offs per Period ■ ITR ■ Cycle Count Results ■ Physical Inventory (Gross and Net) ■ Results (Gross and Net)
16. Risk and Errors. Potential for errors and irregularities is substantially increased. Inventory may also be lost, stolen, destroyed, or temporarily diverted.	■ Cycle Count Procedures ■ Physical Inventory Procedures ■ Inventory Control Procedures ■ Month-End Close ■ GL Reconciliation	5. GL Reconciliation 6. Monthly Closing Procedures 20. Physical Inventory Procedures 21. Cycle Counting Procedures 22. Statistical Sampling Procedures	■ Value of Inventory by Type ■ Value of Inventory Reserve per Period ■ Value of Inventory Write-offs per Period ■ ITR ■ Cycle Count Results ■ Physical Inventory (Gross and Net) ■ Results (Gross and Net)
17. Incorrect Revenue and Cost of Goods Sold. Revenues and related cost of sales may be recorded in the wrong accounting period, as complete and accurate information may not be forwarded to accounting/billing.	■ Period End Sales and Shipment Cutoff Policy ■ Fiscal Closing Calendars	5. GL Reconciliations 6. Monthly Closing Procedures 11. Material Master Data 23. Receiving – Recognition of Inventory and Corresponding Liability 47. Sales Cutoff	■ Revenue Adjustments ■ Supply Chain Process Impact on the Financial Close

Process: Supply Chain Management and Inventory Control			
Process Risk	**Recommended Policies**	**Internal Controls**	**KPIs**
18. Adversely Impacted Operations. Incorrect amounts of materials and supplies may be issued to production or unauthorized quantities of products may be produced.	■ MRP ■ Production Plans	20. Physical Inventory Procedures 21. Cycle Counting Procedures 22. Statistical Sampling Procedures	■ Revenue Adjustments ■ Supply Chain Process Impact on the Financial Close ■ Inventory Days of Supply ■ Inventory Turnover ■ TEI
19. Supplier Performance Issues. Suppliers may be unaware of the company's standards for performance. Suppliers' performance may decrease and damages and delays in delivery may increase. The company may be unable to contractually hold supplier accountable for performance.	■ Supply SLA Reviews	33. Contract Administration 37. Selection of Transportation Carriers	■ Supply SLA Results ■ Results of Supply Management Reviews
20. Incorrect Inventory Classification. Suppliers may improperly classify inventory that may reduce efficiencies in the inventory process.	■ Inventory Classification Policy	23. Receiving – Recognition of Inventory and Corresponding Liability	■ Value of Inventory by Type ■ Value of Inventory Reserve per Period ■ Value of Inventory Write-offs per Period ■ ITR ■ Cycle Count Results ■ Physical Inventory (Gross and Net) ■ Results (Gross and Net)
21. Damaged Inventory. Suppliers may be unaware of the company's standards for damaged goods. The company's assets may be damaged.	■ Damaged Inventory Policy	18. Excess, Obsolete and Defective Inventory 38. Policies and Procedures for Damaged Product 39. Damaged Goods	■ Percentage of Damaged Inventory ■ Percentage of Returns ■ DOS ■ IV ■ DSO

Process: Supply Chain Management and Inventory Control			
Process Risk	**Recommended Policies**	**Internal Controls**	**KPIs**
22. Incorrect Freight Payments. Payments may be made on claims for services that have not been rendered, or duplicate or fraudulent freight claims.	■ Freight Accounting and Claims Process	35. Freight Claims	■ Freight Bill Accuracy ■ Freight Cost per Unit
23. Hazardous Materials. Fines and penalties may be assessed, increasing costs for noncompliance with hazardous materials laws and regulations.	■ Hazardous Materials Policy	36. Hazardous Materials Management	■ Number of Hazardous Material Violations per Period
24. Incorrect Shipments. Shipments may be made to incorrect or unauthorized customers or to incorrect customer locations. Products may have been shipped but not billed or recorded. Products may have been shipped but not billed or recorded. Products that have been authorized for shipment may not have been shipped.	■ Shipping Department Self-Assessments	40. Authorized Shipments 41. Accounting for Shipments 42. Documented Shipments 43. Shipping Records 45. Quantity and Product Verification 49. Customer Complaints 50. Drop Shipments	■ On-Time Shipping Rate ■ Cash-to-Cash Cycle Time ■ Percentage of Returns ■ Percentage of Short Ships and Misships
25. Incorrect Products or Quantities. Incorrect products or quantities may be shipped, or products may be shipped early, late, or in violation of export control and/or customs requirements.	■ Shipping Department Self-Assessments	40. Authorized Shipments 41. Accounting for Shipments 42. Documented Shipments 43. Shipping Records 45. Quantity and Product Verification 49. Customer Complaints 50. Drop Shipments	■ On-Time Shipping Rate ■ Cash-to-Cash Cycle Time ■ Percentage of Returns ■ Percentage of Short Ships and Misships

Process: Supply Chain Management and Inventory Control			
Process Risk	**Recommended Policies**	**Internal Controls**	**KPIs**
26. Lost Shipments. Customer shipments may be lost, misplaced, or misappropriated. The company may not recover for products lost by the carrier. Accountability over products shipped may be lost. Unbilled and/ or misappropriated shipments may not be identified. Back orders or lost sales orders may not be identified and resolved on a timely basis.	■ Shipping Department Self-Assessments	40. Authorized Shipments 41. Accounting for Shipments 42. Documented Shipments 43. Shipping Records 45. Quantity and Product Verification 49. Customer Complaints 50. Drop Shipments	■ Value of Outstanding Shipping Issues ■ Customer Satisfaction

CHAPTER SIXTEEN

Treasury and Cash Management

 OVERVIEW

Many controllers have responsibility for the treasury function along with their other duties. In its broadest sense, the treasury function covers cash management, corporate finance, and financial risk management. The treasury function undertakes a range of complex and skilled tasks, liaises with internal and external stakeholders, and plays a key role in the smooth functioning and value creation of an organization. The main components of the treasury function are included in the following flow chart.

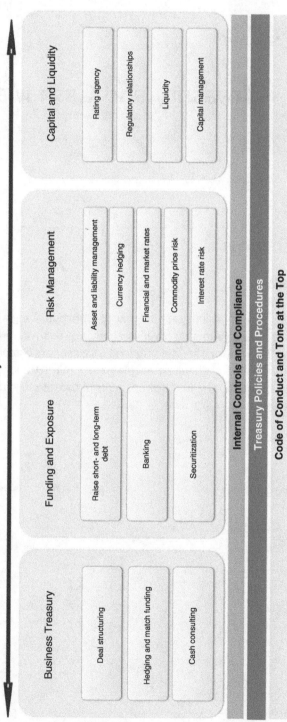

TREASURY AND CASH MANAGEMENT PROCESS FLOW

Treasury Processes

Business Treasury

- Deal structuring
- Hedging and match funding
- Cash consulting

Funding and Exposure

- Raise short- and long-term debt
- Banking
- Securitization

Risk Management

- Asset and liability management
- Currency hedging
- Financial and market rates
- Commodity price risk
- Interest rate risk

Capital and Liquidity

- Rating agency
- Regulatory relationships
- Liquidity
- Capital management

Internal Controls and Compliance

Treasury Policies and Procedures

Code of Conduct and Tone at the Top

CONTROLLER'S TOOL 35 – RESPONSIBILITIES OF THE TREASURY DEPARTMENT

Introduction. In general, the corporate treasury department manages the organization's liquidity risks, financial risks, banking relationships, and working capital. This tool provides additional insight into the details of these responsibilities.

1. Cash Management. This function may seem straightforward, but a great deal of resources and treasury intelligence is used in the cash management function of the world's most successful firms and financial service providers.

2. Foreign Exchange. From the multinational firm's perspective, the treasury management system's role is pivotal to operations. Getting the foreign exchange function wrong can be costly, should the value of cash deteriorate as it crosses borders.

3. Financial Supply Chain. The organization's management of its funds across its supply chain and the transition of those funds through its network is another important responsibility of the treasury department.

4. Risk Management. The treasury department will decide upon issues such as cash levels and exposures to different investments, based on defined risk profiles.

5. Regulation. With the avalanche of regulations that have hit financial markets since the global recession and subsequent attempt by regulators to tighten those markets, the task of the treasurer to keep abreast of regulatory developments has become burdensome. Europe's second Markets in Financial Instruments Directive (MiFID II), for instance, and more recently the GDPR, both of which have ramifications for firms across the globe, give treasurers much to keep up with.

6. Financial Technology. There are several solutions for the treasury function that support cash management, the financial supply chain, and treasury analytics.

CONTROLLER'S TOOL 36 – WHAT ARE THE COMPONENTS OF CASH FLOW?

Introduction. A cash flow statement shows the sources and uses of cash and is typically divided into three components:

1. **Operating Cash Flow.** Operating cash flow, often referred to as working capital, is the cash flow generated from internal operations. It comes from sales of the product or service of the business, and because it is generated internally, it is under the company's control.
2. **Investing Cash Flow**. Investing cash flow is generated internally from nonoperating activities. This includes investments in plant and equipment or other fixed assets, nonrecurring gains or losses, or other sources and uses of cash outside of normal operations.
3. **Financing Cash Flow.** Financing cash flow is the cash coming to and from external sources, such as lenders, investors, and shareholders. A new loan, the repayment of a loan, the issuance of stock, and the payment of dividends are some of the activities that would be included in this section of the cash flow statement.

HOW DOES A COMPANY PRACTICE GOOD CASH FLOW MANAGEMENT?

Good cash management involves the following factors:

1. Knowing when, where, and how cash needs will occur
2. Knowing the best sources for meeting additional cash needs
3. Being prepared to meet these needs when they occur by keeping good relationships with bankers and other creditors

The starting point for good cash flow management is developing a cash flow projection. Smart business owners know how to develop both short-term (weekly, monthly) cash flow projections to help them manage daily cash, and long-term (annual, three-to-five year) cash flow projections to help them develop the necessary capital strategy to meet their business needs. They also prepare and use historical cash flow statements to understand how they used money in the past.

Cash flow management is a process that involves collecting payments, controlling disbursements, covering shortfalls, forecasting cash needs, investing idle funds, and compensating the banks that support these actions. Because global cash management is highly tax- and accounting-oriented, close working relationships with tax and accounting staff are vital. In addition, cash flow management requires coordination between treasury and operations. And in today's volatile markets, it requires powerful electronic tools for gathering diverse financial information and formatting it into useful reports for decision-making.

CONTROLLER'S TOOL 37 – CASH FORECASTS

Introduction. A cash flow forecast can provide an organization with a clear picture of when cash will be received, where it will come from, when to spend cash, and what to spend it on. Using actual commitments and making estimates based on solid data will help to make the cash forecast more realistic and useful.

Cash Flow Forecasts as Part of Integrated Financial Reporting

A cash flow forecast, in order to be useful as a management and control tool, must be based on real data and actual commitments. Historical data on which to base a cash flow forecast will be useful, but must be considered in conjunction with information from the company's business strategy and the budget in order to project a realistic picture of what to expect in terms of future cash flows as an organization moves forward. Actual commitments, defined in terms of amounts and payment terms, will provide a firm basis on which to project cash flows.

In this sense, a cash flow forecast should be considered an integral part of an overall financial planning and control strategy. There should be uniformity among historical financial reports, budgets, and forecasts, in terms of format, types of accounts, and the level of detail presented. This way, the different financial presentations will be comparable, and taken together can be used to describe, evaluate, and manage the operation using the same terms of reference within the same parameters.

Cash Flow Activities as Functions of Each Other

A cash flow forecast can be broken down into the same three basic sections as the statement of cash flows that constitutes one of the basic financial statements:

1. Cash flows from operating activities
2. Cash flows from investing activities
3. Cash flows from financing activities

These three types of cash flow activities are interrelated. They depend on and affect each other. The cash flow forecast should take this into account to provide a complete picture of where cash will come from and how it will be used for the period being forecast. The relationships between the different cash flow activities may depend on the nature of the business, the stage of development of the business and general economic conditions, or conditions within the market or industry in which the business operates.

Ongoing Operations

For example, during a period of relatively normal ongoing operations, the results of the cash flow forecast for operating activities will probably feed the cash flow forecast of investing activities and financing activities. If a cash flow forecast of operating activities shows cash surpluses during certain periods, these surpluses could be incorporated into a short-term investment plan. On the contrary, if cash flows from operations are forecast to show a deficit, this information can be used to plan for the necessary financing.

Startup

The cause and effect relationship, especially during certain stages of a business, such as during startup, may be inverted, and the cash flows available for operating and investing activities will depend on the cash flows generated by financing activities. The amount of financing that can be obtained will determine the capital expenditures that can be made (investing activities) and the amount of working capital that can be used in the business (operating activities).

Growth and Expansion

During a period of growth or expansion, cash flows generated by operations may be used to finance growth, or cash flows from operations may be supplemented by cash flows from financing activities, in order to carry out investing activities, such as making additional capital expenditures to increase production capacity, investing in research and development, launching new lines of products, or starting up or purchasing new lines of business.

Cash Flow Responsibility and Accountability

In a company with separate business units or different lines of business that are relatively autonomous in terms of cash management, separate cash flow forecasts may be prepared according to centers of accountability and responsibility. These different business units may be centralized under a single finance function (in a corporate or home office). For example, if a particular unit generates a cash surplus, the central finance function may take this surplus and allocate it according to the business needs of the overall company. On the contrary, if the cash flow forecast of a particular unit shows a cash deficit, the central finance department will know that this unit will require funding.

The general idea is that cash flow forecasts should be prepared where they are meaningful in terms of the information they provide, and where they are useful in terms of the decisions that can be made based on the information the cash flow forecast provides.

PAYMENT FLOAT

Payment float is the period of time between incurring a debt (obtaining credit on a purchase) and disbursement of the money to repay the debt. For a business, it is prudent to extend this period to the maximum without incurring an interest charge. Both internal and external factors affect the float period. Internal factors (which are controllable by the firm) include the speed with which the firm makes payments on supplier invoices. External factors include the grace period, speed of collection by the supplier, as well as the processing time for checks to clear the bank.

In banking, float is the time between the issuing of a check and payment of the check by the bank. In the past, the farther away the paying bank was from the deposit bank, the longer it would take for the check to clear. During this period the writer collects interest or has access to the funds.

LETTER OF CREDIT

A letter of credit (L/C) is a document typically issued by a bank or financial institution that authorizes the recipient of the letter (the "customer" of the bank) to draw amounts of money up to a specified total, consistent with any terms and conditions set forth in the letter. This usually occurs when the bank's customer seeks to assure a seller (the "beneficiary") that it will receive payment for any goods it sells to the customer.

For example, the bank might extend the L/C conditioned upon the beneficiary's providing documentation that the goods purchased with the line of credit have been shipped to the customer. The customer may use the L/C to assure the beneficiary that, if it satisfies the conditions set forth in the letter, it will be paid for any goods it sells and ships to the customer.

In simple terms, a L/C could be said to document a bank customer's line of credit, and any terms associated with its use of that line of credit. Letters of credit are most commonly used in association with long-distance and international commercial transactions.

Confirmed Letter of Credit

A confirmed letter of credit is an L/C issued by a foreign bank that has been verified and guaranteed by a domestic bank in the event of default by the foreign bank or buyer. Typically this form of an L/C will be sought when a domestic exporter seeks assurance of payment from a foreign importer.

Commercial Letter of Credit

A commercial L/C assures the seller that the bank will provide payment for any goods or merchandise shipped to the bank's customer, assuming the seller provides any required documentation of the transaction and its shipment of the purchased goods.

Irrevocable Letter of Credit

An irrevocable L/C includes a guarantee by the issuing bank that if all of the terms and conditions set forth in the letter are satisfied by the beneficiary, the L/C will be honored.

Revocable Letter of Credit

A revocable L/C may be cancelled or modified after its date of issue by the issuing bank.

Standby Letter of Credit

In the event that the bank's customer defaults on a payment to the beneficiary, and the beneficiary documents proof of its loss consistent with any terms set forth in the letter, a standby L/C may be used by the beneficiary to secure payment from the issuing bank.

FOREIGN EXCHANGE POLICY: MANAGEMENT AND CONTROLS

Companies operating in international markets should establish management policies on foreign exchange. Fluctuations in foreign exchange rates affect the cost competitiveness, profitability, and valuation of a company's international operations. The absence of a foreign exchange management policy leaves a company unprepared to control the potential adverse effects of currency movements. This can lead to increased costs and reduced market share and profits. To avoid these exposures, the company should develop and document a policy statement that describes the company's attitude, objectives, and appropriate responses when managing foreign exchange risk.

The starting point for the formulation of an exposure management policy is to decide exactly what the company has at risk. The following exposures are generally considered in developing a foreign exchange policy:

- **Transaction Exposure.** Generally considered to be the income-statement impact of all payables and receivables denominated in foreign currency. This could include dividends, service fees, royalties, taxes and duties, and the like.
- **Translation Exposure.** Balance sheet exposure that results from the consolidation of financial statements of foreign entities into the "home currency."
- **Corporate Earnings Exposure.** Measures the impact of currency movements on the company's targeted after-tax consolidated earnings.
- **Operating Exposure.** Reflects the effects of exchange rate movements on an entity's projected cash inflows and outflows.
- **Economic Exposure.** Represents the most all-encompassing definition of exposure. It represents all transactions, assets, and liabilities, recorded or anticipated, that will affect the company's cash flow when exchange rates change. This is usually associated with a longer-term (one-to-five year) view of exposure management.

CONTROLLER'S TOOL 38 – FOREIGN EXCHANGE POLICY DEVELOPMENT PROCESS

Introduction. In the proper context, a foreign exchange management policy serves several important functions in addition to the critical control function. An effective policy also helps in assessing treasury performance, providing a framework for analysis, and involving the foreign exchange function in broader corporate decision-making. These benefits can be just as important as the control issues addressed by a formalized policy. The basic policy development process can be summarized as follows:

1. Examine current practices and past experience with regard to foreign exchange management.
2. Define and evaluate exposures, both actual and projected. Evaluate effectiveness of past hedging actions if feasible.
3. Formulate policy guidelines:
    a. Establish priorities for managing exposures.
    b. State corporate objectives clearly.
    c. Ensure compatibility with other corporate goals and philosophies.
    d. Obtain senior management mandate.
4. Develop operational structure:
    a. Decide on degree of centralization.
    b. Evaluate reporting systems and implement needed changes.
    c. Specify approved hedging techniques.
    d. Specify key decision makers/authorized traders.
5. Develop performance evaluation standards.
6. Establish transaction reporting requirements and procedures.
7. Provide for management review of outstanding contracts and activity.
8. Establish a procedure for regular reviews of foreign exchange policies and guidelines. A good policy provides positive framework for action, with room for appropriate modifications and changes over time.
9. Utilize policy review, goal setting, and policy implementation to encourage the integration of foreign exchange management into the broader corporate decision-making process.

 CONTROLLER'S TOOL 39 – CASH MANAGEMENT RULES FOR PETTY CASH

Introduction. Many organizations still use petty cash. But, petty cash funds are not a way to get around cash disbursement controls. They enhance efficiency by providing cash quickly in the following situations:

1. **When the formal system is too costly.** Surprisingly, producing a check can cost as much as $2.50 or more. A $25 purchase is not worth it.
2. **When the formal system is too slow.** It often requires one to five days to process a voucher and produce a check, which is too long for a $25 item needed right away.
3. **For special situations.** Special situations include those such as cashing employee pay-checks or providing advances for travel and conferences (some firms don't allow this).

Typical Problems

Controls. Generally, one custodian is responsible for petty cash and decides who can get petty cash, requires identification for each disbursement, authorizes petty cash payments only for acceptable purposes, observes authorized payout limits, and requests reimbursements. But if the custodian is at a doctor's appointment, no one gets cash, so consider having two or three custodians who coordinate their schedules. A different employee should book reimbursements, and still another should review distributions and amounts.

Shortages. Petty cash funds often run out. To determine how much to keep in the fund, check last year's replenishments. Were they weekly? Monthly? Quarterly? Here are some guidelines:

1. Determine the ideal number of days between replenishment dates. Every 10 days? 20 days? 30 days? The less frequently you replenish the more cash the fund needs.
2. Know how long replenishment takes. Is it same day? 3 days? a week?
3. Decide how many funds to have, as follows:

a. Avg. daily need	$60
b. Replenish fund every	30 days
c. Days needed to replenish	5 days
d. No. of petty cash funds	2 funds
e. Unadjusted funds (a × b)	$60 × 30 days = $1,800
f. Cushion needs (a × c)	$60 × 5 days = $300
g. Adjusted fund (e + f)	$2,100
h. Petty cash per fund (g ÷ d)	$1,050

Security. Keep petty cash in a fireproof, locked, limited access safe, locked metal box, or vault, depending on the fund's size. Do not leave safes and boxes unattended. Limit access to only the petty cash custodian(s).

Reimbursement. Set dollar limits and make sure the custodian observes them. Have clear rules on what can be reimbursed. Prohibit accepting employee IOUs in exchange for cash for personal use.

Replenishment. Replenish before funds run low. Require that all completed petty cash vouchers be in numerical order and in ink (not pencil) with receipts attached. Replenish at least monthly.

Permanent changes. Firms often overlook the need to change the amount in the petty cash fund because it is not systematically reviewed. At least yearly, review the amount as follows: Compare the replenishment each month to the monthly balance. If the amounts replenished are close to the fund balance (within 10 percent), increase the amount. If the replenishments (especially in peak months) are 30 percent less than balance, decrease the amount. Investigate whether employees with legitimate needs were denied petty cash during the year, and adjust decisions about permanent changes accordingly.

CASH MANAGEMENT

The Automated Clearing House Network

The ACH Network is a highly reliable and efficient nationwide batch-oriented EFT system governed by NACHA that provides for the interbank clearing of electronic payments for participating depository financial institutions. The Federal Reserve and Electronic Payments Network act as ACH operators, or central clearing facilities through which financial institutions transmit or receive ACH entries.

ACH payments include:

- Direct deposit of payroll, Social Security, and other government benefits, as well as tax refunds
- Direct payment of consumer bills, such as mortgages, loans, utility bills, and insurance premiums
- Business-to-business payments
- E-checks
- E-commerce payments
- Federal, state, and local tax payments.

Wire Transfers

A wire transfer or credit transfer is a method of transferring money from one person or institution (entity) to another. A wire transfer can be made from one bank account to another bank account or through a transfer of cash at a cash office.

Bank wire transfers are often the most expedient method for transferring funds between bank accounts. A bank wire transfer is affected as follows:

1. The person wishing to do a transfer (or someone they have appointed and empowered financially to act on their behalf) goes to the bank and gives the bank the order to transfer a certain amount of money. IBAN (international bank account number) and BIC (business identifier code) information is given as well so that the bank knows where the money needs to be sent to.
2. The sending bank transmits a message via a secure system (such as SWIFT or Fedwire) to the receiving bank, requesting that it effect payment according to the instructions given.
3. The message also includes settlement instructions. The actual transfer is not instantaneous: funds may take several hours or even days to move from the sender's account to the receiver's account.
4. Either the banks involved must hold a reciprocal account with each other, or the payment must be sent to a bank with such an account (a correspondent bank) to ensure benefit to the ultimate recipient.

Banks collect payment for the service from the sender as well as from the recipient. The sending bank typically collects a fee separate from the funds being transferred, while the receiving bank and intermediate banks through which the transfer travels deduct fees from the money being transferred so that the recipient receives less than the amount the sender sent.

CONTROLLER'S TOOL 40 – INTERNATIONAL PAYMENT METHODS

Introduction. When a business is global, the complexities of international payments (currency, language, customs, regulations, etc.) make cash disbursements more challenging. The table below provides examples of international payment methods.

Method	Usual Time of Payment	Goods Available To Buyer	Risk to Seller	Risk to Buyer	Comments
Cash In Advance	Before shipment	After payment	None	Complete: relies on seller to ship exactly the goods expected, as quoted and ordered	Seller's goods must be special in one way or another or special circumstances prevail over normal trade practices (e.g. goods manufactured to buyer-only specification)
Letter of Credit (See next two items.)			Commercial invoice must match the L/C exactly; dates must be carefully headed; stale documents are unacceptable for collection		L/Cs require total accuracy in conforming to terms, conditions, and documentation
Confirmed Irrevocable Credit	After shipment is made, documents presented to the bank	After payment	Gives the seller a double assurance of payments; depends on the terms of the L/C	Assures shipment is made but relies on exporter to ship goods as described in documents; terms may be negotiated prior to L/C agreement, alleviating buyer's degree of risk	The inclusion of a second assurance of payment (usually a US bank) prevents surprises, and adds assurance that issuing bank has been deemed acceptable by confirming bank; adds cost and an additional requirement to seller

Method	Usual Time of Payment	Goods Available To Buyer	Risk to Seller	Risk to Buyer	Comments
Unconfirmed Irrevocable Credit	Same as above	Same as above	Seller has single bank assurance of payment and seller remains dependent on foreign bank; seller should contact his banker to determine whether the issuing bank has sufficient assets to cover the amount	Same as above	Credit can be changed only by mutual agreement, as stipulated in a sales agreement; becomes open account with buyer's bank as collection agent; foreign bank may have problems making payment in sum or timeliness
Drafts (See next two items.)	Remittance time from buyer's bank to seller's bank may still take one week to one month.		Drafts, by design, should contain terms and conditions mutually agreed upon		A draft may be written with virtually any term or condition agreeable to both parties; when determining draft tenor (terms and conditions), consult with your banker and freight forwarder to determine the most desirable means of doing business in a given country
Sight Draft (with documents against acceptance)	On presentation of draft to buyer	After payment to buyer's bank	If draft not honored, goods must be returned or resold; storage, handling, and return freight expenses may be incurred	Assures shipment but not content, unless inspection or check-in is allowed before payment	A draft can be a collection instrument used to exchange possession and title to goods for payment; seller is essentially drawing a check against the bank account of the buyer; buyer's bank must have preapproval, or seek approval of the buyer prior to honoring the check; payable upon presentation of documents

Method	Usual Time of Payment	Goods Available To Buyer	Risk to Seller	Risk to Buyer	Comments
Time Drafts (with documents against acceptance)	On maturity of the draft	Before payment, after acceptance	Relies on buyer to honor draft upon presentation	Assures shipment but not content; time of maturity allows for adjustments, if agreed to by seller	Payable based upon the acceptance of an obligation to pay the seller at a specified time; although a time draft has more collection leverage than an invoice, it remains only a promissory note, with conditions
Open Account	As agreed, usually by invoice	Before payment	Relies completely on buyer to pay account as agreed	None	All terms of payment, including extra charges and terms should be mutually understood and agreed upon prior to open account initiation; companies conducting ongoing business are candidates for open account terms of payment; seller must measure not only buyer's credit reliability but the country's as well

TABLE OF CONTROLS – TREASURY AND CASH MANAGEMENT

Process: Treasury and Cash Management

1. **Segregation of Duties and Systems Access Controls.** All treasury and cash management activities need to be segregated from company transaction processes. Treasury and cash management staff should only have the systems access required for their job function. Systems access will be reviewed on a periodic basis to ensure there are no intra- or extra-SoD conflicts.

Process: Treasury and Cash Management

---

2. **Control of Payments.** Checks, credits, free product, and the like must only be made when there is:

- An approved marketing program
- Documentation supporting that performance commitments have been met (e.g. valid customer numbers, program identification codes, product codes, media samples, original proofs of performance, photographs of displays, etc.), and appropriate approval has been obtained

3. **Requests for Payment.** The request for payment and the appropriate documentation must be filed and retained in accordance with record retention policies. Check requisitions must be approved by someone independent of the claim processing function.

4. **Authorized Individuals.** Only authorized individuals must be granted access to customer-specific accrual and payment information. Customer-specific accrual and payment data must be subject to periodic independent reviews.

5. **Control of Premium Items.** Premium items, blank check stocks, and bearer drafts must be appropriately stored, safeguarded, and accounted for.

6. **Bank Account Procedures.** Procedures on opening, maintaining, and closing bank accounts must be established. At a minimum, the procedures must cover required approvals, signature authority (including limits), and documentation standards.

7. **Recording of Transactions.** Financing, financial investment, foreign exchange, capital stock, and equity transactions must be promptly recorded and properly classified to facilitate the reporting and required disclosure of external financial information. All recorded balances must be reconciled monthly to the supporting detail (e.g. bank account reconciliations, revolving credit lines, investment subledgers, capital stock, ownership records, etc.). Such reconciliations (contents are known and status is current) must be performed by employees not involved in cash or custodial activities.

8. **Restricted Access.** Access to cash, debt, equity, financial investment and capital stock records, and securities must be restricted.

9. **Responsibilities of Approved Third Parties.** Banks, brokers, independent registrars, transfer agents, or other approved third parties are to be used to account for changes in ownership of the company's issued and unissued shares, the change in the company's debt instruments, and the changes in its financial and publicly traded equity investments.

10. **Foreign Exchange Procedures.** Procedures must be established for approving foreign exchange transactions and ensuring that the transactions are properly documented and recorded in the proper accounts.

11. **Counterparty and Countertrade Exposure.** Procedures must be established to monitor counterparty exposure and market risk related to financing, investing, and foreign exchange activities. Procedures must be established to ensure that countertrade/offset obligations are executed in accordance with corporate policy.

12. **Cash Pooling.** Procedures must be established to ensure that all cash pooling and netting arrangements involving more than one legal entity are executed in accordance with corporate policy.

13. **Board of Director Approval.** The following items and activities must be approved by the BoD and must be documented in minutes of their meetings: banking resolutions and delegations of authority, borrowing resolutions and delegations of authority, all significant debt financing arrangements, and financing of leases. The company financing activity in total must be periodically reviewed with the BoD.

14. **Signing and Authority Limits.** Delegations of signing and authorization limits must be approved by the appropriate CFO of the legal entity. All financing resolutions and authorizations must be reviewed with the appropriate financial institutions periodically or whenever changed.

Process: Treasury and Cash Management

15. **Financing Arrangements**. Financing arrangements must be reviewed with corporate legal and approved by the treasury department. These include: customer financing agreements, debt financing agreements, guarantees and loans in support of third parties, lease and rental of capital assets, programs for factoring or discounting receivables, subsidiary capital stock changes, and interest and foreign currency derivatives. All financing arrangements and foreign exchange contracts must be monitored for compliance to terms, covenants, and underlying obligations.

All financing instruments must be appropriately canceled, or accounted for as canceled by the custodian, upon completion of repayment.

16. **Capital Transactions**. All capital transactions, such as the issuance of stock, stock splits, stock or cash dividends, employee stock options, and so on, must be approved by the BoD in a public company.

17. **Financial and Equity Investment Transactions.** All financial and equity investment transactions must be reviewed for reasonableness and proper approval, be compared to transaction advices or other documentation, and be promptly recorded in the accounts.

18. **Stockholder Information**. All stockholder information is confidential. Such information must be maintained as support for authorized, issued, and outstanding shares, transfers of issued shares, dividends, exercising of employee stock options, and treasury stock.

19. **Financial Investment Policies and Procedures**. Financial investment policies and procedures must exist and be approved in advance by the treasurer or designee and must specify, at a minimum: type, credit quality and maturity of instruments, approved counterparties, counterparty exposure guidelines, and personnel authorized. Any investments outside of policy must be approved individually and in advance by the treasurer.

20. **Purchased Securities**. Where possible, purchased securities must be registered in the name of the company or an appropriate legal subsidiary. Where bearer securities are purchased, appropriate confirmation advices must be received. All securities must be held in safekeeping by the appropriate financial institution, in an in-house safe, or by a designated custodian.

21. **Records of Financial and Equity Investments**. Detailed records of financial and equity investments must be maintained and safeguarded to protect essential information regarding ownership and anticipated income. These records must be kept independent from the custodian and must be reconciled to the securities on hand on a periodic basis. All investment transactions, either financial or equity, must have prior approval, be properly documented, and be promptly recorded in the proper accounts.

Methods of valuation of financial and equity investments, including those within the pension plans, must be developed in accordance with finance policies established by the controller and requirements of governmental reporting bodies. Write-offs and adjustments to the investment accounts must be properly reviewed, evaluated as to worth, and approved by the director of corporate finance in accordance with the finance policy. Foreign currency "spot" transactions (i.e., the purchase and/or sale of foreign currency to satisfy payment obligations due in the next one to three business days) are not "hedging" but require the establishment of operating procedures and controls that must be approved by the treasurer or designee. When feasible, foreign currency obligations between operating units and designated third parties are to be settled through an intercompany netting process. Foreign currency contracts between operating units and designated third parties must be priced, recorded, and accounted for as if they were (independent) third-party contracts.

TABLE OF RISKS AND CONTROLS – TREASURY AND CASH MANAGEMENT

Process: Treasury and Cash Management			
Process Risk	**Recommended Policies**	**Internal Controls**	**KPIs**
1. **Poor segregation of duties and systems access controls may lead to record misuse/ alteration.** Records may be misused or altered by unauthorized employees to the detriment of the company, its owners, stakeholders, and creditors.	■ SoD Controls and Policy ■ Systems Access Controls	1. SoD and Systems Access Controls 2. Control of Payments 3. Requests for Payment 4. Authorized Individuals 5. Control of Premium Items 6. Bank Account Procedures 7. Recording of Transactions 8. Restricted Access 9. Responsibilities of Approved Third Parties 10. Foreign Exchange Procedures 11. Counterparty and Countertrade Exposure 12. Cash Pooling 13. BoD Approval 14. Signing and Authority Limits 15. Financing Arrangements 16. Capital Transactions 17. Financial and Equity Investment Transactions 18. Stockholder Information 19. Financial Investment Policies and Procedures 20. Purchased Securities 21. Records of Financial and Equity Investments	■ Cash visibility percentage estimation ■ Percentage of Payments Succeeding First Time ■ Percentage Forecast Error by Business Unit ■ Funding Buffer ■ Cost of Funds Performance ■ Investment Portfolio Liquidity ■ Hedge Ratio ■ Retrospective Hedge Effectiveness ■ Time Taken to Confirm Deals ■ Asset/Liability Mismatch ■ Forecast Error ■ Cash Visibility ■ Counterparty Limit Usage ■ Cost of Funds Above Benchmark ■ Portfolio Value at Risk ■ Reported Cash That Is Automatically Reconciled

Process: Treasury and Cash Management			
Process Risk	Recommended Policies	Internal Controls	KPIs
2. **Treasury reports may not be accurate.** As a result, critical decisions are made on erroneous information.	■ Treasury Policies and Procedures ■ Treasury Internal Controls	1. SoD and Systems Access Controls 2. Control of Payments 3. Requests for Payment 4. Authorized Individuals 5. Control of Premium Items 6. Bank Account Procedures 7. Recording of Transactions	■ Cash Visibility Percentage Estimation ■ Percentage of Payments Succeeding First Time ■ Percentage Forecast Error by Business Unit ■ Funding Buffer ■ Cost of Funds Performance ■ Investment Portfolio Liquidity ■ Hedge Ratio ■ Retrospective Hedge Effectiveness ■ Time Taken to Confirm Deals ■ Asset/Liability Mismatch ■ Cost of Funds Above Benchmark ■ Portfolio Value at Risk ■ Reported Cash That Is Automatically Reconciled
3. **Cash or securities may be lost, stolen, destroyed, or diverted.**	■ Treasury Policies and Procedures ■ Treasury Internal Controls	1. SoD and Systems Access Controls 14. Signing and Authority Limits	■ Cash Visibility Percentage Estimation ■ Percentage of Payments Succeeding First Time ■ Percentage Forecast Error by Business Unit ■ Funding Buffer ■ Cost of Funds Performance ■ Investment Portfolio Liquidity ■ Hedge Ratio ■ Retrospective Hedge Effectiveness ■ Time taken to confirm deals ■ Asset/liability mismatch

Process: Treasury and Cash Management			
Process Risk	**Recommended Policies**	**Internal Controls**	**KPIs**
4. **Errors and omissions in processing and authorization may occur.** This will result impact the cash management process.	■ Treasury Policies and Procedures ■ Treasury Internal Controls	1. SoD and Systems Access Controls 14. Signing and Authority Limits	■ Percentage of Payments Succeeding First Time ■ Percentage Forecast Error by Business Unit ■ Asset/Liability Mismatch ■ Reported Cash That Is Automatically Reconciled
5. **Financial statements and records may be misstated due to an improper cutoff and valuation.**	■ Treasury Policies and Procedures ■ Treasury Internal Controls	1. SoD and Systems Access Controls 2. Control of Payments 3. Requests for Payment 4. Authorized Individuals 5. Control of Premium Items 6. Bank Account Procedures 7. Recording of Transactions 8. Restricted Access 9. Responsibilities of Approved Third Parties 10. Foreign Exchange Procedures 11. Counterparty and Countertrade Exposure 12. Cash Pooling 13. BoD Approval 14. Signing and Authority Limits 15. Financing Arrangements 16. Capital Transactions 17. Financial and Equity Investment Transactions 18. Stockholder Information 19. Financial Investment Policies and Procedures 20. Purchased Securities 21. Records of Financial and Equity Investments	■ Cash Visibility Percentage Estimation ■ Percentage Forecast Error by Business Unit ■ Asset/Liability Mismatch ■ Cash Visibility ■ Cost of Funds Above Benchmark ■ Portfolio Value at Risk ■ Reported Cash That Is Automatically Reconciled

Process: Treasury and Cash Management			
Process Risk	**Recommended Policies**	**Internal Controls**	**KPIs**
6. Transactions may not be consistent with the global currency requirements of the company.	■ Foreign Exchange Policies and Procedures	10. Foreign Exchange Procedures 11. Counterparty and Countertrade Exposure	■ Percentage of Payments Succeeding First Time ■ Percentage Forecast Error by Business Unit ■ Funding Buffer ■ Cost of Funds Performance ■ Investment Portfolio Liquidity ■ Asset/Liability Mismatch ■ Cash Visibility ■ Counterparty Limit Usage ■ Cost of Funds Above Benchmark ■ Portfolio Value at Risk ■ Reported Cash That Is Automatically Reconciled
7. Financing and investing activities may expose the company to unacceptable levels of counterparty and market risk.	■ Financial Investment Policies and Procedures	17. Financial and Equity Investment Transactions 19. Financial Investment Policies and Procedures 20. Purchased Securities 21. Records of Financial and Equity Investments	■ Cash Visibility Percentage Estimation ■ Percentage of Payments Succeeding First Time ■ Percentage Forecast Error by Business Unit ■ Funding Buffer ■ Cost of Funds Performance ■ Investment Portfolio Liquidity ■ Hedge Ratio ■ Retrospective Hedge Effectiveness ■ Time Taken to Confirm Deals ■ Asset/Liability Mismatch ■ Counterparty Limit Usage

Process: Treasury and Cash Management			
Process Risk	**Recommended Policies**	**Internal Controls**	**KPIs**
8. **The countertrade/ offset arrangement may be illegal or in violation of company policy and code of conduct.**	■ Counterparty and Countertrade Policies and Procedures	11. Counterparty and Countertrade Exposure	■ Cash Visibility Percentage Estimation ■ Percentage of Payments Succeeding First Time ■ Percentage Forecast Error by Business Unit ■ Funding Buffer ■ Cost of Funds Performance ■ Investment Portfolio Liquidity ■ Hedge Ratio ■ Retrospective Hedge Effectiveness ■ Time Taken to Confirm Deals ■ Asset/Liability Mismatch ■ Counterparty Limit Usage
9. **Failure to meet and fulfill countertrade/ offset obligations may lead to problems.** This failure may result in penalties, liquidated damages, potential litigation in foreign countries, and other possible sanctions by foreign governments.	■ Counterparty and Countertrade Policies and Procedures	11. Counterparty and Countertrade Exposure	■ Cash Visibility Percentage Estimation ■ Percentage of Payments Succeeding First Time ■ Percentage Forecast Error by Business Unit ■ Funding Buffer ■ Cost of Funds Performance ■ Investment Portfolio Liquidity ■ Hedge Ratio ■ Retrospective Hedge Effectiveness ■ Time Taken to Confirm Deals ■ Asset/Liability Mismatch ■ Counterparty Limit Usage

Process: Treasury and Cash Management			
Process Risk	**Recommended Policies**	**Internal Controls**	**KPIs**
10. Transactions may result in undesirable legal and/or tax implications.	■ Treasury Policies and Procedures ■ Treasury Internal Controls	1. SoD and Systems Access Controls 2. Control of Payments 3. Requests for Payment 4. Authorized Individuals 5. Control of Premium Items 6. Bank Account Procedures 7. Recording of Transactions 8. Restricted Access 9. Responsibilities of Approved Third Parties 10. Foreign Exchange Procedures 11. Counterparty and Countertrade Exposure 12. Cash Pooling 13. BoD Approval 14. Signing and Authority Limits 15. Financing Arrangements 16. Capital Transactions 17. Financial and Equity Investment Transactions 18. Stockholder Information 19. Financial Investment Policies and Procedures 20. Purchased Securities 21. Records of Financial and Equity Investments	■ Cash Visibility Percentage Estimation ■ Percentage of Payments Succeeding First Time ■ Percentage Forecast Error by Business Unit

CHAPTER SEVENTEEN

Shared Services and Business Process Outsourcing

 **OVERVIEW**

The term *shared services* defines an operational philosophy that involves centralizing those administrative functions of a company that were once performed in separate divisions or locations. Services that can be shared among the various business units of a company include finance, purchasing, inventory, payroll, hiring, and IT. It is a term that is now recognized as applying to the centralization of noncore, support operations. What differentiates shared services from simple centralization is that shared services centers (SSCs) include an element of running these services as a "business" with a separate management team. Some organizations manage their SSC as a profit center in which a transaction fee is charged or allocated to the areas of the company supported.

SSCs first emerged in the early 2000s and today are found in most of the world's successful growth-oriented organizations. Key drivers for shared services have traditionally been cost, but they are increasingly quality of service provision, data, reliability, scale, and flexibility. Running an SSC allows an organization to ramp service provision up or down as required (for example, as a result of M&As). This approach can also drive a focus continuous improvement on the business processes integrated into the model.

Controllers should be aware of all the options available and should be knowledgeable about the decision criteria, risks, and challenges when implementing either an SSC or business process outsourcing (BPO) model. The scope of a SSC or BPO initiative is dependent upon the size of the organization. Large organizations may initiate a complex SSC and BPO model, where smaller organizations may select a simpler SSC model.

The shared services approach is different from the BPO model, in which an external third party is paid to provide a service that was previously the internal responsibility of the organization. However, the goals for considering either a shared service or BPO model are usually the same. These goals include the reduction of cost and the improvements of business process efficiency.

SHARED SERVICES AND BUSINESS PROCESS OUTSOURCING PROCESS FLOW

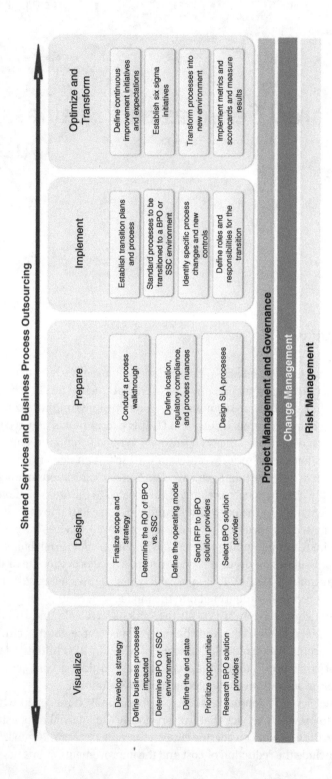

Shared Services and Business Process Outsourcing

Visualize
- Develop a strategy
- Define business processes impacted
- Determine BPO or SSC environment
- Define the end state
- Prioritize opportunities
- Research BPO solution providers

Design
- Finalize scope and strategy
- Determine the ROI of BPO vs. SSC
- Define the operating model
- Send RFP to BPO solution providers
- Select BPO solution provider

Prepare
- Conduct a process walkthrough
- Define location, regulatory compliance, and process nuances
- Design SLA processes

Implement
- Establish transition plans and process
- Standard processes to be transitioned to a BPO or SSC environment
- Identify specific process changes and new controls
- Define roles and responsibilities for the transition

Optimize and Transform
- Define continuous improvement initiatives and expectations
- Establish six sigma initiatives
- Transform processes into new environment
- Implement metrics and scorecards and measure results

Project Management and Governance

Change Management

Risk Management

CONTROLLER'S TOOL 41 – FIVE WAYS THAT HUMAN RESOURCES SHARED SERVICES HELPS SMALL BUSINESS

Introduction. Because small businesses are subject to the same laws and regulations as larger corporations, growing companies face many challenges regarding employee related liabilities (hiring and termination practices, discrimination, etc.) and risks from federal and state employment laws. When a small business executive or manager learns about a potential harassment claim or needs to fire an employee, where can he/she obtain competent and cost effective advice?

Fortune 500 enterprises have used SSCs for years, and studies show that top performing enterprises utilize these services to continually revitalize their organizations with the latest best practices. Here are five additional reasons for a small business to consider HR shared services:

1. Cost minimization via economies of scale, automation, and process improvement (60 percent of companies with shared services HR functions improve client satisfaction, staff productivity, and overall quality while achieving cost reductions of 20–80 percent in HR).
2. Focus allows executives and managers to focus on revenue generating activities – not tactical and administrative people activities.
3. Proactive compliance to minimize risk related to employees and employment laws.
4. Access to best-in-class technologies and processes across divisions and geographic locations.
5. Access to specialized expertise and resources not available internally – owners and executives at most small businesses do not have on-demand access to HR expertise in training, recruiting, employment law, and compensation that is available in the shared services groups of large corporations.

CONTROLLER'S TOOL 42 – THE BENEFITS OF IMPLEMENTING SHARED SERVICES CENTERS

Introduction. The benefit of an SSC is that an organization is able to pull small teams of HR, finance, or IT specialists from the business units themselves and instead locate these teams in one centralized, low-cost location. An added benefit is that focusing only on these support processes means that staff on these teams quickly become expert at what they do.

The shared services model also provides an increasingly attractive career path, given the heightened skill requirements in such centers. Teams tend to focus more on analytics, customer service, and innovation than is the case under the traditional model.

PwC recognizes several global companies as the leaders in SSC implementation. These companies include Hewlett-Packard, Procter & Gamble, and General Electric. PwC notes these reasons for why these organizations have implemented SSCs:

■ **Further simplifying core finance and administration (F&A) processes.** Customization retained since the center was established may no longer be desirable or defensible in the current business climate.
■ **Partnering with internal customers.** Business units may be newly amenable to greater standardization in SLAs, particularly if these changes yield additional savings.

■ **Rebalancing the distribution of talent between headquarters and center operations.** Reductions in operating budgets and overall F&A resource levels can sometimes change the rationale behind where certain skills should reside.

Methodology

A successful move to an SSC model requires a carefully planned and managed transition. The transition should:

- Standardize business processes before the shift
- Consolidate processes and people without losing key employees and disrupting services
- Reengineer systems: the first cost savings usually come from reduced headcounts and redesigned processes
- Communicate a clear vision and early successes to top management
- Win buy-in from all the departments that will use the SSC

Common Uses

As noted in a 2011 Deloitte study, SSCs are used not only to improve cost savings, but also to help organizations respond to the marketplace and pursue rapid growth strategies by:

- Delivering higher-quality service and improved customer satisfaction
- Capturing economies of scale
- Increasing standardization and use of leading-edge technologies
- Freeing up employees to spend more time and resources on their core jobs
- Providing flexibility to quickly add new business units and expand geographically
- Enabling rapid integration of new acquisitions

 CONTROLLER'S TOOL 43 – TYPES OF OUTSOURCING MODELS

Introduction. BPO involves outsourcing processes that are not core to a company but are essential for the smooth operation of the company. The customer transfers complete responsibility for these functions to the service provider, who guarantees certain service quality standards. Similarly to the SSC approach, the processes outsourced include customer service, AP, payroll processing, and inventory management.

Types of Outsourcing Models

---

1. **Global Delivery or Blended Outsourcing Model.** This kind of model allows the service provider to provide its outsourcing services globally. This is preferred choice for large companies.

2. **Hybrid Delivery Model.** This can also be said to be a dual-core model, because the model functions by combining offshore and onshore services together.

3. **Global Shared Services Centers.** This is a model that combines onshore shared services and offshore captive centers. The global center can be run separately with its own budget and responsibilities.

4. **Offshore Multisourcing Model.** This is the practice of using several outsourcing firms and service providers. The advantage in this model is that it is more flexible and provides a solution for business continuity plans.

Types of Outsourcing Models

5. **Classic Outsourcing**. The traditional structure of a classic outsourcing consists of an agreement for the service provider to provide services (based on an agreed scope and an agreed level of services) in return for an agreed pricing structure.

6. **Joint Venture (Between Organization Customer and Service Provider).** In a joint venture, the organization customer and the service provider each contribute capital, intellectual property, personnel, and other resources to design and implement a solution. By definition, a joint venture is a joint organization, regardless of form, in which at least two partners share assets, management, and profits and losses within an agreed joint commercial mission.

7. **Group Captive (Among Multiple Organization Customers for Their Own Captive).** In some industries (such as banking, financial services, and insurance), common regulations impose a compliance burden on competitors. In such cases, competitors may elect to establish a jointly owned "group captive" to perform such compliance-mandated services. Such group captives enable industry players to share information on compliance standards in order to design a standard template of services that meet those standards. Group captives were popular in the 1980s and 1990s before BPOs developed and perfected the classic outsourcing model. A review of group captives offers an insight into this evolution.

8. **Wholly Owned Operating Subsidiary (Captive, or Shared Services Center).** An organization may choose to establish a wholly owned subsidiary to perform particular services for all corporate affiliates. Such an organization is often referred to as a "captive" or a "shared services center." The organization controls all aspects of operations and is able to integrate business process transaction operations with its front-office, customer-facing business.

9. **Virtual Operating Subsidiary.** An organization might create a wholly owned subsidiary in the captive model using its own staff, but operations could be managed by a third-party service provider that guarantees a service level. Such third-party service providers serve as project managers using the organization's resources.

10. **Managed Services (Facilities Management/Operations and Maintenance/Infrastructure Management).** In some cases the organization already possesses all the employees, business processes, and technology necessary to perform the service that it wants to outsource. It may enlist the assistance of a service provider to operate and maintain the service delivery infrastructure.

11. **Build-Operate-Transfer and Build-Own-Operate-Transfer.** These approaches are forms of project financing, wherein a private entity receives a concession from the private or public sector to finance, design, construct, and operate a facility as stated in the concession contract. This enables the project proponent to recover its investment, operating, and maintenance expenses in the project. Due to the long-term nature of the arrangement, the fees are usually raised during the concession period. The rate of increase is often tied to a combination of internal and external variables, allowing the proponent to reach a satisfactory IRR for its investment.

12. **Licensing.** In some cases the organization customer wants to set up a new service delivery center, service architecture, or infrastructure. It may enlist the assistance of a service provider in the design of the operations; the procurement of the necessary equipment, real estate, and technology; and the recruitment, hiring, and training of the personnel for the new service delivery center. Strategic sourcing can be achieved through a licensing model. The organization customer may own a membership list, a trademark, or other intellectual property that can be commercialized for profit.

 ## CONTROLLER'S TOOL 44 – THE ADVANTAGES OF OUTSOURCING

Introduction. Outsourcing offers numerous advantages to companies, as outlined in the following table. The ability to focus on core competencies and reduce cost is considered to be key drivers in the decision-making process.

The Advantages of Outsourcing

1. **Focus on Core Competencies.** Outsourcing enables customers to divert their attention from supplementary tasks and focus on their core functions. Customer care, documentation, IT upgrades, and administrative tasks such as internal audit and payroll processing are the noncore tasks for many companies and consume the time of the management if handled in-house. When these tasks are outsourced, company management can focus on the company's core competencies and bring better services and products into the market.

2. **Cost Savings.** Cost savings is an important consideration in an outsourcing decision. Outsourcing enables companies to reduce their costs on resource management, labor, space, and so on. According to Accenture, outsourcing leads to a cost savings of 25–30 percent. Outsource Partners International estimates the cost savings to reach up to 50 percent when the outsourced work is offshored.

3. **Quality.** Service providers have expert employees along with specialized processes and technology that ensure better quality of output for the customer. However, the customer has to carefully select a supplier that will provide it with the quality of services that it requires.

4. **Flexibility.** Outsourcing provides flexibility to the customer, as the buyer can change a supplier if required. Changing a supplier in case of poor delivery is much easier than changing a full-time employee. Many outsourcing deals incorporate conditions for changes in requirement or termination of the contract.

5. **Time-to-Market.** Outsourcing also enables faster startup, development, and scalability for new operations.

6. **Access to Diverse Technologies.** Service providers have focus on particular services and play in volume. This enables them to keep themselves up to date with the technology required for these services. The customer can thus avoid technology obsolescence and leverage the supplier's access to diverse and advanced technologies.

 ## BUSINESS PROCESS OUTSOURCING

Over a period of time, every industry starts following certain best practices as it develops and matures. The best practices followed in the BPO industry include:

BPO Best Practices

1. Companies outsource critical but noncore business processes that are not strategic to the firm's vision.

2. An inefficient process is not outsourced to a third-party supplier.

3. Companies gather support from its employees before taking the outsourcing plunge.

4. The first step towards this is early communication of the outsourcing decision to the employees and even the shareholders.

5. Sourcing advisors are consulted for negotiating a deal.

6. Supplier is selected based on various criteria such as quality commitment, cost, transparency of operations, data security, and the like.

CONTROLLER'S TOOL 45 – COST-BENEFIT ANALYSIS

Introduction. A cost-benefit analysis is a fairly simple tool to use when making important business decisions. Here are the steps:

Cost Analysis Steps

1. Determine and define the objectives. A cost-benefit analysis must include project objectives and background information so that the reviewer can understand the information even if not intimately familiar with the industry.

2. Document the product's or service's current process. All reviewers involved in the cost-benefit analysis need to understand the details of the business processes so they can make the best decision regarding an alternative.

3. Estimate future requirements and upgrades. Talk with those inside the company or professionals outside the company to find the most realistic estimate.

4. Collect as much detailed cost data for each alternative considered as possible.

5. Choose at least three alternatives. Document and justify the assumptions for each of the alternatives. Always consider the status quo as an alternative and provide the impacts of no change to the current system or process.

6. Estimate the costs involved and determine a total cost.

7. Identify and estimate the value of the benefits.

8. Discount the costs and benefits. Convert the estimate into a common measurement. Calculate the present value, the discounted value, or a future amount with the formula $P = F (1 / (1+I) n)$, where P = Present Value, F = Future Value, I = Interest Rate, and n= Number of Years.

9. Evaluate the alternatives by comparing and ranking the discounted value of each alternative.

10. Perform a sensibility analysis to ensure that the results of your cost-benefit analysis are reliable.

CONTROLLER'S TOOL 46 – INFORMATION FOR SUPPLIER EVALUATION

The organization should collect and record the following general information about the BPO options available:

1. **General Profile**
   This section of the document would give an introductory summary about the service provider. In this section, *location and domain expertise* are important valuation factors. The general profile should include:
   - Name of service provider
   - Location
   - Established year
   - Domain expertise
   - Years of experience in domain
   - Management organization chart
   - Global spread
   - Annual revenue

2. **Clients**

Client details are an indication of the service maturity and reputation of the BPO, and case studies give an insight into the solutions provided for the client. Details regarding previous and current clients of the BPO should be included. The components of this section include:

- Client base in counties and regions
- Previous and current clients of service provider
- Client referrals/testimonials
- Client case studies

3. **Technology and Processes**

This section focuses on technology and processes and includes:

- Software, integrated suites
- Database systems
- Standardized, well-documented development processes
- Secure development environment
- Standardized project management system
- Standardized delivery mechanism
- Agreed mode of communication between client and provider
- Communication technologies, such as e-mail, chat, and video-conferencing software
- Flexibility and scalability of technology solutions and processes

If a company is opting for multisource solutions, then it must ensure that software systems are compatible throughout the BPOs being considered.

4. **Human Capital**

This section focuses on the management and employees that will be supporting the business process or processes being considered for outsourcing. The details of this section include:

- Profile of managers, including qualifications and experience
- Number of employees
- Qualifications and skill set of employees
- Experience of employees
- Communication and language skills of employees
- Pay and benefits of employees
- Attrition rate
- Training initiatives for employees

5. **Infrastructure**

Depending on whether a company is opting for a third-party outsourcing model or a virtual captive model, it is important to evaluate the physical infrastructure of the service provider. Information considered for the infrastructure review includes:

- Office space
- Hardware requirements, including servers, workstations, peripherals
- Telecommunication links such as broadband Internet and phone links.

6. **Quality**

The quality initiatives of the BPO should include:

- Quality certifications, such as Six Sigma
- Documented quality assurance (QA) process

- Established roles and responsibilities for the QA process
- A QA metrics program

7. **Pricing**

Pricing consideration should include:
- Cost of solution
- Terms and conditions of the contract

8. **Cultural Fit**

The cultural fit of the BPO is an important consideration and should include the following review components:
- Workplace ethics
- Responsiveness to client needs
- Cultural differences, including language

9. **Value Proposition**

The value proposition would include the key differentiators that would make a particular BPO a better choice than others. Considerations for value propositions include:
- Flexibility and willingness to go the extra mile for the client
- Rapid development environment
- Orientation towards long-term partnerships
- Cutting-edge technology
- Ability to create long-term intellectual capital for the client
- A partner-player for the client, helping it to grow its business

 ## CONTROLLER'S TOOL 47 – CONSIDERATIONS IN IMPLEMENTING SERVICE LEVEL AGREEMENTS AND METRICS

Introduction. An important step in the decision-making process is to establish a set of SLAs and internal control requirements that will establish performance expectations for the BPO.

An SLA is a negotiated agreement between two parties in which one is the customer and the other is the actual service provider. This can be a legally binding formal or informal contract. An SLA should contain operating norms that describe how the process is governed, managed, and controlled. An SLA should also include a set of operating metrics that are reported on a monthly or quarterly basis. As an example, a good set of metrics for AP would include cost per invoice, DPO, invoices paid on time, outstanding credit balances, paid credits, and number of suppliers on the supplier master. The following considerations apply:

Considerations for Service Level Agreements and Metrics

---

1. Does the firm have a standard set of metrics?

2. Does the firm have an SLA process?

3. Previous experience with AP and track record?

4. Do the SLAs meet your needs and help achieve business objectives?

5. What corrective action is taken if the SLAs are not accomplished?

6. Will the firm agree to periodic status review meetings?

7. Does the contract have an exit clause for nonperformance?

8. How is the process managed?

9. How are system or process changes addressed?

10. Is communication an issue?

11. What is the time frame for implementation?

12. How is the implementation managed?

TABLE OF CONTROLS – SHARED SERVICE CENTERS AND BUSINESS PROCESS OUTSOURCING

Process: Shared Service Centers and Business Process Outsourcing

1. **There is a well-defined governance process.** The SSC is has a well-defined organization structure with a clear chain-of-command to address escalated issues if needed.

2. **The shared services center and/or business process outsourcing entity utilize(s) automation.** In the past two decades, companies have moved transaction-processing activities to low-cost geographies to take advantage of labor arbitrage. These efforts aim to improve organizational capabilities, drive processes improvement, reduce costs and execute strategy. Robotic process automation (RPA) enables shared services leaders to achieve productivity increases and cost reductions. Gartner research finds more than 80 percent of shared services organizations have implemented RPA technology to automate routine, repetitive, rule-based activities. RPA enables shared services leaders to achieve productivity increases and cost reductions in excess of those provided by labor arbitrage alone.

3. **The organization uses global process owners for standardization.** Many shared-services projects target cost and productivity improvements within a single process (such as AP). The most advanced companies often go well beyond those limitations and appoint GPOs for end-to-end processes such as O2C or P2P.

4. **There is an Investment in training and a recognition of the importance of employees.** As SSCs look to increase the value they provide to business-unit customers, successful organizations don't treat employee training as a discretionary cost; rather, they see training and development as an investment.

5. **The organization provides data analytics.** Data analytics allows these teams to simplify complex information, use that information in different ways at different times, and be better prepared for strategic planning.

6. **There is a focus on operational excellence.** There are continuous improvements in operations that are evidenced by metrics and positive SLA results.

7. **The shared services center and/or business process outsourcing entity are/is forward thinking.** Forward-thinking firms expand both the geographic scope and the breadth of their service offerings. For these companies, there are no opt-out options for business units. The SSC serves every country, location, business unit, and employee of the company. Progressive companies expand the scope to include expert functions and don't limit the criteria to whether the SSC yields the same kind of cost savings as those achieved by taking on high-volume transaction processing.

TABLE OF RISKS AND CONTROLS – SHARED SERVICE CENTERS AND BUSINESS PROCESS OUTSOURCING

Process: Shared Service Centers and Business Process Outsourcing			
Process Risk	**Recommended Policies**	**Internal Controls**	**KPIs**
1. Companies don't plan for the startup costs. This seems to be widely forgotten when it comes to shared services.	■ Operational and SLA Processes	1. There is a well-defined governance process. 2. The SSC and/or BPO utilize automation. 3. The organizations use GPOs for standardization. 4. There is an investment in training and a recognition of the importance of employees. 5. The organization provides data analytics. 6. There is a focus on operational excellence 7. The SSC and/or BPO are forward thinking.	■ Customer Satisfaction ■ SLAs Achieved ■ Financial Performance ■ Percentage of Processes Automated ■ Cost per Transaction ■ Cost per Transaction vs. Goal ■ Transaction Defects
2. Transaction costs increase. Even with new technology, there is a risk of creating additional layers of management and coordination. Unfortunately reform proponents often overlook this trade-off, focusing on production-cost savings rather than the transaction-cost burden for clients.	■ Operational and SLA Processes	1. There is a well-defined governance process. 2. The SSC and/or BPO utilize automation. 3. The organizations use GPOs for standardization. 4. There is an investment in training and a recognition of the importance of employees. 5. The organization provides data analytics. 6. There is a focus on operational excellence. 7. The SSC and/or BPO are forward thinking.	■ Customer Satisfaction ■ SLAs Achieved ■ Financial Performance ■ Percentage of Processes Automated ■ Cost per Transaction ■ Cost per Transaction vs. Goal ■ Transaction Defects

Process: Shared Service Centers and Business Process Outsourcing			
Process Risk	**Recommended Policies**	**Internal Controls**	**KPIs**
3. Service quality is reduced. Standardization of back-office processes brings advantages but also risks, including excessive concern for processes over outcomes and slower decision-making.	■ Operational and SLA Processes	1. There is a well-defined governance process. 2. The SSC and/or BPO utilize automation. 3. The organizations use GPOs for standardization. 4. There is an investment in training and a recognition of the importance of employees. 5. The organization provides data analytics. 6. There is a focus on operational excellence. 7. The SSC and/or BPO are forward thinking.	■ Customer Satisfaction ■ SLAs Achieved ■ Transaction Defects
4. There is functional duplication. By sharing services, managers are expected to end duplicated activities and eliminate redundant capacity.	■ Operational and SLA Processes	1. There is a well-defined governance process. 2. The SSC and/or BPO utilize automation. 3. The organizations use GPOs for standardization. 4. There is an investment in training and a recognition of the importance of employees. 5. The organization provides data analytics. 6. There is a focus on operational excellence. 7. The SSC and/or BPO are forward thinking.	■ Customer Satisfaction ■ SLAs Achieved ■ Financial Performance ■ Percentage of Processes Automated ■ Cost per Transaction ■ Cost per Transaction vs. Goal ■ Transaction Defects
5. The company's systems, technology, tools, and management capability aren't a good fit for centralized processing.	■ Operational and SLA Processes	2. The SSC and/or BPO utilize automation.	■ Percentage of Processes Automated

Process: Shared Service Centers and Business Process Outsourcing			
Process Risk	**Recommended Policies**	**Internal Controls**	**KPIs**
6. There is a lack of reporting and metrics for the business processes supported.	■ Operational and SLA Processes	6. There is a focus on operational excellence.	■ Customer Satisfaction ■ SLAs Achieved ■ Financial Performance ■ Percentage of Processes Automated ■ Cost per Transaction ■ Cost per Transaction vs. Goal ■ Transaction Defects
7. Regulatory requirements are not achieved – putting the company at risk.	■ Operational and SLA Processes	1. There is a well-defined governance process. 3. The organizations use GPOs for standardization.	■ Customer Satisfaction ■ SLAs Achieved ■ Financial Performance ■ Percentage of Processes Automated ■ Cost per Transaction ■ Cost per Transaction vs. Goal ■ Transaction Defects
8. There is a delay in the financial close due to additional SSC and/ or BPO consolidation points.	■ Operational and SLA Processes	1. There is a well-defined governance process. 2. The SSC and/or BPO utilize automation. 3. The organizations use GPOs for standardization. 4. There is an investment in training and a recognition of the importance of employees. 5. The organization provides data analytics. 6. There is a focus on operational excellence. 7. The SSC and/or BPO are forward thinking.	■ Customer Satisfaction ■ SLAs Achieved ■ Financial Performance ■ Percentage of Processes Automated ■ Cost per Transaction ■ Cost per Transaction vs. Goal ■ Transaction Defects

CHAPTER EIGHTEEN

Dashboards, Data Validation, Analytics, Metrics, and Benchmarking

OVERVIEW

Controllers need to know how their areas of responsibilities perform compared to those of their peers and leading-edge companies worldwide. Benchmarking provides a method of collecting business process improvement ideas. Implementing these value-added process improvements to replace activities that don't add value allows business processes to contribute positively to the company's financials and competitive position. Benchmarking provides the avenue to benefit from process improvements others have implemented while stimulating new ideas. Benchmarking results identify best practices and potential areas for implementing process improvements.

DASHBOARDS, DATA VALIDATION, ANALYTICS, METRICS, AND BENCHMARKING PROCESS FLOW

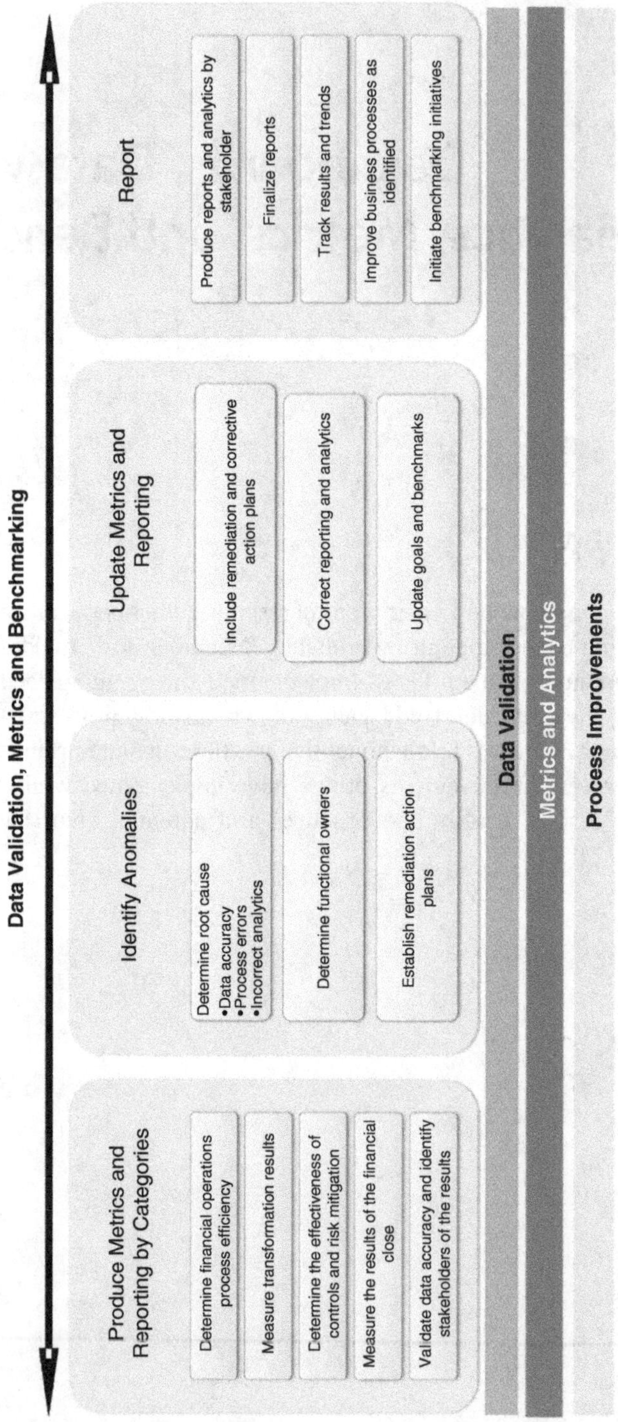

Data Validation, Metrics and Benchmarking

Produce Metrics and Reporting by Categories

- Determine financial operations process efficiency
- Measure transformation results
- Determine the effectiveness of controls and risk mitigation
- Measure the results of the financial close
- Validate data accuracy and identify stakeholders of the results

Identify Anomalies

- Determine root cause
  - Data accuracy
  - Process errors
  - Incorrect analytics
- Determine functional owners
- Establish remediation action plans

Update Metrics and Reporting

- Include remediation and corrective action plans
- Correct reporting and analytics
- Update goals and benchmarks

Report

- Produce reports and analytics by stakeholder
- Finalize reports
- Track results and trends
- Improve business processes as identified
- Initiate benchmarking initiatives

Data Validation

Metrics and Analytics

Process Improvements

CONTROLLER'S TOOL 48 – KEY CONSIDERATIONS FOR DASHBOARD TECHNOLOGY

Introduction. A data dashboard is an information management tool that visually tracks, analyzes and displays KPIs, metrics, and key data points to monitor the health of a business, department, or specific process. It is customizable to meet the specific needs of a department and company. The table below outlines some key considerations to consider for successful implementation.

Key Considerations for Dashboard Technology

1. Carefully align the KPIs being selected for your dashboards with the company's overall business goals.

2. Establish a hierarchy of KPIs, from enterprise-wide strategic metrics (market share, profitability, etc.) to more tactical line-of-business benchmarks.

3. Continuously review the KPIs being used and update or change them as necessary to assure relevance in today's continually evolving business environment.

4. Measure company performance against the established KPIs.

5. Develop a process to measure how and whether dashboard tools are being utilized – a fancy solution isn't of much use if it's not being used.

6. Establish training programs to educate end users at all levels.

7. Create a dashboard implementation team that includes cross-functional employees as well as senior managers. This will help you design the dashboard with end users in mind.

8. Strive for dashboards that are easily readable and understandable. Too many KPIs can get in the way of this objective.

CONTROLLER'S TOOL 49 – TYPES OF BENCHMARKING

Introduction. Benchmarking is an integral part of reporting and monitoring performance metrics. Controllers compare the performance of their products or processes externally to those of competitors and best-in-class companies, as well as internally to other operations within their own firm that perform similar activities. Additionally, organizations track performance by comparing their own results over time (e.g. month to month, year to year). There are three common types of benchmarking initiatives: (1) internal, (2) industry/volume, and (3) world class. The details for each type are provided in this controller's tool.

1. **Internal Benchmarking**

   Benchmarking works well in an organization because accounting and other measurement principles are similar. Measurement criteria are standardized and well understood. These benefits are magnified if the units being measured are homogeneous. The organization has the resources to drill down to details when analyzing differences.

   In such an environment, the starting point is reasonably even/level. From there, the company can observe differences in performance. Organizations have been very effective in benchmarking internally.

   For example, a hotel chain can compare properties and furnish data on the cost per room, associates hours/square foot of hotel space, guest occupancy percentage, and so forth. Using various criteria, the hotel chain could rank its properties best to worst, highlighting the high performers and exploring the essence of their success. To continue the example, evaluating the results could reveal that the property in Las Vegas is benefiting from a boom in that market, while another property near the bottom has been adversely affected by hurricanes. As a result, external metrics – for example, occupancy percentage of the properties relative to competition, quality level, and price points – become relevant. The Las Vegas property may be at 80 percent occupancy, but comparable hotels may be at 95 percent. If the hurricane-area property is at 50 percent occupancy while its competitors are at 35 percent, which property is better managed? Within the chain, differences in size, construction, services, amenities, and quality all have an impact.

Internal benchmarking can involve the following:

- **Homogeneous units.** Unit A versus units B, C, and D
- **Individuals.** Key entry associates Mary, John, and Kate versus budget, standard, last month, and each other
- **Overall progress or tracking trends.** This month versus budget, last month, and last year

2. **Industry/Volume Benchmarking**

Staying within your industry increases the likelihood of finding similar processes, thus providing more relevant and compelling comparisons.

Additionally, an entity gets the most value when it compares itself to organizations similar to itself in volume as well as in process. High-volume transaction business processes generally have lower per-transaction costs. As a result, higher-volume units should be benchmarked.

If lower transaction costs are attributable to economies of scale and more advanced technology, smaller business processes will not be able to replicate the economies of scale but can consider the advanced technology as a possibility, as automation continues to become more affordable.

3. **World Class Benchmarking**

In world class benchmarking, a company compares a business process to the best in class. This may mean crossing industry lines in order to obtain new ideas. For example, Motorola wanted to improve its order entry/fulfillment and sought out Lands' End, a best-in-class company, whose core business relied upon that process. Many companies have studied process leaders like Walmart for supply chain quality and FedEx for tracking excellence, in spite of differences in industry and scale.

Collecting Benchmark Data

Data collection involves identifying and assembling the data components that are pertinent to the business process area. Some considerations are included below.

Cost

- Salaries, whose differences are based upon scale, experience, and the skill mix required. Consider the following when collecting salary data:
  - Indirect salaries, including remote processors and related costs
  - Managerial salaries, which may or may not include part or all of the salary of a department manager, such as a controller

- Benefit costs, including Social Security taxes, unemployment taxes, pension, medical costs, and other perks that differ based upon benefit plans
- IT software and hardware, remembering that the business process owner may be considered to be the client for systems supporting the process
- Equipment, including equipment depreciation and interest on the undepreciated portion in the department, and including furniture and fixtures
- Occupancy, recognizing that geographical differences influence real estate value, property taxes, construction, and utilities, while company standards influence the work environment
- Travel
- Training
- Telecommunications, both inbound and outbound
- Delivery, including postage and express mail

Due to the variability of the use and nature of the above elements, a simple salary and benefit cost is most often preferred. In an effort to level the playing field on varying costs and systems, many organizations use cost per full time employee equivalent.

Payroll/Overhead

- Managers/administrators
- Regular associates
- Part-time associates
- Contract associates
- Full-time equivalents
- Open positions
- Overtime hours paid
- Sick pay
- Vacation pay
- Business days

Analyzing Benchmark Results

1. **Evaluation of Improvement Opportunities.** In order to make recommendations for change that is suitable for its environment and to increase the likelihood of success, participants should ask the following questions about the benchmark study:
   - **Who are the leaders?** Preferably leaders in the industry and volume categories.
   - **How did they do it?** Are they at our level of progress? How long did it take?
   - **How are the leaders organized?** Look at the relationships. Are they less bureaucratic and more empowering?
   - **How are we unique?** Every organization is unique. Does our uniqueness capture/serve our segment?
   - **Are our differences necessary?** Although some uniqueness is essential, other differences may not be vital and may be superfluous, adding cost and effort to the process. This may ultimately result in substandard service.
   - **Can we apply the approach?** Is it achievable in our organization?
   - **What is most revealing?** What are the salient differences?

- **Which programs close the gaps?** Do not give up if you cannot achieve their level of success overnight. Strive for a single step of progress at a time.
- **What are our priorities?** Identify the most important areas to improve.
- **What are the barriers to change?** What obstacles are going to impede a successful implementation? Are they real or perceived?
- **How can we gain advantage?** Develop a vision for winning!

2. **Factors Affecting Metrics.** Benchmarking and metrics often go together. Like benchmarking, there are several considerations to address when developing a metrics program.

   - Environment with internal controls – have controls been established based upon internal and external risks?
   - Risk avoidance, or the willingness of management to take risks or spend money to exercise control
   - Departmental administration other than finance, or quasi accounting functions performed at the operating level
   - Degree/quality of automation, or the status of system development and integration
   - Training of associates
   - Experience of associates
   - Time in business
   - Industry practices
   - Management's access to data/information
   - Nature and differentiation of inquiries
   - Expected response/service level
   - Retention/retrieval system
   - Error tolerance
   - Level of standardization/complexity

3. **Pitfalls in Benchmarking and Metrics.** Do not focus too narrowly on one metric or KPI. As an example, a one-dimensional reduction in AP cost per invoice will have trade-offs, such as sacrificing quality aspects, as well as affecting control, internal service, and supplier relations. Unfortunately, some of these components of success are difficult to measure. Consider total cost when considering process improvement because some improvements could add expense in other areas, such as IT, software, hardware, and various other services, including outsourcing

   Process improvements should be carefully prioritized. It is also critical to understand the impacts on internal controls. The organization needs to consider the feasibility of a process improvement and determine if a similar company or organization has benefited. Lastly, a process improvement that works well in a SAP environment may not work well in an Oracle or legacy environment.

4. **Summary of Benchmarking Benefits.** There are several important benefits to implementing a benchmarking project, which include the following results;

   - **Forces an external view.** This is a competitive world where change occurs rapidly.
   - **Broadens perspective to see beyond the barriers.** Learning about others helps a company understand itself.
   - **Nurtures outside-the-box thinking.** Successful organizations adapt and improve.
   - **Identifies innovation, breakthroughs, and trends**. What is happening, or are we missing something?

- **Identifies competitive position.** Where do we stand?
- **Assists in goal setting and decision-making.** Where do we want to be?
- **Supports process development.** The best companies are doing it; are we only mediocre, or are we missing something?
- **Provides organizations with an accelerated change methodology.** This was the winner's road map; here are the lessons they learned.
- **Builds confidence that objectives can be reached.** If Proctor & Gamble can do it, why can't we at Colgate do it?
- **Eliminates activities that don't add value.** Dell eliminated it, why should Hewlett-Packard continue with it?

 ## CONTROLLER'S TOOL 50 – IMPLEMENTING METRICS

Introduction. When defining metrics, it's important to define what needs to be measured and to follow the step-by-step process in the list below that's illustrated in the diagram that follows.

1. Identify the process.
2. Gather data.
3. Analyze outcomes.
4. Report results.
5. Improve the process.

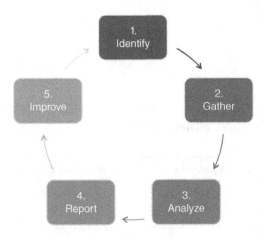

1. **Identify**
   - Define the components of the process to be measured.
   - Review the process.
   - Determine what should be measured.
   - Start simple!
   - Ensure that the data is available and easy to collect.

2. **Gather**
   - Don't start from scratch.
   - Use a template to gather the data.
   - Include your team in the process.
   - Define the time period for measurement.
   - Determine when to start.

3. **Analyze**
   - Do the outcomes make sense?
   - Are there areas of concern?
   - How do results stack up?
   - Set a target for comparison.
   - Internal processes
   - Other companies
   - Similar industries
   - Establish goals.
   - Review.

4. **Report**
   - Do the outcomes make sense?
   - Are there areas of concern?
   - How do results "stack up"?
   - Set a target for comparison.
   - Review internal processes.
   - Evaluate other companies.
   - Evaluate like industries.
   - Establish goals.
   - Review.

5. **Improve**

TABLE OF CONTROLS – DATA VALIDATION, ANALYTICS, METRICS, AND BENCHMARKING

Process: Data Validation, Analytics, Metrics, and Benchmarking

---

1. Goals and Stakeholders. Establish goals for the analytics, metrics, and benchmarking initiative and ensure that stakeholders are identified for the business processes to be included.

2. Data Validation. Ensure that data is validated and is reflected accurately with no missing or duplicated data.

3. Defined Benchmarking Project. Determine approach, define the benchmarking project, and specify if the initiative will include another company or an internal process.

4. Visibility of Spending. Spending results are tracked, analyzed, and reported to business stakeholders.

5. Strategic Sourcing Opportunities. Strategic sourcing opportunities are identified to leverage suppliers and positively impact working capital. With few exceptions, Fortune 1000 organizations are burdened with an oversized base of suppliers. Given that the average Fortune 1000 company buys approximately 400–500 commodities and maintains a global supplier base of over 50,000 suppliers, there is an average of over 100 suppliers per commodity.

Process: Data Validation, Analytics, Metrics, and Benchmarking
6. Business Process Metrics. Implement metrics to report business process results, identify process improvements, and address payment issues in a timely manner. Metrics should focus on cost, process efficiency, internal controls, and customer service impacts to the payments process.
7. Reporting and Analytics Process. Develop a reporting process so that the results of metrics and analytics are reported in a timely and consistent manner.

TABLE OF RISKS AND CONTROLS – DATA VALIDATION, ANALYTICS, METRICS, AND BENCHMARKING

Process: Data Validation, Analytics, Metrics and Benchmarking

Process Risk	Recommended Policies	Internal Controls	KPIs
1. Goals and expectations are not defined or achieved.	▪ Company KPI Process ▪ Company Business Process Scorecards (See KPI Library)	1. Establish Goals and Stakeholders 2. Data Validation 3. Define a Benchmarking Project 4. Visibility to Spending 5. Strategic Sourcing Opportunities 6. Business Process Metrics 7. Develop a Reporting and Analytics Process	▪ KPIs by Business Process
2. Data is not validated. Results are inaccurate, which will impact the decision-making process.	▪ Data Reconciliation Process	2. Data Validation	▪ Percentage of Data Accuracy
3. Benchmarking initiatives are not well defined. Expectations are not achieved and business decisions are inaccurate.	▪ Company Benchmarking Policies	3. Define a Benchmarking Project	▪ Number of Benchmarking Initiatives
4. Business process metrics are not defined. There will be inconsistent calculations and results. Business process improvements may not be identified.	▪ Company KPI Process ▪ Company Business Process Scorecards (See KPI Library)	7. Develop a Reporting and Analytics Process	▪ KPIs by Business Process
5. There are spending anomalies and trends. Opportunities to address a spending issue for a specific supplier or commodity are not visible to the company, causing potential payment problems.	▪ Spend Reporting Process	4. Visibility to Spending	▪ Strategic Sourcing Cost Savings ▪ Unapproved Items in PO Workflow

Process: Data Validation, Analytics, Metrics and Benchmarking			
Process Risk	**Recommended Policies**	**Internal Controls**	**KPIs**
6. **Strategic sourcing opportunities are not identified**. Opportunities for strategic sourcing are not identified or acted open. Strategic sourcing is an approach to supply chain management that formalizes the way information is gathered and used so that an organization can leverage its consolidated purchasing power to find the best possible values in the marketplace.	■ Spend Reporting Process ■ Strategic Sourcing Program	5. Strategic Sourcing Opportunities	■ Strategic Sourcing Cost Savings
7. **There is a loss of visibility of analytics and metrics results.**	■ Company KPI Process ■ Company Business Process Scorecards (See KPI Library)	6. Business Process Metrics 7. Develop a Reporting and Analytics Process	■ KPIs by Business Process ■ Percentage of Data Accuracy ■ Number of Remediation Issues

7

Information Technology Risk

SECTION INTRODUCTION

Imagine waking up to discover that your IT systems have been hacked. Your company's financial results have been leaked to the media, your confidential business plans have been compromised, and your employees' personal files have been posted on the Internet. The market loses confidence in your organization, your share price takes a dive, and your directors are found to be personally responsible for inadequate risk management practices.

Every organization uses information; most are dependent on it. Information is an asset that, like other important business assets, is essential to your business and consequently needs to be suitably protected. This is especially important in the increasingly interconnected business environment, where information is now exposed to a growing number and a wider variety of threats and vulnerabilities.

CHAPTER NINETEEN

Information Technology Controls and Cybersecurity

 OVERVIEW

In the world of enterprise IT, governance is something controllers often think about. Controllers want to know how many IT projects are outstanding. Organizations should have a basic framework by which all decisions are made. The six components of the COBIT (Control Objectives for Information and Related Technologies) framework are depicted in the following process flow.

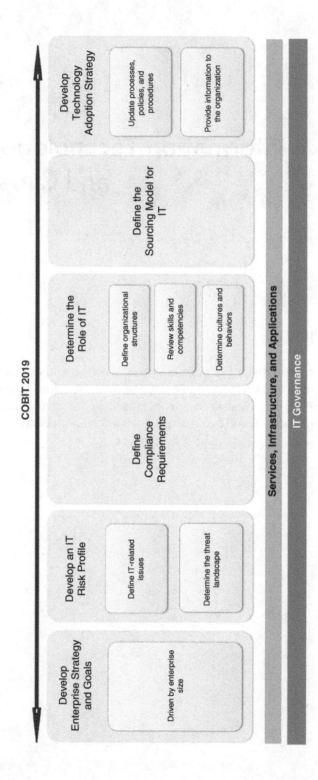

INFORMATION TECHNOLOGY CONTROLS AND CYBERSECURITY PROCESS FLOW

COBIT 2019

Develop Enterprise Strategy and Goals

Driven by enterprise size

Develop an IT Risk Profile

Define IT-related issues

Determine the threat landscape

Define Compliance Requirements

Determine the Role of IT

Define organizational structures

Review skills and competencies

Determine cultures and behaviors

Define the Sourcing Model for IT

Develop Technology Adoption Strategy

Update processes, policies, and procedures

Provide information to the organization

Services, Infrastructure, and Applications

IT Governance

ACCESS CONTROL

One of the most important internal controls an organization of any size should establish is access control – the doorway to all IT systems and corporate resources. Computer access control applies to all information resources: desktops, servers, mainframes, networks, and so forth. The objective of computer access control is to assure the integrity, availability, and confidentiality of company information and the facilities that process, store, or transmit such information.

A system of access control reduces the risk of information being disclosed, contaminated, misused, or destroyed, whether by accidental or intentional means. It is based upon proper authorization and establishes a basis for internal control by enabling separation of responsibility both within and among owner, user, and service-provider functions. Restricting an individual's access to resources based upon need to know and establishing individual accountability are essential principles in achieving effective access and internal control.

Access controls specify how the business will monitor its IT resources and how they should be used. The most commonly used access controls include user accounts, consisting of passwords and usernames; login and resource access rights; and the establishment of privileged system accounts. Two common methods of user authentication are:

> **Single-factor authentication:** An authentication/identification method based on "something you know," where the primary method of identifying the user is a password.
> **Two-factor authentication:** An authentication/identification method based on "something you have plus something you know." The user's information, if captured, cannot be used by itself by unauthorized individuals to gain entry into a computer system or application. It requires processing something that is unique to the individual and a PIN that ensures that the individual is indeed who they say they are. Time-dependent random number generators and cryptographic techniques are examples of such an authentication technique.

Those responsible for IT security should keep the following in mind:

1. **Security Administration Procedures.** Owners/service providers of equipment, in coordination with unit and department managers, must appoint security administrators. The security administrator function should be segregated from computer operations, systems development, and support when practical. Responsibility for managing and controlling the security administration function must remain with the company. Management must make periodic reviews of accounts and privileges assigned by security administrators.
2. **Transferred or Terminated Employees.** System administrators must follow established procedures to maintain computer accounts for users who are transferred within the company, and to deactivate employee computer accounts upon the employee's transfer or termination from the company on a timely basis. Security administrators have the authority to delete or activate accounts of terminated employees without reference to the owner or the owner's manager. Procedures must also be in place to detect active computer accounts assigned to terminated employees.
3. **Segregation of Duties.** Computer systems or programs are considered in production status if relied upon by management for planning, conducting, recording, or reporting business, engineering, or manufacturing operations. IT departments, end users, or suppliers may

develop software for production systems. Production systems may operate on mainframe, departmental, or personal computers, or over WAN/LAN networks. The following controls must exist to protect production computer software and data files:

- Every application and system must have an identified owner who has ultimate responsibility to satisfy application system control and audit requirements.
- Where systems are used in an environment outside the original owner's control, the user becomes the owner and has the responsibility to ensure that appropriate controls are utilized.
- Individual accountability is to be established for all systems activities and information processed (e.g. data content, programming, and systems operation).
- Data processing personnel directly supporting the system must be permitted access to application programs.
- Control and audit features are to be considered prior to purchase or licensing, or if developed, during the user-requirement phase. These features are to be implemented at the time that the system becomes operational.

4. **Multiple Systems Access.** Supervisors must ensure access granted to multiple systems does not compromise SoD.

 ## USER ACCOUNTS

The creation and management of user accounts is vital to an organization, because access controls are built around user accounts. The purpose of user accounts is to grant employees access to specific network systems and resources.

User access is based on an employee job description and responsibilities. This login information should be set up on the network's operating system. Although employees only need one user account for access to network resources, system administrators must have an additional account that enables them to perform system maintenance work. Any unused user accounts should be disabled as soon as possible. In addition, user accounts should be disabled after an employee is terminated or leaves the organization.

A key aspect of all user accounts is the creation of a username and password. The company's IT department should establish the employee's username. Because many usernames are based on the employee's first and last name, passwords should be hard to guess. To help employees create effective and secure passwords, companies should incorporate the following rules as part of their IT security policies:

- Passwords should contain at least six characters.
- Passwords should contain at least one number, as well as one uppercase and lowercase letter.
- Passwords should be changed every 60 days.
- At least one symbol should be incorporated in addition to numbers and upper- and lowercase letters.
- Consider multifactor authentication processes in which a code is sent through another channel (cell phone or e-mail) that has to be input after the user name and password are validated (tokenization). Multifactor authentication, also known as MFA or multistep

verification, adds another layer of security, supplementing the username and password model with a code that only a specific user has access to (typically sent to something they have immediately to hand).

These rules should be implemented as a system-wide policy on the operating system. If a separate authentication process is used for specific applications, the same rules should be part of the application's use policy. In addition, companies may want to consider the use of separate usernames and passwords – or at least a different password – for each system, so that not all systems are affected when a security breach occurs. Although this is more difficult for employees to manage, this alternative offers more effective security.

 ## LOGIN AND RESOURCE ACCESS REQUESTS

The username and password allow employees access to a company's network resources. As a result, companies must hold employees accountable for all activity associated with their user accounts. For example, employees should not share their passwords with anyone, write them down on paper, or store them in their computers. If they reveal their password to IT support staff, systems must be reset to prompt the employee for a password change when the user logs into the system again.

Furthermore, the user account should be set up to allow employees three login attempts only. After the third failed login attempt, the system should disable the account. To reestablish the user account, the employee must contact the company's network administrator or customer service department. Finally, access requests to network resources should come from the employee's direct supervisor, and the company's IT policies and procedures should indicate who needs to implement all access requests.

 ## INTERNAL SERVICE LEVEL AGREEMENTS

An internal SLA is a contract that defines the kinds of services the user can expect from the IT department. Although small businesses may not be required to have an SLA, there should be a documented process for all IT operations that states the expected timing of the delivery of services to the business and the expected results. In many midsize companies, SLAs that define yearly expected services and how job requests will be escalated are developed between the IT department and the department needing services.

 ## MANAGEMENT AND CONTROL

The way organizations choose to manage and control data depends on how data is classified and who the data owner – the primary employee responsible for managing and coordinating the data's use, such as determining who has data access rights, approving changes, and determining the appropriate backup and recovery times – is. Classifying information helps to ensure that the right kind of security control is implemented. Possible classification categories include:

- Restricted (i.e. data with a highly monitored distribution list, such as reports of major business issues that could harm the company's reputation)
- Confidential (i.e. information that is limited to data owners, such as a list of department budgets)
- Internal (i.e. data that is restricted to corporate employees, such as an employee satisfaction survey)
- Public (i.e. information that is available to the public, such as published quarterly profit reports)

When dealing with restricted or confidential data, companies may consider the use of encryption or attorney–client privileges to safeguard the information's integrity and privacy. Organizations also should make sure corporate data is backed up regularly and that the data owner is an employee.

VULNERABILITY AND THREAT MANAGEMENT

One of the main reasons data controls are established is to manage potential software and hardware risks. During the IT planning process, organizations should consider the following guidelines:

1. IT departments should implement a documented process for receiving software updates and security patches from suppliers.
2. Companies should draft a test and implementation plan that defines how patches and updates will be conducted, and follow established change management protocols.
3. Organizations should consider conducting an ethical attack at least once per year to verify system vulnerabilities, especially if an external website is available to the public. The ethical attack can be performed by a third-party supplier or the IT department.
4. Software and hardware applications should undergo an ethical attack before production.

CONTROLLER'S TOOL 51 – CONTROL OBJECTIVES FOR INFORMATION AND RELATED TECHNOLOGIES

COBIT 5 was introduced in April 2012 by the Information Systems Audit and Control Association (ISACA) as a revision to the previous version. The main purpose of COBIT 5 is to provide a system of IT governance to large complex organizations. The components of COBIT 5 are summarized below.

Summary of the Components of COBIT 5

Five Principles

1. Meeting stakeholder needs
2. Covering the enterprise end to end

3. Applying a single integrated framework
4. Enabling a holistic approach
5. Separating governance from management

Enterprise Enablers

1. Principles, policies, and frameworks
2. Processes
3. Organizational structures
4. Culture, ethics, and behavior
5. Information
6. Services, infrastructure, and applications
7. People, skills, and competencies

Benefits

The COBIT 5 framework provides the following benefits to organizations:

- Maintains high-quality information to support business decisions
- Achieves strategic goals and realize business benefits through the effective and innovative use of IT
- Achieves operational excellence through reliable, efficient application of technology
- Maintains IT-related risk at an acceptable level
- Optimizes the cost of IT services and technology
- Supports compliance with relevant laws, regulations, contractual agreements, and policies

The Purpose of COBIT 5

COBIT 5 provides a comprehensive framework that assists enterprises in achieving their objectives for the governance and management of enterprise information and technology assets. Simply stated, it helps enterprises create optimal value from IT by maintaining a balance between realizing benefits and optimizing risk levels and resource use.

COBIT 5 enables IT to be governed and managed in a holistic manner for the entire enterprise, taking in the full end-to-end business and IT functional areas of responsibility while considering the IT-related interests of internal and external stakeholders. COBIT 5 is generic and useful for enterprises of all sizes, whether commercial, not-for-profit, or public sector.

Using COBIT 5 to Reduce Risk

Because COBIT 5 is business oriented, the framework can deliver value and govern and manage IT-related business risk.

The goals stated in the COBIT 5 framework are:

- Determine stakeholder needs and governance objectives (value creation).
- Identify enterprise goals that can support stakeholder needs. If the balanced scorecard is used to develop these goals, then a common set of terms can be used to communicate the goals.
- Select IT-related goals (for each enterprise goal) that will facilitate the achievement of the goals.

- Achieve IT-related goals. This requires the successful application and use of enablers.
- Present the proposed set of needs, goals, and enablers to executive management as a means of delivering effective governance and management of IT-related technology.

CONTROLLER'S TOOL 52 – OTHER IT INTERNAL CONTROL FRAMEWORKS AND CONSIDERATIONS

Introduction. This tool provides some additional internal control frameworks and resources for the IT process that a controller should be aware of when developing an IT controls structure.

Information Technology Infrastructure Library

ITIL, created by the UK government, runs a close second to COBIT. It offers eight sets of management procedures in eight books: service delivery, service support, service management, infrastructure management, software asset management, business perspective, security management, and application management. ITIL is a good fit for organizations concerned about operations.

Capability Maturity Model Integration

The CMMI method, created by a group from government, industry, and Carnegie Mellon's Software Engineering Institute, is a process improvement approach that includes 22 process areas. It is divided into appraisal, evaluation, and structure. CMMI is particularly well suited to organizations that need help with application development, lifecycle issues, and improving the delivery of products throughout the lifecycle.

IT General Controls

ITGCs, also referred to as general computer controls, are defined as controls other than application controls that relate to the environment within which computer-based application systems are developed, maintained, and operated, and which are therefore applicable to all applications. The objectives of general controls are to ensure the proper development and implementation of applications, and the integrity of program and data files and of computer operations. Like application controls, general controls may be either manual or programmed.

Global Technology Audit Guide

GTAG was developed by the Institute of Internal Auditors in straightforward business language to address a timely issue related to IT management, control, and security. To date, the IIA has released guides on the following topics:

- *GTAG 1: Information Technology Controls*
- *GTAG 2: Change and Patch Management Controls: Critical for Organizational Success*
- *GTAG 3: Continuous Auditing: Implications for Assurance, Monitoring, and Risk Assessment*
- *GTAG 4: Management of IT Auditing*

- *GTAG 5: Managing and Auditing Privacy Risks*
- *GTAG 6: Managing and Auditing IT Vulnerabilities*
- *GTAG 7: Information Technology Outsourcing*
- *GTAG 8: Auditing Application Controls*
- *GTAG 9: Identity and Access Management*
- *GTAG 10: Business Continuity Management*
- *GTAG 11: Developing the IT Audit Plan*
- *GTAG 12: Auditing IT Projects*
- *GTAG 13: Fraud Prevention and Detection in the Automated World*
- *GTAG 14: Auditing User-Developed Applications*
- *GTAG 15: Information Security Governance*
- *GTAG 16: Data Analysis Technologies*

CONTROLLER'S TOOL 53 – IT FRAMEWORK AND INTERNAL CONTROL CONSIDERATIONS FOR SMALL BUSINESSES

Introduction. All small businesses should consider focusing on some basic IT controls to ensure that data and company access are protected. We can break IT controls into three categories:

1. **Data.** Management relies on an application system or data warehouse to process or maintain data (e.g. transactions or other relevant data) related to significant accounts or disclosures or reports used in the operation of relevant control.
2. **Passwords.** (1) Create a strong long password, (2) apply password encryption, (3) implement two-factor authentication, (4) add advanced authentication methods, (5) test passwords, (6) don't use dictionary words, (7) use a different password for every account, (8) secure mobile phones, (9) change the passwords of all ex-employees, and (10) use password tools to avoid writing down reminders.
3. **System Access.** System access should be assigned to ensure that data and systems are protected and segregation of duties (SoD) violations do not occur. As an example, human resources data needs to be secured with HR-only access. System access rights should be reviewed on a monthly to quarterly basis to ensure that user rights are properly established. Build this review into an internal controls program for IT.

According to Deloitte, "Granting any new user access is the initial step for maintaining a controlled environment on the IT application. An inappropriate user access could result in posting of unauthorized financial transactions. Excessive access to business application needs to be granted based on roles and responsibilities of users. Provision of access that is not in line with the user's job responsibilities could lead to posting of unauthorized financial transactions."[1]

---

[1]General IT controls (GTIC): Risk and impact. Deloitte Risk Advisory (November; accessed August 2, 2020). https://www2.deloitte.com/content/dam/Deloitte/in/Documents/risk/in-ra-general-it-controls-noexp.pdf.

1. **Compensating Controls.** In small companies when SoD is not always possible, use compensating controls and additional reviews when appropriate.
2. **Automated Controls.** Management relies upon the application system to perform certain automated functions that are relevant to the company. Review these controls to make sure that data is not being changed or manipulated.
3. **System-Generated Reports and Analytics.** Throughout all business processes, management relies on an application, data warehouse query, or report writer to generate a report that is used in the operation of relevant controls. Correct data will facilitate the decision-making process.

 ## CONTROLLER'S TOOL 54 – KEY COMPONENTS OF SUCCESSFUL IT GOVERNANCE

Introduction. Here are some strategies that support a successful IT governance structure, as recommended by the IT Governance Institute.

IT Governance Strategies

- **Executive Engagement.** The tone is set at the top, with senior business and IT executives visibly and actively committed to mandating and enforcing policies, leading by example, keeping staff informed, and taking appropriate and timely action. This will show employees that implementing the framework is not extracurricular work.

- **Policies as Strategic Tools.** Formally adopting strong IT-related policies produces an optimal balance of clear guidance and direction along with some necessary flexibility to address practical day-to-day needs.

- **Defined Hierarchy of Governing Bodies.** Although the tone and direction will be set at the top, the lead decision maker must delegate implementation responsibility to the managers and technical experts best equipped to handle normal operations. Leadership should create formal governing bodies, each with its own charter and scope of authority, to provide the necessary structure to make these decisions in a clear, transparent, and predictable manner. Committees such as the IT executive steering committee, IT risk management committee, and architecture and technology selection committee will have the requisite expertise, participation, consistency, and authority to respond accurately and promptly to changes in marketplace conditions.

- **Delegation of Authority and Precedent.** Decisions should be delegated to individuals uniquely equipped to make them based on their position, experience, and skills. Clearly document the scope of authority, guidance, and considerations for all common decisions.

- **Business Alignment.** IT project prioritization and budget development decisions should always support business strategy and priorities.

- **Proactive Liaison and Communications.** IT should establish a liaison so that each business unit has at least one senior IT executive to advocate for it. The most senior of the business liaisons should sit on the IT executive steering committee.

- **Metrics and Reporting.** The holy grail of effective management is the ability to passively gather and objectively report balanced metrics capturing the key aspects of IT performance and delivery, such as revenue and operation costs, reliability, customer satisfaction, project delivery, spending, risk and security, quality, and compliance. The highest-level summaries should be presented regularly to the IT executive steering committee, with drill-downs reported more frequently to appropriate line managers.

- **Procedures, Standards, and Controls of Appropriate Weight.** Procedures and standards and controls (especially passive preventative ones) that can be readily implemented and objectively observed should be clear and practical and should be documented. Resist the tendency to design in the highest degree of control at every point along the process flow. Instead, evaluate potential controls to determine if they provide sufficient marginal benefit to justify the additional costs.

- **Independent Scrutiny.** Self-reported information can be less transparent than independently obtained data, leading to potential problems. Management should establish policy monitors to review day-to-day activities for compliance.

- **Training and Awareness Program.** Through computer-based training, regular reminders, and management discussion forums, employees must be instructed on their specific roles and responsibilities in the governance and control framework. Training should leave employees knowing exactly what they need to do and why, and where to go for help.

- **Easy-to-Use Tools.** Create a "light touch" tool set for capturing only must-have information to promote proper governance. When possible, data should be automatically captured from preexisting sources, keystrokes minimized, and response times accelerated.

TABLE OF CONTROLS – INFORMATION TECHNOLOGY CONTROLS AND CYBERSECURITY

Process: Information Technology Controls and Cybersecurity

1. Acceptable Use Policy. This is a document that describes what rights employees have with regard to the usage of computer systems. The policy might state, for example, that employees are forbidden to browse gambling or pornographic sites while at work or from any company-owned computer. All employees should sign an acceptable use policy when their employment first begins, as well as at their annual performance review. Disregarding the terms of the policy should be grounds for discipline or dismissal.

2. Remote Access Policy. This provides standards for methods and times that employees may connect to the corporate network from a remote location, including from home and/or mobile devices. Remote access policies can be enforced technically and are important to have in place as a safeguard against improperly transmitting confidential data to insecure or unauthorized sources.

3. Authorized Business Purpose. This policy states that information resources should be used only for authorized business purposes. These resources include, but are not limited to, Microsoft Outlook, the Internet, the intranet, computer systems, personal computers, and mobile devices. The use of these resources for nonbusiness purposes, such as but not limited to distributing chain letters and jokes, private business ventures, advertisements, and so on, is prohibited. Like any company property, these resources and their use are subject to monitoring and/or inspection at any time.

4. Security Controls for Cloud-Based Applications. Once developed and deployed, applications and systems must be operated securely. Unlike physical servers, disks, and networking devices, software defines the cloud virtual infrastructure. Consequently, the infrastructure can be treated as source code, which should be managed in a source code control system, with change control procedures enforced. Source code control systems have been proven effective in managing software development. These same practices can be adapted to manage cloud infrastructure. Changes to production resources should require independent approval prior to implementation by a system manager.

5. Resource Protection. All resources in an employee's custody should be protected against accidental or unauthorized modification, disclosure, or destruction. Information classified as restricted or confidential must be handled appropriately to protect it against unauthorized disclosure, as follows:

- This type of information should not be transmitted or received outside the company except in extraordinary cases.
- Confidential information on a personal computer hard drive, diskette, and tape or other magnetic media must be encrypted. It should not be placed on personal equipment at home.
- Personal computer hard drives, diskettes, tapes, and other magnetic media containing confidential information must be destroyed when disposed of.
- Voice mail messages containing information classified as restricted or confidential should be identified as such at the beginning of the message.
- Cellular or portable telephones must not be used to access restricted or confidential information unless the transmission is encrypted.
- Passwords should be kept secret, changed frequently, and established as ones that cannot be easily guessed.
- A logged-on session should never be left unattended/unsecured.
- Supervision should be immediately notified if there is a suspicion or a possibility that the security of company information has been compromised or that such an attempt has been made.
- Owners should ensure that appropriate controls are utilized upon assuming that role. When systems are used in an environment outside the original owner's control, the user becomes the owner; obtain management approval before using personal equipment and software to process company data or information.
- All software installed on company computers should be properly licensed. Illegal copies of software must not be received, made, used, or distributed.
- Management approval should be obtained before installing or executing software on company-owned computers.
- Users should ensure that approved virus detection software is installed, active, and up to date on all workstations assigned for their use. At a minimum each workstation must be checked daily, or each time it is used if less than daily.
- Computer data files, programs, and software should be periodically backed up to ensure continuity of business operations in the event of hardware, software, or application failure or an extended outage.
- Management authorization should be obtained before removing computer equipment and data files (including those removed for disposal) containing company information.
- Information software and hardware must be maintained and operated to ensure that their availability and integrity are consistent with their importance.

6. Access and Control System. Computer access control applies to all information resources: desktops, servers, mainframes, networks, and the like. The objective of computer access control is to assure the integrity, availability, and confidentiality of company information and the facilities that process, store, or transmit such information. A system of access control reduces the risk of information being disclosed, contaminated, misused, or destroyed, whether by accidental or intentional means. It is based upon proper authorization and establishes a basis for internal control by enabling separation of responsibility both within and among owner, user, and service provider functions. Restricting an individual's access to resources based upon need to know and establishing individual accountability are essential principles in achieving effective access and internal control.

7. Multiple Systems Access. IT supervisors and business process owners must ensure access granted to multiple systems does not compromise corporate SoD policies.

8. Segregation of Duties Policies. The owner must ensure the following key control elements are present:

- SoD
- Procedures to resolve problems
- Procedures to manage changes

9. Segregation of Duties for Production Applications. Computer applications or programs are considered in production status if relied upon by management for planning, conducting, recording, or reporting business, engineering, or manufacturing operations. IT departments, end users, and suppliers may develop software for production applications.

    a Every application must have an identified owner who has ultimate responsibility to satisfy application system control and audit requirements.

    b. Where applications are used in an environment outside the original owner's control, the user becomes the owner and has the responsibility to ensure that appropriate controls are utilized.

    c. Individual accountability is to be established for all application activities and information processed (e.g. data content, programming, and systems operation).

    d. Data processing personnel directly supporting the application must be permitted access to application programs.

    e. Control and audit features are to be considered prior to purchase or licensing, or if developed, during the user requirement phase. These features are to be implemented at the time the application becomes operational.

10. Continuity of Critical Information. For critical information, software, and hardware, owners must ensure that documented and periodically tested plans are in place to provide for the continuation of services in the event of a prolonged interruption.

11. On-Premise Restricted Access. If applications are not cloud based, management may designate certain computing and telecommunications areas as requiring restricted access. Access to restricted computing and telecommunications areas must be limited to authorized individuals on a need-to-know basis. Examples of restricted areas are product design departments, computer centers, telecommunications closets and switch rooms, and network file server locations. The following control techniques must be employed for these areas:

■ Physical access to computer and network hardware, software, data, and documentation must be specifically authorized by management and restricted to only those personnel requiring such access for performance of assigned functional responsibilities.

■ All entrances/exits to restricted computing and telecommunication areas must be physically secured.

■ All keys, keycards, badges, and combinations used to limit access to restricted computing and telecommunication areas must be confiscated and/or access denied by management upon employee termination or transfer. Access lists to these areas must be reviewed on at least an annual basis.

■ All physical access to computer hardware, software, data, and documentation by suppliers and suppliers must be specifically authorized by management. All suppliers and suppliers must be supervised by authorized personnel.

■ All removal of computer and telecommunications equipment and data files containing proprietary information must be specifically authorized by management, recorded, and reconciled. All data files removed must be handled in accordance with their classification.

12. Authorized Company Asset Removal. All removal of computer equipment, telecommunications equipment, and data files (including those removed for disposal) containing company information must be specifically authorized by management. All data files removed must be handled in accordance with their security classification.

13. Environmental Requirements. Physical computer and telecommunication sites must be prepared and maintained in accordance with the environmental requirements specified by the supplier for the equipment.

14. Regular Inventories. Periodic inventories of computer and telecommunication software and hardware must be performed on a regular basis and reconciled.

15. Error Logs. All computer and telecommunication hardware and software problems/errors must be recorded, monitored, and analyzed to ensure timely identification and correction.

16. Security Administration Procedures. Owners/service providers of equipment, in coordination with unit and department managers, must appoint security administrators. The security administrator function should be segregated from computer operations, systems development, and support when practical. Responsibility for managing and controlling the security administration function must remain with the company. Management must make periodic reviews of accounts and privileges assigned by security administrators.

17. Transferred or Terminated Employees. System administrators must follow established procedures to maintain computer accounts for users who are transferred within the company and to deactivate employee computer accounts upon the employee's transfer or termination from the company on a timely basis. Security administrators have the authority to delete or activate accounts of terminated employees without reference to the owner or the owner's manager. Procedures must also be in place to detect active computer accounts assigned to terminated employees.

18. Approved Protocols and Services. Only tested and approved protocols and services will be allowed over company networks.

19. Network Management. Network service providers must utilize configuration, performance, fault, accounting, and security management tools to monitor and manage networks.

20. Standardized Network Addresses. Network addresses must be obtained and maintained as specified in the company network standards. If no standards exist, they should be developed.

21. Information Encryption. Users must ensure that any information is encrypted, including e-mail, fax, voice, video, and data classified as company confidential when it is transmitted over the network. In other words, any information classified as company confidential must not be transmitted unless it is encrypted. Passwords must be encrypted during network transmission.

22. Defined Owners. Each network component or service must have a defined owner.

23. Network Connection Authorization. Every network connection must be authorized by the company unit requesting the connection and the owner of the network segment to which the connection is requested. Every network connection must be documented by the owner/service provider.

24. Accountability for Access. Access to or actions through a network that would compromise the security of other units on the network are not to be permitted by any company unit. Company units that authorize a non-company person or unit to access the company's network are accountable for their actions.

25. Accountability for Network Security. Network service providers are responsible for monitoring the use of the network, preventing any security deficiencies, notifying information security services if any security deficiencies or misuse of the network are discovered, and taking proactive corrective action to remedy the deficiencies or to prevent the misuse from continuing.

26. User Acceptance Process. This process includes testing that will adequately test each system function and condition defined by the detailed logical and physical design. Specifications for conversion to the proposed system that will ensure the integrity of processing procedures and data. User procedures should document both the manual and application-supported activities required to execute a business process, including how users interact with the application and how that interaction is controlled. User procedures should reasonably answer questions on system operation, error correction, and control. Operations documentation detail how to operate the application system and should include procedures for restarting the application in the event of a hardware or software failure as well as training to sufficiently enable users to independently operate and control system processing.

27. Change Control Process. Changes to the production hardware and/or software environment must be tested. Tests must include sufficient conditions to ensure the new system configuration operates as intended. Testing must also include evidence that all requirements were tested to the satisfaction of the ultimate users of the system.

- **Financial Management Review.** If the system change will result in the creation of journal entries or changes in journal entry account distribution, the change must be approved by financial management.
- **Software Configuration Management.** Organizations and departments with responsibility for hardware or software must document and implement plans and procedures for software configuration management. Software configuration management includes version control, change, promotion/migration, and release management and status reporting.
- **System Development Methodology.** Organizations and departments with responsibility for hardware or software must follow an approved, documented system development methodology when making maintenance changes to the production environment. The methodology and formality employed should be appropriate for the size of the project.
- **Documented Contingency Plans.** Organizations or departments with responsibility for hardware or software must document a contingency plan to be followed in the event that the change to the production environment is not successful.
- **System-Wide Version Controls.** If distributed systems are designed with multiple copies of the same programs and data files on more than one computer, system-wide version controls must be developed to ensure proper versions of programs and data files are used throughout the system.

28. Digitized/Electronic Transaction Controls. Paperless transactions must include evidence of proper authorization. Effective controls must be in place to ensure the integrity of electronic authorizations.

- **Authentic Transaction Sources.** Controls must be in place to ensure the authenticity of the transaction source. The authentication and security requirements must be defined and agreed to by the company. These requirements must be based on the classification category of the information (e.g. confidential, controlled, restricted) and must meet the minimum requirements identified in the "Management and Control" section in this chapter.
- **Timely Exchange of Transactions.** The service provider, whether external or internal, is responsible for implementing system controls to ensure that paperless transactions are exchanged within the period of time agreed to by the trading partners.
- **Transaction Integrity and Accuracy.** The integrity and accuracy of paperless transactions must not be altered by either internal or external service providers.
- **Transaction Integrity and Audit Trails.** Each component of the paperless processing system, from manual entry and computer operations to application edits and system security, must encompass the controls necessary to ensure transaction integrity. In addition, there must be adequate audit trails at key points in the transmission path to provide verification of such integrity and security.

TABLE OF RISKS AND CONTROLS – INFORMATION TECHNOLOGY CONTROLS AND CYBERSECURITY

	Process: Information Technology Controls and Cybersecurity		
Process Risk	Recommended Policies	Internal Controls	KPIs
1. Applications and systems may not be properly maintained and controlled without owner sponsorship.	■ Business Process Ownership of Application	3. Authorized Business Purpose 22. Defined Owners	■ Number of Company Applications ■ Number of Company Applications without Business Owners ■ Percentage of Projects Aligned with the Organization's Strategic Plan/Initiatives ■ Percentage of Projects Stopped in the Evaluation Phase Versus the Execution Phase ■ Percentage of Projects That Meet or Exceed the Business Case Value Expectation ■ Percentage of Project Phases Completed on Time ■ Percentage of Projects Achieving Quality Targets ■ Percentage of Projects at or Under Budget ■ Percentage of Applications Not Covered by External Vendor Support Agreements ■ Percentage of Hardware Units Not Easily Procured/Replaced Through Strategic Vendors ■ Number and Duration of Unplanned Outages ■ Percentage of SLAs Met or Exceeded ■ Customer Satisfaction Rate ■ Number of Complaints Logged Related to System Issues ■ Cost of Downtime ■ Budget Percentage Devoted to Innovation ■ Change Request Cycle Time ■ Change Success Rate ■ First Response Time ■ Number of Noncompliance Events ■ Number of SoD/User Access Issues

Process: Information Technology Controls and Cybersecurity			
Process Risk	**Recommended Policies**	**Internal Controls**	**KPIs**
2. **IT personnel may seek approval for application or system changes from someone other than the owner.**	Change Control Policies	3. Authorized Business Purpose 22. Defined Owners	■ Number of Company Applications ■ Number of Company Applications Without Business Owners ■ Percentage of Projects Aligned with the Organization's Strategic Plan/Initiatives ■ Percentage of Projects Stopped in the Evaluation Phase Versus the Execution Phase ■ Percentage of Projects That Meet or Exceed the Business Case Value Expectation ■ Percentage of Project Phases Completed on Time ■ Percentage of Projects Achieving Quality Targets ■ Percentage of Projects at or Under Budget ■ Percentage of Applications Not Covered by External Vendor Support Agreements ■ Percentage of Hardware Units Not Easily Procured/Replaced Through Strategic Vendors ■ Number and Duration of Unplanned Outages ■ Percentage of SLAs Met or Exceeded ■ Customer Satisfaction Rate ■ Number of Complaints Logged Related to System Issues ■ Cost of Downtime ■ Budget Percentage Devoted to Innovation ■ Change Request Cycle Time ■ Change Success Rate ■ First Response Time ■ Number of Noncompliance Events ■ Number of SoD/User Access Issues

Process: Information Technology Controls and Cybersecurity			
Process Risk	**Recommended Policies**	**Internal Controls**	**KPIs**
3. Management personnel may change responsibilities without transferring ownership of applications.	■ Change Control Policies	27. Change Control Policies	■ Number of Company Applications Without Business Owners
4. Adequate resources may not be available to meet business requirements and growth.	■ Resource Protection Plans and Policies	5. Resource Protection	■ Percentage of Projects Aligned with the Organization's Strategic Plan/Initiatives ■ Percentage of Projects That Meet or Exceed the Business Case Value Expectation ■ Percentage of Project Phases Completed on Time ■ Percentage of Projects Achieving Quality Targets ■ Percentage of Projects at or Under Budget ■ Percentage of Applications Not Covered by External Vendor Support Agreements
5. The responsibilities associated with operating and/or maintaining application software operations and application documentation may not be clearly defined.	■ Resource Protection Plans and Policies	1. Acceptable Use Policy 3. Authorized Business Purpose	■ Percentage of SLAs Met or Exceeded ■ Customer Satisfaction Rate ■ Budget Percentage Devoted to Innovation

Process: Information Technology Controls and Cybersecurity			
Process Risk	Recommended Policies	Internal Controls	KPIs
6. Business, manufacturing, or engineering systems may become dysfunctional, resulting in productivity and revenue losses, or critical data could be destroyed.	■ User Access Policies	2. Remote Access Policy 4. Security Controls for Cloud-Based Applications 6. Access and Control System 7. Multiple Systems Access 8. SoD Policies 9. SoD for Production Applications 10. Continuity of Critical Information 11. On-Premise Restricted Access 15. Error Logs 16. Security Administration Procedures 18. Approved Protocols and Services 21. Information Encryption 24. Accountability for Access	■ Number of Company Applications ■ Number of Company Applications Without Business Owners ■ Percentage of Projects Aligned with the Organization's Strategic Plan/Initiatives ■ Percentage of Projects Stopped in the Evaluation Phase Versus the Execution Phase ■ Percentage of Projects that Meet or Exceed the Business Case Value Expectation ■ Percentage of Project Phases Completed on Time ■ Percentage of Projects Achieving Quality Targets ■ Percentage of Projects at or Under Budget ■ Percentage of Applications Not Covered by External Vendor Support Agreements ■ Percentage of Hardware Units Not Easily Procured/Replaced Through Strategic Vendors ■ Number and Duration of Unplanned Outages ■ Percentage of SLAs Met or Exceeded ■ Customer Satisfaction Rate ■ Number of Complaints Logged Related to System Issues ■ Cost of Downtime ■ Budget Percentage Devoted to Innovation ■ Change Request Cycle Time ■ Change Success Rate ■ First Response Time ■ Number of Noncompliance Events ■ Number of SoD/User Access Issues

		Process: Information Technology Controls and Cybersecurity	
Process Risk	**Recommended Policies**	**Internal Controls**	**KPIs**
7. **Operational efficiency and reliability may be impaired and significantly disrupt processing.**	■ User Access Policies	2. Remote Access Policy 4. Security Controls for Cloud-Based Applications 6. Access and Control System 7. Multiple Systems Access 8. SoD Policies 9. SoD for Production Applications 10. Continuity of Critical Information 11. On-Premise Restricted Access 16. Security Administration Procedures 18. Approved Protocols and Services 21. Information Encryption 24. Accountability for Access	■ Change Request Cycle Time ■ Change Success Rate ■ First Response Time ■ Number of Noncompliance Events ■ Number of SoD/User Access Issues
8. **Duplicate infrastructures may be developed, increasing overall costs.**	■ Business Case Requirements ■ Assigned Business Process Owners	1. Acceptable Use Policy 3. Authorized Business Purpose 6. Access and Control System 7. Multiple Systems Access 22. Defined Owners 24. Accountability for Access	■ Cost of Downtime

Process: Information Technology Controls and Cybersecurity			
Process Risk	Recommended Policies	Internal Controls	KPIs
9. Company information may be disclosed, lost, or contaminated, which may adversely affect the organization's competitive position.	■ User Access Policies ■ SoD Policies	2. Remote Access Policy 4. Security Controls for Cloud-Based Applications 6. Access and Control System 7. Multiple Systems Access 8. SoD Policies and Procedures 9. SoD for Production Applications 10. Continuity of Critical Information 11. On-Premise Restricted Access 16. Security Administration Procedures 18. Approved Protocols and Services 21. Information Encryption 24. Accountability for Access	■ Number of Company Applications ■ Number of Company Applications Without Business Owners ■ Percentage of Projects Aligned with the Organization's Strategic Plan/Initiatives ■ Percentage of Projects Stopped in the Evaluation Phase Versus the Execution Phase ■ Percentage of Projects That Meet or Exceed the Business Case Value Expectation ■ Percentage of Project Phases Completed on Time ■ Percentage of Projects Achieving Quality Targets ■ Percentage of Projects at or Under Budget ■ Percentage of Applications Not Covered by External Vendor Support Agreements ■ Percentage of Hardware Units Not Easily Procured/Replaced Through Strategic Vendors ■ Number and Duration of Unplanned Outages ■ Percentage of SLAs Met or Exceeded ■ Customer Satisfaction Rate ■ Number of Complaints Logged Related to System Issues ■ Cost of Downtime ■ Budget Percentage Devoted to Innovation ■ Change Request Cycle Time ■ Change Success Rate ■ First Response Time ■ Number of Noncompliance Events ■ Number of SoD/User Access Issues

Process: Information Technology Controls and Cybersecurity			
Process Risk	**Recommended Policies**	**Internal Controls**	**KPIs**
10. Passwords to user computer or network accounts may be disclosed and allow unauthorized access to data and programs.	■ User Access Policies ■ SoD Policies	2. Remote Access Policy 4. Security Controls for Cloud-Based Applications 6. Access and Control System 7. Multiple Systems Access 8. SoD Policies 9. SoD for Production Applications 10. Continuity of Critical Information 11. On-Premise Restricted Access 16. Security Administration Procedures 18. Approved Protocols and Services 21. Information Encryption 24. Accountability for Access	■ Number of Noncompliance Events ■ Number of SoD/User Access Issues
11. Unauthorized use, disclosure, modification, destruction, or theft of applications and data could occur.	■ User Access Policies ■ SoD Policies	2. Remote Access Policy 4. Security Controls for Cloud-Based Applications 6. Access and Control System 7. Multiple Systems Access 8. SoD Policies and Procedures 9. SoD for Production Applications 10. Continuity of Critical Information 11. On-Premise Restricted Access 16. Security Administration Procedures 18. Approved Protocols and Services 21. Information Encryption 24. Accountability for Access	■ Number of Noncompliance Events ■ Number of SoD/User Access Issues

Process: Information Technology Controls and Cybersecurity			
Process Risk	**Recommended Policies**	**Internal Controls**	**KPIs**
12. Computer and telecommunication hardware may be used by unauthorized personnel to bypass normal security and operating controls and gain access to confidential applications and data.	■ User Access Policies	2. Remote Access Policy 4. Security Controls for Cloud-Based Applications 6. Access and Control System 7. Multiple Systems Access 8. SoD Policies 9. SoD for Production Applications 10. Continuity of Critical Information 11. On-Premise Restricted Access 16. Security Administration Procedures 18. Approved Protocols and Services 21. Information Encryption 24. Accountability for Access	■ Number of Noncompliance Events ■ Number of SoD/User Access Issues
13. Access to production data files and programs may be granted without proper authorization.	■ User Access Policies	2. Remote Access Policy 4. Security Controls for Cloud-Based Applications 6. Access and Control System 7. Multiple Systems Access 8. SoD Policies 9. SoD for Production Applications 10. Continuity of Critical Information 11. On-Premise Restricted Access 16. Security Administration Procedures 18. Approved Protocols and Services 21. Information Encryption 24. Accountability for Access	■ Number of Noncompliance Events ■ Number of SoD/User Access Issues

Process: Information Technology Controls and Cybersecurity			
Process Risk	**Recommended Policies**	**Internal Controls**	**KPIs**
14. Unauthorized access attempts may be made on a regular basis without detection.	■ User Access Policies	2. Remote Access Policy 4. Security Controls for Cloud-Based Applications 6. Access and Control System 7. Multiple Systems Access 8. SoD Policies 9. SoD for Production Applications 10. Continuity of Critical Information 11. On-Premise Restricted Access 16. Security Administration Procedures 18. Approved Protocols and Services 21. Information Encryption 24. Accountability for Access	■ Number of Noncompliance Events ■ Number of SoD/User Access Issues
15. Sensitive information may be accessed and/ or disclosed to unauthorized personnel.	■ User Access Policies	2. Remote Access Policy 4. Security Controls for Cloud-Based Applications 6. Access and Control System 7. Multiple Systems Access 8. SoD Policies and Procedures 9. SoD for Production Applications 10. Continuity of Critical Information 11. On-Premise Restricted Access 16. Security Administration Procedures 18. Approved Protocols and Services 21. Information Encryption 24. Accountability for Access	■ Number of Noncompliance Events ■ Number of SoD/User Access Issues

Process: Information Technology Controls and Cybersecurity			
Process Risk	Recommended Policies	Internal Controls	KPIs
16. Special access privileges may be granted that result in unnecessary or unauthorized access to production data files.	■ User Access Policies	2. Remote Access Policy 4. Security Controls for Cloud-Based Applications 6. Access and Control System 7. Multiple Systems Access 8. SoD Policies 9. SoD for Production Applications 10. Continuity of Critical Information 11. On-Premise Restricted Access 16. Security Administration Procedures 18. Approved Protocols and Services 21. Information Encryption 24. Accountability for Access	■ Number of Noncompliance Events ■ Number of SoD/User Access Issues
17. Users may be given access to data files and programs that are not required for their job functions.	■ User Access Policies	2. Remote Access Policy 4. Security Controls for Cloud-Based Applications 6. Access and Control System 7. Multiple Systems Access 8. SoD Policies 9. SoD for Production Applications 10. Continuity of Critical Information 11. On-Premise Restricted Access 16. Security Administration Procedures 18. Approved Protocols and Services 21. Information Encryption 24. Accountability for Access	■ Number of Noncompliance Events ■ Number of SoD/User Access Issues

Process: Information Technology Controls and Cybersecurity			
Process Risk	**Recommended Policies**	**Internal Controls**	**KPIs**
18. Data may not be accurately or completely transferred.	■ Digitized/ Automated Transactions	28. Digitized/Electronic Transaction Controls	■ Number of Noncompliance Events ■ Number of SoD/User Access Issues
19. Transmissions may not have adequate error correction.	■ Digitized/ Automated Transactions	28. Digitized/Electronic Transaction Controls	■ Percentage of SLAs Met or Exceeded ■ Customer Satisfaction Rate ■ Number of Complaints Logged Related to System Issues ■ First Response Time ■ Number of Noncompliance Events ■ Number of SoD/User Access Issues
20. Proprietary data may be disclosed to unauthorized personnel during transmission.	■ Digitized/ Automated Transactions ■ User Access Policies	21. Information Encryption 23. Network Connection Authorization 28. Digitized/Electronic Transaction Controls	■ Percentage of SLAs Met or Exceeded ■ Customer Satisfaction Rate ■ Number of Complaints Logged Related to System Issues ■ First Response Time ■ Number of Noncompliance Events ■ Number of SoD/User Access Issues
21. Applications may be implemented that do not meet user requirements or comply with software quality standards.	■ User Acceptance Testing (UAT) Requirements	26. User Acceptance Process	■ Percentage of Projects Achieving Quality Targets
22. Roles and responsibilities may be unclear, resulting in increased development cycle times or application inadequacies.	■ UAT Requirements	27. Change Control Process	■ Percentage of Projects Aligned with the Organization's Strategic Plan/Initiatives ■ Percentage of Projects Stopped in the Evaluation Phase Versus the Execution Phase ■ Percentage of Projects That Meet or Exceed the Business Case Value Expectation ■ Percentage of Project Phases Completed on Time ■ Percentage of Projects Achieving Quality Targets

Process: Information Technology Controls and Cybersecurity			
Process Risk	Recommended Policies	Internal Controls	KPIs
23. Applications may be implemented without approval of the system design, proper testing, or conversion resulting in erroneous processing.	■ Implementation Review and Approval Policies ■ UAT Requirements	26. User Acceptance Process	■ Percentage of Projects Aligned with the Organization's Strategic Plan/Initiatives ■ Percentage of Projects Stopped in the Evaluation Phase Versus the Execution Phase ■ Percentage of Projects That Meet or Exceed the Business Case Value Expectation ■ Percentage of Project Phases Completed on Time ■ Percentage of Projects Achieving Quality Targets
24. Users may not actively participate in the development process, which could result in incorrect decisions during the design and testing phases.	■ Implementation Review and Approval Policies ■ UAT Requirements	26. User Acceptance Process	■ Percentage of SLAs Met or Exceeded ■ Customer Satisfaction Rate ■ Number of Complaints Logged Related to System Issues ■ Number of Company Applications Without Business Owners
25. Improper selection of solutions to business problems may result from incomplete evaluation of alternatives.	■ Business Case Requirements	1. Acceptance Use Policy 3. Authorized Business Purpose	■ Percentage of SLAs Met or Exceeded ■ Customer Satisfaction Rate ■ Number of Complaints Logged Related to System Issues ■ Number of Company Applications Without Business Owners
26. The application design may not be properly documented and communicated, resulting in uncontrolled or erroneous processing.	■ Business Case Requirements	26. User Acceptance Process	■ Percentage of SLAs Met or Exceeded ■ Customer Satisfaction Rate ■ Number of Complaints Logged Related to System Issues

SECTION EIGHT

Business Continuity and Physical Security Risk

 SECTION INTRODUCTION

Business Continuity

The objective of disaster recovery and business continuity planning for computer systems and telecommunications is to ensure the continuance of the company's applications in the event of unanticipated computer processing disruptions, such as operational failures or site disasters that destroy or prevent access to the computer or telecommunication equipment, data, and software.

The recovery plan is not intended to duplicate a normal business environment but to minimize the potential loss of assets, lessen the impact on customers, and keep the company in business. Through decisive action, which is based on advanced planning, business disruptions and losses can be minimized.

The only applications that management may choose to exempt from this standard are those that can be reproduced from other existing information and/or are not inputs to a critical application, or those that would incur more expense from following the standard than the application is worth to the company in the event of destruction by a disaster.

Additionally, applications that are critical to the successful operation of the company should be prioritized, and acceptable downtime should be determined when establishing business continuity plans.

Physical Security

Physical security is the protection of personnel, hardware, programs, networks, and data from physical circumstances and events that could cause serious losses or damage to an enterprise,

427

agency, or institution. This includes protection from fire, natural disasters, burglary, theft, vandalism, and terrorism.

The three main components of physical security are:

1. **Obstacles.** Obstacles can be placed in the way of potential attackers and sites can be hardened against accidents and environmental disasters. Such measures can include multiple locks, fencing, walls, fireproof safes, and water sprinklers.
2. **Surveillance and Notification Systems.** Surveillance and/or notification systems – such as lighting, heat sensors, smoke detectors, intrusion detectors, alarms, and cameras – can be put in place.
3. **Apprehension/Recovery Methods.** Methods of apprehending attackers can be implemented (preferably before any damage has been done) so as to allow for quick recovery from accidents, fires, or natural disasters. Recovery methods would include the business continuity plan.

CHAPTER TWENTY

Business Continuity and Physical Security

 ## OVERVIEW – BUSINESS CONTINUITY

The business continuity plan (BCP) is used by organizations of all sizes to detail how business will continue if a disaster or emergency occurs. The BCP documents department, employee, and supplier information; inventory; emergency procedures; and post-disaster plan for all business operational functions.

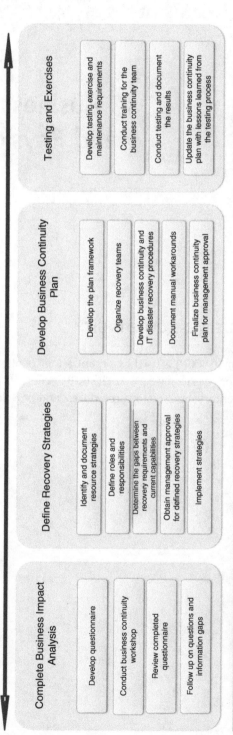

BUSINESS CONTINUITY PROCESS FLOW

BUSINESS CONTINUITY AND DISASTER RECOVERY: KEY DEFINITIONS

Business continuity plan: A BCP comprises the prearranged plans and procedures that critical business functions will execute to ensure business continues relatively unscathed until computer and telecommunications facilities are reestablished following a disaster.

Critical application: A critical business application is one that the company must have to support major revenue activities, movement of goods to customers (particularly those that can spoil or that are time-critical for the customer), and/or a strategic manufacturing process, or to fulfill contractual or regulatory obligations. In addition, an application is defined as critical if the application's availability is deemed by management to be vital to the continued functioning of company business. Examples of critical applications are customer service support, order entry, inventory control, manufacturing resource planning, purchasing, warehouse control, quality assurance, and financial systems.

Disaster: A loss of computing or telecommunication resources to the extent that routine recovery measures cannot restore normal service levels within 24 hours, which impacts the company's business significantly.

Disaster recovery: The restoration of computing and telecommunication services following an outage resulting from a disaster. Disaster recovery is a small subset of business continuity. It is also sometimes confused with work area recovery (which has to do with the loss of the physical building in which the business is conducted), also only a part of business continuity.

Vital business assessment: A process required to determine what business functions and supporting applications are critical for the company to continue to conduct business in the event of a disaster.

CONTROLLER'S TOOL 55 – BUSINESS CONTINUITY: PERSONNEL

Introduction. The business continuity planning process should encompass the steps that are needed if a disruption in business or a disaster occurs. The plan should consider the business process and IT impacts as well as the applications that are maintained in the cloud.

Business Continuity: Personnel

---

1. Document internal key personnel with backups. These are key employees that are integral to the functioning of your business processes. A controller should identify the key employees for each business process. It's important to identify backups.

Consider which job functions are critically necessary every day. Think about who fills those positions when the primary jobholder is on vacation.

Make a list of all those individuals with all contact information, including business phone, home phone, cell phone, pager, business e-mail, personal e-mail, and any other possible way of contacting them in an emergency situation where normal communications might be unavailable.

2. Identify who can telecommute. Some people in your company might be perfectly capable of conducting business from a home office.

3. Document external contacts. If you have critical suppliers, contractors, or consultants, build a special contact list that includes a description of the company (or individual) and other critical information about them, including key personnel contact information. Include on your list people such as attorneys, bankers, IT consultants, and solution providers. The list should include anyone that you might need to call to assist with various operational issues.

4. Document critical equipment and access to ERP Systems. Determine if a copy machine and fax are necessary if ERP access is not possible. **Identify critical files and documents.** These include articles of incorporation, key supplier financial contracts, utility bills, banking information, critical HR documents, building lease papers, and tax returns.

5. Identify your contingency location. This is the place you will conduct business while your primary offices are unavailable. Depending on the situation, it could be a hotel – or telecommuting may be a viable option.

6. Make a how-to list. It should include step-by-step instructions on what to do, who should do it, and how. Your organization's policies and procedures are critical. Public companies can use SOX documentation. Ensure that business processes are assigned to a lead person, as covered in step 1 of this table. Key processes should be prioritized.

7. Put the information together. A BCP is useless if all the components are scattered all over the company. Each key process business should have an electronic folder (and backup) with all the key information. If necessary, the contents of the folder can be printed.

8. Communicate. Make sure everyone in your company is familiar with the BCP. Hold mandatory training classes for each and every employee. Schedule refreshers periodically.

10. Test the plan. All BCPs should be tested to make sure all the key components have been identified and the plan can be executed. Schedule refreshers of tests of the plan periodically.

11. Plan to update the plan. No matter how good your plan is, and no matter how smoothly your test runs, it is likely there will be events not covered by your plan.

12. Review and revise. Every time something changes, update all copies of your BCP and initiate the BCP communication process again. With all the changes in technology, it's important to ensure that the plan is never outdated.

13. Consider next steps. Consider the next steps for recovery and identify what needs to happen to bring the organization, region, country, or division back on line.

CONTROLLER'S TOOL 56 – BUSINESS CONTINUITY: INFORMATION TECHNOLOGY

IT BCPs provide step-by-step procedures for recovering disrupted systems and networks. The goal of this process is to minimize any negative impacts to company operations. The IT business continuity process identifies critical IT systems and networks; prioritizes their recovery time objective; and delineates the steps needed to restart, reconfigure, and recover them. A comprehensive IT BCP also includes all the relevant supplier contacts, sources of expertise for recovering disrupted systems, and a logical sequence of action steps to take for a smooth recovery

According to National Institute for Standards and Technology (NIST) publication *Contingency Planning for Information Technology Systems* (NIST SP 800-34), the following summarizes the ideal structure for an IT disaster recovery plan:

Business Continuity: Information Technology

1. Develop the business contingency planning policy statement. A formal policy provides the authority and guidance necessary to develop an effective contingency plan.

2. Conduct the business impact analysis. The business impact analysis helps to identify and prioritize critical IT systems and components.

3. Identify preventive controls. These are measures that reduce the effects of system disruptions and can increase system availability and reduce contingency lifecycle costs.

4. Develop recovery strategies. Thorough recovery strategies ensure that the system can be recovered quickly and effectively following a disruption.

5. Develop an IT contingency plan. The contingency plan should contain detailed guidance and procedures for restoring a damaged system.

6. Test, train on, and execute the plan. Testing the plan identifies planning gaps, whereas training prepares recovery personnel for plan activation; both activities improve plan effectiveness and overall agency preparedness. Execute the plan to ensure that it works.

7. Plan maintenance. The plan should be a living document that is updated regularly to remain current with system enhancements.

In addition, management must be committed to supporting and taking part in this effort.

- Define your business continuity efforts in terms of business processes.
- Document the impact of an extended loss of operations and key business functions.
- Select teams that will give you the balance needed to develop a proper plan.
- Develop a BCP that is easy to develop and easy to maintain.
- Define how to integrate continuity planning issues into ongoing business planning and system development processes to ensure that the plan is viable over time.
- Consider integrating the testing of the BCP for a business function into internal controls programs. This will help to ensure continuous business continuity.

 ## TABLE OF CONTROLS – BUSINESS CONTINUITY

Process: Business Continuity

---

1. Recovery Priority. Application owners must classify their application's recovery priority. This priority must be used by computer and telecommunications equipment owners/service providers to determine the sequence of restarting selected critical application systems in the event of an unanticipated processing disruption. The priority assessment should include the following:

a. Conduct a vital business assessment to quantify the risk in terms of dollars, production volume, or other measurable terms due to partial or total loss of processing the application.

b. Assess the lead time between loss of application processing and adverse impact on operations as part of determining acceptable downtime.

c. Obtain agreement from company unit management on the classification as to critical or noncritical.

2. Alternative Equipment and/or Facilities. The owners and service providers of computer systems and telecommunications, and equipment and facilities, in coordination with application owners, are responsible for arranging for alternative equipment and/or computing facilities. Alternative equipment and/or facilities should be adequate to recover selected mission-critical computer and telecommunication platforms. BCPs must include a determination of the most effective alternative processing method for both critical and noncritical applications. Alternatives include:

a. Working from home or processing at another company site.

b. Processing at a conditioned site maintained by a recovery site supplier; or not processing applications until computer equipment and/or sites normally reserved for noncritical operations only are restored.

c. A plan detailing cloud-based applications, IT, and user personnel requirements and special skills needed in the event of an unanticipated processing disruption.

d. Storage of critical computer vital records, replacement forms, supplies, and documentation in the cloud or in an offsite storage facility. Storage at a place of residence is not an acceptable long-term solution. Preference should be given to using a professional offsite supplier at a distance of 4–80 miles from storage of the original data.

3. Documentation and Testing. Detailed BCPs must be documented and tested at least annually to ensure recovery can be accomplished. Where tests of the full plan are found to be impractical due to business conditions or the cost of testing, test plans must be developed and implemented to test portions of the plan. The alternative to a full test is a complete paper walk-through with an audit of the offsite vital records. Business process owners must participate in the test to certify business recovery capability.

4. Annual Review of Plans. System owners/service providers, in conjunction with application owners, must review and update their BCPs at least annually or more frequently when significant changes are made to the applications, hardware, or software.

5. Recovery Time Targets. Owners/service providers responsible for developing BCP arrangements must specify and publish to users the target times for recovery of:

 a. Mission critical functions

 b. Normal service

 Users must be informed that no service will be available during the specific recovery period.

6. Tested Business Continuity Plans. Users are responsible for developing and testing their plans in conjunction with service providers to continue their business operations during the recovery period. Where the plan is to cease operations during this period, this fact must be documented.

 ## TABLE OF RISKS AND CONTROLS – BUSINESS CONTINUITY

Process: Business Continuity			
Process Risk	**Recommended Policies**	**Internal Controls**	**KPIs**
1. **The company may incur a severe disruption of engineering and/or manufacturing, or business operations may not be able to recover in the event of an unanticipated processing disruption**. This risk could be further compounded by the lack of the correct vital records in the offsite storage facility.	■ BCPs ■ Risk Management Policies and Procedures	1. Recovery Priority 2. Alternative Equipment or Facilities 3. Documentation and Testing 4. Annual Review of Plans 5. Recovery Time Targets 6. Tested BCPs	■ Percentage of Downtime ■ Number of Days to Recovery ■ Frequency of Business Continuity Plan Tests Performed ■ SLA Performance ■ OLA Performance ■ Date of Last Plan Update ■ Cloud Computing Plans Reviewed/Obtained

Process: Business Continuity			
Process Risk	**Recommended Policies**	**Internal Controls**	**KPIs**
2. The company could sustain substantial financial loss and regulatory fines if critical computer systems and equipment are severely damaged or destroyed.	▪ BCPs ▪ Risk Management Policies and Procedures	1. Recovery Priority 2. Alternative Equipment or Facilities 3. Documentation and Testing 4. Annual Review of Plans 5. Recovery Time Targets 6. Tested BCPs	▪ Percentage of Downtime ▪ Number of Days to Recovery ▪ Frequency of Business Continuity Plan Tests Performed ▪ SLA Performance ▪ OLA Performance ▪ Date of Last Plan Update ▪ Cloud Computing Plans Reviewed/ Obtained
3. Critical systems may not be recovered first.	▪ BCPs ▪ Risk Management Policies and Procedures	5. Recovery Time Targets	▪ Percentage of Downtime ▪ Number of Days to Recovery ▪ Frequency of Business Continuity Plan Tests Performed ▪ SLA Performance ▪ OLA Performance ▪ Date of Last Plan Update ▪ Cloud Computing Plans Reviewed/ Obtained
4. The disaster recovery plans may not be effective, which would jeopardize the company's ability to continue its business.	▪ BCPs ▪ Risk Management Policies and Procedures	6. Tested BCPs	▪ Percentage of Downtime ▪ Number of Days to Recovery ▪ Frequency of Business Continuity Plan Tests Performed ▪ SLA Performance ▪ OLA Performance ▪ Date of Last Plan Update ▪ Cloud Computing Plans Reviewed/ Obtained

Process: Business Continuity			
Process Risk	**Recommended Policies**	**Internal Controls**	**KPIs**
5. Company assets – such as product, property, material, and technology – may be stolen, damaged, or otherwise compromised.	■ BCPs ■ Risk Management Policies and Procedures	1. Recovery Priority 2. Alternative Equipment or Facilities 3. Documentation and Testing 4. Annual Review of Plans 5. Recovery Time Targets 6. Tested BCPs	■ Percentage of Downtime ■ Number of Days to Recovery ■ Frequency of Business Continuity Plan Tests Performed ■ SLA Performance ■ OLA Performance ■ Date of Last Plan Update ■ Cloud Computing Plans Reviewed/Obtained
6. An inadequate strategy may cause irreparable harm to market share, resulting in a significant financial loss to shareholders.	■ BCPs ■ Risk Management Policies and Procedures	1. Recovery Priority 2. Alternative Equipment or Facilities 3. Documentation and Testing 4. Annual Review of Plans 5. Recovery Time Targets 6. Tested BCPs	■ Percentage of Downtime ■ Number of Days to Recovery ■ Frequency of Business Continuity Plan Tests Performed ■ SLA Performance ■ OLA Performance ■ Date of Last Plan Update ■ Cloud Computing Plans Reviewed/Obtained
7. The company's ability to conduct business may be significantly impaired.	■ BCPs ■ Risk Management Policies and Procedures	1. Recovery Priority 2. Alternative Equipment or Facilities 3. Documentation and Testing 4. Annual Review of Plans 5. Recovery Time Targets 6. Tested BCPs	■ Percentage of Downtime ■ Number of Days to Recovery ■ Frequency of Business Continuity Plan Tests Performed ■ SLA Performance ■ OLA Performance ■ Date of Last Plan Update ■ Cloud Computing Plans Reviewed/Obtained

Process: Business Continuity			
Process Risk	**Recommended Policies**	**Internal Controls**	**KPIs**
8. Inadequate plans may cause a significant delay in implementing the business continuity strategy and damage to the company's reputation, resulting in a significant loss of business.	∎ BCPs ∎ Risk Management Policies and Procedures	1. Recovery Priority 2. Alternative Equipment or Facilities 3. Documentation and Testing 4. Annual Review of Plans 5. Recovery Time Targets 6. Tested BCPs	∎ Percentage of Downtime ∎ Number of Days to Recovery ∎ Frequency of Business Continuity Plan Tests Performed ∎ SLA Performance ∎ OLA Performance ∎ Date of Last Plan Update ∎ Cloud Computing Plans Reviewed/Obtained

OVERVIEW – PHYSICAL SECURITY

According to *CSO* magazine, physical security is the protection of people, property, and physical assets from actions and events that could cause damage or loss.[1] Though often overlooked in favor of cybersecurity, physical security is equally important. And, indeed, it has grown into a $30 billion industry. All the firewalls in the world can't help you if an attacker removes your storage media from the storage room.

The growing sophistication of physical security through technologies such as artificial intelligence and the Internet of things means IT and physical security are becoming more closely connected, and as a result security teams need to be working together to secure both the physical and digital assets.

---

[1] *CSO* magazine is a magazine for chief security officers. *CSO Magazine* is a magazine for chief sustainability officers.

PHYSICAL SECURITY PROCESS FLOW

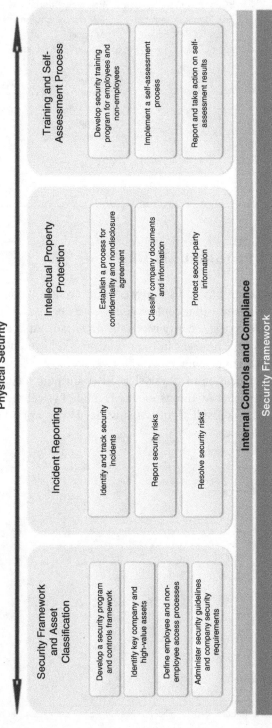

SECURITY CONTROLS: KEY DEFINITIONS

Administrative security controls: These are primarily policies and procedures put into place to define and guide employee actions in dealing with the organization's sensitive information. For example, a policy might dictate that HR conduct background checks on employees with access to sensitive information, while procedures would indicate how this should be done.

Another example of an administrative control is requiring that information be classified and detailing the process to classify and review those information classifications. Furthermore, the organization security awareness program is an administrative control used to make employees cognizant of their security roles and responsibilities. Note that administrative security controls in the form of a policy can be enforced or verified with technical or physical security controls.

Technical security controls: These controls are also called logical controls, and they are devices, processes, protocols, and other measures used to protect sensitive information. Examples include logical access systems, encryptions systems, antivirus systems, firewalls, and intrusion detection systems.

Physical security controls: These are devices and means to control physical access to sensitive information and to protect the availability of the information. Examples are physical access systems (fences, mantraps, guards), physical intrusion detection systems (motion detectors, alarm systems), and physical protection systems (sprinklers, backup generators). Administrative and technical controls depend on proper physical security controls being in place. An administrative policy allowing only authorized employees access to the data center do little good without some kind of physical access control.

Preventive security controls: These controls are put into place to prevent intentional or unintentional disclosure, alteration, or destruction of sensitive information. Some examples of preventive controls are:

- A policy, for example a directive that unauthorized network connections are prohibited
- A firewall, or hardware/software that blocks unauthorized network connections
- A locked wiring closet, which would prevent unauthorized equipment from being physically plugged into a network switch.

Detective security controls: These controls are like burglar alarms. They detect and report an unauthorized or undesired event (or an attempted undesired event). Detective security controls are invoked after the undesirable event has occurred. Examples of detective security controls are log monitoring and review, system audit, file integrity checkers, and motion detection.

Corrective security controls: These are used to respond to and fix a security incident. Corrective security controls also limit or reduce further damage from an attack. Some examples are:

- A procedure to clean a virus from an infected system
- A guard checking and locking a door left unlocked by a careless employee
- Updating firewall rules to block an attacking IP address

Recovery security controls: These controls put a system back into production after an incident. Most BCP activities fall into this category. For example, a BCP may include a recovery security control specifying that after a disk failure, data is to be restored from a backup tape.

Directive security controls: These are the equivalent of administrative controls. Directive controls direct that some action be taken to protect sensitive organizational information. The directive can be in the form of a policy, procedure, or guideline.

Deterrent security controls: These are controls that discourage security violations: for instance, a sign that says "Unauthorized Access Prohibited" may deter a trespasser from entering an area. Similarly, the presence of security cameras might deter an employee from stealing equipment, and a policy that states that access to servers is monitored could deter unauthorized access.

Compensating security controls: These are controls that provide an alternative to normal controls that cannot be used for some reason: for instance, a certain server may not be able to have antivirus software installed because it interferes with a critical application. A compensating control would be to increase monitoring of that server or isolate that server on its own network segment.

 ## CONTROLLER'S TOOL 57 – ISO/IEC 17799:2005

ISO/IEC 17799:2005 – a standard developed jointly by the International Organization for Standardization and the International Electrotechnical Commission – establishes guidelines and general principles for initiating, implementing, maintaining, and improving information security management in an organization. The objectives outlined provide general guidance on the commonly accepted goals of information security management. The control objectives and controls in ISO/IEC 17799:2005 are intended to be implemented to meet the requirements identified by a risk assessment. ISO/IEC 17799:2005 is intended as a common basis and practical guideline for developing organizational security standards and effective security management practices, and to help build confidence in interorganizational activities. There are 10 sections:

1. **Business Continuity Planning**
   The objectives of this section are to counteract interruptions to business activities and to critical business processes from the effects of major failures or disasters.
2. **System Access Control**
   The objectives of this section are (1) to control access to information, (2) to prevent unauthorized access to information systems, (3) to ensure the protection of networked services, (4) to prevent unauthorized computer access, (5) to detect unauthorized activities, and (6) to ensure information security when using mobile computing facilities.
3. **System Development and Maintenance**
   The objectives of this section are (1) to ensure security is built into operational systems; (2) to prevent loss, modification, or misuse of user data in application systems; (3) to protect

the confidentiality, authenticity, and integrity of information; (4) to ensure IT projects and support activities are conducted in a secure manner; and (5) to maintain the security of application system software and data.

4. **Physical and Environmental Security**

   The objectives of this section are (1) to prevent unauthorized access, damage and interference to business premises and information; (2) to prevent loss, damage, or compromise of assets and interruption to business activities; and (3) to prevent compromise or theft of information and information processing facilities.

5. **Compliance**

   The objectives of this section are (1) to avoid breaches of any criminal or civil law, of any statutory, regulatory or contractual obligations, and of any security requirements; (2) to ensure compliance of systems with organizational security policies and standards; and (3) to maximize the effectiveness of and to minimize interference to/from the system audit process.

6. **Personnel Security**

   The objectives of this section are (1) to reduce risks of human error, theft, fraud, or misuse of facilities; (2) to ensure that users are aware of information security threats and concerns, and are equipped to support the corporate security policy in the course of their normal work; and (3) to minimize the damage from security incidents and malfunctions and learn from such incidents.

7. **Security Organization**

   The objectives of this section are (1) to manage information security within the company; (2) to maintain the security of organizational information processing facilities and information assets accessed by third parties; and (3) to maintain the security of information when the responsibility for information processing has been outsourced to another organization.

8. **Computer and Network Management**

   The objectives of this section are (1) to ensure the correct and secure operation of information processing facilities; (2) to minimize the risk of systems failures; (3) to protect the integrity of software and information; (4) to maintain the integrity and availability of information processing and communication; (5) to ensure the safeguarding of information in networks and the protection of the supporting infrastructure; (6) to prevent damage to assets and interruptions to business activities; and (7) to prevent loss, modification, or misuse of information exchanged between organizations.

9. **Asset Classification and Control**

   The objectives of this section are to maintain appropriate protection of corporate assets and to ensure that information assets receive an appropriate level of protection.

10. **Security Policy**

    The objectives of this section are to provide management direction and support for information security.

TABLE OF CONTROLS – PHYSICAL SECURITY

Process: Physical Security

---

1. **Security Program Administration.** Management must designate a specific employee (or employees) to be responsible for the administration, maintenance, and implementation of the local security program.

2. **Trained and Capable Physical Security Employees.** Management should ensure that security personnel or those providing security functions are appropriately prepared for discharging their responsibilities by:

- Having a documented training program, including any specialized training that is appropriate for the site or company unit
- Consistently and uniformly applying and supporting security procedures
- Having a written agreement, consistent with ICS (internal control standards) and approved by the legal, risk management, and worldwide corporate security departments, that defines performance expectations whenever contract guard services are being used
- Conducting a preemployment and drug screening process (e.g. interview of references, criminal records check, and confirmation of education and prior employment) in accordance with appropriate national and local laws

3. **Security Guidelines.** The ICS must be used to form the basis of all security programs. All security guidelines and procedures must be maintained and available to all affected employees. All policies and procedures related to security must be submitted to corporate security for approval. Issues arising from this approval process will be referred to the director of corporate security for resolution.

4. **Incident Reporting.** Management will develop procedures for documenting and reporting incidents (e.g. fraud, theft, embezzlement, or unlawful or unethical practices or conditions) that result in the actual or potential loss of company assets. Additionally, serious operational security incidents or high-profile losses must be reported promptly to corporate security.

5. **Security and Related Forums**. Security and related personnel will participate with corporate security in formally established geographic and/or divisional security forums to discuss security issues, risks, and appropriate countermeasures.

6. **Identification of Critical Assets.** Management will develop and implement an annual process for identifying the critical assets entrusted to their organization. The process should include discussions with other appropriate organizations (e.g. technical and business intelligence, other organizations involved in the business flow). The assets considered should include physical assets, information systems, intellectual property, and proprietary information. An asset should be considered as key if the loss of or inability to use the asset would significantly impact revenue and/or the ability to meet customers' needs and/or maintain a competitive position. The characterization of critical assets should include:

- Description
- Function in the business (how asset is used)
- Why the asset has value (e.g. essential for operations, competitive advantage)
- Description of the form(s)
- Who uses the asset
- Where the asset is located
- How access to or use of asset is controlled
- How security is maintained
- Recovery process in the event the asset is compromised, destroyed, or stolen

7. **Critical Asset Security.** The process for identification should also include controlled distribution of this confidential information to appropriate personnel to ensure consistent and comprehensive awareness of those assets that require special security consideration. The identification of these assets will be the basis of the entire risk profile and business continuity planning.

8. **Identification of Company Property.** The placement and wording of the notices(s) should be appropriate and consistent with any applicable lease provisions and with local legal requirements regarding trespassing and liability statutes.

9. **Physical Security Measures.** All facilities used by the company must be designed to protect against unauthorized entry, theft, property damage, and injury to personnel. Techniques should include:

- Electronic access control
- Intrusion detection system
- Interior detection
- Protective fencing for utilities, electrical substations, chemical storage, communication equipment, and other vital areas
- Exterior protective lighting that provides daylight visibility of CCTV recordings
- Local remote alarm system monitoring
- Security personnel as required
- Alarm and emergency response capabilities
- Critical asset areas afforded increased protection

10. **Employee Access.** Employee access to sites and facilities should be controlled. These controls should be by visual acceptance (security officer, reception, or responsible person on site) of the employee's corporate identification badge or by electronic access control. Site procedures for controlling company employee access shall address the following issues:

- Days and hours when access is permitted
- Business justification for being on site
- Use of nondisclosure and confidentiality agreements

11. **Non-Employee Access.** Non-employees (e.g. contractors, contract employees, joint venture employees, company retirees, visitors, subsidiary employees, and suppliers) should have business justification for entering the site, should be granted explicit access authorization, and should have controlled access to the site. Site procedures for controlling non-employee access must address the following issues:

- Days and hours when access is permitted
- Business justification for being on site
- Use of nondisclosure and confidentiality agreements
- Company host responsibility for non-employee access to the site
- Authorized personnel who can grant non-employee access to a specific site

12. **Property Control Procedures.** The intent of this standard is to describe specific standards related to controlling physical assets while individuals are entering and leaving the premises. Management will establish property control policies and procedures, including:

- Paper or electronic removal documentation with sufficient information (e.g. asset number, individual charged with responsibility, time period asset will be off premises) to account for the whereabouts of corporate assets assigned to individual employees
- Paper or electronic documentation that tracks non-company assets (e.g. tools and equipment) that are brought on premises to ensure accountability for the asset when it is removed from the premises
- Inspection procedures appropriate for the site to assist in the safeguard of assets
- An audit process to verify the effectiveness of controls

TABLE OF RISKS AND CONTROLS – PHYSICAL SECURITY

Process: Physical Security			
Process Risk	**Recommended Policies**	**Internal Controls**	**KPIs**
1. Security for company employees and visitors may be inadequate.	■ Corporate Security Policy ■ Security Training Programs ■ Security Guidelines ■ Incident Reporting Processes	1. Security Program Administration 2. Trained and Capable Physical Security Employees 3. Security Guidelines 4. Incident Reporting 5. Security and Related Forums 6. Identification of Critical Assets 7. Critical Asset Security 8. Identification of Company Property 9. Physical Security Measures 10. Employee Access 11. Non-Employee Access 12. Property Control Procedures	■ Security Cost as a Percentage of Total Company Revenue ■ Number of Security FTEs (Full-Time Equivalents) as a Percentage of Total Company FTEs ■ Number of Nuisance Alarms by Facility ■ Number of Security Incidences by Facility ■ Cost of a Security Incident ■ Average Response Time to a Security Incident ■ Cycle Time to Resolve a Security Incident
2. There is an inability to respond to security incidents.	■ Corporate Security Policy ■ Security Training Programs ■ Security Guidelines ■ Incident Reporting Processes	4. Incident Reporting 5. Security and Related Forums 12. Property Control Procedures	■ Number of Security Incidences by Facility ■ Cost of a Security Incident ■ Average Response Time to a Security Incident
3. The disaster/ emergency plans may not be effective.	■ Corporate Security Policy ■ Security Training Programs ■ Security Guidelines ■ Incident Reporting Processes	8. Identification of Company Property	■ Time to Recover from an Emergency ■ Percentage of BCPs in place
4. Improperly trained security personnel may not be able to adequately respond to a situation/ incident requiring their involvement.	■ Security Training Programs	2. Trained and Capable Physical Security Employees	■ Percentage of Security Personnel Trained ■ Pass/Fail Rate of Security Tests

Process: Physical Security			
Process Risk	**Recommended Policies**	**Internal Controls**	**KPIs**
5. **Company assets, such as product, property, material, and technology, may be stolen, damaged, or otherwise compromised.**	■ Corporate Security Policy ■ Security Training Programs ■ Security Guidelines ■ Incident Reporting Processes	1. Security Program Administration 2. Trained and Capable Physical Security Employees 3. Security Guidelines 4. Incident Reporting 5. Security and Related Forums 6. Identification of Critical Assets 7. Critical Asset Security 8. Identification of Company Property 9. Physical Security Measures 10. Employee Access 11. Non-Employee Access 12. Property Control Procedures	■ Number of Security Incidences by Facility ■ Cost of a Security Incident ■ Average Response Time to a Security Incident ■ Security Cost as a Percentage of Total Company Revenue ■ Number of Security FTEs as a Percentage of Total Company FTEs ■ Number of Nuisance Alarms by Facility
6. **Unauthorized access to and/or disclosure of proprietary information could adversely affect the company's competitive position and reputation.**	■ Corporate Security Policy ■ Security Training Programs ■ Security Guidelines ■ Incident Reporting Processes	9. Physical Security Measures 10. Employee Access 11. Non-Employee Access	■ Security Cost as a Percentage of Total Company Revenue ■ Number of Security FTEs as a Percentage of Total Company FTEs ■ Number of Nuisance Alarms by Facility
7. **The company's ability to conduct business may be significantly impaired.**	■ Corporate Security Policy ■ Security Training Programs ■ Security Guidelines ■ Incident Reporting Processes	1. Security Program Administration 2. Trained and Capable Physical Security Employees 3. Security Guidelines 4. Incident Reporting 5. Security and Related Forums 6. Identification of Critical Assets 7. Critical Asset Security 8. Identification of Company Property 9. Physical Security Measures 10. Employee Access 11. Non-Employee Access 12. Property Control Procedures	■ Security Cost as a Percentage of Total Company Revenue ■ Number of Security FTEs as a Percentage of Total Company FTEs ■ Number of Nuisance Alarms by Facility

	Process: Physical Security		
Process Risk	**Recommended Policies**	**Internal Controls**	**KPIs**
8. Security response to major incidents may be slowed and ultimately impede resolution.	■ Incident Reporting Processes	4. Incident Reporting 5. Security and Related Forums	■ Average Response Time to a Security Incident
9. Unauthorized or unlawful entry may be attempted or made into company premises without detection.	■ Incident Reporting Processes	9. Physical Security Measures 10. Employee Access 11. Non-Employee Access	■ Security Cost as a Percentage of Total Company Revenue ■ Number of Security FTEs as a Percentage of Total Company FTEs ■ Number of Nuisance Alarms by Facility
10. Records and data may be destroyed, stolen, or altered by unauthorized individuals.	■ Corporate Security Policy ■ Security Training Programs ■ Security Guidelines ■ Incident Reporting Processes	9. Physical Security Measures 10. Employee Access 11. Non-Employee Access	■ Number of Nuisance Alarms by Facility
11. Required documentation of non-employee access to company property is not maintained.	■ Corporate Security Policy ■ Security Training Programs ■ Security Guidelines ■ Incident Reporting Processes	11. Non-Employee Access	■ Number of Nuisance Alarms by Facility

Leadership and Change Management Risk

 SECTION INTRODUCTION

Leadership is that interpersonal influence that gets individuals or groups to act or perform as the leader desires. Leaders are self-motivated and recognize their own strengths and weaknesses. They are able to effectively influence others within a direct reporting structure, virtual team environment, or membership organization, and even across diverse cultures and geographies. And effective leaders are cognizant of the nuances in communication and management styles. There's no time when leadership is more valuable than during crises, when leaders must tap into all of the skills previously listed while they're under duress and confronting difficult situations.

The controller's role may differ in small and large organizations and in private and public companies. However, the controller is always looked upon as an accounting leader for the organization. Some organizations may refer to the controller as the chief accounting officer and others may have a separate position for this role. Government and nonprofit organizations may refer to the controller as the comptroller.

In some smaller organizations the controller may assume the responsibilities usually held by the chief financial officer. Some organizations may have the controller assume the role of acting CFO when the CFO is not available.

A large public organization may have divisional, functional, regional, subsidiary, and business-unit controllers. These controllers require the same skill sets as corporate controllers.

The controller's role in all organizations is always expanding to include more responsibilities, as executive management understands the impact that the controller has on the company. Since the controller has responsibilities for all accounting activities, business processes, and financial reporting, he or she is in a position to have an organization-wide view of the company. Some organizations with unique experience and visibility promote the controller to chief operating officer.

Due to traditional and expanding responsibilities, it is important for the controller to be comfortable not only with the role of accounting leader, but also that of a business leader for the organization.

CHAPTER TWENTY ONE

Leadership and Managing Change

 OVERVIEW

From a simplistic viewpoint, one might say strong leaders see the big picture and reach for the sky, while good managers focus their attention on staying grounded and ensuring that nothing falls through the cracks on the way to achieving business goals. One thing is undeniable: both strong leadership and effective management are critical to organizational success and sustainability. The following process flow stresses the importance of leadership and change management skills for a controller.

LEADERSHIP AND CHANGE MANAGEMENT PROCESS FLOW

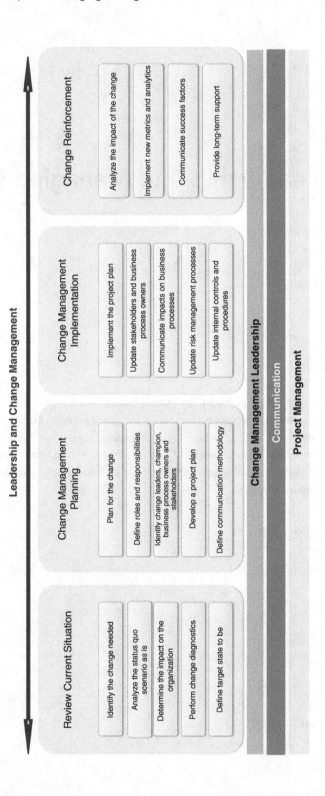

Leadership and Change Management

Change Management Leadership

Communication

Project Management

Review Current Situation
- Identify the change needed
- Analyze the status quo scenario as is
- Determine the impact on the organization
- Perform change diagnostics
- Define target state to be

Change Management Planning
- Plan for the change
- Define roles and responsibilities
- Identify change leaders, champion, business process owners and stakeholders
- Develop a project plan
- Define communication methodology

Change Management Implementation
- Implement the project plan
- Update stakeholders and business process owners
- Communicate impacts on business processes
- Update risk management processes
- Update internal controls and procedures

Change Reinforcement
- Analyze the impact of the change
- Implement new metrics and analytics
- Communicate success factors
- Provide long-term support

CONTROLLER'S TOOL 58 – THE HENRI FAYOL PRINCIPLES OF BUSINESS MANAGEMENT

Introduction. French management theorist Henri Fayol (1841–1925) developed principles of management based on his personal work experiences in a mining and metallurgical company. He was little known outside France until the late 1940s when Constance Storrs published her translation of Fayol's 1916 book *Administration Industrielle et Generale*. Fayol is looked upon as a key influence in the classical school of management, and his teachings are often compared to the task-oriented management style of Frederick Taylor at Bethlehem Steel. In 1911, Taylor published *The Principles of Scientific Management* in the United States. His five principles for business management — planning, organizing, controlling, coordinating, and commanding — are still used today in leadership literature and education. His principles can be defined as follows:

1. **Planning** is the decision-making process that defines the actions needed. This process includes gathering information, generating alternatives, and moving forward with a decision based on the information provided.

2. **Organizing** is the manner in which all resources are properly used and deployed. Resources include people, time, and money.

3. **Controlling** refers to how managers govern their staffs by meetings, metrics, and KPIs. Controlling also refers to the number of meetings a manager may have and how the discipline of action-item tracking is implemented.

4. **Coordinating** is about teamwork. Fayol's management theory states that in order to have a productive, efficient, and effective organization, people must work together as one team with a common goal.

5. **Commanding** requires that managers articulate clearly what is expected from subordinates. For managers to positively motivate their staff, they must model timely and accurate communication.

 ## CONTROLLER'S TOOL 59 – LEADERSHIP TRAITS

Introduction. In the seventh edition of *Organizational Behavior*, authors John R. Schermerhorn Jr., James G. Hunt, and Richard N. Osborn describe traits critical to leadership.

"Influence, vision, communication, knowledge, charisma, and creative thinking all are hallmarks of good leaders. Unlike management, leadership stems from the core of a personality. And although leadership skills can be nurtured and developed, it is my belief that they cannot be taught to those who don't already possess key tendencies. One either has what it takes to be a leader or doesn't. That is why some people are considered to be born leaders."[1]

Traits with Positive Implications for Successful Leadership	
Energy and Adjustment or Stress Tolerance	Vitality and emotional resilience
Prosocial Power Motivation	Need for power, exercised primarily for the benefit of others
Achievement Orientation	Need for achievement, desire to excel, drive for success, willingness to assume responsibilities, and a concern for task objectives

[1]Schermerhorn, John R., Hunt, James G., and Osborn, Richard N. (2001). *Organizational Behavior*. 7th edition update. Wiley.

Traits with Positive Implications for Successful Leadership	
Energy and Adjustment or Stress Tolerance	Vitality and emotional resilience
Emotional Maturity	Well adjusted in interpersonal situations
Self-Confidence	Confidence in one's self and performance as a leader
Integrity	Ethical and trustworthy behavior
Perseverance or Tenacity	Ability to overcome obstacles; strength of will
Cognitive Ability and Intelligence	Ability to gather and interpret complex information
Task-Relevant Knowledge	Knowledge about the process, company, and industry
Flexibility	Ability to respond appropriately to changes in the environment

 ## CONTROLLER'S TOOL 60 – COMMUNICATION FOR CONTROLLERS

Introduction. Appropriate communication of a milestone, event, or action plan helps to establish and differentiate true leaders. There are two styles of communication:

1. **Directive Communication**

   Arthur F. Carmazzi is the principal founder of Directive Communication International™, a company focusing on leadership development and change management. On his company website, he defines directive communication as setting "the emotional and decision-making base for optimizing the way people interact with each other in an organization, team or group. It enables individuals the ability to specifically and positively direct enthusiasm and action for themselves and the people around them. It exposes individuals to the mental, emotional, and physical triggers that will lead to improvement in their quality of life in and out of work."

2. **Consultative Communication**

   Consultative communication implies that both parties are collaborating. Some leaders look at consultative communication as way to slow things down.

   Consultative communication can be used in a face-to-face discussion as well as in a team environment, such as in a staff meeting or project status meeting. Consultative communication results in collaboration and helps team members feel that they are valued and respected.

 ## CONTROLLER'S TOOL 61 – GUIDELINES FOR ACTIVE LISTENING

Introduction. The concept of active listening involves encouraging the speaker to state what they really mean and stems from the work of counselors and therapists. The goal of active listening is to help associates express themselves, offer suggestions, and get to the root cause of a matter. Here are some guidelines for the active listening process:

Guidelines for Active Listening

1. Listen for the content of the message and organize it into key components.

2. Listen for feelings about the key points being conveyed.

3. Ensure that you respond appropriately to feelings with compassion.

4. Be cognizant if there is overreaction to the situation.

5. Watch for verbal and nonverbal indications and be prepared to reconvene the discussion if necessary.

6. Repeat and paraphrase the key points that were conveyed.

7. Wait until the speaker is finished.

8. Do not plan your response until the speaker is finished.

9. Never interrupt to state your own opinion.

10. Maintain eye contact if you are in a face-to-face meeting.

TABLE OF CONTROLS – LEADERSHIP AND MANAGING CHANGE

Process: Leadership and Managing Change

1. **Well-Defined Change Management Processes.** Change management is a collective term for all approaches to preparing, supporting, and helping individuals, teams, and organizations in making organizational change.

2. **Job Descriptions.** Wikipedia defines a job description as a written narrative that describes the general tasks, or other related duties, and responsibilities of a position.

3. **Tone at the Top. Tone at the top** is a term that originated in the field of accounting and is used to describe an organization's general ethical climate, as established by its BoD, audit committee, and senior management.

4. **Organizational Structure**. An organizational structure defines how activities such as task allocation, coordination, and supervision are directed towards the achievement of organizational aims. Organizational structure affects organizational action and provides the foundation on which standard operating procedures and routines rest.

5. **Leadership Training.** Leadership and management training courses are specialized programs designed to help you learn new leadership techniques and refine old skills to run your team, including assertive communication, motivation methods, and coaching. The manager is an employee who is responsible for planning, directing, and overseeing the operations and fiscal health of a business unit, division, department, or an operating unit in an organization. The manager is responsible for overseeing and leading the work of a group of people in many instances.

6. **Delegation of Authority.** DoA means division of authority and its powers downwards to the subordinate. Delegation is about entrusting someone else with doing parts of your job. DoA can be defined as subdivision and suballocation of powers to subordinates in order to achieve effective results.

7. **Human Resources Recruitment Policy.** A recruitment policy is a statement that defines how you hire. It outlines your company's preferred hiring practices and promotes consistency within your employee recruiting process.

8. **Internal Controls Program.** A company's internal controls program is implemented across all functions and business processes.

TABLE OF RISKS AND CONTROLS – LEADERSHIP AND MANAGING CHANGE

Process: Leadership and Managing Change			
Process Risk	**Recommended Policies**	**Internal Controls**	**KPIs**
1. **Accountability is unclear.** Without defined roles and responsibilities, there is a lack of account-ability and company goals are not achieved.	▪ Job Descriptions ▪ Organization Structure	1. Well-Defined Change Management Process 2. Job Descriptions 3. Tone at the Top 4. Organizational Structure 5. Leadership Training 6. DoA 7. HR Recruitment Policy 8. Internal Controls Program	▪ Percentage of Company Goals Achieved per Strategic Plan
2. **Change is not properly managed.** This causes additional risk to a company.	▪ Change Management Process	1. Well-Defined Change Management Process	▪ Number of Internal Controls Issues Requiring Remediation
3. **Unfair or inappropriate hiring practices.**	▪ HR Policies and Hiring Practices	7. HR Recruitment Policy	▪ Number of Hiring Issues Requiring Remediation or Legal Action ▪ Number of Ethics Issues Reported to the Ethics Hotline
4. **Without a good leader, there can be bad management, as evidenced by the lack of integrity.**	▪ Tone at the Top	3. Tone at the Top 5. Leadership Training	▪ Number of Ethics Issues Reported to the Ethics Hotline
5. **Poor leadership may lead to poor or inap-propriate communi-cation.**	▪ Job Descriptions	3. Tone at the Top 5. Leadership Training	▪ Number of Ethics Issues Reported to the Ethics Hotline
6. **Poor leadership can put the company at risk and can cause reputational damage.**	▪ Tone at the Top ▪ HR Policies and Hiring Practices	3. Tone at the Top 5. Leadership Training	▪ Number of Hiring Issues Requiring Remediation or Legal Action ▪ Number of Ethics Issues Reported to the Ethics Hotline

Process: Leadership and Managing Change			
Process Risk	**Recommended Policies**	**Internal Controls**	**KPIs**
7. **Poor leadership can cause financial harm and possible business failure.** Poor leadership may result in significant lawsuits.	▪ Tone at the Top	3. Tone at the Top 5. Leadership Training	▪ Budget Variance Percentages ▪ Cost Center Expense Overages ▪ Number of DoA Issues
8. **Financial statements and records may be misstated due to improper leadership and awareness.**	▪ Tone at the Top ▪ DoA	3. Tone at the Top 5. Leadership Training	▪ Budget Variance Percentages ▪ Cost Center Expense Overages ▪ Number of DoA Issues
9. **Unapproved transactions may result in undesirable legal and/or tax implications.**	▪ Tone at the Top ▪ DoA	4. Organizational Structure 6. DoA	▪ Number of DoA Issues

CHAPTER TWENTY TWO

Trends, Process Transformation, and Digitization

 OVERVIEW

When a company thinks about improving working capital, the initial thought is to pay invoices later, thus extending DPO. The company may not consider the alternatives described in this chapter as ways to reduce cost in financial transaction processing by implementing digitization and process transformation.

TRENDS, PROCESS TRANSFORMATION, AND DIGITIZATION PROCESS FLOW

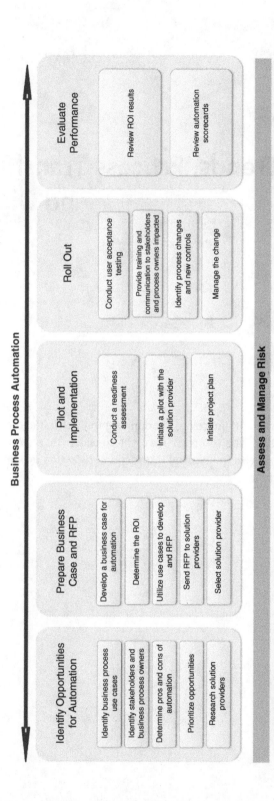

Business Process Automation

Identify Opportunities for Automation
- Identify business process use cases
- Identify stakeholders and business process owners
- Determine pros and cons of automation
- Prioritize opportunities
- Research solution providers

Prepare Business Case and RFP
- Develop a business case for automation
- Determine the ROI
- Utilize use cases to develop and RFP
- Send RFP to solution providers
- Select solution provider

Pilot and Implementation
- Conduct a readiness assessment
- Initiate a pilot with the solution provider
- Initiate project plan

Roll Out
- Conduct user acceptance testing
- Provide training and communication to stakeholders and process owners impacted
- Identify process changes and new controls
- Manage the change

Evaluate Performance
- Review ROI results
- Review automation scorecards

Assess and Manage Risk

Link Budgets and Forecasts to the Strategic Plan

CONTROLLER'S TOOL 62 – BLOCKCHAIN USES

Introduction. As controllers consider process transformation, they should consider solutions using blockchain. Blockchain is ubiquitous. Wherever you turn there's a new application of this remarkable technology. It is already disrupting the financial services industry and some banks are even issuing their own cryptocurrency accounts, apparently in direct competition to their own traditional core business. But the impact will go much further than that and I believe it will fundamentally alter the way we do business with each other, not only the way we use money.

Blockchain is an open ledger in which every transaction on a network is recorded and available for authorized participants to see and verify. It can be thought of as a secured spreadsheet, in that it sits in a cloud where multiple parties can review it but no one can change it. Bitcoin popularized blockchain technology, which was proposed in 2008 in a white paper by Satoshi Nakamoto (pseudonym).

Application	Use Case
Currency	■ Cross-Border Payments ■ Escrow and Custody Services ■ Supply Chain and Trade Finance ■ Customer Acquisition and Loyalty
Assets	■ Financial Securities and Trading ■ Logistics and Asset Tracking ■ Intellectual Property Rights ■ Real Estate and Property
Contracts	■ Supply Chain Management ■ Digital Rights Management ■ Insurance ■ Legal
Data	■ Identity Management ■ File Storage and Sharing ■ Electronic Medical Records ■ Auditing and Compliance
P2P	■ Internet of Things ■ Voting and Governance Systems ■ Collaborative Economy

Business Process Improvement

BPI attempts to reduce variation and/or waste in processes so that the desired outcome can be achieved with better utilization of resources. BPI is a systematic approach to help organizations to archive significant changes in the way they do business. BPI can be the product of Business Process Reengineering, Redesign, and Benchmarking. BPI works by:

- Defining the organization's strategic goals and purposes: Who are we, what do we do, and why do we do it?
- Determining the organization's customers or stakeholders: Who do we serve?
- Aligning the business processes to realize the organization's goals: How do we do it better? Aligning business processes can lead to the implementation of an SSC or a BPO process.

Business Process Automation

BPA is the strategy a business uses to automate processes in order to reduce costs. It consists of integrating applications, restructuring labor resources, and using software applications to automate specific business processes. There is ongoing discussion as to whether BPA is a distinct field of activity in its own right or merely a subset of a wider activity.

The BPI rationale is that before any process can be automated, it is necessary to define (often at a very strategic level or enterprise-wide) all of the business processes running inside an organization. From this effort the processes can be redefined, and where necessary optimized, through automation.

The BPA approach states that until a process is automated there is no real value in analyzing and defining it, that the cycle of business change is so rapid that there simply isn't time to define every process before choosing which ones to address with automation, and that delivering immediate benefits creates more value. However, moving directly to a BPA approach may cause some issues, since an inefficient process may be automated without addressing processing improvements first.

CONTROLLER'S TOOL 63 – IDENTIFYING SAAS IMPOSTERS

Introduction. In today's IT landscape, many organizations have adopted a cloud-first approach to business systems. Yet with so many vendors offering SaaS solutions, how do you know which vendor will enable you to achieve the true benefits SaaS has to offer? What are the characteristics to look for when considering a software as-a-service (SaaS) solution, and what are the real impacts on modern businesses? This controller's tool will provide the questions you should ask and the answers you should expect when looking for a SaaS solution so that you can identify SaaS imposters.

Question	Answer: Imposter	Answer: Genuine Supplier
1. Are upgrades/updates included in the SaaS subscription fee?	Additional service fees are required to apply the new software.	Yes, they are included as part of your subscription fee.
2. Will we always be using the most recent release of the software?	Only if you pay an additional fee for upgrades.	Yes, all our customers are always using most recent version of the software.
3. How often will new versions/capabilities be delivered?	Every 18 months, but our customers usually skip releases to save on the cost of upgrades.	Multiple times per year. Each release is incremental, vigorously tested, and should not cause major disruption to your business.
4. Do you support configuration options or customizations through new upgrades and updates?	We support customizations, but upgrades may destabilize customizations and require additional fees to support OR no customizations are allowed.	Configuration options are provided and fully supported by the supplier through all updates. Only acceptance testing is required on the part of the customer for each update.

CONTROLLER'S TOOL 64 – 10 CRITICAL REQUIREMENTS FOR CLOUD APPLICATIONS

Introduction. According to Admin Kripaa's post on the Ramco Systems blog, "in the enterprise software industry's rush to fulfill rising demand, some providers may skip requirements that are critical to delivering the true benefits of cloud applications. Industry pioneers for cloud applications that use the SaaS delivery model know shortcuts don't exist. Applications, architectures, and processes must be built from the ground up to produce superior, modern alternatives to the traditional on-premise software and maintenance model." The post outlines these 10 critical requirements for cloud applications:[1]

1. True multitenancy

2. Regularly delivered, supplier-managed updates

3. Seamless integration on demand

4. Business-driven configurability

5. World-class data center and security

6. High-performance, sustainable IT Infrastructure

7. Predictable total cost of ownership model

8. Faster deployment

9. Internal controls

10. Liberation from nonstrategic IT issues

PROCESS DIGITIZATION

All organizations require IT solutions to run their organization more effectively and efficiently. A controller plays a critical role in the IT solution selection, implementation, and post-implementation processes.

The controller must ensure that the solution does not put the organization at risk or impact the financial closing process. The controller should ensure that the IT solution links to the strategic plan of the organization and helps the company achieve its business objectives. The controller must also ensure that the solution does not negatively impact a financially significant business process or impact existing internal controls programs. Lastly, an internal controls program may need to be revised if there is a major implementation. Controller's Tool 65 outlines the types of solutions to consider.

[1]Kripaa, Admin (2011). 10 critical requirements for cloud applications. Ramco Systems blog (accessed April 20, 2020). https://blogs.ramco.com/10-critical-requirements-for-cloud-applications

CONTROLLER'S TOOL 65 – TYPES OF IT SOLUTIONS TO CONSIDER

Introduction. A controller and his or her staff can be daunted by the types and number of IT solutions available to support financial operations. The matrix below was developed to provide an overview of the IT solutions that can be explored to meet an organizational need. Understanding the types of solutions available is an important step in the selection process and is good information to have before developing the business case.

IT Solution Category	Description	Reference (if Applicable)
Accounting Software	Accounting software is application software that records and processes accounting transactions within functional modules such as AP, AR, payroll, and trial balance. It functions as an accounting information system. It may be developed in-house by the company or organization using it, be purchased from a third party, or be a third-party application software package with local modifications. It varies greatly in its complexity and cost. **Core Modules** ■ AR – where the company enters money received ■ AP – where the company enters its bills and pays money it owes ■ GL – the company's "books" ■ Billing – where the company produces invoices to clients/customers ■ Stock/inventory – where the company keeps control of its inventory ■ PO – where the company orders inventory ■ Sales order – where the company records customer orders for the supply of inventory ■ Cash book – where the company records collection and payment	https://en.wikipedia.org/wiki/Accounting_software
Accounts Payable Automation	AP automation is slowly becoming standard among effective and cost-conscious organizations of all sizes. By using a software system for AP automation, companies shorten their payment cycles, cut down on AP-related costs, and increase control over the AP cycle. Reducing costs and improving efficiency and productivity are the main goals for AP departments and automation is the key to achieving these goals.	

IT Solution Category	Description	Reference (if Applicable)
Accounts Receivable (Billing) Automation	Automated billing is an action in which the invoicing for goods and services occurs without the need to prepare the invoice manually. Many billing systems of this type provide the ability to generate and send electronic copies of the invoices to customers. The use of this type of billing software makes it possible to manage the invoicing process with greater efficiency, saving the company both time and money. There are several features that are common to automated billing software. In most cases, the software is designed to allow the creation of customer profiles that contain all the data needed to accurately prepare the invoice. This data will include the customer name, billing address, billing contact, and an e-mail address if the invoice is to be sent electronically. In most cases the automated billing program will collect data from other sources that have to do with customer usage or allow for the manual entry of orders once they are fulfilled. The processes within the billing system then apply the proper rates for each order and create an invoice. Depending on how the automated billing system is configured, the invoice may be printed out, along with a companion envelope, immediately after the invoice generation. However, it is possible to set up the software so that invoices are automatically printed at a specific time of day. There are even some examples of software that will prompt machinery to fold the invoice, insert it into a pre-addressed envelope, and seal the envelope. When e-mail is used as the delivery medium, the system may expedite the delivery immediately after generating the invoice or manage the e-mail process at a specific time of day, an approach that allows business owners to survey invoices before they are sent out.	https://www.wisegeek.com/what-is-automated-billing.htm

IT Solution Category	Description	Reference (if Applicable)
Requirements for Integrating ERM, Compliance, and Business Processes	Most solutions today are static (not business process based) and only address one specific regulation or risk management approach. Furthermore, it is typical that business units and divisions within a company develop their own unique solutions, which leads to miscommunication and lost opportunities because of the lack of coordination, alignment, and common goals. The right technology solution can facilitate addressing these issues and improve the overall performance of the company. Such a solution needs to meet the following criteria: ■ A single system that can align and link objectives, components, and entities. ■ Compliance-designed business process management (BPM) based on automating iterative processes with flexibility and extensibility. ■ Automate all aspects of the enterprise risk approach, multi-compliance requirements, and business processes from a single system. ■ Automated alerts, issue management, and remediation. ■ Ability to distribute specific tasks to individuals in business units for action to eliminate unnecessary and complex system access and reduce training and support costs. ■ Customize your requirements to specifically meet your needs. ■ Integrate existing systems and monitor at a transaction level if required. ■ Shared central repository with granular security access to control very precisely what can be accessed. ■ Complete real-time continuous control tracking, monitoring, audit and documentation management.	http://compliancy.com/ solutions_enterprise_risk_ management.html

IT Solution Category	Description	Reference (if Applicable)
Budgeting	Managers need direct access to budget data and actuals throughout the year and in real time. They need to be able to access views that allow comparisons between markets, channels, products, and so forth. Without this, managers have no way of using the budget effectively as a management tool. Spreadsheets are two dimensional. A good budget system provides a financial reporting system that goes beyond two dimensions by providing you with a multidimensional view that allows the controller to: <ul><li>Examine your operation from different perspectives – by GL account, manager, project, location, product line, and customer, or any other areas of your operation – to determine variances and trends and make changes in line with goals and forecasts</li><li>Measure performance using a multitude of variables – product line, manager, division, location, channel, and so on – to answer questions</li></ul>	
Business Process Automation	According to Wikipedia, "business process automation (BPA), also known as business automation or digital transformation,[1] is the technology-enabled automation of complex business processes.[2] It can streamline a business for simplicity, achieve digital transformation, increase service quality, improve service delivery or contain costs. It consists of integrating applications, restructuring labor resources and using software applications throughout the organization.[3] Robotic process automation is an emerging field within BPA that uses artificial intelligence."	https://en.wikipedia.org/wiki/Business_process_automation

IT Solution Category	Description	Reference (if Applicable)
Types of Cloud Computing	Types of cloud services: IaaS, PaaS, SaaS, FaaS Cloud computing services fall into four categories: infrastructure as a service (IaaS), platform as a service (PaaS), software as a service (SaaS), and FaaS (functions as a service). These are sometimes called the cloud computing stack, because they build on top of one another. 1. **Infrastructure as a service (IaaS).** IaaS is the most basic category of cloud computing services that allows you rent to IT infrastructure (servers or VMs) from a cloud provider on a pay-as-you-go basis. 2. **Platform as a service (PaaS).** PaaS refers to the supply of an on-demand environment for developing, testing, delivering, and managing software applications. It is designed to quickly create web or mobile apps, without worrying about setting up or managing the underlying infrastructure of servers, storage, network, and databases needed for development. 3. **Software as a service (SaaS).** SaaS is a method for delivering software applications over the Internet as per the demand and on a subscription basis. SaaS helps you host and manage the software application and underlying infrastructure and handle any maintenance (software upgrades and security patching). 4. **Functions as a service (FaaS).** FaaS adds another layer of abstraction to PaaS, so that developers are completely insulated from everything in the stack below their code. Instead of handling the hassles of virtual servers, containers, and application runtimes, they upload narrowly functional blocks of code and set them to be triggered by a certain event. FaaS applications consume no IaaS resources until an event occurs, reducing pay-per-use fees.	https://www.esds.co.in/blog/cloud-computing-types-cloud/#sthash.bytnv6sr.dpbs

IT Solution Category	Description	Reference (if Applicable)
Customer Relationship Management Systems	CRM is a widely implemented model for managing a company's interactions with customers, clients, and sales prospects. It involves using technology to organize, automate, and synchronize business processes – principally sales activities, but also marketing, customer service, and technical support activities. The overall goals are to find, attract, and win new clients; nurture and retain those the company already has; entice former clients back into the fold; and reduce the costs of marketing and client service. CRM is a company-wide business strategy and includes customer-interface departments as well as other departments. Tools and workflows can be complex, especially for large businesses. Previously these tools were generally limited to simple CRM solutions that focused on monitoring and recording interactions and communications. Software solutions then expanded to embrace deal tracking, territories, opportunities, and the sales pipeline itself.	http://en.wikipedia.org/wiki/Customer_relationship_management
E-commerce	E-commerce is the buying and selling of goods and services on the Internet, especially the World Wide Web. In practice, this term and a newer term, e-business, are often used interchangeably. For online retail selling, the term *e-tailing* is sometimes used. E-commerce can be divided into: ■ E-tailing, or virtual storefronts, on websites with on-line catalogs, sometimes gathered into a virtual mall ■ The gathering and use of demographic data through web contacts ■ EDI, the business-to-business exchange of data ■ E-mail and fax and their use as media for reaching prospects and established customers (for example, with newsletters) ■ Business-to-business buying and selling ■ The security of business transactions	http://searchcio.techtarget.com/definition/e-commerce

IT Solution Category	Description	Reference (if Applicable)
Enterprise Resource Planning Systems	ERP systems' definition implies a conglomeration of multimodule applications software packages that integrate activities of different functional departments. In this regard it is important to know that the term *ERP* entails not only those software packages but also an effective combination of business strategies, users, and the hardware required to run ERP software.	
	ERPs are cross-functional, enterprise-wide systems that handle manufacturing, HR management, order entry, AR and AP, GL, purchasing, warehousing, and transportation for an organization. Contrary to popular belief, an ERP system is not part of a back-office system, as it deals with customers as well as other people. ERP systems attempt to cover all the basic operations of any given organization, such as nonprofit organizations, nongovernmental organizations, government agencies, private corporations, and so forth.	
Ethics Hotlines	The most effective hotlines offer 24-hour, 365-day access to a skilled interviewer. For the best results, and to simplify communication, organizations should provide a single mechanism for reporting all workplace issues. Reports should be disseminated quickly to designated parties. The hotline should also be promoted with educational materials directed to everyone in the organization, including employees and suppliers.	
	Using a centralized reporting mechanism, information should be disseminated to the most appropriate parties, which likely includes HR, the audit committee of the BoD, and the legal and loss prevention departments, among others. Dual dissemination of complaints related to fraud acts as a system of checks and balances by ensuring that no single person is in possession of this highly sensitive information. This protects the integrity of the reporting mechanism.	
	The hotline program's case management system should provide a centralized database for documenting the steps taken by the organization to investigate allegations reported via the hotline.	

IT Solution Category	Description	Reference (if Applicable)
Fixed Asset Automation	Tracking assets is an important concern of every company, regardless of size. Fixed assets are defined as any "permanent" object that a business uses internally, including, but not limited to, computers, tools, software, or office equipment. While employees may use a specific tool or tools, the asset ultimately belongs to the company and must be returned. Therefore, without an accurate method of keeping track of these assets, it would be very easy for a company to lose control of them. Asset-tracking software allows companies to track what assets it owns, where each is located, who has it, when it was checked out, when it is due for return, when it is scheduled for maintenance, and the cost and depreciation of each asset. The reporting option that is built into most asset-tracking solutions provides prebuilt reports, including assets by category and department, check-in/check-out, net book value of assets, assets past due, audit history, and transactions.	https://en.wikipedia.org/wiki/Fixed_assets_management
Continuous Controls Monitoring (CCM)	Continuous controls monitoring (CCM) is a set of technologies to reduce business losses through continuous monitoring and reducing the cost of audits through continuous auditing of the controls in financial and other transactional applications.	https://www.gartner.com/en/information-technology/glossary/continuous-controls-monitoring-ccm
Inventory Controls Systems	An inventory control system is a system that encompasses all aspects of managing a company's inventories: purchasing, shipping, receiving, tracking, warehousing and storage, turnover, and reordering. In different firms the activities associated with each of these areas may not be strictly contained within separate subsystems, but these functions must be performed in sequence in order to have a well-run inventory control system. Computerized inventory control systems make it possible to integrate the various functional subsystems that are a part of the inventory management into a single cohesive system. In today's business environment, even small and midsize businesses have come to rely on computerized inventory management systems.	http://www.inc.com/encyclopedia/inventory-control-systems.html

IT Solution Category	Description	Reference (if Applicable)
Payroll Solutions	The term *payroll* encompasses every employee of a company who receives a regular wage or other compensation. Some employees may be paid a steady salary, while others are paid for hours worked or the number of items produced. All of these different payment methods are calculated by a payroll specialist, and appropriate paychecks are issued. Companies often use objective measuring tools such as time cards or time sheets completed by supervisors to determine the total amount of payroll due each pay period. After a payroll accountant multiplies an employee's hours by his or her pay rate, the gross income amount is entered into a calculator or computer program. Regular deductions, such as tax withholdings, FICA (social security) payments, medical insurance, union dues, charitable contributions, and so on, are then categorized and subtracted. The remaining balance is then converted to a check and becomes the employee's net pay for that time period. Payroll departments also identify the employer and employees using a federal code and keep a running tally of total income and deductions for the fiscal year. Payroll accounting software makes it easy for companies to process payroll and handle all of the accounting tasks that go along with recording and processing payroll. For small business owners, keeping enough cash in a payroll account is often one of their highest priorities. Even if the business itself hasn't become profitable, employees must still be compensated for their services. This is why many smaller companies prefer to keep their payroll obligations as low as possible until they've reached a certain level of profitability.	http://payroll.intuit.com/payroll_resources/payroll_101/ http://www.wisegeek.com/what-is-payroll.htm
Project Accounting	Project accounting allows companies to accurately assess the ROI of individual projects and enables true performance measurement. Project managers are able to calculate funding advances and actual versus budgeted cost variances using project accounting. Project accounting can also have an impact on the investment decisions that companies make. As companies seek to invest in new projects with low upfront costs, less risk, and longer-term benefits, the costs and benefit information from a project accounting system provides crucial feedback that improves the quality of such important decisions. If a company has several ongoing internal and customer focused projects, it is important to consider a software solution to enable accurate tracking and accounting.	

IT Solution Category	Description	Reference (if Applicable)
Project Management	Project management software is a term covering the many types of software applications – including software for estimation and planning, scheduling, cost control and budget management, resource allocation, collaboration software, communication, quality management and documentation, and administration systems – that are used to deal with the complexity of large projects or programs.	https://www.pmi.org/
Regulatory Compliance	Regulatory compliance software is a software solution for companies struggling with rapidly changing legal requirements. Regulatory compliance software is used in a wide variety of industries, including the accounting, environmental, and medical fields. Many industries are heavily regulated by their home government, and complying with these regulations can be difficult, as it involves a great deal of paperwork and knowledge of constantly evolving regulations. Software companies respond to a demonstrated need and create regulatory compliance software to assist companies and make them more efficient. Regulatory compliance software is especially vital for the medical industry, transparent accounting practices, and companies that deal with environmental hazards. The software is designed to manage and organize data so that companies can quickly access it, giving auditors access to company records along with proof that the company is complying with legal mandates. Additionally, it helps to improve safety records within the company by keeping companies in compliance with safety procedures.	http://www.wisegeek.com/what-is-regulatory-compliance-software.htm
Travel and Expense Solutions	Businesses leverage all sorts of tools and technology to operate as efficiently as possible. Yet, for various reasons, companies often overlook expense management or put it on the backburner. For instance, some businesses: ■ Don't believe they're big enough to automate expense management ■ Have legacy technologies or processes that "work just fine" and therefore aren't upgraded ■ Feel more comfortable with known quantities like spreadsheets and paper expense reports	https://www.concur.com/newsroom/article/what-is-expense-management-automation

DEVELOPING THE BUSINESS CASE

A business case captures the reasoning for initiating an investment for the organization. It is often presented in a well-structured written document but may also sometimes come in the form of a short verbal argument or presentation. Some organizations may require a business case as a component of their capital budgeting process.

The business case describes who will be affected and how. The who and how typically revolve around individual or organizational behavioral changes in a process known as change management. The business case breaks out specific alternatives that were examined and their associated impacts, risks, costs, and benefits. Those alternatives focus more on technical components, contributing to the overall business solution.

 ## CONTROLLER'S TOOL 66 – THE BUSINESS CASE TEMPLATE

Introduction. This comprehensive template can be used when presenting the business case for initiating any project, transformation, or digitization initiative.

1. Executive Summary

This section should provide general information on the issues surrounding the business problem and the proposed project or initiative created to address it. Usually this section is completed last, after all other sections of the business case have been written. This is because the executive summary is exactly that – a summary of the detail that is provided in subsequent sections of the document.

Issue

This section should briefly describe the business problem that the proposed project will address. This section should not describe how the problem will be addressed, only what the problem is.

Anticipated Outcomes

This section should describe the anticipated outcome if the proposed project or initiative is implemented. It should include how the project will benefit the business and describe what the end state of the project should be.

Recommendation

This section summarizes the approach for how the project will address the business problem. This section should also describe how desirable results will be achieved by moving forward with the project.

Justification

This section justifies why the recommended project should be implemented and why it was selected over other alternatives. Where applicable, quantitative support should be provided. The impact of not implementing the project should also be stated.

2. Business Case Analysis Team

This section describes the roles of the team members who developed the business case. It is imperative that participants and roles are clearly defined in the business case analysis and that those participants and roles are kept current throughout the life of any project initiated.

Role	Description	Name/Title
Executive Sponsor	Provides executive support for the project	
Technology Support	Provides all technology support for the project	
Controller	Provides financial analysis and internal controls support	
Process Improvement	Advises team on process improvement techniques	
Project Manager	Manages the business case and project team	
Software Support	Provides all software support for the project	

3. Problem Definition

Problem Statement

This section describes the business problem that this project was created to address. The problem may be a process or a technology, or may be oriented towards a product/service. This section should not include any discussion related to a solution.

Organizational Impact

This section describes how the proposed project will modify or affect the organizational processes, tools, hardware, and/or software. It should also explain any new roles that would be created or how existing roles may change as a result of the project.

Technology Migration

This section provides a high-level overview of how the new technology will be implemented and how data from the legacy technology will be migrated. This section should also explain any outstanding technical requirements and obstacles that need to be addressed.

4. Project Overview

This section describes high-level information about the project and should include a description, goals and objectives, performance criteria, assumptions, constraints, and milestones. This section consolidates all project-specific information into one chapter, allowing for an easy understanding of the project since the baseline business problem, impacts, and recommendations have already been established.

Project Description

This section describes the approach the project will use to address the business problem(s). Description of the approach should include what the project will consist of, a general description of how it will be executed, and the purpose of the project.

Goals and Objectives

This section lists the business goals and objectives that are supported by the project and how the project will address them.

Project Performance

This section describes the measures that will be used to gauge the project's performance and outcomes as they relate to key resources, processes, or services.

Project Assumptions

This section lists the preliminary assumptions for the proposed project. As the project is selected and moves into detailed project planning, the list of assumptions will most likely grow as the project plan is developed. However, for the business case there should be at least a preliminary list from which to build.

Project Constraints

This section lists the preliminary constraints for the proposed project. As the project is selected and moves into detailed project planning, the list of constraints will most likely grow as the project plan is developed. However, for the business case there should be at least a preliminary list from which to build.

5. Major Project Milestones

This section lists the major project milestones and their target completion dates. Since this is the business case, these milestones and target dates are general and in no way final. It is important to note that as the project planning moves forward, a baseline schedule including all milestones will be completed.

Milestones/Deliverables	Target Date
Project Charter	
Project Plan Review and Completion	
Project Kickoff	
Phase I Complete	
Phase II Complete	
Phase III Complete	
Phase IV Complete	
Phase V Complete	
Closeout/Project Completion	

6. Strategic Alignment

All projects should support the organization's strategy and strategic plans in order to add value and maintain executive and organizational support. This section provides an overview of the organizational strategic plans that are related to the project. This includes the strategic plan, what the plan calls for, and how the project supports the strategic plan.

Strategic Plan	Goals/Objectives	Relationship to Project

7. Cost-Benefit Analysis

Many consider this one of the most important parts of a business case, as it is often the costs incurred or the savings yielded by a project that will affect final approval to go forward. It is important to quantify the financial benefits of the project as much as possible in the business case. This is usually done in the form of a cost-benefit analysis. The purpose of this is to illustrate the costs of the project and compare them with the benefits and savings to determine if the project is worth pursuing.

Action	Action Type	Description	First Year Costs (- Indicates Anticipated Savings)

Net First-Year Savings	

8. Alternatives Analysis

All business problems may be addressed by any number of alternative projects. While the business case is the result of having selected one such option, a brief summary of considered alternatives should also be included – one of which should be the status quo, or doing nothing. The reasons for not selecting the alternatives should also be included.

No Project (Status Quo)	Reasons for Not Selecting Other Alternatives

9. Approvals

The business case is a document with which approval to move forward with the creation of a project is granted or denied. Therefore, the document should receive approval or disapproval from its executive review board

Approver Name	Title	Signature	Date
	CEO and President		
	CFO		
	Controller		
	Executive VP		

TABLE OF CONTROLS – TRENDS, PROCESS TRANSFORMATION, AND DIGITIZATION

Process: Trends, Process Transformation, and Digitization

1. **Analysis of the Current Process.** The current process, or as-is state, is analyzed to determine if improvements can be made to improve efficiency and reduce cost in the current environment.

2. **Definition of the Future State.** The to-be state of the process after transformation is well defined.

3. **Business Case and Funding.** A business case is developed to propose a solution and get approval for funding.

4. **Project Sponsor.** The transformation has a defined sponsor for the initiative.

5. **Project Management.** A project manager is assigned to the effort to ensure that the project is implemented as planned and status reporting is in place.

6. **Data Accuracy.** Data is validated and reconciled for the transformation initiative.

7. **Transformation Metrics.** Metrics are defined to determine the ROI of the transformation project as well as the impact on cost, process efficiency, and cycle time.

8. **Testing and Training**. Testing and user training is completed by those impacted by the transformation.

9. **Project Implementation Approval**. The implementation of the transformation is approved by the project sponsor and business process owner.

10. **Post-implementation Review**. The project is reviewed to capture lessons learned, failures, and successes.

TABLE OF RISKS AND CONTROLS – TRENDS, PROCESS TRANSFORMATION, AND DIGITIZATION

Process: Trends, Process Transformation, and Digitization			
Process Risk	**Recommended Policies**	**Internal Controls**	**KPIs**
1. **The transformation is completed without understanding or correcting current process.**	▪ Business Case Requirements ▪ Project Management Process	1. Analysis of the Current Process 2. Definition of the Future State 3. Business Case and Funding 6. Data Accuracy 7. Transformation Metrics 8. Testing and Training 9. Project Implementation Approval 10. Post-implementation Review	▪ Number of Users Relative to the Number of Licenses Purchased ▪ Number of Processes Performed on New Solution ▪ Percentage Cost-per-Transaction Reduction ▪ ROI for Solutions Implemented ▪ Amount of New Revenue Attributed to Digital Investments ▪ Percentage of Data Accuracy
2. **The future state is not defined.** The future state of the process after transformation is not defined and expectations are not established.	▪ Business Case Requirements ▪ Project Management Process	2. Definition of the Future State 3. Business Case and Funding	▪ Number of Users Relative to the Number of Licenses Purchased ▪ Number of Processes Performed on New Solution ▪ Percentage Cost-per-Transaction Reduction ▪ ROI for Solutions Implemented ▪ Amount of New Revenue Attributed to Digital Investments ▪ Percentage of Data Accuracy
3. **The solution is not approved or funded.** This may impact the company's forecast and budget.	▪ Business Case Requirements ▪ Project Management Process	1. Analysis of the Current Process 2. Definition of the Future State 3. Business Case and Funding	▪ Number of Users Relative to the Number of Licenses Purchased ▪ Number of Processes Performed on New Solution ▪ Percentage Cost-per-Transaction Reduction ▪ ROI for Solutions Implemented ▪ Amount of New Revenue Attributed to Digital Investments ▪ Percentage of Data Accuracy

Process: Trends, Process Transformation, and Digitization			
Process Risk	**Recommended Policies**	**Internal Controls**	**KPIs**
4. The data used for the transformation is incorrect. Data is not reconciled or validated, resulting in inaccurate reporting and results.	■ Data and Account Reconciliation Processes	6. Data Accuracy	■ Percentage of Data Accuracy
5. There is no project management discipline throughout the project.	■ Project Management Process	4. Project Sponsor 5. Project Management 9. Project Implementation Approval 10. Post-implementation Review	■ Number of Project Milestones Achieved on Time
6. Solution results are implemented without testing the functionality.	■ Project Management Process	8. Testing and Training	■ Number of Issues Identified in the Testing Process
7. Solution users are not trained on how to use all the capabilities of the system.	■ Project Management Process	8. Testing and Training	■ Number of Users Trained
8. There are no measurements to determine project success.	■ Project Management Process	7. Transformation Metrics	■ Number of Users Relative to the Number of Licenses Purchased ■ Number of Processes Performed on New Solution ■ Percentage Cost-per-Transaction Reduction ■ ROI for Solutions Implemented ■ Amount of New Revenue Attributed to Digital Investments ■ Percentage of Data Accuracy

Process: Trends, Process Transformation, and Digitization			
Process Risk	**Recommended Policies**	**Internal Controls**	**KPIs**
9. **The implementation of the project is not approved.** The project is implemented without validation of success factors.	▪ Project Management Process	9. Project Implementation Approval	▪ Number of Users Relative to the Number of Licenses Purchased ▪ Number of Processes Performed on New Solution ▪ Percentage Cost-per-Transaction Reduction ▪ ROI for Solutions Implemented ▪ Amount of New Revenue Attributed to Digital Investments ▪ Percentage of Data Accuracy
10. **There is no post-implementation project review to determine the impact and results on business processes.** Lessons learned are not documented or communicated.	▪ Project Management Process	10. Post-implementation Review	▪ Number of Users Relative to the Number of Licenses Purchased ▪ Number of Processes Performed on New Solution ▪ Percentage Cost-per-Transaction Reduction ▪ ROI for Solutions Implemented ▪ Amount of New Revenue Attributed to Digital Investments ▪ Percentage of Data Accuracy

PART FOUR

Glossary

Access Controls These are the procedures and controls that limit or detect access to critical network assets to guard against loss of integrity, confidentiality, accountability, or availability. Access controls provide reasonable assurance that critical resources are protected against unauthorized modification, disclosure, loss, or impairment.

Account Number Defines the accounting transaction type for the transaction and includes a system-generated number tied to a company's chart of accounts.

Accounting Policy Basic concepts, assumptions, policies, methods and practices used by a company for maintaining accounting principles and summarization into financial statements as prescribed by GAAP (generally accepted accounting principles). A policy can be described as what needs to happen to ensure that accounting cycles are working within boundaries of internal control.

Accounting Procedure The routine steps in processing accounting data during an accounting period. In sequence, (1) occurrence of the transaction, (2) classification of each transaction in chronological order (journalizing), (3) recording the classified data in ledger accounts (posting), (4) preparation of financial statements, and (5) closing of nominal accounts. A procedure ensures that a policy is properly executed and explains the how. Other procedures or policies will be referenced if applicable.

Accruals Accruals are adjustments for (1) revenues that have been earned but are not yet recorded in the accounts, and (2) expenses that have been incurred but are not yet recorded in the accounts. The accruals need to be added via adjusting entries so that the financial statements report these amounts.[1]

Artificial Intelligence (AI) AI textbooks define the field as the study of intelligent agents, meaning any device that perceives its environment and takes actions that maximize its chance of successfully achieving its goals. Colloquially, the term *artificial intelligence* is often used to describe machines (or computers) that mimic cognitive functions that humans associate with the human mind, such as learning and problem-solving.

Assertions Financial statement assertions are claims made by an organization's management regarding its financial statements. The assertions form a theoretical basis from which external auditors develop a set of audit procedures confirming that all of the information contained within the financial statements has been accurately recorded.

Audit Committee The audit committee's role includes the oversight of financial reporting, the monitoring of accounting policies, the oversight of any external auditors, regulatory compliance, and discussion of risk management policies with management. The audit committee may approve and review the status of the company's annual internal audit plan and is usually apprised of any suspicions of fraud reported via the ethics hotline process.

Benchmarking According to Wikipedia, "benchmarking is the practice of comparing business processes and performance metrics to industry bests and best practices from other companies. Dimensions typically measured are quality, time, and cost."[2]

Best Practices Implementation of the highest quality, most advantageous, repeatable processes achieved by applying the experiences of those with the acquired skill or proficiency. Best practices are achieved by implementing processes, templates, and checklists that will improve cycle time, reduce cost, and provide the foundation for continuous improvement.

Blockchain   Blockchain is an open ledger in which every transaction on a network is recorded and available for authorized participants to see and verify. It can be thought of as a secured spreadsheet, in that it sits in a cloud where multiple parties can review it but no one can change it. Bitcoin popularized blockchain technology, which was proposed in 2008 in a white paper by Satoshi Nakamoto (pseudonym).

Budget Process   A budget process refers to the process by which companies create and approve an annual budget. Most companies track results on a monthly basis through internal reporting processes where actual expenses are compared with the approved budget for a cost center or operating unit. This monthly review identifies excessive spending, which could reflect a control issue.

Business Continuity Planning   The process of developing advance arrangements and procedures that enable an organization to respond to an event in such a manner that critical business functions continue with planned levels of interruption or essential change.

Business Continuity Program   This is an ongoing program supported and funded by executive staff to ensure that business continuity requirements are assessed, resources are allocated, and recovery strategies and procedures are completed and tested.

Business Unit   A logical element or segment of a company (such as accounting, production, or marketing) representing a specific business function with a definite place on the organizational chart under the domain of a manager. A business unit is also called a department, division, or functional area.

Cash Pooling   The primary target of cash pooling is the optimization and use of surplus funds of all companies in a group in order to reduce external debt and increase available liquidity. Interest benefits in particular can be achieved in multiple ways for pool participants on the payable side and on the receivable side.

Change in Accounting Principle   When a company adopts an alternative generally accepted accounting principle in place of a previously used principle to account for the same type of transaction or event, that action is called a change in accounting principle. The term *accounting principle* includes not only accounting principles and practices but also the methods of applying them.

Cifas   "Cifas is a not-for-profit fraud prevention membership organization. Cifas is the UK's leading fraud prevention service, managing the largest database of instances of fraudulent conduct in the country. Throughout the UK, Cifas experts and services help protect individuals and organizations from the growing and increasingly sophisticated threat of fraud and financial crime. Since 1988, Cifas has helped its members and customers protect themselves from billions of pounds worth of fraud losses."[3]

Collection Effectiveness Index (CEI)   "The collection effectiveness index, also known as the CEI, is a calculation of a company's ability to retrieve its accounts receivable from customers. CEI measures the amount collected during a time period against the amount from receivables in the same time period."[4]

Common Chart of Accounts   In accounting, a common chart of accounts is a numbered list of the accounts that comprise a company's general ledger. A company should establish accounting policies and rules for the use of specific account numbers. As a best practice, a simplified chart of accounts will enable a faster close. The accounting department should monitor the use of accounts and identify and correct any anomalies.

Company Code   The business transactions relevant for financial accounting are entered, saved, and evaluated at the company-code level. You usually create a legally independent company in ERP systems (e.g. the applicable ERP system) with one company code.

Compensating Control   In some cases, an employee will perform all activities within a process; under this scenario, SoD does not exist and risk cannot be identified or mitigated in a timely manner. As a result, the implementation of additional compensating controls should be considered. A compensating control reduces the vulnerabilities in ineffectively segregated functions. A compensating control can reduce the risk of errors, omissions, irregularities, and deficiencies, which can improve the overall business process.

Consolidation Software An effective and consistent reporting process requires a reliable database, which is often achieved by using dedicated consolidation and reporting software. This software allows for an automated process, a reliable audit trail, and a protected database.

Contingency Plan A contingency plan is defined as a set of measures to deal with emergencies caused by failures due to human action or natural disasters that impact the operation of a company. Contingency planning includes the prearranged plans and procedures that critical business functions will execute to ensure business continuity until computer and telecommunications facilities are reestablished following a disaster.

Continuous Auditing (CA) CA is an automatic method used to perform auditing activities, such as control and risk assessments, on a more frequent basis. Technology plays a key role in continuous audit activities by helping to automate the identification of exceptions or anomalies, analyze patterns within the digits of key numeric fields, review trends, and test controls, among other activities.

Continuous Controls Monitoring (CCM) Gartner defines "CCM as a set of technologies to reduce business losses through continuous monitoring, reducing the cost of audits through continuous auditing of the controls in fiscal and other transactional applications."[5]

Contra Revenue " Contra revenue is a deduction from the gross revenue reported by a business, which results in net revenue. Contra revenue transactions are recorded in one or more contra revenue accounts, which usually have a debit balance (as opposed to the credit balance in the typical revenue account)."[6]

Controller A financial controller is a senior-level executive who acts as the head of accounting and oversees the preparation of financial reports, such as balance sheets and income statements A financial controller, who may also be referred to as a financial comptroller, usually reports to an organization's chief financial officer (CFO).

Corruption Perceptions Index "The corruption perceptions index is produced by Transparency International and ranks 180 countries and territories by their perceived levels of public-sector corruption according to experts and businesspeople. It uses a scale of 0 to 100, where 0 is highly corrupt and 100 is very clean. More than two-thirds of countries score below 50 on 2018's index, with an average score of just 43. It reveals that the continued failure of most countries to significantly control corruption is contributing to a crisis in democracy around the world. While there are exceptions, the data shows that despite some progress, most countries are failing to make serious inroads against corruption."[7]

Cost Center The designated accounting location in which costs are incurred, defined as a subunit of a legal entity and in some cases the business unit depending on how the business unit code is utilized. All cost centers are assigned to a company's legal entity; however, only some cost centers may be assigned to business or operating units. The assignment of a cost center is distinguished by an area of responsibility, location, or accounting method.

Cost Management Cost management comprises the fiscal processes, reporting, and analytics that support cost accounting, inventory accounting, and cost analysis.

Counterparty A counterparty is the other party that participates in a financial transaction; every transaction must have a counterparty in order for the transaction to go through. More specifically, every buyer of an asset must be paired up with a seller who is willing to sell, and vice versa.

Countertrade "Countertrade is a reciprocal form of international trade in which goods or services are exchanged for other goods or services rather than for hard currency. This type of international trade is more common in developing countries with limited foreign exchange or credit facilities. Countertrade can be classified into three broad categories: barter, counterpurchase, and offset."[8]

Critical Application A critical business application is one that a company must have to support major revenue activities, movement of goods to customers, a strategic manufacturing process, or to fulfill contractual or regulatory obligations. In addition, an application is defined as critical if its availability is deemed by management to be vital to the continued functioning of company business. Examples of critical applications are customer service support, order entry, inventory control, manufacturing resource planning, purchasing, warehouse control, quality assurance, and finance.

Critical Process   A critical business process is one that if disrupted or made unavailable for any length of time will have a significant negative impact on the success of the business.

Customer Relationship Management (CRM)   CRM is an approach to managing a company's interaction with current and potential customers. CRM systems use technology to manage a company's relationships and interactions with customers and potential customers. Such systems use data analysis about customers' history with a company to improve business relationships with customers, specifically focusing on customer retention and ultimately driving sales growth.

Cycle Counting   Cycle counting is a popular inventory counting solution that allows businesses to count a number of items in a number of areas within the warehouse without having to count the entire inventory. Cycle counting is a sampling technique where the count for the whole warehouse is inferred from the count of a certain number of items.

Cycle Time   Cycle time is the total time from the beginning to the completion of a process. Cycle time includes process time, during which a unit is acted upon to bring it closer to an output, and delay time, during which a unit of work is spent waiting to take the next action.

Data Model   A data model establishes data definitions and processes for reference, ensures data rules are utilized, and provides a schematic view of the underlying components comprising the data that drives the fiscal function.

Days Payable Outstanding (DPO)   "DPO refers to the average number of days it takes a company to pay back its accounts payable. Therefore, DPO measures how well a company is managing its accounts payable. A DPO of 20 means that on average it takes a company 20 days to pay back its suppliers."[9]

Days Sales Outstanding (DSO)   DSO represents the average number of days it takes credit sales to be converted into cash or how long it takes a company to collect its account receivables. DSO can be calculated by dividing the total accounts receivable during a certain time frame by the total net credit sales. This number is then multiplied by the number of days in the period of time.

Debt Covenant   Debt covenants are agreements between a company and a creditor, usually stating limits or thresholds for certain financial ratios that the company may not breach.

Delegation of Authority (DoA)   As one of the critical corporate controls for a company, a DoA policy is sometimes confused with an SoD policy. Although the two both provide the foundation of good internal controls and corporate governance, the DoA policy focuses on the establishment of approval levels for specific business transactions to specific individuals within the company.

Disaster   A disaster is defined as a loss of computing or telecommunication resources to the extent that routine recovery measures cannot restore normal service levels within 24 hours, impacting the company's business significantly.

Due Diligence   Due diligence is the investigation or exercise of care that a reasonable business or person is expected to take before entering into an agreement or contract with another party, or an act with a certain standard of care. It can be a legal obligation, but the term will more commonly apply to voluntary investigations.

Enterprise Resource Planning (ERP) System   An ERP system is business process management software that allows an organization to use a system of integrated applications to manage the business and automate many back-office functions related to technology, services, and human resources. Examples of ERP systems are the applicable ERP system, Oracle, Microsoft Dynamics, and Sage.

External Audit   "An external audit is a periodic audit conducted by an independent qualified auditor with the aim to determine whether the accounting records for a business are complete and accurate. According to Wikipedia, "an external auditor performs an audit, in accordance with specific laws or rules, of the financial statements of a company, government entity, other legal entity, or organization, and is independent of the entity being audited. Users of these entities' fiscal information, such as investors, government agencies, and the general public, rely on the external auditor to present an unbiased and independent audit report." The Sarbanes–Oxley Act, or SOX, has imposed stringent requirements on external auditors in their evaluation of internal controls and financial reporting for public companies listed on stock exchanges in the United States.[10]

External Reporting   Companies prepare external financial statements to report their business information to outside observers, including potential investors, stakeholders, shareholders, and the SEC.

Federal Risk and Authorization Management Program (FedRAMP)   FedRAMP "is a government-wide program that provides a standardized approach to security assessment, authorization, and continuous monitoring for cloud products and services. FedRAMP enables agencies to rapidly adapt from old, insecure legacy IT to mission-enabling, secure, and cost-effective cloud-based IT. FedRAMP created and manages a core set of processes to ensure effective, repeatable cloud security for the government. FedRAMP established a mature marketplace to increase utilization and familiarity with cloud services while facilitating collaboration across government through open exchanges of lessons learned, use cases, and tactical solutions."[11]

Financial Accounting Standards Board (FASB)   FASB is a private, nonprofit organization standard-setting body whose primary purpose is to establish and improve GAAP within the United States in the public's interest.

Financial Architecture   The structure in which components, processes, and systems for a finance function are organized and integrated. Financial architecture is used to set the foundation for all finance and accounting processes and systems.

Financial Hierarchy   A company's financial hierarchy is usually structured with retained earnings at the top, followed by debt financing, and then external equity financing at the bottom. It is supported by a structure of cost centers.

Fixed Assets   A fixed asset is a long-term tangible piece of property that a firm owns and uses in its operations to generate income. Fixed assets are not expected to be consumed or converted into cash within one to two years. Fixed assets are known alternatively as property, plant, and equipment, PP&E, and capital assets.

Financial Planning and Analysis (FP&A)   FP&A is a group within a company's finance organization that provides senior management with a forecast of the company's profit and loss (income statement) and operating performance for the upcoming quarter and year.

Fiscal Close   The fiscal close process establishes a cutoff of fiscal activity so that a company can generate monthly, quarterly and annual financial reports for stakeholders and shareholders.

Forecast Process   A fiscal forecast is a financial management tool that presents estimated information based on past, current, and projected fiscal conditions. It helps to identify future revenue and expenditure trends that may have an immediate or long-term influence on strategic goals.

Fraud   According to the US Department of Justice, "fraud occurs when a person or business intentionally deceives another with promises of goods, services, or financial benefits that do not exist, were never intended to be provided, or were misrepresented. Typically, victims give money but never receive what they paid for. Millions of people in the United States are victims of fraud crimes each year. "Virtually anyone can fall prey to fraudulent crimes. Con artists do not pass over anyone due to such factors as a person's age, finances, educational level, gender, race, culture, ability, or geographic location. In fact, fraud perpetrators often target certain groups based on these factors."[12]

General Accounting   Financial processes that support the fiscal close, general accounting, and intercompany processes.

General Data Protection Regulation (GDPR) "The GDPR applies to personal data, meaning any information relating to an identifiable person who can be directly or indirectly identified, in particular by reference to an identifier. This definition provides for a wide range of personal identifiers to constitute personal data, including name, identification number, location data, or online identifier, reflecting changes in technology and the way organizations collect information about people."[13]

Global Technology Audit Guide (GTAG) GTAG was developed by the Institute of Internal Auditors in straightforward business language to address a timely issue related to IT management, control, and security.

Hedging Hedging against investment risk means strategically using financial instruments or market strategies to offset the risk of any adverse price movements. Hedging, for the most part, is a technique not by which you will make money but by which you can reduce potential loss.

Highly Significant Transaction A highly significant transaction is one that could reasonably result in a 10% or greater variance in revenues or would result in a 5% or greater variance in the net worth (assets minus liabilities).

Hire-to-Retire (H2R) As defined on Chapter 5 of this author's book, *The Internal Controls Toolkit*,[14] H2R is a human resources process that includes everything that needs to be done over the course of an employee's career with a company. The following are high-level process steps:

■ **Human Resources Planning:** Human resource management planning such as work design.
■ **Recruiting:** Recruiting processes such as relationship building, employer branding, job posting, job fairs, and interviewing.
■ **Employee Management:** Everything that is required to manage an employee such as onboarding, performance management, training and development, and benefits and compensation processes.
■ **Redeploy:** The processes related to an employee being redeployed such as foreign work assignments.
■ **Payroll:** The control and delivery of payroll.
■ **Retire:** The processes related to an employee leaving such as exit interviews and retirement benefits.

Human Capital Management (HCM) HCM is considered to be essential for acquiring and retaining high-performing employees. HCM plays an essential role in helping the organization's human resources department increase the overall productivity of employees. HCM functions are focused on hiring talented employees, providing orientation and onboarding best practices, training employees to best utilize their skills and talents, and retaining employees by providing job satisfaction and a well-defined career path.

Imprest System According to Wikipedia, "The imprest system is a form of financial accounting system. The most common imprest system is the petty cash system. The base characteristic of an imprest system is that a fixed amount is reserved, which after a certain period of time or when circumstances require, because money was spent, it will be replenished."[15]

Intercompany Accounting Intercompany accounting is the process of recording financial transactions between different legal entities within the same parent company.

Internal Audit The internal audit department is an independent, objective assurance and consulting activity designed to add value, improve an organization's operations, and identify and mitigate risk.

Internal Controls The integrated framework approach defines internal control as a "process, effected by an entity's board of directors, management, and other personnel, designed to provide reasonable assurance regarding the achievement of objectives in the following categories: (a) reliability of financial reporting, and (b) effectiveness and efficiency of operations, and compliant with applicable laws and regulations."[16]

Internal Reporting Internal financial reporting traditionally means compiling and distributing generic reports that show a company's past, short-term fiscal performance with budget results. Internal reporting can also be generated by divisions, profit centers, and regions.

International Accounting Standards (IAS) IAS are older accounting standards that were replaced in 2001 by International Financial Reporting Standards (IFRS), issued by the International Accounting Standards Board (IASB), an independent, not-for-profit organization, and the IFRS Foundation.

International Financial Reporting Standards (IFRS)   IFRS standards were issued by the IFRS Foundation and the IASB to provide a common global language for business affairs so that company accounts are understandable and comparable across international boundaries.

Internet of Things (IoT)   IoT is a system of interrelated computing devices and mechanical and digital machines provided with unique identifiers and the ability to transfer data over a network without requiring human-to-human or human-to-computer interaction.

Information Technology Laboratory (ITL)   ITL is one of six research laboratories within NIST, a globally recognized and trusted source of high-quality, independent, and unbiased research and data. ITL's mission, to cultivate trust in IT and metrology, is accomplished using its world-class measurement and testing facilities and encompassing a wide range of areas of computer science, mathematics, statistics, and systems engineering.

IT General Control (ITGC)   ITGCs are the basic controls that can be applied to IT systems, such as applications, operating systems, databases, and supporting IT infrastructure. The objectives of ITGCs are to ensure the integrity of the data and processes that the systems support.

Key Performance Indicator (KPI)   A KPI is a measurable value or metric that demonstrates how effectively a process is working.

Market Counterparty   Within the financial services sector, the term *market counterparty* is used to refer to governments, national banks, national monetary authorities, and international monetary organizations, such as the World Bank Group, which acts as the ultimate guarantor for loans and indemnities. The term may also be applied, in a more general sense, to companies acting in this role.[17]

Mergers and Acquisitions (M&A)   In a merger, the boards of directors for two companies approve the combination and seek shareholders' approval. After the merger, the acquired company ceases to exist and becomes part of the acquiring company.

MiFID II   The second Markets in Financial Instruments Directive is a legislative framework instituted by the EU to regulate financial markets in the bloc and improve protections for investors. Its aim is to standardize practices across the EU and restore confidence in the financial industry, especially after the 2008 financial crisis.

National Institute of Standards and Technology (NIST)   According to its website, "The National Institute of Standards and Technology (NIST) was founded in 1901 and is now part of the US Department of Commerce. NIST is one of the nation's oldest physical science laboratories. Congress established the agency to remove a major challenge to US industrial competitiveness at the time—a second-rate measurement infrastructure that lagged behind the capabilities of the United Kingdom, Germany, and other economic rivals."[18]

Net Income   Net income is equal to net earnings (profit), calculated as sales less cost of goods sold, selling, general and administrative expenses, operating expenses, depreciation, interest, taxes, and other expenses.

Net Value   A net (sometimes written "nett") value is the resultant amount after accounting for the sum or difference of two or more variables. In economics, it is frequently used to imply the remaining value after accounting for a specific, commonly understood deduction.

Order-to-Cash (O2C)   Order-to-cash (OTC or O2C) is a set of business processes that involve receiving and fulfilling customer requests for goods or services. It is a top-level, or context-level, term used by management to describe the finance-related component of customer sales

PEST Analysis   PEST analysis is a simple and widely used tool that helps analyze the political, economic, socio-cultural, and technological changes in a business environment. Looking at the impacts of these four quadrants provides an understanding of big-picture changes and exposures that impact a company.

Physical Inventory   Physical inventory is an actual count of the goods in stock. A physical inventory can involve counting, weighing, and otherwise measuring items, as well as asking third parties for counts of inventory items that have been consigned to them.

Policy Controls   Policy controls are the general principles and guides for action that influence decisions. They indicate the limits to choices and the parameters or rules to be followed by a company and its employees. Major policies should be reviewed, approved, and communicated by senior management. Policies are derived by:
■   Considering the business environment and process objectives   Identifying the potential categories of risks that the environment poses towards achievement of the objectives

Procedure Controls   Procedure controls prescribe how actions are to be performed consistent with policies. Procedures should be developed by those who understand day-to-day actions.

Process   A process is a systematic series of actions directed to some end, and a continuous action or operation taking place in a definite manner.

Process Flow   A process flow communicates the actual process currently in place. It is a picture of the flow and sequence of work steps, tasks, or activities and includes the flow or sequence of steps throughout the process, the person responsible for each task, and the decision points and their impact on the flow of work.

Procure-to-Pay (P2P)   Procure-to-pay is a term used in the software industry to designate a specific subdivision of the procurement process. Procure-to-pay systems enable the integration of the purchasing department with the accounts payable department and consider all the supporting processes.

Profit Center   A profit center is an area of responsibility for which an independent operating profit is calculated.

Project   According to the Project Management Institute, a project is temporary in that it has a defined beginning and end in time, and therefore defined scope and resources. Furthermore, a project is unique in that it is not a routine operation, but a specific set of operations designed to accomplish a singular goal.

Project Accounting   Project accounting is a specific form of accounting that corresponds to a defined project. This accounting process helps to adequately track, report, and analyze fiscal results and implications.

Public Accounting Oversight Board (PCAOB)   PCAOB is a nonprofit corporation established by the US Congress to oversee the audits of public companies in order to protect investors and the public interest by promoting informative, accurate, and independent audit reports. PCAOB also oversees the audits of brokers and dealers, including compliance reports filed pursuant to federal securities laws, to promote investor protection.

Record-to-Report (R2R)   According to Wikipedia, "R2R is a finance and accounting management process which involves collecting, processing and delivering relevant, timely and accurate information used for providing strategic, financial and operational feedback to understand how a business is performing."[19]

Related Party   A related party is a person or an entity that is related to the reporting entity. A person or a close member of that person's family is related to a reporting entity if that person has control, joint control, or significant influence over the entity or is a member of its key management personnel.

Request for Information (RFI)   Some organizations may choose to initiate an RFI, which focuses on obtaining information from solution providers. The RFI is not as formal as the RFP process, but may require similar information.

Request for Proposal (RFP)   An RFP is a document that reflects the detailed requirements by a prospective buyer in order to receive vendor offerings. Usually dedicated to automation solutions, an RFP is issued to select any kind of products (tangibles) and services (nontangibles).

Review Controls   These controls include an ongoing self-assessment process, as required by the Sarbanes–Oxley Act of 2002. A self-assessment is a series of questions that validate the effectiveness of the control environment. A self-assessment must be conducted every fiscal quarter; in some situations, the manager of the operating unit may elect to conduct a self-assessment test more frequently. It is imperative that all weaknesses found in the testing process are remediated through a corrective action and follow-up process.

Revenue Revenue is the amount of money that a company actually receives during a specific fiscal period, including discounts and deductions for returned merchandise. It is the top line or gross income figure from which costs are subtracted to determine net income.

Revenue Recognition Revenue is one of the most important measures used by investors in assessing a company's performance and prospects. However, previous revenue recognition guidance differs between GAAP and IFRS—and many believe both standards are in need of improvement.

Return on Investment (ROI) ROI is a performance measure used to evaluate the efficiency of an investment. ROIs are also used in the decision-making process when selecting an automated solution, new equipment, or other capital expenditures.

Roll Forward According to VentureLine, "in accounting, this is the systematic establishment of new accounting period balances by using (rolling forward) prior accounting period data. There are two approaches: (1) Roll forward both asset and liabilities on a consistent basis from a consistent earlier date (possibly the last annual review) or, (2) take the most up-to-date asset and liability figures as the starting point (which may be at different dates) to produce roll-forward estimates of assets and liabilities.

In securities, roll forward is when an investor replaces an old options position with a new one having a later expiration date but the same strike price."[20]

Sarbanes–Oxley (SOX) Act 2002 SOX can be divided into three main points:

1. The scope of an external audit firm has been restricted in which CPAs no longer have the right to set standards for their practice.
2. There are new duties for boards of directors in general and for audit committees in particular. Corporate governance provisions include a required code of ethics or standards of business conduct.
3. There are new requirements for the CEO and CFO. Each SEC filing (10-K and 10-Q) stating that:
    a. The report fairly represents in all material respects the company's operations and fiscal condition.
    b. The report does not contain any material misstatements or omit to state a material fact necessary in order to make the statements made, in light of the circumstances under which the statements were made, not misleading.
    c. The report containing financial statements complies with Section 13(a) or 15(d) of the Securities and Exchange Act of 1934.
    d. The company's control system is in place and effective.

Securities and Exchange Commission (SEC) The SEC is an independent agency of the US federal government responsible for protecting investors, maintaining fair and orderly functioning of securities markets, and facilitating capital formation. The SEC has a three-part mission: protect investors; maintain fair, orderly, and efficient markets; and facilitate capital formation.

Segregation of Duties (SoD) An SoD control is one of the most important controls that your company can have. Adequate SoD reduces the likelihood that errors (intentional or unintentional) will remain undetected by providing for separate processing by different individuals at various stages of a transaction and for independent reviews of the work performed. The SoD control provides four primary benefits: (1) the risk of a deliberate fraud is mitigated as the collusion of two or more persons would be required in order to circumvent controls, (2) the risk of legitimate errors is mitigated as the likelihood of detection is increased, (3) the cost of corrective actions is mitigated as errors are generally detected relatively earlier in their lifecycle, and (4) the organization's reputation for integrity and quality is enhanced through a system of checks and balances.

Significant Deficiency This is a single control deficiency, or combination of control deficiencies, that adversely affects the company's ability to initiate, authorize, record, process, or report external fiscal data reliably. There is more than a remote likelihood that a misstatement of the company's annual or interim financial statements that is more than inconsequential will not be prevented or detected.

Single-Factor Authentication   An authentication method based on "something you know," where the primary method of identifying the user is a password.

Standard Operating Procedures   Standard operating procedures are formal written guidelines that denote daily operational procedures, assist in long-range planning, and provide instructions for incident responses.

Standards of Internal Control   These standards define a series of internal controls that address the risks associated with key business processes, subprocesses, and entity-level processes. They have resulted from over 30 years of experience in the finance, accounting, and internal controls field. The standards are a body of work that leverages experience at large technology companies. They were developed when implementing internal control programs for approximately 80 business processes and subprocesses, which include payroll, the fiscal closing process, logistics, procurement, accounts payable, and accounts receivable.

Super User   A user of an ERP with special privileges needed to administer and maintain the system, or a system administrator. The special privileges may include the ability to process a fiscal transaction and make changes in the general ledger to modify the transaction. Super-user privileges must be monitored to ensure that access rights are not used to incorrectly modify or falsify a transaction, which would result in risk to the company.

Supervisory Controls   Supervisory controls are situations in which managers ensure that all employees understand their responsibilities and authorities, and the assurance that procedures are being followed within the operating unit. A supervisory control can also be considered as a compensating control in which a supervisory review is necessary to augment SoD controls.

Supply Chain Management   In commerce, supply chain management – the management of the flow of goods and services – involves the movement and storage of raw materials, of work-in-process inventory, and of finished goods from point of origin to point of consumption.

Supply Chain Finance (SCF)   SCF is a set of tech-based business and financing processes that lower costs and improve efficiency for the parties involved in a transaction. SCF works best when the buyer has a better credit rating than the seller and can thus access capital at a lower cost. Unlike traditional factoring, where a supplier wants to finance its receivables, reverse factoring is a financing solution initiated by the ordering party in order to help its suppliers to finance its receivables more easily and at a lower interest rate than what would normally be offered.

SWOT Analysis   According to Wikipedia, "SWOT analysis (or a SWOT matrix) is a strategic planning technique used to help a person or organization identify strengths, weaknesses, opportunities, and threats related to business competition or project planning. It is intended to specify the objectives of the business venture or project and identify the internal and external factors that are favorable and unfavorable to achieving those objectives."[21]

Systems Access Policy   A systems access policy applies to both domestic and international financial and operational systems and is an integral part of SoD. The scope of a systems access policy is worldwide and applies both to the approval of new access requests and the establishment of an internal controls environment for general system access. A systems access policy ensures that transactions cannot be systematically generated to create SoD control issues. There are two types of SoD controls that must be in place: (1) control of security object privileges, and (2) control of multiple security profiles.

System for Award Management (SAM)   SAM is an official website of the US government. There is no cost to use SAM. Controllers can use this site to:
◼ "Register to do business with the US government
◼ Update or renew your entity registration
◼ Check status of an entity registration
◼ Search for entity registration and exclusion records"[22]

Transparency International "Transparency International is one global movement sharing one vision: a world in which government, business, civil society and the daily lives of people are free of corruption. The organization focuses on the creation of international anticorruption conventions, the prosecution of corrupt leaders and seizures of their illicitly gained riches, national elections won and lost on tackling corruption, and companies held accountable for their behavior both at home and abroad."[23]

Two-Factor Authentication Two-factor authentication is based on "something you have plus something you know." It requires processing something that is unique to the individual and a PIN that ensures that the individual is indeed who they say they are. Time-dependent random number generators and cryptographic techniques are examples of such an authentication technique.

Work Instruction A work instruction is a step-by-step document that depicts the actions needed to complete an activity at the transaction level and is a detailed document that may include "keystroke" information. This is a very detailed how-to document.

Endnote

1 Averkamp, Harold (n.d.). What are accruals? AccountingCoach (accessed January 1, 2019). https://www.accountingcoach.com/blog/what-are-accruals.

2 Wikipedia (n.d.). Benchmarking entry (accessed March 2, 2019). https://en.wikipedia.org/wiki/Benchmarking.

3 Cifas (n.d.). Who we are. Cifas website, What Is Cifas? (accessed April 13, 2020). https://www.cifas.org.uk/about-cifas/what-is-cifas.

4 Wilkinson, Jim (2016). Collection effectiveness index (CEI). The Strategic CFO website, WikiCFO (May 19; accessed on May 4, 2020). https://strategiccfo.com/cei.

5 Gartner (n.d.). Continuous controls monitoring (CCM) definition. Gartner website, Information Technology Glossary (accessed March 2, 2019). https://www.gartner.com/it-glossary/continuous-controls-monitoring-ccm.

6 AccountingTools (2019). Contra revenue (April 18; accessed July 30, 2020). https://www.accountingtools.com/articles/what-is-contra-revenue.html.

7 Transparency International (2018). Corruption Perceptions Index 2018 (accessed April 13, 2020). https://www.transparency.org/cpi2018.

8 Kenton, Will (2020). Countertrade definition. Investopedia, Advanced FOREX Trading Concepts (March 28; accessed April 13, 2020). https://www.investopedia.com/terms/c/countertrade.asp.

9 Corporate Finance Institute (n.d.). What is days payable outstanding? CFI website (accessed May 4, 2020). https://corporatefinanceinstitute.com/resources/knowledge/accounting/days-payable-outstanding.

10 Wikipedia (n.d.). External auditor entry (accessed March 2, 2019). https://en.wikipedia.org/wiki/External_auditor.

11 FedRAMP (n.d.). About us. FedRAMP website (accessed April 13, 2020). https://www.fedramp.gov/about.

12 US Department of Justice, US Attorney's Office – District of Alaska (2020). Financial fraud crimes; financial fraud crime victims. US DOJ website, US Attorney's Office – District of Alaska (February 5; accessed May 4, 2020). https://www.justice.gov/usao-ak/financial-fraud-crimes.

13 European Union (n.d.). General Data Protection Regulation (GDPR). EU website, GDPR FAQs (accessed January 4, 2019). https://eugdpr.org/the-regulation/gdpr-faqs.

14 Doxey, Christine H. (2019). The hire to retire (H2R) process. *The Internal Controls Toolkit*. Wiley F&A, ch. 5, p. 133.

15 Wikipedia (n.d.). Imprest system entry (accessed May 4, 2020). https://en.wikipedia.org/wiki/Imprest_system.

16 COSO (2013). Integrated Framework Executive Summary (accessed August 3, 2020). https://www.coso.org/Documents/990025P-Executive-Summary-final-may20.pdf.

17 Wikipedia (n.d.). Counterparty entry (accessed April 13, 2020). https://en.wikipedia.org/wiki/Counterparty.

18 National Institute of Standards and Technology (2017). About NIST. NIST website (June 14; accessed April 13, 2020). https://www.nist.gov/about-nist.

19 Wikipedia (n.d.). Record to report entry (accessed May 4, 2020). https://en.wikipedia.org/wiki/Record_to_report.

20 VentureLine. Definition of roll forward. VentureLine website (accessed August 3, 2020). https://www.ventureline.com/accounting-glossary/R/roll-forward-definition/.

21 Wikipedia (n.d.). SWOT analysis entry (accessed August 3, 2020). https://en.wikipedia.org/wiki/SWOT_analysis.

22 System for Award Management (SAM) (n.d.). SAM description (accessed April 13, 2020). https://www.sam.gov/SAM.

23 Transparency International (n.d.). Our organization. Transparency International website (accessed April 13, 2020). https://www.transparency.org/whoweare/organisation.

Index of Controller's Tools

Introduction. This index provides the listing of all the tools for controllers that are included in this book and provides a quick glance at an inventory of all the helpful tools provided.

Index of Controller's Tools

Index of Controller's Tools

Section	Chapter	Chapter Title	Controller's Tool Number	Name of Controller's Tool
2 **STRATEGIC PLANNING AND MERGERS AND ACQUISITIONS RISK**	7	Strategic Planning and Mergers and Acquisitions	15 16	Sample Strategic Plan Table of Contents Mergers and Acquisitions Due Diligence Checklist
3 **INTERNAL CONTROL RISK**	8	Internal Control Program	17 18 19	Roles and Responsibilities for Internal Controls Internal Control Best Practices for Privately Held Companies Leveraging Internal Control Basics to Implement a Control Self-Assessment Program
4 **COMPLIANCE RISK**	9	Regulatory Compliance	20	Regulatory Compliance Toolkit
5 **PAYMENT RISK**		Section Introduction	21	Overview of Payment Business Processes, Subprocesses, Risk Impacts, and Indicators
6 **FINANCIAL OPERATIONS RISK**	13	Record-to-Report	22 23 24 25	Monthly Closing Best Practices 15 Best Practices to Simplify Your Financial Close General Financial Statement Fraud Red Flags Fraud Red Flags for Lenders and Investors
	14	Budgets, Forecasts, and Capital Budgeting	26 27 28 29 30 31 32	Types of Budgeting The Budgeting Process Budget Process Best Practices Types of Financial Forecasting Models The Forecasting Process for Small Businesses Controller's Areas of Responsibility for the Capital Budget and Fixed Assets Alternative Methods for Capital Budgeting
	15	Supply Chain Management and Inventory Control	33 34	Blockchain Features That Enable Supply Chain Financing Supply Chain Performance Metrics

Index of Controller's Tools

Section	Chapter	Chapter Title	Controller's Tool Number	Name of Controller's Tool
	16	Treasury and Cash Management	35	Responsibilities of the Treasury Department
			36	What Are the Components of Cash Flow?
			37	Cash Forecasts
			38	Foreign Exchange Policy Development Process
			39	Cash Management Rules for Petty Cash
			40	International Payment Methods
	17	Shared Services and Business Process Outsourcing	41	Five Ways That Human Resources Shared Services Helps Small Business
			42	The Benefits of Implementing Shared Services Centers
			43	Types of Outsourcing Models
			44	The Advantages of Outsourcing
			45	Cost-Benefit Analysis
			46	Information for Supplier Evaluation
			47	Considerations in Implementing Service Level Agreements and Metrics
	18	Dashboards, Data Validation, Analytics, Metrics, and Benchmarking	48	Key Considerations for Dashboard Technology
			49	Types of Benchmarking
			50	Implementing Metrics
7 INFORMATION TECHNOLOGY RISK	19	Information Technology Controls and Cybersecurity	51	Control Objectives for Information and Related Technologies
			52	Other IT Internal Control Frameworks and Considerations
			53	IT Framework and Internal Control Considerations for Small Businesses
			54	Key Components of Successful IT Governance
8 BUSINESS CONTINUITY AND PHYSICAL SECURITY RISK	20	Business Continuity and Physical Security	55	Business Continuity: Personnel
			56	Business Continuity: Information Technology
			57	ISO/IEC 17799:2005

Index of Controller's Tools

Key Performance Indicator Library

Introduction. This library was developed as a reference and summarizes the KPIs that a controller should consider. The library can be used to obtain KPI information for every process that is included in this book. The KPIs provided here can be used to establish or improve the direction of a metrics and analytics program for a defined business process. These KPIs can also be used for internal and external benchmarking activities.

Section	Chapter	Name of Chapter/Process	Key Performance Indicators (KPIs)
1 CORPORATE AND REPUTATIONAL RISK	3	The Controller and Risk Management	▪ Number of Risks Identified per Period ▪ Number of Risks Requiring Remediation ▪ Number of Risks That Occurred More Than Once ▪ Predicted Risk Severity Compared to Actual Severity ▪ Number of Risks That Were Not Identified ▪ Cost of Risk Management ▪ Number of Risks Mitigated
	4	The Controller and Ethics	▪ Number of Ethics Issues Reported by Period ▪ Number of Ethics Hotline Calls ▪ Number of Root Causes of Ethics Issues by Type ▪ Number of Fraudulent Activities ▪ Value of Fraudulent Activities ▪ Number of Ethics Issues Remediated ▪ Percentage of Employees Trained ▪ Revenue Impact of Ethics Violations ▪ Media Impact of Ethics Violations ▪ Risk Assessment Results ▪ Self-Assessment Results ▪ Percentage of Employees Trained ▪ Revenue Impact of Ethics Violations

Section	Chapter	Name of Chapter/Process	Key Performance Indicators (KPIs)
	5	The Controller and Corporate Governance	■ Number of Ethics Issues Reported by Period ■ Number of Ethics Hotline Calls ■ Revenue Impact of Ethics Violations ■ Risk Assessment Results ■ Self-Assessment Results ■ Budget Accuracy Percentage ■ Variance Amount per Financial Close ■ Number of Remediation Issues ■ Number of Ethics Issues Reported by Period ■ Number of Ethics Hotline Calls ■ Number of Ethics Issues Remediated ■ Number of Post-Close Adjustments ■ Value of Post-Close Adjustments ■ Average Percentage of Salary Increases per Financial Period ■ Number of Promotions per Quarter ■ Number of Instances Where Salaries Are Above Pay Grades ■ Number of Root Causes of Ethics Issues by Type ■ Number of Fraudulent Activities ■ Value of Fraudulent Activities
1 CORPORATE AND REPUTATIONAL RISK	6	Entity-Level Controls	■ Percentage of Strategic Deliverables Achieved ■ Percentage Budget Accuracy ■ Percentage Revenue Increase ■ Budget Accuracy Percentage ■ Variance Amount per Financial Close ■ Number of Remediation Issues ■ Number of Ethics Issues Reported by Period ■ Number of Ethics Hotline Calls ■ Number of Root Causes of Ethics Issues by Type ■ Number of Ethics Issues Remediated ■ Number of Post-Close Adjustments ■ Value of Post-Close Adjustments ■ Number of Fraudulent Activities ■ Value of Fraudulent Activities ■ Risk Assessment Results ■ Number of Remediation Activities from the Internal Audit Process ■ Number of Remediation Activities from Self-Assessment Results ■ Revenue Impact of Ethics Violations ■ Media Impact of Ethics Violations ■ Risk Assessment Results

Section	Chapter	Name of Chapter/Process	Key Performance Indicators (KPIs)
2 STRATEGIC PLANNING AND MERGERS AND ACQUISITIONS RISK	7	**Strategic Planning and Mergers And Acquisitions**	■ Percentage of Strategic Deliverables Achieved ■ Percentage Budget Accuracy ■ Percentage Revenue Increase ■ Percentage of Company Goals Achieved ■ Percentage of Cost Savings ■ Percentage of Cycle Time Improvements ■ Percentage of Company Goals Achieved ■ Percentage of Critical Operations with Contingency Plans ■ Percentage of Contingency Plans Test ■ Customer Retention Percentage ■ Employee Attrition Rate ■ System Conversion Percentage ■ System Adoption Percentage ■ Actual vs. Budget ■ Number of Outstanding M&A Issues ■ System Conversion Percentage ■ System Adoption Percentage ■ Number of Fraudulent Issues ■ Value of Fraudulent Issues ■ Number of Issues Reported via the Ethics Hotline ■ Types of Issues Reported ■ Number of Employee Complaints
3 INTERNAL CONTROL RISK	8	**Internal Control Program**	■ Number of Outstanding SoD Issues ■ Number of SoD Issues Mitigated ■ Value of Outstanding SoD Issues ■ Number of Outstanding Internal Audit Issues ■ Number of Fraudulent Issues ■ Value of Fraudulent Issues ■ Number of Outstanding Internal Control Issues ■ Employee Attrition Rate ■ Number of Issues Reported via the Ethics Hotline ■ Types of Issues Reported ■ Number of Employee Complaints ■ Cycle Time to Close ■ Number of Post-Close Adjustments ■ Number of Financial Statement Adjustments ■ Number of GL Variances
4 COMPLIANCE RISK	9	**Regulatory Compliance**	■ Number of Noncompliance Incidences per Quarter (by Company and Business Unit) ■ Value of Company Fines ■ Value of Fines per Business Unit ■ Number of Corrective Action Plans ■ Percentage Revenue Increase/Decrease

Section	Chapter	Name of Chapter/Process	Key Performance Indicators (KPIs)
5 PAYMENT RISK	10	Procure-to-Pay 1.0 Procurement 1.1 Supplier Selection and Management	■ Number of Active Suppliers in the Supplier Master File ■ Number and Percentage of One-Time Suppliers ■ Number and Percentage of Fraudulent Suppliers ■ Number and Percentage of Suppliers Under Contract ■ Savings from Strategic Sourcing Initiatives ■ Supplier Service Level Agreements (SLAs) ■ Number and Percentage of Supplier On-boarding Issues ■ Number and Percentage of Compliance Issues Identified ■ Value of Compliance Fines ■ Number and Percentage of Suppliers Under Contract ■ Value of Pricing Issues ■ Inventory Level Trends ■ Number and Value of Excessive Inventory by SKU Number
		Procure-to-Pay 1.0 Procurement 1.2 Contract Management	■ Percentage Compliance with Contract Policy and Approval Process ■ Percentage of Correct Usage of Contract Types ■ Percentage Compliance with Company Templates ■ Number of Pricing Issues Found in Correct Reviews ■ Number of Pricing Issues by Supplier ■ Percentage Supplier Using SLAs ■ SLA Scorecard Results by Supplier ■ Percentage Compliance with Company Templates ■ Percentage Compliance with Right-to-Audit Clauses
5 PAYMENT RISK	10	Procure-to-Pay 1.0 Procurement 1.3 Purchasing and Ordering	■ Number of Non-PO Invoices Processed ■ Number of Fraudulent POs ■ Adherence to PO Policies ■ Number of Import and Export Issues Reported per Period ■ Amount of Compliance Fines Paid per Period ■ Value of Clearing Account Variances ■ Value of Unmatched Invoices per Period ■ Value of Outstanding Accruals per Period ■ Gross and Net Inventory Cycle Count Variances ■ Value of Inventory Write-Offs ■ Value of Pricing Issues ■ Number and Value of Duplicate/Erroneous Payments Identified per Period ■ Number and Value of Duplicate/Erroneous Payments by Reason ■ Unapproved Items in PO Workflow ■ Value of Intellectual Property Loss

Section	Chapter	Name of Chapter/Process	Key Performance Indicators (KPIs)
		Procure-to-Pay	■ Strategic Sourcing Cost Savings
			■ Unapproved Items in PO Workflow
			■ Number of Fraudulent POs
		1.0 Procurement	■ Number of Fraudulent Suppliers
			■ Adherence to PO Policies
		1.4 Reporting, Metrics, and Analytics	■ Cost per RFP
			■ Cost per Contract
			■ Cost per PO
			■ PO Workflow Defects
			■ Unapproved Items in PO Workflow
			■ Non-PO Invoices
			■ Number of P-Cards Implemented
			■ Monthly Supplier Spending on P-Cards
			■ Value of P-Card Rebates
			■ Percentage of Diversity Suppliers Used
			■ Value of Spend for Diversity Suppliers
5 **PAYMENT RISK**	10	**Procure-to-Pay**	■ Number of SoD Reviews Performed
			■ Number of SoD Conflicts Identified
			■ Number of SoD Conflicts Mitigated
		2.0 Accounts Payable	■ Number of System Access Reviews Performed
			■ Number of Systems Access Issues Identified
		2.1 Supplier Master File	■ Number of Systems Access Issues Mitigated
			■ Number of Active Suppliers in the Supplier Master File
			■ Number of Suppliers Paid Electronically
			■ Number of Invoices Paid by Check, P-Card, Wire, and ACH
			■ Number and Value of Payment Issues Stopped per Payment Run
			■ Value of Payment Issues by Payment Type
			■ Number of Controls Reviewed
			■ Cycle Time for the Remediation of Control Issues
			■ Number and Percentage of New Suppliers Established in the Supplier Master File
			■ Number of Active Suppliers in the Supplier Master File
			■ Number of Invalid Suppliers Identified
			■ Number of Suppliers Identified on Compliance "Watch Lists"
			■ Number of Suppliers Requiring Additional Due Diligence Verification
			■ Number of Suppliers Paid Electronically
			■ Number and Value of Payment Issues Stopped per Payment Run
			■ Value of Payment Issues by Payment Type
			■ Number and Percentage of New Suppliers Established in the Supplier Master File
			■ Number of Inactive Suppliers (with No Activity in the Last 18 Months)
			■ Number of Suppliers with Invalid Data (Returned Checks or Other Payment Issues)
			■ Number of Employee and Supplier Master File Cross-Checks Performed
			■ Number of Matches Identified and Remediated

Section	Chapter	Name of Chapter/Process	Key Performance Indicators (KPIs)
5 **PAYMENT RISK**	10	**Procure-to-Pay** **2.0 Accounts Payable** **2.2 Invoice Processing**	■ Number of SoD Reviews Performed ■ Number of SoD Conflicts Identified ■ Number of SoD Conflicts Mitigated ■ Value and Number of Instances of Fraud ■ Percentage of First Time Matches ■ Percentage of On-Time Payments ■ Percentage of Inventory Cycle Count Issues ■ Percentage of Inventory Quality Issues ■ Number and Percentage of New Suppliers Established in the Supplier Master File ■ Number of Active Suppliers in the Supplier Master File ■ Number of Inactive Suppliers (with No Activity in the Last 18 Months) ■ Number of Suppliers with Invalid Data (Returned Checks or Other Payment Issues) ■ Number of Invalid Suppliers Identified ■ Number of Invoices Paid by Check, P-Card, Wire, and ACH ■ Number and Value of Payment Issues Stopped per Payment Run ■ Value of Payment Issues by Payment Type ■ Number of Suppliers Identified on Compliance "Watch Lists" ■ Number of Suppliers Requiring Additional Due Diligence Verification ■ Number and Value of Pre-Close and Post-Close Adjustments ■ Number and Value of Monthly Accruals ■ Number and Value of Outstanding Accruals by Reason

Section	Chapter	Name of Chapter/Process	Key Performance Indicators (KPIs)
5 **PAYMENT RISK**	10	**Procure-to-Pay** **2.0 Accounts Payable** **2.3 Payment Process**	■ Number of SoD Reviews Performed ■ Number of SoD Conflicts Identified and Mitigated ■ Number and Value of Payment Issues and Errors Identified and Mitigated ■ Value of Payment Issues by Payment Type ■ Percentage and Number of Invoices Paid by Check, P-Card, Wire, and ACH ■ Number and Value of Payment Issues Stopped per Payment Run ■ Number of Inactive Suppliers (With No Activity in the Last 18 Months) ■ Number of Suppliers with Invalid Data (Returned Checks or Other Payment Issues) ■ Number of Invalid Suppliers Identified ■ Number of Suppliers Identified on Compliance "Watch Lists" ■ Number of Suppliers Requiring Additional Due Diligence Verification ■ Number and Value of Pre-Close and Post-Close Adjustments ■ Number and Value of Monthly Accruals ■ Number and Value of Outstanding Accruals by Reason
5 **PAYMENT RISK**	10	**Procure-to-Pay** **2.0 Accounts Payable** **2.4 Accounting Process**	■ Number of GL Accounts Reconciled per Month ■ Value and Aging of Variances ■ Cycle Time to Complete the Close ■ Number and Value of Adjusting Entries ■ Number and Value of Pre-Close and Post-Close Adjustments ■ Number and Value of Monthly Accruals ■ Number and Value of Outstanding Accruals by Reason ■ Number and Value of Unclaimed Supplier Payments ■ Number and Value of Escheatment Items by State

Section	Chapter	Name of Chapter/Process	Key Performance Indicators (KPIs)
		Procure-to-Pay 2.0 Accounts Payable 2.5 Customer Service	■ Average Customer Service Ratings ■ Number and Type of Customer Service Inquiries (Internal and External) ■ Source of Customer Service Inquiries ■ Value and Percentage of Payment Issues Identified ■ Value and Percentage of Payment Issues Corrected ■ Payment Issues by Supplier ■ Cycle Time for Resolution ■ Adherence to Established SLAs ■ Number of AP Payment Process Impacts Identified ■ Number of AP Process Impacts Implemented
		Procure-to-Pay 2.0 Accounts Payable 2.6 Reporting, Metrics, and Analytics	■ Number and Percentage of Payment Issues Identified and Stopped ■ Value of Cost Savings Opportunities Identified in the AP Process ■ Strategic Sourcing Cost Savings ■ Percentage and Number of Fraudulent Payments ■ Number of Fraudulent Suppliers ■ Percentage Adherence to AP Policies ■ Percentage of E-invoices Processed ■ Cost per Invoice ■ Cycle Time to Process an Invoice ■ PO Workflow Defects ■ Unapproved Items in PO Workflow ■ Non-PO Invoices
		Procure-to-Pay 2.0 Accounts Payable 2.7 P-Cards	■ Number of SoD Reviews Performed ■ Number of SoD Conflicts Identified and Mitigated ■ Number and Value of P-Card Payment Issues and Errors Identified and Mitigated ■ Number and Percentage of P-Card Issues as Compared to Supplier Payments Issued ■ Number and Percentage of P-Card Violations ■ Number of P-Cards Issued ■ Number and Percentage of P-Card Privileges Revoked ■ Number and Value of Pre-Close and Post-Close Adjustments

Section	Chapter	Name of Chapter/Process	Key Performance Indicators (KPIs)
5 PAYMENT RISK	10	Procure-to-Pay 2.0 Accounts Payable 2.8 Travel and Entertainment	▪ Number of SoD Reviews Performed ▪ Number of SoD Conflicts Identified and Mitigated ▪ Number and Value of T&E Payment Issues and Errors Identified and Mitigated ▪ Number and Percentage of T&E Issues as Compared to Total T&E Payments Issued ▪ Number and Percentage of Corporate Card Violations ▪ Number of Corporate Cards Issued ▪ Number and Percentage of Corporate Card Privileges Revoked ▪ Number and Value of Pre-Close and Post-Close Adjustments
	11	Hire-to-Retire 3.0 Human Resources 3.1 Human Resources Process Hire-to-Retire 4.0 Payroll 4.1 Payroll Processing Process	▪ Number of SoD Reviews Performed ▪ Number of SoD Conflicts Identified and Mitigated ▪ Number and Value of Payroll Payment Issues and Errors Identified and Mitigated ▪ Number of New Hires ▪ Number of Transfers ▪ Number of Terminations ▪ Number of Hiring Violations Identified ▪ Number of Hiring and Discriminatory Issues Identified ▪ Number and Value of Payroll Payment Issues and Errors Identified and Mitigated ▪ Number and Value of Employee Benefit Issues Identified and Mitigated ▪ Number and Value of Pre-Close and Post-Close Adjustments ▪ Number of Regulatory Issues Identified and Mitigated ▪ Number of Unauthorized Employee Records Identified ▪ Number of CSAs Performed ▪ Number of SoD Reviews Performed ▪ Number of SoD Conflicts Identified and Mitigated ▪ Number and Value of Payroll Payment Issues and Errors Identified and Mitigated ▪ Number and Value of Fines Incurred ▪ Number and Value of Payroll Exceptions Identified ▪ Number of Special Payments Paid Per Period ▪ Number of Unauthorized Employee Records Identified. ▪ Number of CSAs Performed ▪ Cost to Process Payroll Results ▪ Cycle Time for Each Payroll Process ▪ Number and Value of Pre-Close and Post-Close Adjustments for the Payroll Process

Section	Chapter	Name of Chapter/Process	Key Performance Indicators (KPIs)
5	11	Hire-to-Retire	■ Number of SoD Reviews Performed
			■ Number of SoD Conflicts Identified and Mitigated
PAYMENT RISK		4.0 Payroll	■ Number and Value of Payroll Payment Issues and Errors Identified and Mitigated
			■ Value of Variances Reported in Payroll Bank Accounts
		4.2 Payroll Payment Process	■ Aging of Variances Reported in Payroll Bank Accounts
			■ Payroll Payments by Payment Type (ACH, Check, Other)
			■ Number and Value of Payroll Exception Payments
			■ Percentage of ACH Payments Issued
			■ Percentage of Nonwage Payments Issued
			■ Number and Value of Unclaimed Wages (by State)
			■ Number and Value of Pre-Close and Post-Close Adjustments
		Hire-to-Retire	■ Number and Percentage of Payroll Issues Identified and Stopped
			■ Value of Cost Savings Opportunities Identified in the Payroll Process
			■ Percentage and Number of Fraudulent Payments
		4.0 Payroll	■ Number of Fraudulent Employees
			■ Percentage Adherence to Payroll Policies
		4.3 Reporting, Metrics, and Analytics	■ Percentage of Manual Checks Issued
			■ Percentage of ACH Payments Issued
			■ Percentage of Nonwage Payments Issued
			■ Cycle Time to Process a Payroll Transaction
			■ Unapproved Items in Time and Attendance Records in Workflow
			■ Value and Aging of Unclaimed Payroll Payments
			■ Value and Aging of Unclaimed Wages
	12	Order-to-Cash	■ Customer Satisfaction Ratings
		5.0 Order-to-Cash	■ Customer Contract Accuracy Percentage
			■ Percentage of Billing Errors
		5.1 Sales	■ Billing Accuracy Percentage
			■ Percentage of Pricing Errors
			■ Days Sales Outstanding (DSO)
			■ Number of Cases Reported
			■ Product Delivery Cycle Time
			■ Number and Value of Revenue Account Adjustments per Period
			■ Collection Effectiveness Index (CEI)
		Order-to-Cash	■ Number of SoD Reviews Performed
		5.2 Customer Master File	■ Number of SoD Conflicts Identified
			■ Number of SoD Conflicts Mitigated
			■ Number of Systems Access Reviews Performed
			■ Number of Systems Access Issues Identified
			■ Number of Systems Access Issues Mitigated
			■ Customer Master File Accuracy Percentage
			■ Number of Credit Reviews Performed
			■ Number of Changes to Credit Limits
			■ Number of Customer Accounts Denied Credit
			■ Number of Active Customers in the Customer Master File
			■ Number of Customers Submitting Payments Electronically
			■ Number of Controls Reviewed
			■ Cycle Time for the Remediation of Control Issues
			■ Cost of Compliance Remediation

Section	Chapter	Name of Chapter/Process	Key Performance Indicators (KPIs)
5 PAYMENT RISK	12	**Order-to-Cash** **5.3 Credit Analysis**	■ Number of SoD Reviews Performed ■ Number of SoD Conflicts Identified ■ Number of SoD Conflicts Mitigated ■ Number of Systems Access Reviews Performed ■ Number of Systems Access Issues Identified ■ Number of Systems Access Issues Mitigated ■ Number of Credit Reviews Performed ■ Number of Changes to Credit Limits ■ Number of Customer Accounts Denied Credit ■ DSO ■ CEI ■ AR Aging ■ Value of Write-offs per Period ■ Value of Customer Refunds per Period ■ Customer Refunds Issues by Reason ■ Number of Management Adjustments per Period ■ Cash-Flow Forecast and Reporting Accuracy ■ Average Customer Satisfaction Rating ■ Number of Customers Submitting Payments Electronically ■ Number of Controls Reviewed ■ Cycle Time for the Remediation of Control Issues ■ Number of Active Customers in the Customer Master File ■ Number of Customers Submitting Payments Electronically ■ Number and % of Customers Submitting ACH Remittances ■ Cycle Time for the Remediation of Control Issues ■ Value of Compliance Fines ■ Cost of Compliance Remediation
		Order-to-Cash **5.4 Order Fulfillment and Invoicing**	■ Average Customer Satisfaction Rating ■ Percentage and Value of Inventory Control Issues ■ Number of SoD Reviews Performed ■ Number of SoD Conflicts Identified ■ Number of SoD Conflicts Mitigated ■ Number of Systems Access Reviews Performed ■ Number of Systems Access Issues Identified ■ Number of Systems Access Issues Mitigated ■ Percentage and Value of Revenue Reversals ■ CEI ■ AR Aging ■ AR Aging by Customer ■ Value of Write-offs per Period ■ DSO ■ Number of Credit Reviews Performed ■ Number of Changes to Credit Limits ■ Number of Customer Accounts Denied Credit ■ Number and Value of Pre-Close and Post-Close Adjustments to the GL

Section	Chapter	Name of Chapter/Process	Key Performance Indicators (KPIs)
		Order-to-Cash **5.5 Accounts Receivable and Collections**	■ DSO ■ CEI ■ Value of Write-offs per Period ■ Value of Customer Refunds per Period ■ Customer Refunds Issues by Reason ■ Value and Number of Customer Refunds Issued ■ Percentage of Customer Refunds Compared to AR Sub-ledger Balance ■ Number of Management Adjustments per Period ■ Cash Flow Forecast and Reporting Accuracy ■ Average Customer Satisfaction Rating ■ Percentage and Value of Inventory Control Issues ■ Number of SoD Reviews Performed ■ Number of SoD Conflicts Identified ■ Number of SoD Conflicts Mitigated ■ Number of Systems Access Reviews Performed ■ Number of Systems Access Issues Identified ■ Number of Systems Access Issues Mitigated ■ Percentage and Value of Revenue Reversals ■ Value of Write-offs per Period ■ Value of AR Account Reconciliation Variances ■ Value and Percentage of Disputed Invoices ■ AR Aging by Customer ■ Number and Value of Pre-Close and Post-Close Adjustments to the GL ■ Customer Master File Accuracy Percentage ■ AR Data Accuracy Percentage
5 **PAYMENT RISK**	**12**	**Order-to-Cash** **5.6 Cash Application and Management**	■ Number of SoD Reviews Performed ■ Number of SoD Conflicts Identified ■ Number of SoD Conflicts Mitigated ■ Number of Systems Access Reviews Performed ■ Number of Systems Access Issues Identified ■ Number of Systems Access Issues Mitigated ■ AR Aging by Customer ■ CEI ■ DSO ■ First-Time Customer Payment Match ■ Number and Value of Cash Application Issues ■ Cash Application Accuracy Percentage ■ Cash Flow Reporting Accuracy Percentage ■ Variance and Trend Analysis for Cash Flow Reporting Changes to Working Capital Reporting ■ Cycle Time to Remediate a Customer Payment Issue ■ Value of AR Fraud Instances ■ Average Customer Satisfaction Rating ■ Value of AR Account Reconciliation Variances ■ Number and Value of Pre-Close and Post-Close Entries to the GL

Section	Chapter	Name of Chapter/Process	Key Performance Indicators (KPIs)
		Order-to-Cash 5.7 Reporting, Metrics, and Analytics	■ Number and Percentage of O2C Issues Identified and Remediated ■ Value of Cost Savings Opportunities Identified in the O2C Process ■ DSO ■ CEI ■ AR Aging ■ AR Aging by Customer ■ Value of AR Write-offs ■ Unapplied Cash ■ Cycle Time to Apply Cash ■ First-Time Customer Payment Matches ■ Unapplied Cash
6 FINANCIAL OPERATIONS RISK	13	Record-to-Report	■ Number of Adjustments After Cutoffs ■ Number of Post-Close Entries ■ Number of Management Adjustments ■ Number of GL Accounts with Variances ■ Days to Close ■ Number of Financial Statement Corrections (Restatements) ■ Amount of Cash Account Variances ■ Types and Numbers of Cash Forecasting Issues ■ Amount of Intercompany Variances ■ Purchase Price Variance (PPV) Trends ■ Number of Ethics Violations Reported via Hotline ■ Trend Analysis of Accruals ■ Amount of AP Clearing Account Variances ■ Number of Open POs ■ Amounts of Open POs ■ Variance Amount – Budgets to Actuals ■ Variance Amount – Forecast to Actuals
	14	Budgets, Forecasts, and Capital Budgeting	■ Percentage Budget Variance ■ Percentage Strategic Goals Achieved ■ Value of Unapproved Expenditures ■ Percentage Variance Actuals to Capital Budgets ■ ROI on Capital Investments ■ Percentage Accuracy of Fixed-Asset Inventories ■ Amount of Fixed Asset Write-offs

Section	Chapter	Name of Chapter/Process	Key Performance Indicators (KPIs)
	15	**Supply Chain Management and Inventory Control**	■ Number of SoD Conflicts ■ Number of Internal Control Issues ■ Cost per Supply Chain Employee ■ Employee Salaries as a Percent of Revenue ■ Perfect Order Measurement ■ Fill Rate ■ Supply Chain Cycle Time ■ Average Payment Period for Production Materials ■ DOS ■ IV ■ Inventory DOS ■ Cash-to-Cash Cycle Time ■ Customer Order Cycle Time ■ Amount of Scrap Inventory on Hand ■ Scrap Inventory Turnover ■ Returned Orders ■ Supply Chain Department Cost as a Percentage of Revenue ■ Value of Inventory Write-offs per Period ■ TEI ■ Percentage of Order Defectives ■ Percentage of Damaged Inventory ■ Percentage of Returns ■ Percentage of Customer Returns Compared to Total Sales ■ Percentage of Short Ships and Misships ■ Value of Inventory with a Quality Block ■ Value of Inventory by Type ■ Value of Inventory Reserve per Period ■ Value of Inventory Write-offs per Period ■ ITR ■ Cycle Count Results (Gross and Net) ■ Physical Inventory (Gross and Net) ■ On-Time Shipping Rate ■ Days Sales Outstanding (DSO) ■ Revenue Adjustments ■ Supply Chain Process Impact on the Financial Close ■ Inventory Turnover ■ Supply SLA Results ■ Results of Supply Management Reviews ■ Freight Bill Accuracy ■ Freight Cost per Unit ■ Number of Hazardous Material Violations per Period ■ Value of Outstanding Shipping Issues ■ Customer Satisfaction

Section	Chapter	Name of Chapter/Process	Key Performance Indicators (KPIs)
6 FINANCIAL OPERATIONS RISK	16	Treasury and Cash Management	■ Cash Visibility Percentage Estimation ■ Percentage of Payments Succeeding First Time ■ Percentage Forecast Error by Business Unit ■ Funding Buffer ■ Cost of Funds Performance ■ Investment Portfolio Liquidity ■ Hedge Ratio ■ Retrospective Hedge Effectiveness ■ Time Taken to Confirm Deals ■ Asset/Liability Mismatch ■ Forecast Error ■ Cash Visibility ■ Cost of Funds Above Benchmark ■ Portfolio Value at Risk ■ Reported Cash That Is Automatically Reconciled ■ Counterparty Limit Usage
6 FINANCIAL OPERATIONS RISK	17	Shared Services and Business Process Outsourcing	■ Customer Satisfaction ■ SLAs Achieved ■ Financial Performance ■ Percentage of Processes Automated ■ Cost per Transaction ■ Cost per Transaction vs. Goal ■ Transaction Defects
	18	Dashboards, Data Validation, Analytics, Metrics, and Benchmarking	■ KPIs by Business Process ■ Percentage of Data Accuracy ■ Number of Benchmarking Initiatives ■ KPIs by Business Process ■ Strategic Sourcing Cost Savings ■ Unapproved Items in PO Workflow ■ Number of Remediation Issues

Section	Chapter	Name of Chapter/Process	Key Performance Indicators (KPIs)
7 INFORMATION TECHNOLOGY RISK	19	Information Technology Controls and Cybersecurity	■ Number of Company Applications ■ Number of Company Applications Without Business Owners ■ Percentage of Projects Aligned with the Organization's Strategic Plan/Initiatives ■ Percentage of Projects Stopped in the Evaluation Phase Versus the Execution Phase ■ Percentage of Projects That Meet or Exceed the Business Case Value Expectation ■ Percentage of Project Phases Completed on Time ■ Percentage of Projects Achieving Quality Targets. ■ Percentage of Projects at or Under Budget ■ Percentage of Applications Not Covered by External Vendor Support Agreements ■ Percentage of Hardware Units Not Easily Procured/Replaced Through Strategic Vendors ■ Number and Duration of Unplanned Outages ■ Percentage of SLAs Met or Exceeded ■ Customer Satisfaction Rate ■ Number of Complaints Logged Related to System Issues ■ Cost of Downtime ■ Budget Percentage Devoted to Innovation ■ Change Request Cycle Time ■ Change Success Rate ■ First Response Time ■ Number of Noncompliance Events ■ Number of SoD/User Access Issues
8 BUSINESS CONTINUITY AND PHYSICAL SECURITY RISK	20	Business Continuity and Physical Security	■ Percentage of Downtime ■ Number of Days to Recovery ■ Frequency of Business Continuity Plan Tests Performed ■ SLA Performance ■ OLA Performance ■ Date of Last Plan Update ■ Cloud Computing Plans Reviewed/Obtained ■ Security Cost as a Percentage of Total Company Revenue ■ Number of Security FTEs (Full-Time Equivalents) as a Percentage of Total Company FTEs ■ Number of Nuisance Alarms by Facility ■ Number of Security Incidences by Facility ■ Cost of a Security Incident ■ Average Response Time to a Security Incident ■ Cycle Time to Resolve a Security Incident ■ Time to Recover from an Emergency Percentage of BCPs in Place ■ Percentage of Security Personnel Trained ■ Pass/Fail Rate of Security Tests

Section	Chapter	Name of Chapter/ Process	Key Performance Indicators (KPIs)
9 LEADERSHIP AND CHANGE MANAGEMENT RISK	21	**Leadership and Managing Change**	▪ Percentage of Company Goals Achieved per Strategic Plan ▪ Number of Internal Controls Issues Requiring Remediation ▪ Number of Hiring Issues Requiring Remediation or Legal Action ▪ Number of Ethics Issues Reported to the Ethics Hotline ▪ Budget Variance Percentages ▪ Cost Center Expense Overages ▪ Number of DoA Issues
	22	**Trends, Process Transformation, and Digitization**	▪ Percentage Cost-per-Transaction Reduction ▪ ROI for Solutions Implemented ▪ Amount of New Revenue Attributed to Digital Investments ▪ Percentage of Data Accuracy ▪ Number of Project Milestones Achieved on Time ▪ Number of Issues Identified in the Testing Process ▪ Number of Users Trained ▪ Number of Users Relative to the Number of Licenses Purchased ▪ Number of Processes Performed on New Solution

Index